Deciphering Shakespeare's Plays

A Practical Guide to the
Twenty Best-Known and Enduring Works

CYNTHIA GREENWOOD

CALPURNIA PRESS

Published by Calpurnia Press, 1113 Willard Street, Houston, Texas 77006

Copyright ©2018, 2008 by Cynthia Greenwood

All rights reserved. No part of this book may be reproduced, stored in a retrieval system, or transmitted by any means, electronic, mechanical, photocopying, recording, or otherwise, without written permission from the publisher. For information, address is 1113 Willard Street, Houston, Texas 77006.

ISBN: 978-0-9988978-0-6 (Paperback Edition)
ISBN: 978-0-9988978-1-3 (E-book Edition)

Library of Congress Control Number 2017909262

Credits and permissions are listed on pages xix-xx and are considered a continuation of the copyright page. Every effort has been made to inform each theatrical expert who is quoted in this guide about the 2018 revision.

Originally published as *The Complete Idiot's Guide to Shakespeare's Plays*, now revised and updated.

Cover design (2018 edition): Adina Cucicov
Book design (2018 edition): Adina Cucicov
Cover image: Kenneth Branagh (as Hamlet) in *Hamlet* (1996). Photo courtesy of Columbia Pictures/Photofest.
Back cover image: *William Shakespeare*, by William Blake (1800).

Printed in the United States of America

Published by Calpurnia Press
1113 Willard Street
Houston, TX 77006

*For Bob
and my parents, James and Janet.*

Contents at a Glance

PART 1: SHAKESPEARE AND HIS WORLD 1

Chapter 1: Shakespeare's England 3
What kind of world did Shakespeare live in? Look at his life in the context of English social class, politics, religion, and cosmology during the late Renaissance.

Chapter 2: A Man of the Theatre 11
Besides being a great poet and playwright, Shakespeare was an actor, an influential member of the Lord Chamberlain's Men, and a shareholder in the Globe. A look at the art and business of theatre in Shakespeare's time.

Chapter 3: Heady Theatre in London's Earliest Playhouses 23
What were those early Elizabethan playhouses and audiences actually like?

PART 2: PLAYS ARE FOR THE STAGE 37

Chapter 4: Experiencing Shakespeare on the Stage 39
How to think about and enjoy Shakespeare's plays as scripts for performance.

Chapter 5: Shakespeare's Music 47
What makes Shakespeare's language so musical, witty, verbally complex, and intoxicating to our ears?

Chapter 6: How Shakespeare's Plays Were Published 57
Persistent questions about Shakespeare's lost manuscripts, the First Folio, multiple script versions, and when he wrote his plays.

PART 3: THE COMEDIES..73

Chapter 7: The Taming of the Shrew...75
A popular, lively marriage farce, The Taming of the Shrew *is steeped in controversy. Director Sidney Berger talks about the challenges of staging this entertaining comedy.*

Chapter 8: A Midsummer Night's Dream...89
A Midsummer Night's Dream *is full of fairy magic, potions, spells, and labyrinthine plotting. Read F. Murray Abraham's ideas about playing Bottom, a rich part for the actor.*

Chapter 9: The Merchant of Venice..105
Still popular, The Merchant of Venice *remains highly controversial among directors, playgoers, and critics. Actor Scott Wentworth talks about playing Antonio, and director Sidney Berger talks about the play's merits and why it is difficult to stage.*

Chapter 10: Much Ado About Nothing..121
Much Ado about Nothing *is a romantic comedy full of love, intrigue, and mistaken identity. Actor Jeffrey Bean talks about the play's insight into modern relationships.*

Chapter 11: The Merry Wives of Windsor..137
A festive comedy like no other, The Merry Wives of Windsor *offers us a window into rural Elizabethan life. Director Rutherford Cravens talks about adapting the play's setting.*

Chapter 12: As You Like It..151
In the great pastoral comedy As You Like It, *"court" meets "country" as everyone escapes into the Forest of Arden. Director Penny Metropulos muses about staging the play in the context of the American West.*

Chapter 13: Twelfth Night, or What You Will..167
Shakespeare's twilight comedy, Twelfth Night, *is a masterwork of cross-dressing, disguise, and carnival madness. Actors Rutherford Cravens and Jeffrey Bean talk about the role of Shakespeare's clowns, while director Robert Hupp offers views about staging* Twelfth Night.

Chapter 14: Measure for Measure..183
Measure for Measure *is a pessimistic drama that probes virtue, vice, and profound ideas about justice and mercy. Understand why many directors consider it a problem comedy.*

PART 4: THE HISTORIES 197

Chapter 15: Richard III 199
Richard III, *featuring Shakespeare's irresistibly wicked king, has been a crowd pleaser throughout the ages.*

Chapter 16: Henry IV, Part I 217
A brilliant ensemble play about civil rebellion, Henry IV, Part I *plunges us into the antics of Prince Hal and Falstaff, Shakespeare's most famous comic character. Actor Mark Mineart offers tips about performing King Henry.*

Chapter 17: Henry V 231
Henry V, *a stunning epic about war, showcases England's invasion of France during the Hundred Years War. Continuing the Henry IV saga, Hal tests his authority as king.*

PART 5: THE TRAGEDIES 245

Chapter 18: Romeo and Juliet 247
Romeo and Juliet *is a sublime early tragedy about family feuding and star-crossed lovers. Its high-pitched word combat is as electric as its sword fighting. Director Roseann Sheridan talks about casting Benvolio as a woman.*

Chapter 19: Julius Caesar 265
Julius Caesar *is an early Roman tragedy that still pleases playgoers. Savor the penetrating portraits of Brutus, Mark Antony, and Cassius amid the rise and fall of the ancient world's most powerful leader.*

Chapter 20: Hamlet, Prince of Denmark 279
Hamlet *is a world-famous, self-consciously theatrical play that mulls life, love, death, and despair through the mind of a giant amongst protagonists. Director Michael Kahn talks about Shakespeare's ambiguity, and fight director Jack Young analyzes how Shakespeare imagined the fencing match.*

Chapter 21: Othello, the Moor of Venice 299
Othello *is an intimate revenge tragedy with a tight, fast-moving plot. Go behind the scenes with director Roseann Sheridan during the 2007 Texas Shakespeare Festival.*

Chapter 22: King Lear 315
King Lear *is a tour de force of Western drama that profoundly explores the human condition and the meaning of life. Actor Charles Krohn muses about performing the role of King Lear. Director Jack Young talks about staging the play's violence, and director Kate Pogue examines what goes into staging* King Lear.

Chapter 23: Macbeth 333
Macbeth, *a great tragedy set in medieval Scotland, explores the dark face of evil against a backdrop of prophecies, witchcraft, and Celtic imaginings. Essays by actors Simon Russell Beale and Sian Thomas shed light on the roles of Macbeth and Lady Macbeth.*

Chapter 24: Antony and Cleopatra 349
Antony and Cleopatra *is a steamy tragedy about doomed lovers who co-ruled the Roman empire. Director Joseph Graves looks at what makes Antony a challenging role.*

PART 6: THE ROMANCES 363

Chapter 25: The Winter's Tale 365
A poignant romance, The Winter's Tale *offers an enduring story of human suffering, separation, and reconciliation.*

Chapter 26: The Tempest 377
The Tempest *is a great romance and unique achievement about the power of illusion and the artist. Actor Bree Welch talks about performing the role of Miranda.*

APPENDICES 391

Appendix A: Shakespeare's Lesser-Known Plays 393
Appendix B: The Collaborative Plays 401
Appendix C: Glossary of Elizabethan English 409
Appendix D: Resources on Shakespeare's Plays 415

INDEX 419

Contents

Introduction xv
Acknowledgments xix
PART 1: SHAKESPEARE AND HIS WORLD 1
Chapter 1: Shakespeare's England 3
    Shakespeare's Early Life and Education 4
    Life in London 5
    Aristocracy and Social Class 6
    Trade and Social Mobility 7
    The Political and Religious Context 8
    The Reign of Elizabeth I 8
    The Rule of James I 9
    Shakespeare's Upward Mobility and Court Connections 10
Chapter 2: A Man of the Theatre 11
    A Man of the Theatre 12
    A Poet and a Player 12
    Shakespeare the Actor and the Elizabethan Player's Life 13
    Passing Muster with the Master of the Revels 14
    A Poet Makes Inroads as a Dramatist 15
    Shakespeare and the Lord Chamberlain's Men 16
    A Debt to Christopher Marlowe 16
    A Note About Shakespeare's Sources 17
    From Poet and Playwright to Sharer in the Globe 17
    Shakespeare's Peers and Collaboration 19
    Shakespeare's Legacy and Impact on Modern Theatre 20

Chapter 3: Heady Theatre in London's Earliest Playhouses 23
    A New, Heady Theatre for the Masses 24
    The Flight to the Suburbs 25
    The Theatre, The Curtain, The Rose, and The Swan 25
    The Globe 27
    The Ornate Stage and Amphitheatre 28
    Interior Details 28
    For-Profit Theatre with Widespread Appeal 30
    Who Were Those Early English Playgoers? 31
    Raucous, "Red-Light" Entertainment 32
    Inside the Playhouse 32
    The Actors 33
    Did Shakespeare Direct His Plays? 34

PART 2: PLAYS ARE FOR THE STAGE 37

Chapter 4: Experiencing Shakespeare on the Stage 39
    Entertainment for the Ear 40
    Remember—Each Play Is a Script 41
    The Dramatic Experience and the Integral Role of the Actor 42
    Shakespeare's Scripts Offer Freedom of Interpretation 43
    Shakespeare in Live Performance 44

Chapter 5: Shakespeare's Music 47
    The Artistry of Shakespeare's Verse Line 48
    Punning, Figures of Speech, and Elaborate Wordplay 50

Chapter 6: How Shakespeare's Plays Were Published 57
    Playwriting—A Less Noble Profession 58
    The First Folio of 1623 60
    Multiple Script Versions Put Scholars in a Muddle 63
    How Many Plays Did Shakespeare Actually Write? 66
    Trust Me: Hamlet Is Funny—A Mini-Lesson in Genre 69

PART 3: THE COMEDIES 73

Chapter 7: The Taming of the Shrew 75
    Sly's Dream—The Play-Within-the-Play 78
    Making Sense of the Shrew and Bully Farce 84
    The Taming of the Shrew—A Chronology of Notable Screen Productions 87

Chapter 8: A Midsummer Night's Dream 89
    Let's Get to Know the Lovers and the Plots 93
    Oberon Toys with Mortals 96
    Three Weddings 98
    Puck's Last Word on the Grave 99
    Staging *A Midsummer Night's Dream* 100
    F. Murray Abraham as Bottom 101

Chapter 9: The Merchant of Venice 105
    Bassanio's Expensive Wish 109
    Shylock Calls in His Pound of Flesh 112
    Attending to the Language—An Actor Inhabits Antonio 115
    Our Modern Empathy for Shylock—A Problem for Directors 117

Chapter 10: Much Ado About Nothing 121
    Two Lovers Fight a "Merry War" 124
    Under Cover—Romancing Hero by Proxy 125
    Don Pedro Plays Cupid, the Matchmaker 127
    Shaming Hero (For Shame, Claudio!) 128
    Faking Death to Reclaim Virtue 129
    A Bride in Disguise 131
    Two Kinds of Relationships 132

Chapter 11: The Merry Wives of Windsor 137
    No Royals Here! A True English, Middle-Class Comedy 140
    Falstaff Plays the Lecher for Easy Cash 141
    Courting Anne Page 144
    A Tryst with Herne the Hunter 146
    A Director's View 147
    Other Notable Productions 148

Chapter 12: As You Like It 151
    Court Intrigue—A Duke Usurps His Brother 155
    Court Versus Country? Is There Life After the Forest of Arden? 159
    As You Like It at the Oregon Shakespeare Festival 161
    Rosalind—An Actress for All Time 163

Chapter 13: Twelfth Night, or What You Will 167
    Royal Houses of Sentiment and Mourning 171
    Shipwrecked and Washed Ashore, Viola Goes Under Cover 171
    Plotting Against Malvolio 174

    Witty Fools and Buffoons—Two Actors Talk About Shakespeare's Clowns........176
    Robert Hupp Interprets *Twelfth Night* for the Stage........179
Chapter 14: Measure for Measure........183
    To Reform Vienna, a Duke Relinquishes Power........186
    A Plan with a Bed Trick........189
    The Energy of *Measure for Measure* Onstage........194

PART 4: THE HISTORIES........197

Chapter 15: Richard III........199
    A Cruel and Charming Tyrant........204
    Shakespeare's Take on the Wars of the Roses........205
    A Villain Gets to Work........205
    Old Queen Margaret Curses and Prophesies........207
    On a Murder Rampage........208
    "My Kingdom for a Horse"........211
    The Play's Lessons and Sources........212
    How Big-Time Actors Have Re-created Richard........212
    Richard III in the Late Twentieth Century........214

Chapter 16: Henry IV, Part I........217
    King Henry Is Tired and Disillusioned........221
    Rebellion Is Brewing........224
    Concerns About Kingship and the Growth of a King........227
    Actors on Acting: How to Play a Plausible King Henry........228

Chapter 17: Henry V........231
    "O for a Muse of Fire"—Gentles, Let Your Imaginations Run Wild!........235
    Henry Gets Down to Business—Contemplating War and Catching Traitors........236
    Rallying the Troops at Harfleur and Agincourt........238
    A Bloody Victory at Agincourt........239
    To Seal His Conquest, Henry Proposes to Princess Katherine........242
    Henry V in Performance........244

PART 5: THE TRAGEDIES........245

Chapter 18: Romeo and Juliet........247
    Family Feud in "Fair Verona"........250
    A Ruse, a Letter, and a Sleeping Potion........258
    Romeo and Juliet on Stage and Screen........261

Chapter 19: Julius Caesar 265
   Rome Is Dissatisfied on the Feast of Lupercal 269
   Brutus Is Lured into a Conspiracy 270
   Mark Antony Incites the Rabble 272
   Antony and Octavius Get Even 273
   Brutus Falls on His Sword 274
   A Word About Roman History and Shakespeare's Fascination 275

Chapter 20: Hamlet, Prince of Denmark 279
   A Specter Stalks 283
   A Cycle of Revenge Destroys Two Families 289
   Intriguing Patterns and Themes in *Hamlet* 292

Chapter 21: Othello, the Moor of Venice 299
   A Secret Marriage in Venice 302
   More Lies Until Othello Collapses into a Fit 307
   Creating a Production of *Othello* at the Texas Shakespeare Festival 311

Chapter 22: King Lear 315
   Lear's Foolhardy Test and Cordelia's Banishment 319
   Lear Rages Against His Daughters and the Elements 322
   What the Journeys of Edgar, Gloucester, and Lear Teach Us 325
   Actor Charles Krohn Muses about Performing Lear 326

Chapter 23: Macbeth 333
   Three Hags on a Heath—An Uncanny Prophecy 337
   Royal Shakespeare Company Actors Interpret the Macbeths 344

Chapter 24: Antony and Cleopatra 349
   Rome Suffers While Antony Dallies with Cleopatra 354
   Octavius and Antony's Rivalry Leads to War 356

PART 6: THE ROMANCES 363

Chapter 25: The Winter's Tale 365
   The Proverbial Storm—Leontes' Jealous Obsession 368
   A Foundling in Bohemia—Perdita's Awakening 371

Chapter 26: The Tempest 377
   Prospero's Magic Isle 381
   Subterfuge Against the King of Naples 383
   Exploring Illusion Versus Reality 385
   Actor Bree Welch Interprets the Role of Miranda for the Houston
      Shakespeare Festival 387

APPENDICES 391

    Appendix A: Shakespeare's Lesser-Known Plays 393
    Appendix B: The Collaborative Plays 401
    Appendix C: Glossary of Elizabethan English 409
    Appendix D: Resources on Shakespeare's Plays 415

INDEX 419

Introduction

Do you remember your first experience with a play by William Shakespeare? Did you look forward to reading *Romeo and Juliet* and then get bogged down during the love scenes? Perhaps you loved *Othello*. With evil Iago, it reads like a juicy soap opera. But I bet the archaic language was slow going. Or *Richard III*? Sensational melodrama, but why did he need so many characters? How are we supposed to keep them all straight?

The truth is, reading Shakespeare's plays can be a chore for just about everyone. Most of us approach them for the first time as readers. And that's where we make our mistake. Don't forget: Shakespeare wrote his plays to entertain you, to sell tickets! (If you're studying the plays in English class, keep that in mind.)

How to Approach This Book

There is a world of actors, directors, and other professionals outside your radar who get immersed in Shakespeare, day in and day out. They make a living doing it. Shakespeare comes alive for them because they breathe the fresh air of his verse. They speak his prose. They grapple with his powerful soliloquies. With this book, we aim to bring you closer to their world.

This guide to Shakespeare's plays is written for the beginner of any age as well as students who tackle the plays in English literature and theatre courses. We devote individual chapters to 20 of Shakespeare's best-known and most popular plays. You'll find descriptions of major characters as well as easy-to-read plot synopses. We look at theme and other useful interpretations. Take a look at the original interviews with actors and directors who regularly perform in and stage the plays. Wherever possible, we put the plays in a dramatic context.

In the following chapters, we invite you to approach the plays as Shakespeare himself intended——as live works for performance.

Part 1, "Shakespeare and His World," puts Shakespeare and his playwriting career in their cultural and historical context. What kind of world did Shakespeare live in? We look at Shakespeare's life and career within the highly commercial and collaborative theatre business of Elizabethan London. You'll get insights into his work as an actor or "player," how his playwriting career developed, impressions of how others perceived his work and talent, the evolution of England's early theatres, and what Shakespeare's audiences were like.

Part 2, "Plays Are for the Stage," presents the plays as scripts for live performance and explores the mysteries surrounding Shakespeare's original manuscripts, early editions of his plays, and the treasured First Folio.

Part 3, "The Comedies," introduces you to eight of the most popular Shakespearean comedies that are staged and taught. These include *The Taming of the Shrew*, *The Merchant of Venice*, and the great festive comedies *As You Like It*, *Twelfth Night*, and *Measure for Measure*, Shakespeare's best-known problem comedy.

Part 4, "The Histories," covers three of Shakespeare's best-loved history plays, including the juicy *Richard III* and brilliant *Henry IV, Part I*. Each of these plays is performed and taught frequently.

Part 5, "The Tragedies," includes Shakespeare's seven greatest and enduring tragedies. These include those written early in his career, like *Romeo and Juliet*, and the four iconic works—*Hamlet*, *Othello*, *King Lear*, and *Macbeth*.

Part 6, "The Romances," surveys two romances highly acclaimed by directors, critics, and scholars—*The Winter's Tale* and *The Tempest*.

One final note as you review individual plays: consider the genre distinctions in this book as useful categories for ease of reference. But categories can mislead you. There is much in these comedies that's deadly serious! Shakespearean comedy is defined by a set of conventions inherited from classical drama, European medieval romance, and English miracle and morality plays. Villains like the evil Don John in *Much Ado About Nothing* ensure that the comedies have darker moments of suspense. And don't despair! Shakespeare supplied his signature wit and humor to lighten the mood of his great tragedies. Trust me. In the midst of its Danish court intrigue and long-winded speeches, *Hamlet* has many funny moments! (Note: all quotations from Shakespeare's plays are taken from the second edition of *The Riverside Shakespeare: The Complete Works*.)

Interludes

Interspersed throughout each chapter are helpful sidebars to guide you further. These brief interludes include definitions of Elizabethan words, puns, and terms; close readings of famous speeches and soliloquies; historical factoids; useful analysis of theme or imagery; and entertaining stage, film, and TV productions you might want to watch on your own.

In these sidebars we define key literary, archaic, and historical terms to help you follow each play's action. By the way, the title of this interlude comes from Horatio's response to Hamlet, signaling that he is reluctant to end their conversation.

The memorable lines in Shakespeare's plays are almost infinite. Their meaning is not always clear. Here, we go *verse by verse* (or *line by line*) to give you a closer understanding of verse style, hidden humor, a key speech, a theme, or an insight into character.

TIMELESS SOLILOQUIES

Here, we go in-depth to help you decipher and interpret longer speeches or soliloquies with special significance.

"A KINGDOM FOR A STAGE"

To make the plays come alive, we offer a dramatic flavor through tips and tidbits about early and modern stage productions. We also offer tips about great performances and useful adaptations on TV and the big screen.

Acknowledgments

I extend a special thanks to the generous theatre colleagues who have supported a revised edition of this guide. They include Raymond Caldwell, Jeffrey Bean, Diana Howie, and Ron Severdia. In preparing this manuscript, I continue to benefit from the assistance of editors Randy Ladenheim-Gil and Janette Lynn. I could not have completed this project without the tremendous professional and moral support of Debra Kass Orenstein, my literary property attorney. And I sincerely appreciate the encouragement of Regina Ryan, my agent.

I am extremely grateful to the expert stage directors and actors who graciously agreed to be interviewed for this book. All were enthusiastic and spoke with me on short notice, taking time away from busy rehearsal and performance schedules. I also thank them for reviewing chapters and offering suggestions: Raymond Caldwell, Sidney Berger, Scott Wentworth, Jeffrey Bean, Rutherford Cravens, Penny Metropulos, Robert Hupp, Mark Mineart, Roseann Sheridan, Michael Kahn, Charles Krohn, Kate Pogue, Jack Young, Joseph Graves, and Bree Welch. Further, I am indebted to Raymond Caldwell, Joseph Graves, Sidney Berger, Penny Metropulos, and Mark Mineart for putting me in touch with their trusted colleagues. A big thanks to Michael Kahn, Liza Llorenz, and Lauren Beyea at Shakespeare Theatre Company in Washington, D.C., for accommodating my tight schedule. I am very grateful to Georgianna Ziegler, Head of Reference at the Folger Shakespeare Library, for her generous assistance and review.

A special thanks goes to the late Sidney Berger for welcoming me into Houston Shakespeare Festival rehearsals of *Love's Labor's Lost*, as well as his *Acting Shakespeare* course at University of Houston, so I could get the player's perspective. I also thank Raymond Caldwell and Roseann Sheridan for permission to watch *Othello* rehearsals at the Texas Shakespeare Festival. I want to thank Randy Ladenheim-Gil, my original acquisitions editor at Penguin/Alpha Books, for her enthusiasm and patience, as well as Megan Douglass, my development editor, for her meticulous efforts. I'm especially grateful to my husband, Robert Molder, and my father, James R. Greenwood, for keeping my readers in mind as they read the book. I sincerely thank Anne Lewis for reading part of the manuscript; Janet Greenwood, my mother, for her moral support; and my students at Wharton County Junior College who shared my enthusiasm for Shakespeare. (A big hug for my close cousin and Shakespeare connoisseur, Ardis Collins, for introducing me to the superb repertory at Stratford, Ontario, many years ago!)

Part 1
Shakespeare and His World

Part 1. Shakespeare and His World

Before you delve into Shakespeare's comedies, histories, and tragedies, it helps to know something about Renaissance (or early modern) England. What was it like to live in London and the surrounding countryside during Shakespeare's time? What kind of place did Shakespeare discover when he left Stratford-upon-Avon to work in London as an actor and poet?

Here we explore the social, cultural, political, and religious context in which Elizabeth I and James I ruled and Shakespeare wrote. How did the country's rigid class distinctions and economy figure into the world of the plays? Let's face it—life wasn't easy back then. There was no cure for the plague; public executions were the norm; and religious differences spilled over into every segment and layer of society.

What do we know about Shakespeare, the actor, after he arrived in London and became a playwright? We'll look at how Shakespeare's career as poet, playwright, and Globe shareholder evolved. Obviously, no Elizabethan playwright produced plays in a vacuum, and this section touches on the earliest examples of English drama.

Undoubtedly, Shakespeare wrote great plays, but how did London's early public playhouses, their impresarios, and their patrons influence and react to those plays? This section puts the playwright squarely in the highly social world of acting, playgoing, and the noble patronage on which it all depended.

Chapter 1

Shakespeare's England

> **INTRODUCTION**
> - The social and cultural context of Shakespeare's career as a playwright
> - Young William's early life and education in Stratford-upon-Avon
> - How Shakespeare's plays represent rural and urban English life and class variety
> - Political and religious concerns during the reign of Elizabeth I and James I
> - Evidence tying Shakespeare's successful theatre career to a prosperous lifestyle in Stratford

A majority of scholars believe that Shakespeare wrote at least 38 plays and collaborated on others, starting around 1589 and ending in 1613, a prolific 24-year span. During these fruitful years, he lived in London and worked as a player for several acting troupes. These included the famous court-sponsored company called the Lord Chamberlain's Men, a company that would later become known as the King's Men. Beginning in 1599, he also earned a decent living as a shareholder in the Globe theatre. He frequently performed for nobles at court, including Queen Elizabeth I and her successor, King James I. His traceable writing career roughly spanned the last 14 years of Elizabeth's reign and the first 10 years that James I ruled.

For England, a prosperous country of about five million people, these were years of great social, religious, and political upheaval. The gap between rich and poor was significant. Outbreaks of the plague posed a constant threat to the public, especially in London, in many different spheres.

Largely rural, England was full of lush, thick forests. A majority of the English lived in villages within counties resembling Shakespeare's native Warwickshire. Many farmed and ploughed the land. As the wool industry flourished, though, farmland was converted to pasture, putting farmers and their workers out of business. Riots were not uncommon during the 1580s and 1590s, as the raising of sheep became more lucrative and widespread. The medieval lifestyle of the farmer was disappearing.

In Shakespeare's pastoral comedy *As You Like It*, the shepherd Corin upholds the dignity of a "true laborer," saying: "I earn that I eat, get that I wear, owe no man hate, envy no man's happiness." He adds, "the greatest of my pride is to see my ewes graze and my lambs suck."

Let's look more closely at Shakespeare's world and the daily lives of his fellow English citizens.

Shakespeare's Early Life and Education

Born in the rural market town of Stratford-upon-Avon, William Shakespeare was baptized on April 26, 1564, at Holy Trinity Church. He was the oldest son of five surviving children born to Mary Arden and John Shakespeare. John worked as a glover and wool dealer. Most likely, young William attended the grammar school in Stratford-upon-Avon from age 7 until age 15. There he received rigorous instruction in Latin grammar, the principles of ancient rhetoric, and the study of composition. He studied a variety of classical works—Latin comedies by Plautus, Virgil's epic *Aeneid*, Ovid's *Metamorphoses*, and the writings of Roman orators like Cicero.

For many in England, a grammar school education provided the means for social advancement. It gave Shakespeare the means to prosper as a man of the theatre, allowing him to rake in profits as a Globe playhouse shareholder and hobnob with nobles at court. In 1597, sometime after he had written *Romeo and Juliet* and *A Midsummer Night's Dream*, Shakespeare purchased a large house in Stratford called New Place.

When playwright Ben Jonson denigrated Shakespeare by writing that he knew "small Latin and less Greek," he started centuries of debate about the quality of Shakespeare's learning and education. The rigor of a grammar school education in the 1570s far exceeded that of many high school and university liberal arts programs today.

Shakespeare probably left school at age 15. Many have speculated about it, but nobody knows what he did for the next three years. At age 18 he married Anne Hathaway, who was pregnant and eight years older than he. The couple had three children. Susanna was born in 1583, and the twins Hamnet and Judith came two years later. In 1592 the first record appears that alludes to Shakespeare's own writing.

As he wrote and acted in plays, Shakespeare stayed mostly in London, but records show that, on occasion, he traveled back to Stratford-upon-Avon in Warwickshire, his birthplace and where his family lived. The beauty and richness of the rural Warwickshire of Shakespeare's youth undoubtedly inspired plays like *The Merry Wives of Windsor*, *As You Like It*, and many others.

The Merry Wives of Windsor is the only play set in a small, rural English village resembling the playwright's native Warwickshire. In the first scene of Act four, Mistress Quickly interrupts constantly as Sir Hugh Evans gives young William Page a Latin lesson similar to the many that young Shakespeare must have endured at the King's New School in Stratford.

Life in London

More than one-quarter of England's population lived in London when Shakespeare started his writing career. Much like today, rural inhabitants flocked to the city in hopes of a better life. Sometime in his early to mid-twenties, Shakespeare may have taken one of two rutted, well-traveled roads between Stratford and London, probably on foot. One took him through Oxford and the other through Banbury, on the way south. The journey would have taken him about four days, notes Dennis Kay in *William Shakespeare: His Life and Times*.

Part 1. Shakespeare and His World

Shakespeare's Globe playhouse sits in the lower-left portion of this engraving by Claes Jansz Visscher of Amsterdam. Visscher's panorama depicts London as it appeared during the early 1600s, not long after Shakespeare was writing his great tragedies. Note St. Paul's Church (top left) and the Bankside in Southwark (bottom foreground), where the Globe and other public playhouses were situated. Small boats for hire by Londoners are pictured on the Thames, the city's main thoroughfare and avenue of international trade.

(Public domain image from Library of Congress Prints and Photographs Division, Washington, D.C.)

When Shakespeare first arrived in London, maybe late in the 1580s, the new sights, smells, and crowds might have shocked him. By 1600, the city's already dense population had grown to 200,000. The city was still encircled by its ancient wall and city gates—Aldgate (east), Ludgate (west), Aldersgate (north), and Bridgegate (south). Sanitation was poor in the city, and human waste washed into the Thames and Fleet Rivers. The city must have had a rank smell! Back in those days, London Bridge was lined with shops, houses, and taverns. Each time Shakespeare approached the bridge, he would've been assaulted by a display of severed heads adorning pikes. A traitor's punishment! Shakespeare's plays document the life and colorful speech of Londoners, which Shakespeare encountered daily inside markets, shops, taverns, inns, and brothels. The *Henry IV* plays spotlight a lively tavern in the now-defunct section of Eastcheap, where Prince Hal and Falstaff's friendship flourished. By 1590, Shakespeare lived in Southwark, south of the Thames, where the earliest playhouses were built. (Read more about these early public playhouses in Chapter 3.)

Aristocracy and Social Class

In Shakespeare's time, England retained rigid class divisions in spite of a growing middle class that prospered in London's mercantile economy. According to Russ McDonald's analysis in *The Bedford Companion to Shakespeare: An Introduction with Documents*, England was divided into distinct social groups during Shakespeare's playwriting years.

The aristocracy included England's wealthiest citizens, the royals and nobles who owned large country estates with beautiful castles that required lots of upkeep! (Portia, the rich heiress of *The Merchant of Venice* who owned a glittering estate in Belmont, is a perfect example.) Some aristocrats occupied high-ranking positions at court in London; others served in Parliament, McDonald notes. Keep in mind that a majority of Shakespeare's plays centered on the lives and realm of aristocrats and nobles. This was the fashion in Renaissance drama, poetry, and prose romance.

The gentry were descended from aristocrats and almost as rich, but in general they owned less land. Some members of the gentry had lucrative business holdings, similar to the father of Viola De Lesseps in the movie *Shakespeare in Love*. Others, known as gentlemen, were rich landowners in their own right. Citizens included city dwellers that worked in various trades or ran shops or inns. Citizens who lived off of their own farms or pastureland were considered yeomen. Laborers and servants were one step lower—laborers might have worked the land or herded sheep and servants worked inside the house. (Many of Shakespeare's Fools or court jesters, considered servants to his kings, are among his most brilliant and witty dramatic creations!) Members of this class were one step above indigents and vagrants.

Trade and Social Mobility

Many types of trade and industry drove London's mercantile economy. Livery companies controlled the city's trade in goods and services. Drapers, butchers, fishmongers, and other skilled craftsmen such as hatmakers, goldsmiths, and shoemakers were rigidly organized into the guilds of freemen and apprentices that dated back to the Middle Ages. Teenagers between 14 and 17 would begin apprenticeships to skilled craftsmen lasting at least seven years. During this period apprentices were under the tight authority of their masters. Apprenticing offered boys (and a few women) a chance to climb the social ladder and settle into a well-paid trade. Boy actors began their careers by apprenticing to one of London's many acting companies. It is possible that sometime after Shakespeare's marriage or the birth of his children, he apprenticed to one of the acting companies with which he is associated. In Chapter 2, we'll say more about Shakespeare's multifaceted career in the theatre.

The Political and Religious Context

England endured the Wars of the Roses—the bloody conflicts between the Lancastrian and Yorkist nobles in the fifteenth century—before the Tudor kings ushered in an era of stability. This prolonged jockeying for the throne captured Shakespeare's imagination. In the history plays (see Part 4), you'll read more about how the English nobles fell out before Henry Tudor killed King Richard III at the Battle of Bosworth Field. Henry Tudor's son was the iconoclastic Henry VIII, who broke away from the Catholic Church in 1534 and established the Church of England. (He had six wives, remember, two of whom were executed!) During Henry's long reign from 1509 to 1547, he ushered in a period of Protestant religious reforms. Besides going head-to-head with the Pope, his ambitious foreign policy ruffled feathers with Spain, France, and other European powers.

The Reign of Elizabeth I

Henry VIII's daughter Elizabeth took the throne in 1558, six years before Shakespeare was born. Her people and her advisors expected her to marry, but she never found a suitable mate. Questions about her succession dogged her reign until she died in 1603. Early on, she sought to stabilize the religious unrest fomented by her Catholic sister's reactionary policies toward religion. Between 1553 and 1558, Queen Mary (a.k.a. Bloody Mary) had essentially halted the system of Protestant reforms championed by her father, King Henry VIII. She repealed Protestant laws and executed many prominent Protestant reformers! Reversing this trend, Queen Elizabeth I put the Church of England back on the path of Protestant reform.

Chapter 1. Shakespeare's England

PTOLEMY AND RENAISSANCE COSMOLOGY

Medieval England still believed in Ptolemy of Alexandria's ancient theories of astronomy, namely the view that the earth was the planetary king at the center of the universe. It took a long time for late Renaissance England to shake off this view. Even though Copernicus issued his treatise asserting that the earth revolved around the sun in 1543, Ptolemy's system often held sway in late Renaissance literary allusions to the cosmos. Shakespeare's plays were no exception. Implicit in many great poems and plays is an idea of order and harmony in the universe. This system of medieval and Renaissance cosmology is highly complex.

Still, religious unrest stemming from the Protestant Reformation and the growing power of more extreme Puritans unsettled life for the average citizen. (Elizabeth herself had been excommunicated by the Catholic Church and often feared for her life.) While Elizabeth ruled, she displayed a savvy tolerance for Puritan and Catholic extremists within the Anglican Church. The queen's policies toward the practice of religion forced changes upon the ritual and worship of Catholics. These changes must have been jarring. The Holy Trinity Church in Stratford, for example, was stripped of statues and images of Catholic saints, which were considered idolatrous. Altars disappeared and communion tables were brought in. A generation accustomed to the Catholic liturgy found themselves forced to adopt the Anglican rituals of the Book of Common Prayer.

The Rule of James I

James VI of Scotland became King James I of England in 1603 after Queen Elizabeth died. The Scottish king brought England many years of political stability. He continued Elizabeth's policies of religious tolerance and compromise. During his reign, in 1611, the authoritative version of the Bible was published, which is known today as the King James Bible. King James's rule is also distinguished by England's signing of a treaty with Spain, increased settlement of England's colonies, and increased trade overseas. In 1603, Shakespeare's acting company, the Lord Chamberlain's Men, received a new patent from the king and, henceforth, went by the title of the King's Men. The prestigious company performed many of Shakespeare's plays at court.

Shakespeare's Upward Mobility and Court Connections

Although Shakespeare's successful career took root in London, he still supported and maintained his ties to Stratford-upon-Avon. Evidence that Shakespeare's flourishing acting, writing, and business career allowed him to improve his style of living in Stratford is seen in many surviving documents. When Shakespeare bought the New Place estate in Stratford in 1597 at age 33, his theatre career must have been flourishing. Still acting, he appeared in Ben Jonson's comedy *Every Man in His Humor* in 1598 and the tragedy *Sejanus* in 1603. In 1598, printed editions of his *Richard II*, *Richard III*, and *Love's Labor's Lost* carried his name on the title page. In 1599, he was listed as an occupant of the new Globe theatre. In 1602, he bought more land and a cottage in Stratford, in Chapel Lane. Many records also link him and his plays with the courts of Elizabeth I and James I. In 1604, Shakespeare and eight of his fellow King's Men received red livery cloth for King James's coronation procession.

FACTS TO REMEMBER
- Contrary to Ben Jonson's dismissal of it, Shakespeare's grammar school education in Stratford gave him a solid grounding in Latin, Greek, Roman stage comedy, Ovid, and the rigors of classical rhetoric.
- Shakespeare vividly captured the flavor of London's streets, shops, taverns, and brothels throughout his plays.
- Shakespeare's plays are colored by a cross section of English social classes—from aristocrats, gentry, and citizens, to yeomen, servants, and beggars.
- Education and apprenticeships to guilds gave many teenagers of humble origins opportunities for upward mobility.
- Queen Elizabeth I and King James I, who reigned while Shakespeare wrote great plays, managed to stabilize fervent religious divisions within England's Anglican church.
- Records of land and home purchases in Stratford-upon-Avon demonstrate Shakespeare's success in the theatre business. Other documents link him directly with the courts of Elizabeth I and James I.

Chapter 2
A Man of the Theatre

> **INTRODUCTION**
> - Putting Shakespeare's theatre career in perspective
> - Shakespeare's accomplishments as a poet
> - What we know about Shakespeare's acting career
> - After writing notable early plays, Shakespeare joins the Lord Chamberlain's Men
> - Dramatic voices and influences on Shakespeare's plays
> - Shakespeare moves from actor and playwright to shareholder in the Globe theatre

Today, because of TV, film, and the powerful influence of the Internet and social media, Shakespeare has become a celebrity of mass media and our market-driven culture. To some, Shakespeare's plays are regarded as sacred documents. But looking at Shakespeare as a literary genius can mislead you. Consider this: We have no evidence that Shakespeare expressed any interest in publishing his plays while he was alive. During his lifetime, it was acceptable for poets to publish their works for posterity, not playwrights. (Remember that the modern novel had not even been born yet!)

Imagine what the day-to-day realities must have been for Shakespeare and his acting troupe, the Lord Chamberlain's Men. Yes, Shakespeare wrote great plays, but the theatre business was highly competitive. The company was under pressure to produce plays frequently. City officials closed the theatres often after outbreaks of the plague. As Shakespeare sweated over his beautiful blank verse, he and his company weathered the same financial pressures as small theatre managers, Broadway producers, and Hollywood movie moguls. Shakespeare was an artist, but he was also a businessman.

A Man of the Theatre

What do we know about Shakespeare's acting career? What acting companies did he work for? Who influenced his early plays, and who were his greatest rivals? Under what conditions did actors and playwrights work during those days? Did Shakespeare's plays ever get censored? Shakespeare and the Lord Chamberlain's Men thrived in a highly commercial environment. Within this atmosphere, playwriting was not always a solo effort. Dramatists sometimes collaborated on plays, much like the team who writes for television's *The Simpsons*. Let's look closely at Shakespeare as a man of the theatre.

A Poet and a Player

We don't know exactly what year Shakespeare left his wife and family in Stratford-upon-Avon and headed for London. It could have been sometime after 1585, when his twins Hamnet and Judith were born. The details of Shakespeare's career between 1585 and 1592 are mysterious. Many believe that Shakespeare arrived in London during the late 1580s to seek his fortune as a poet. His two highly acclaimed narrative poems, *Venus and Adonis* and *The Rape of Lucrece*, were dedicated to Henry Wriothesley, the third Earl of Southampton, in 1593 and 1594, respectively. These dedications suggest that the earl was Shakespeare's patron. Positive allusions to *Lucrece* around this time tell us the poems were well regarded. It's possible Shakespeare was also writing his beautiful sonnets by this time.

Chapter 2. A Man of the Theatre

Shakespeare the Actor and the Elizabethan Player's Life

As he grew up, it's likely that Shakespeare saw theatrical productions in the vicinity of Stratford performed by touring actors. (In Shakespeare's day, by the way, actors were called *players*.) We don't know the specific roles he performed, but Shakespeare is listed as a "principal actor" along with 25 other players in the First Folio. (The First Folio is the first printed collection of Shakespeare's plays, appearing in 1623.) He also had a major role in Ben Jonson's comedy *Every Man in His Humor*, in 1598, and the tragedy *Sejanus*, in 1603. He is supposed to have played the Ghost in *Hamlet*, but there's no real proof that he did. He's also rumored to have played Adam, the old man, in *As You Like It*.

It's likely that Shakespeare didn't take his acting as seriously as he did his writing. Or perhaps his true talents didn't lie in that direction. (By the way, a person who wrote poems or plays at this time was considered a *poet*. There was no such word as *playwright*.) In Elizabethan England, actors didn't have a stellar reputation. Many regarded them with suspicion and hostility because of their itinerant lifestyle. Their reputation as dissolute vagrants probably improved as public playhouses were built outside the City of London. Only young boys and men were allowed to act onstage. Women didn't take to the stage until after the English monarchy was restored in 1660. (Read more about early London playhouses in Chapter 3.)

Unless you worked for an acting company that had the support of a noble, the nomadic life of acting was a tough way to make a living. In the late sixteenth century, theatre was an odd business. London city officials and their vocal constituencies objected to the theatres because they encouraged bad conduct. But the queen and other aristocrats liked their entertainment. So noble patrons sponsored the acting companies to protect their own and the actors' interests. During this period, all performances in public theatres were considered "rehearsals" for official court performances. Essentially, the playhouses provided the companies a way to earn money and practice before performing at the court. (Read Chapter 3 to learn more about the Elizabethan theatres, their locations, their audiences, and why London officials and Puritans did not like them.)

VERSE BY VERSE

The life and work of an actor has never been easy. In *Shakespeare and Co.*, Stanley Wells details the incredible demands placed on actors in Shakespeare's day. They had little time to learn their lines or rehearse them before a new show opened. They also memorized and performed multiple roles at a time.

Below, Wells catalogues myriad challenges facing actors during Shakespeare's day, as well as the talents they needed to have:

> They had to be physically fit, and many of them needed to be able to fence, to fight, to sing, to dance, to play musical instruments. They had to speak highly wrought, rhetorically complex language, to give at least an impression of understanding classical allusions, and quite often to speak in languages other than English.

Frequent outbreaks of the plague closed the theatres for months on end, leaving players unemployed or forcing them to leave town and perform in the provinces. In 1593, an outbreak of the plague closed the theatres for two years. Like today's actors, who risk accidents in rehearsal or performance, acting could be very dangerous.

Passing Muster with the Master of the Revels

Before acting companies could perform new plays, they had to have them reviewed and licensed by the queen's Master of the Revels. The Lord Chamberlain's Men would submit Shakespeare's scripts to make sure their content did not offend the court. This practice also ensured that nothing seditious made it into public performance. Some scripts got censored. The queen's Master censored the scene in Shakespeare's *Richard II* when the king is deposed. Ben Jonson was accused of writing seditious content in his lost play called *The Isle of Dogs*. As a result, he was sent to prison for several weeks.

Chapter 2. A Man of the Theatre

A Poet Makes Inroads as a Dramatist

Presumably, while he wrote his sonnets and enjoyed recognition for his long poems, Shakespeare was causing a stir with his playwriting. It's amazing that the first record we have alluding to Shakespeare's playwriting career comes across as harsh and biting. In 1592, Robert Greene attacked Shakespeare in a pamphlet called *Greene's Groatsworth of Wit*:

> ... for there is an upstart Crow, beautified with our feathers that, with his tiger's heart wrapped in a player's hide, supposes he is as well able to bombast out a blank verse as the best of you: and being an absolute *Johannes factotum*, is in his own conceit the only Shake-scene in a country.

What exactly is he saying, and what does it mean? Greene's phrase "with his Tiger's heart wrapped in a player's hide," gives us a parody of Shakespeare's verse in his early play *Henry VI, Part III*. ("O tiger's heart wrapped in a woman's hide!") "Player's hide" suggests that Shakespeare is an actor who writes plays. Obviously, the playwright's *Henry VI* plays (summarized in Appendix A) were creating competition for established playwrights. Shakespeare, branded as an "upstart Crow," was coming into his own!

Ben Jonson was Shakespeare's best-known contemporary and rival during the 1600s. Even though Jonson denigrated Shakespeare's knowledge of classical languages, he gives him high praise in the 1623 First Folio. *The Oxford Dictionary of Shakespeare* excerpts one writer's thoughts (published in 1662) on the differences between the two dramatists:

> "Many were the wit-combats betwixt him and Ben Jonson; which two I behold like a Spanish great galleon and an English man of war: Master Jonson (like the former) was built far higher in learning; solid, but slow in his performances. Shakespeare, with the English man of war, lesser in bulk, but lighter in sailing, could turn with all tides, tack about, and take advantage of all winds, by the quickness of his wit and invention."
>
> —*The History of the Worthies of England*, Thomas Fuller

Part 1. Shakespeare and His World

Shakespeare and the Lord Chamberlain's Men

The theatres reopened in 1594 after being shuttered because of the plague. By this time, some scholars believe Shakespeare had already written his *Henry VI* history trilogy, *The Two Gentlemen of Verona* (a comedy), *The Taming of the Shrew* (a comedy), *Titus Andronicus* (a tragedy), and *Richard III* (a history). In the late 1580s, as he was acting and writing, Shakespeare most likely worked for one or more acting companies. Scholars can't be sure, but he may have been employed by the Queen's Men, Pembroke's Men, or the Lord Strange's Men.

It is certain that in 1594, Shakespeare, Richard Burbage, and five others formed the Lord Chamberlain's Men, sponsored by Henry Carey, Lord Hunsdon, who served under Queen Elizabeth I. For Shakespeare, working as both actor and playwright for a theatrical troupe with ties to the court would have been a dream come true. For the next couple of years, the troupe rose to prominence, performing for Elizabeth's court and for the public at the Theatre, the first public playhouse in Shoreditch. Shakespeare helped distinguish the company by delivering his manuscripts of *Richard II*, *A Midsummer Night's Dream*, and *Romeo and Juliet*. These plays were well received at the time.

A Debt to Christopher Marlowe

Today Shakespeare is celebrated as a genius without parallel, but he certainly didn't write in a vacuum. As a matter of fact, at various stages of his playwriting career, you can see clear influences of other dramatists' styles.

Christopher Marlowe was a great voice of Elizabethan theatre, and one that Shakespeare may have viewed as his greatest rival. Marlowe wrote plays for the Admiral's Men, a company whose dealings are wryly explored in the film *Shakespeare in Love* (1998). The author of a great narrative poem *Hero and Leander*, as well as the plays *Tamburlaine* and *Dr. Faustus*, Marlowe is one of the few Elizabethan dramatists whose works are still performed today. If Marlowe's life hadn't been cut short in a tavern fight in 1593, the landscape of the theatre world may have looked very different.

Marlowe is credited with originating the style of blank verse used in drama of the era. (Read more about blank verse in Chapter 5.) With *Dr. Faustus*, he pioneered a new kind of tragedy centered on one person's inevitable fall resulting from inherent limitations. Although his and Shakespeare's comedic visions are drastically different, the language of Shylock in Shakespeare's *The Merchant of Venice* draws inspiration from Marlowe's portrait of Barabas in *The Jew of Malta*. Shakespeare's allusion to Marlowe's *Hero and Leander* in his own play *As You Like It* is a rare nod to the writing of a contemporary.

A Note About Shakespeare's Sources

Nowadays, it's fashionable for playwrights and novelists to invent completely new plots for readers. There was no such expectation for playwrights during Shakespeare's day. Shakespeare had a brilliant knack for taking plots from romantic tales and biographies and constructing highly complex, unique plots of his own. We could name dozens of his direct and indirect sources, but here are some of the major ones.

For Roman plays like *Julius Caesar* and *Antony and Cleopatra*, he used material from Plutarch's *Lives of the Noble Grecians and Romans*, translated by Thomas North. In spotlighting the reigns of English kings in his histories, he relied on Raphael Holinshed's *Chronicles of England, Scotland, and Ireland*; Edward Hall's *The Union of the Two Noble and Illustre Families of Lancaster and York*; and *A Mirror for Magistrates*. He also used Holinshed and other sources as he created *Macbeth* and other tragedies. For his *The Comedy of Errors*, Shakespeare borrowed from two plays by Plautus, the Roman dramatist, and read them in the original Latin. For other comedies, Shakespeare read widely, adapting medieval and Renaissance tales and romances written in English, Portuguese, and Italian, for instance.

From Poet and Playwright to Sharer in the Globe

A couple of years after Shakespeare joined the Lord Chamberlain's Men, the company ran into a few difficulties with the man who owned the land beneath the Theatre. He refused to renew their lease. Because the troupe owned the playhouse, they disassembled the timbers of the Theatre and used them to build a new theatre south of the Thames. In 1599, this new theatre, christened the Globe, opened for business. Shakespeare became 1 of 10 shareholders in the Globe, a new status that led to personal prosperity for him and his family. It also afforded him a stable environment that contributed to the maturity of his playwriting.

John Heminges and Henry Condell, respected actors of the Lord Chamberlain's Men, put together the first collection of Shakespeare's plays. Known to us as the First Folio, the volume was published in 1623, seven years after Shakespeare died. Its title page, shown here, features Martin Droeshout's engraving of Shakespeare's portrait and the only such portrait known to be authentic.

(Public domain image obtained via Wikimedia Commons.)

When Shakespeare wrote *Julius Caesar* and *Hamlet* between 1599 and 1600, he launched a great period of dramatic achievement. For unexplained reasons, he moved away from writing comedies and histories. His last true comedy, written around 1601-1602, is *Twelfth Night*. Extremely well wrought, it looks ahead to the darker problem comedies like *Measure for Measure* and *All's Well That Ends Well*. No one knows why Shakespeare abandoned comedy to write tragedies like *King Lear* and *Macbeth*. Some suggest the death of his son Hamnet in 1596 darkened his vision and fueled his cycle of darker plays. Or perhaps audiences were clamoring for tragedy at that time, and Shakespeare adapted his output to suit public tastes.

When Queen Elizabeth died in 1603 and King James I took the throne, his court issued the Lord Chamberlain's Men a royal patent and changed their title to the King's Men. Shakespeare became their most important playwright. Plays such as *Othello*, *King Lear*, and *Macbeth* were performed for James I and his court.

In 1608, Shakespeare became part owner of Blackfriars, an indoor public theatre where night performances could be staged by candlelight. At this point he began writing plays for more sophisticated and aristocratic audiences. Shakespeare's output was slowing down, although he didn't stop taking his drama in new directions. Shakespeare retired to Stratford sometime before he died in 1616. It's not clear exactly when, or if, he wrote one or more of his late romances before or after he left London. With *The Winter's Tale* and *The Tempest*, he was giving audiences plays with fairytale romance and hopeful endings.

Shakespeare's Peers and Collaboration

In an article titled "The Mirror of Life" in the April 2007 issue of *Harper's Magazine*, Jonathan Bate says that despite our current view of Shakespeare as a "unique genius," in his own day, he was "but one in a constellation of theatrical stars." Bate notes that toward the end of Shakespeare's career, dramatists such as Ben Jonson, George Chapman, John Fletcher, Francis Beaumont, Thomas Kyd, Thomas Dekker, and Thomas Heywood, among others, had each created reputations for themselves.

Scholars continue to explore the highly collaborative nature of playwriting during Shakespeare's lifetime. Many agree that several of Shakespeare's later plays, once solely attributed to him, were co-written with another playwright. *Henry VIII* and *Timon of Athens* are good examples. Many experts in Elizabethan and Jacobean drama now attribute revisions of *Measure for Measure* and *Macbeth* to Thomas Middleton, author of *A Game at Chess* and *The Changeling*. Experts now claim that Shakespeare contributed elegant lines to *The Spanish Tragedy*, Thomas Kyd's drama that influenced Shakespeare's *Hamlet*.

According to scholar Gary Taylor and a team of editors of the 2016 *New Oxford Shakespeare Modern Critical Edition*, stylometric computer software analysis used to pinpoint authorship has revealed that the lesser-known *Henry VI, Parts I, II, and III* (among the first plays composed by Shakespeare) were co-authored by Shakespeare and his iconic rival, Christopher Marlowe. Among other new co-author attributions, the *New Oxford Shakespeare* credits Middleton with adapting Shakespeare's late comedy, *All's Well That Ends Well*. Read Appendix B to learn more about these co-authored plays.

Some who make their living by studying and teaching Shakespeare tend to get wrapped up in the beauty of his output. But they forget that he also aimed to entertain. No doubt he revised his plays so they would work better on the stage. Some are seriously focused on putting Shakespeare's career into its performance context. Nowadays, more and more experts consider that Shakespeare revised some of his plays, including *Hamlet*.

Shakespeare's Legacy and Impact on Modern Theatre

Shakespeare seems to be a fixture in the public imagination. In 2000, listeners of BBC's Radio 4 voted him Britain's Man of the Millennium. Shakespeare's persistent appeal in the twenty-first century stems, in part, from the timeless quality and inherent adaptability of his characters and dramatic plots. His plays continue to be adapted for film and television. Joseph Graves, artistic director of the Beijing Institute of World Theatre and Film affiliated with Peking University, says Shakespeare is such a hot ticket in China that as many as 4,000 people have appeared to watch his plays in villages outside Beijing! In a recent count online, there are close to 190 theatres and festivals that stage Shakespeare's plays in their repertory or summer programs. In Stratford-upon-Avon, home of world-class productions by the Royal Shakespeare Company, the Royal Shakespeare Theatre is undergoing redevelopment to the tune of 50 million pounds. Let's face it—Shakespeare has become big business for stage and screen impresarios.

Chapter 2. A Man of the Theatre

FACTS TO REMEMBER

- Shakespeare and the Lord Chamberlain's Men were popular with the court and London playgoers, but they still experienced business and financial pressures similar to stage and movie producers today.
- In the early 1590s, Shakespeare published two acclaimed narrative poems—*Venus and Adonis* and *The Rape of Lucrece*—which were dedicated to Henry Wriothesley, the third Earl of Southampton.
- Although actors had a bad reputation during Shakespeare's day, they were a highly talented lot in a hazardous, demanding profession.
- When Shakespeare became part owner in the Globe, his income increased and his playwriting matured.
- Shakespeare drew upon an array of plays, biographies, tales, and romances written in English, Latin, Italian, and Portuguese. He read some in their original languages and some in English translations.
- Unlike dramatists and novelists today, Shakespeare and his peers weren't expected to invent new plots for their plays.
- Queen Elizabeth's Master of the Revels screened all plays for offensive content before they were performed. If necessary, the plays were censored.

Chapter 3
Heady Theatre in London's Earliest Playhouses

> **INTRODUCTION**
> - How theatre-going differed in Shakespeare's day
> - Why and where London's earliest playhouses were built
> - The look and feel of the interior of an Elizabethan amphitheatre
> - The kinds of patrons Shakespeare's plays attracted
> - The importance of Elizabethan costumes
> - Tips about how early Elizabethan plays were produced

Exactly what motivates you to buy a ticket for a play or a Broadway-style musical? Maybe your friends are touting a show they've seen or you've read a promising review. So you buy a ticket. At $100 a pop, you feel compelled to get all dressed up, go out for an early dinner, and head to the theatre. When you're seated and comfortable, you might look around and take note. Everyone looks as well-heeled and well-coifed as you do.

When it's time to switch off your cell phone, the house lights go down and the audience gets hushed. Then you sit back, watch, and listen (and hope to get your money's worth!). You reserve your applause for the moment before the intermission. And heckling—well, that's only allowed in sports arenas, not the theatre. Compared to being in an early London playhouse, you might as well be in church!

To municipal and religious officials in London, the theatre during Shakespeare's time had a bad reputation. Not surprisingly, it was hugely popular. How did playgoing back then become so appealing? In this chapter, we'll look at the origins of this art form and how the early playhouses originated. We'll talk about Shakespeare's Globe theatre and the look and feel of those early stages. Exactly who performed Shakespeare's plays and what was their importance?

A New, Heady Theatre for the Masses

Today we speak in terms of going to *see* a play. During the heyday of Shakespeare's oral culture, you spoke about going to *hear* a play. When Puck addresses the amateur actors in *A Midsummer Night's Dream*, he conveys the primacy of the spoken word:

> What, a play toward? I'll be an auditor,
> An actor too perhaps, if I see cause.
> (III.1.79-80)

The look and feel of London's open-air playhouses in the late sixteenth century was nothing like the hushed intimacy of our own soft-seated auditoriums. Going to a playhouse during the Renaissance was like heading off to watch the Super Bowl or World Series baseball. On holidays, some Elizabethan playhouses could pack in as many as 3,000 spectators.

The public playhouse also provided a relatively new form of mass entertainment. Before 1576, when the first playhouses were built, dramatic entertainment consisted of morality plays performed by itinerant actors on a bare wooden platform in a country or urban square. Early on, acting troupes performed in the yards of the inns where they lodged. And many folks went in for popular spectator sports like bear baiting, a bloody spectacle resembling today's bullfights or cockfights.

Chapter 3. Heady Theatre in London's Earliest Playhouses

Experiencing a play in Shakespeare's time was a very different experience compared to what you're used to. For starters, public plays were performed in open-air theatres in the middle of the afternoon. To hear a play by Marlowe or Shakespeare, laborers and middle-class businessmen had to leave work early, which didn't sit well with London city officials!

What's more, traveling to the theatre was not an easy jaunt and carried some risk. To do it, playgoers ventured from the city into London's seedy, outer neighborhoods, where prostitutes and brothel owners plied their trade. In this area they might rub shoulders with patrons of the Paris Garden, where they watched bears and bulls being baited and attacked by dogs.

The Flight to the Suburbs

Here's a summary of how the first successful playhouses sprang up and eventually dotted London's suburbs. These outlying areas included Shoreditch—north of the Thames River and about a mile from the East End—and the Bankside, south of the river. Here theatre owners could obtain a license from the Master of the Revels, a court official, and remain safely outside the reach of meddling London officials.

The Theatre, The Curtain, The Rose, and The Swan

The first commercial playhouse was the Theatre, built in 1576 near Finsbury Fields in Shoreditch. James Burbage and a company of actors leased the land that it occupied. This multipurpose theatre resembled a bear-baiting arena, with an open courtyard and backstage areas that served as a backdrop and dressing rooms for the actors.

Dutch humanist scholar Johannes de Witt's sketch of the Swan Theatre (as copied by his friend Aernout van Buchell), from around 1596, is the only existing document that depicts actors inside an Elizabethan playhouse.

(Public domain figure by Aernout van Buchell, after Johannes de Witt, via Wikimedia Commons.)

Soon after Burbage built the Theatre, another businessman came along and wanted a piece of the action. So he constructed a playhouse known as the Curtain, where leading actor Richard Burbage often performed. An entrepreneur named Henry Laneman may have owned the Curtain, but some historians believe it was Philip Henslowe. Whoever he was, he must have done well because he built another playhouse on the Bankside, south of the Thames, about ten years later. Built in 1587, this theatre was called the Rose. Philip Henslowe, a savvy entrepreneur (and brothel owner!) owned the Rose and managed its resident company, known as the Admiral's Men. Eventually, this company performed Shakespeare's most important history plays.

Many popular Elizabethan plays were performed at the Rose theatre, and it drew enormous crowds. As a matter of fact, we have a lot to thank Henslowe for. If it weren't for his diary of accounts, known as Henslowe's *Diary*, in which he recorded payments to players and playwrights, we wouldn't know as much about the business side of things during that time.

The Globe

By 1599, Richard and Cuthbert Burbage—sons of James Burbage—oversaw the Theatre, where Shakespeare and the Lord Chamberlain's Men often performed. When the landlord refused to renew their lease, the Burbages had to find a new home, so they dismantled the Theatre and used the materials to erect the Globe. For the first time in his career, Shakespeare became a one-tenth owner in a public theatre and one of five "sharers" in the Globe. The Lord Chamberlain's Men made their home at the Globe, performing great Shakespearean plays between 1599 and 1603. Queen Elizabeth died during that year so they changed their name to the King's Men, after James I took the throne.

Shakespeare wrote his greatest plays for audiences at the Globe theatre on the Bankside. The original theatre, shown here, burned down after a cannon went off backstage during a performance of Henry VIII.

(Illustration by Robert Perry Molder.)

The Ornate Stage and Amphitheatre

When he built the Theatre, James Burbage essentially took the platform stage and roomy pit designed for spectators in popular bear-baiting arenas and transformed them. Even though no replica or drawing of the original Globe theatre exists, scholars and historians of theatre have deduced quite a lot from records, documents such as Henslowe's *Diary*, recent excavations on the Bankside, and, of course, the plays themselves.

As you read Shakespeare's plays, remain aware of the stage and setting that Shakespeare was writing for. Theatrical historians have reconstructed many characteristics of the Elizabethan stage straight from speeches and stage directions in his plays.

Interior Details

The Globe interior was constructed as a polygon, based upon the design of the bear-baiting ring. The stage was a bare wooden platform made from oak timbers. Based on its rival playhouse, the Fortune, we surmise that the Globe was 27½ feet deep and 43 feet wide and surrounded on three sides by multistoried galleries (the balcony seating) with space enough for seated spectators and "groundlings" to pack themselves in. The groundlings stood in the yard or pit for the entire performance.

A canopy or roof covered the platform stage, supported by two large wooden columns that were colorfully decorated to look like marble. The roof ceiling was painted with ornate designs representing the "heavens," while a trapdoor onstage opened into an area below the stage that could signify "hell" and function as a storage area for props. The players entered and exited the stage from two large middle doors, which were each flanked by an additional door. Actors used these outer "upstage" doors in many different ways.

In his Prologue to *Henry V*, Shakespeare invites his audiences to suspend their disbelief and imagine "mighty" French and English kingdoms battling on a tiny stage. He also makes literal references to physical playhouse details:

CHAPTER 3. HEADY THEATRE IN LONDON'S EARLIEST PLAYHOUSES

> ...   Can this cockpit hold
> The vasty fields of France? Or may we cram
> Within this wooden O the very casques
> That did affright the air at Agincourt?
> O, pardon! Since a crooked figure may
> Attest in little place a million,
> And let us, ciphers to this great accompt,
> On your imaginary forces work.
> Suppose within the girdles of these walls
> Are now confin'd two mighty monarchies,
>   ...
> Piece out our imperfections with your thoughts;
>   ...
> Think, when we talk of horses, that you see them
> Printing their proud hoofs i' th' receiving
> earth;
> (I.Prologue.11-20; 23; 26-27)

The "wooden O" of line 13 probably refers to the round shape of the Curtain theatre, where this play was performed in 1599. This single reference gave historians a big clue about the probable shape of the Globe.

Flash forward from the Curtain theatre in 1599 to the darkened interior of a modern theatre. Where would a school play or a Broadway show be without sets or a curtain to signal act and scene changes? At the Globe and other public playhouses, there was no such thing. Scene changes were signaled as actors in one scene left the stage, and others entered for the next scene. Also, as the players spoke their lines, the audience would pick up clues about setting.

In *Romeo and Juliet*, however, many scene transitions leave much to the imagination because there is no clear-cut exodus of one group of actors followed by another. After Romeo and Juliet meet at the Capulet dance in Act two, scene 1, Mercutio and Benvolio are looking for Romeo outside the orchard wall. As Mercutio rambles on about various types of love, Romeo remains quiet, presumably inside the wall underneath Juliet's window. Then Mercutio exits, signaling the end of scene 1, but when scene 2 starts, Romeo finishes

Mercutio's couplet, making the scene transition seamless. Suddenly Romeo is gazing at Juliet's window, forcing us (and Shakespeare's audience) to imagine Romeo inside the orchard wall in a location different from scene 1.

Props also offered a key visual ingredient about scene location. Without scenery or backdrops, a small sword or a letter in the hands of a player had no small effect. In addition, players relied on elaborate and expensive costumes to convey a character's position or a change in scene. Costumes were an acting company's most valuable asset.

To change into their costumes, Elizabethan actors used the *tiringhouse*, located backstage or behind the façade. Elizabethan costumes not only conveyed a character's nobility or lowborn status, they also gave the audience an important clue about where a scene took place. Fancy costumes also allowed the players of female parts to effectively disguise their male gender. In costume, actors were believable as dukes and kings, credible as vulgar fools, or whatever the role required.

The New Globe on London's Bankside, as near as possible, authentically reproduces the original Globe. To the best of their knowledge, architects and artisans have re-created a stunning replica of the interior and exterior of this exquisite playhouse.

For-Profit Theatre with Widespread Appeal

Like today, the business of Elizabethan theatre started and thrived as a commercial enterprise. (Well, until the Puritan Long Parliament shut the theatres down in 1642.) Playwrights and acting companies, who depended on the patronage of earls and other nobles, served managers like Henslowe, who staged a different play every afternoon.

In those first Elizabethan playhouses, rival theatre companies like the Admiral's Men and Lord Chamberlain's Men competed for patrons. Believe me, these houses did the business. If you were a tourist visiting London for a week's hiatus, you could see a different play every day! How different from theatres on Broadway or London's West End, which run the same play for weeks, months, or even years!

Chapter 3. Heady Theatre in London's Earliest Playhouses

Despite their business acumen and knack for entertaining, theatre managers were dogged by city officials who threatened to close them down. They were also bad-mouthed by pious Puritans who claimed they were downright immoral.

The amphitheatre at the Swan or the Globe playhouse probably held between 2,000 and 3,000 on major holidays. (That's huge compared to some of the biggest theatres on Broadway or in London's West End!) Admission was one penny for the groundlings, who stood in the yard or pit surrounding the stage. The cost was two pennies if you wanted access to a gallery section encircling the stage. You paid even more if you sat down in the galleries.

Indoor theatre existed during this time, but these venues were considered private. At the Blackfriars theatre, for instance, young boys performed classical-style dramas with highly stylized, formal rhetoric. Court masques with fancy costumes, music, and stage machinery were produced at Blackfriars, amid warmth and candlelight. These dramas appealed to nobles and highborn citizens and might cost as much as sixpence for admission if you sat in the gallery. If you sat in the yard closest to the stage, you paid more, not unlike the patron pecking order in modern theatres.

Who Were Those Early English Playgoers?

Just who was drawn to Shakespeare's plays? These plays attracted people from all walks of life. In *Shakespeare Alive!* Joseph Papp (late esteemed producer of the New York Shakespeare Festival) and Elizabeth Kirkland described the public theatre in Shakespeare's time as a "democratic gathering":

> Because plays were so affordable, accessible, and fun, they drew people from a wide range of social classes. Young noblemen studying at the Inns of Court, prosperous merchants and traders, well-to-do lawyers and doctors, grocers and glovemakers and booksellers and bakers and their families, enthusiastic teenage apprentices, poor peddlers, humble household servants, and menial workers—all crowded in through the same two doors before separating to go upstairs to the galleries or straight through to the yard...

Raucous, "Red-Light" Entertainment

The earliest Elizabethan playhouses had a bad reputation for a variety of reasons. Before playhouses were built, actors, considered lowborn and disreputable, wandered the countryside and performed at the inns where they lodged. This type of entertainment caught on and inn-yard play-acting became more popular and commercial. London city officials began regulating inn-yard entertainment in 1574, forcing theatre entrepreneurs to relocate. After this year, the purpose-built theatres that sprang up were built in the suburbs, where there were fewer restrictions on public behavior. Because the playhouses could pack in large crowds, they were seen as extremely dangerous during outbreaks of the deadly bubonic plague. City officials also feared that large crowds were prone to rioting.

Anything could happen at the playhouse. A play by Marlowe or Shakespeare might start around 2 P.M. and finish in the late afternoon. Obviously, in the days before electricity, you couldn't see a play after dark. Elizabethans also risked their personal safety if they didn't leave the theatre and get home before dark. Some historians note that fights occasionally broke out among the groundlings that paid a penny for admission. The spectators might shout out their reactions to the people on stage. The whole experience was a lively one.

Inside the Playhouse

So what was all the scandal and excitement about? Elizabethan drama, particularly works written by Shakespeare, offered the London public a diversion never seen before. This drama blended beautiful, rhetorical speeches with ingenious comedy, burlesque, and bawdy jokes.

Beginning with the crowd-puller *Richard III* and the farcical *The Taming of the Shrew*, Shakespeare was inventing theatre that anyone could relate to, not just wealthy people. Shakespeare treated his public to stories about lovers, husbands and wives, fathers and daughters, and the world of both city and country folks. These plays included characters from all walks of life. There was something for everyone.

The bawdy passion of *Romeo and Juliet* was a far cry from the preachy mystery plays held over from medieval times. This was heady theatre like nothing ever seen before.

As its name suggests, drama on the Globe's stage reflected the world and all of the people in it. As Shakespeare's playwriting evolved, he began blending the blank verse and rhyme found in his early comedies with an artful use of prose. Though highly stylized, this prose sounded closer to the natural rhythms of conversation. In turn, his characters became more rounded, more complex, and more self-aware. The portraits in his festive comedies and mature tragedies were so penetrating they offered playgoers a mirror of their own souls.

Around 1600, as Shakespeare began churning out great comedies like *Twelfth Night*, the public just couldn't stay away. During this time he also wrote *Hamlet*, and his position as one of the court's most important playwrights was assured. He was successful, part owner of the Globe, and a playwright supported by the Lord Chamberlain's Men under the queen. After Queen Elizabeth's death in 1603, his company became known as the King's Men under the new king, James I.

The Actors

During the Renaissance the success of plays onstage depended on the actors' performances. But unlike today, the entire show hinged on their talents because the acting company had no creative or technical team and no visual machinery to entertain and distract the audience. Theatre historians believe Elizabethan actors didn't need close direction like many actors do today. Scenery wasn't necessary in those days because the script signaled key setting changes between scenes.

Absent the visual sets we take for granted, Shakespeare wrote plays that entertained with poetry and language, and the actors were the conduits of the spoken word. Today, on the other hand, resident theatre companies spend thousands of dollars on scenery, relying largely on backdrops and elaborate sets. Without our fancy visual displays today, we would be lost. Shakespeare, however, asked his audiences to use their own imaginations.

Women were not allowed on the Elizabethan stage. Young boys who hadn't reached puberty performed female roles. Long before our own age of mass printing and instant electronic communication, Shakespeare's was a culture that relied on and prized the spoken word. In Hamlet's play-within-the-play for the Danish court, the prince coaches the visiting players on technique, cautioning them on the dangers of overdoing it.

> Speak the speech, I pray you, as I pronounc'd
> it to you, trippingly on the tongue, but if you mouth it,
> as many of our players do, I had as live the town-crier spoke my
> lines. Nor do not saw the air too much with
> your hand, thus, but use all gently, for in the very
> torrent, tempest, and, as I may say, whirlwind of your
> passion, you must acquire and beget a temperance that
> may give it smoothness.
> (III.2.1-8)

Actors today take a whole lot for granted. Imagine for a moment how different things would be if you were a player in one of Shakespeare's plays. You audition; you get the part; but you can't rush out and simply buy the latest Variorum or Oxford edition of *Hamlet* in paperback! Original scripts were scarce and they belonged to the acting company. The bookkeeper or theatre manager, who copied all the parts, would give you a scroll containing only your lines and the cues from a preceding part that prompted you to walk onstage.

It's likely that Elizabethan actors were just more adept at recitation and memorization than modern actors. They could be relied upon to use the English language artfully and rhetorically to entertain their audiences. Their gift for speaking verse and powers of memorization are rarely found today.

Did Shakespeare Direct His Plays?

As modern theatre has evolved, the importance of the director has grown considerably. When Shakespeare was acting and writing his own plays, though, close direction of actors' movements wasn't needed. Why is that? Largely because Shakespeare crafted his scripts so that the verse and stage directions conveyed all of the information the actors would ever need.

In *A Midsummer Night's Dream's* play-within-the-play, Peter Quince, Nick Bottom, and company give us an intriguing glimpse into how an early play might have been cast and rehearsed. The playhouse manager would assign roles to the actors and pass out scrolls containing the parts. During the show, he would stand in the wings and prompt the actors, based on the entrances and exits marked up in his script.

> **FACTS TO REMEMBER**
> - London's first open-air playhouses, which drew large, colorful crowds from all walks of life, offered the same kind of relaxed atmosphere as you find in today's sports arenas.
> - Costing as little as a penny, plays in Shakespeare's time were less exclusive and more broadly appealing than today.
> - Before Shakespeare's Globe was built in 1599, London's open-air playhouses included the Theatre, the Curtain, the Swan, and the Rose.
> - Built in London's outlying suburbs in "red light" districts, the early playhouses were loathed by city officials and religious folks.
> - The Elizabethan stage consisted of a canopied wooden platform, surrounded by three-tiered balcony seating and a large pit where the groundlings stood.
> - Because there was little scenery on the Elizabethan stage, costumes and props were very important.

Part 2
Plays Are for the Stage

Part 2. Plays Are for the Stage

Before we talk about Shakespeare's plays, we have to get a few things straight. Since literary criticism became a professional academic pursuit, people have fallen in love with the language and poetry of Shakespeare's plays. By putting words, verses, and speeches under a microscope, scholars have enhanced our knowledge of Shakespeare's meaning and artistic method.

But wait! A play is very different from a sonnet by John Donne or a poem by Wallace Stevens. Remember, Shakespeare wrote his plays for the stage. These works are scripts, pure and simple, and you must remember this. They had to be adapted and changed to work effectively in front of an audience.

The following chapters encourage you to think about the plays as works for the stage. Take a break from literary analysis for a moment. We'll talk about the importance of the spoken word in Shakespeare's day to help you make better sense of Shakespeare's own words.

Shakespeare was influenced by the form and fashion of his own time. We'll look at the unique rhetorical style and substance of Shakespeare's language and wordplay. But let's not forget that without actors who live and breathe and the directors who produce the plays, these beautiful words and speeches are not as powerful.

Last, but not least, we'll consider when and how Shakespeare's plays were published and clarify some confusing facts about the published editions.

Chapter 4
Experiencing Shakespeare on the Stage

> **INTRODUCTION**
> - Benefits of experiencing Shakespeare inside the theatre
> - Tips to help you enjoy the dramatic experience
> - Pitfalls of analyzing character, theme, and fixed ideas about genre
> - Thoughts about Shakespeare's scripts from experts
> - Watching Shakespeare "live" in North America

Now that we've introduced you to the world of Elizabethan theatre during Shakespeare's time, it's time to fast-forward a few centuries to today's Shakespearean enterprise. As time passes, the spoken idiom of Shakespeare's plays becomes more difficult to understand and interpret. You're probably asking, how can I possibly watch Shakespeare and understand him? So much of his Elizabethan vocabulary has vanished! What about all that cryptic poetry and verse, the myriad allusions and endless puns? So difficult to decipher!

Do you know the lyrics of all your favorite rock songs? Trying to catch every word during a performance is like trying to hear every lyric at a rock concert. I speak for countless actors, directors, and critics when I say—there is more to a Shakespeare play than just words. No doubt you get more out of watching

Macbeth in the theatre if you read the play beforehand. But don't be fooled by what your teachers tell you. When Shakespeare wrote his scripts, he set out to reenact a compelling story using talented players who were skilled at the art of providing poetic entertainment for your ear.

One last caveat—the Shakespearean critical industry is a gargantuan enterprise. Each year, scholars write dozens of new books; at any given moment in North America, theatre critics are reviewing a new performance for readers. Reviews and journal articles are useful, but even knowledgeable critics can lead you astray. Go to the theatre, watch the plays, and be your own judge.

Entertainment for the Ear

We can thank theatrical historians and esteemed director and playwright Harley Granville-Barker for reminding us what it was like to watch a Shakespeare play at the Globe in 1599. To Shakespeare's generation, the spoken language was still the most important medium of communication. At the Stratford-upon-Avon grammar school where Shakespeare was educated, students became proficient in Latin grammar and learned some basic Greek. The playwright would have learned the art of spoken rhetoric by studying the writings of Cicero and Quintilian, two brilliant Roman orators famed for their prose style.

As we discussed in Chapter 3, Shakespeare's audiences flocked to the Globe to "hear" a play, not see it. In writing his plays, Shakespeare provided countless clues about setting and stage business into his verse, to help the actors and audience. To appreciate Shakespeare's plays, it wasn't necessary for the audience to read the plays beforehand. Elaborate sets that conveyed a drama's time or place were unnecessary. Simple costumes communicated whether a character was a duke or a gravedigger. Remember that many of those who stood in the pit at the Globe were illiterate. Shakespeare wrote for them, as well as for the well-coifed nobles who sat in the upper tiers. For them and for you, hearing an Elizabethan play should be akin to hearing music; it is entertainment for the ear.

For the past 200 years, great poets, playwrights, and men of letters have dissected the written texts of Shakespeare's plays. This is a laudable, painstaking exercise that has brought us closer to the discrepancies among multiple versions of a single play and the meanings inherent in Elizabethan English,

CHAPTER 4. EXPERIENCING SHAKESPEARE ON THE STAGE

a dialect accessible to language scholars. But Shakespeare's dialect is not Mandarin Chinese, nor is it as foreign as the Middle English of Chaucer's *Canterbury Tales*. It is still possible for a modern English speaker to follow the spoken dialect of Queen Elizabeth I, especially in the theatre.

Remember—Each Play Is a Script

We have no reason to believe that Shakespeare had an interest in writing his plays for publication. (We'll look into this question further in Chapter 6, when we discuss how Shakespeare's plays were published.) But for now, remember that Shakespeare wrote his plays as scripts to be performed in public playhouses for paying customers, as well as for nobles at the court.

Think about the Elizabethan commercial enterprise as something akin to today's film and TV industry. If Shakespeare lived today, it is possible that he would have written for film or television, as well as for the stage. Dramatist Tom Stoppard, for example, who has written cerebral dramas like *The Coast of Utopia* and *The Invention of Love*, also co-authored the film script for *Shakespeare in Love*.

Shakespeare in Love *(1998) lends insight into the cutthroat, highly collaborative theatre business that Shakespeare navigated in the early 1590s, after writing early works like* The Two Gentlemen of Verona. *Here, Shakespeare (Joseph Fiennes) struggles with his muse while writing* Romeo and Juliet.

(Photo courtesy of Miramax/Photofest.)

The Dramatic Experience and the Integral Role of the Actor

We all realize, of course, that Shakespeare is an integral part of the Western canon of great literary works. No matter how much I tout the importance of "hearing" a play in performance, most English speakers are introduced to Shakespeare in their junior high or high school English classes. Realizing that our academic study of Shakespeare so often precedes our enjoyment of his plays inside the theatre, here are a few tips to ensure that your English teachers don't sour you on the thrill of Shakespearean drama.

Many of us were taught to study plays using principles of literary analysis. Doing a close reading of a novel by Virginia Woolf or a poem by Emily Dickinson is a useful exercise. You can read and reread the text to gain a deeper understanding of character and theme. But applying such principles to drama can be slippery because each actor who plays Henry V or Prince Hamlet, for example, interprets the role differently. Actors lend personal nuances to a role's soliloquy and dialogue, shading the role differently in any given production. The same thing holds true for film. Laurence Olivier's Henry V is mature and sardonic, while the younger Kenneth Branagh comes across as serious and intense. Which characterization was Shakespeare's intent? Neither and both, because Shakespeare's language leaves room for interpretation and ambiguity. His language is all we have to go on and all that we really need.

In *William Shakespeare: Writing for Performance*, John Russell Brown observes that Shakespeare experienced special challenges in writing for the stage. He conceived each part by imagining how words and actions could work together. Shakespeare's characterization is dynamic and determined by a character's words, actions, and interplay with other characters. Brown writes, "None of the characters is independent: all are made progressively clear by interaction with one another." He also suggests that the life that Shakespeare gave his characters is far from abstract and fixed "constructs" imagined by critics. "Like audiences at the Globe,

> who came again and again to a favorite play, [Shakespeare] would not have been satisfied by any one performance which gave life to them."

To understand the variety of potential interpretations that a given scene provides for actors, consider the charged moment after Gertrude summons Hamlet into her "closet," or bedchamber, following Hamlet's production of *The Mousetrap*. Gertrude is upset because Hamlet has offended Claudius, his stepfather. But Hamlet chooses this moment to angrily interrogate her about how she could so quickly remarry after holding such affection for King Hamlet, her former husband. Actors play this scene in myriad ways—some Hamlets seem both tender and frustrated with Gertrude. Others get so physical and violent with her that they throw her on the bed. Other Hamlets, insanely jealous, have gotten sexual with Gertrude, intimating that an incestuous attraction existed between mother and son!

Keep in mind that Shakespeare wrote his plays centuries before drama and poetry became subjects of academic criticism. In the First Folio, Shakespeare's characters are listed under the heading Dramatis Personae, meaning "the persons of the plays." To this day, classical actors in Britain and North America are trained to view their role or "part" primarily in terms of what the lines themselves reveal. The tendency for actors to psyche out a character's deeply rooted motivations started in the twentieth century.

Shakespeare's Scripts Offer Freedom of Interpretation

When we begin addressing individual plays in Chapter 7, we'll learn how directors find room for individual interpretation of Shakespeare's plays within the scripts themselves. For each production, directors decide how to cast actors, block scenes, cut scenes and lines, and design sets and costumes based upon factors such as the size of their budget as well as the nature of their performance space. Actors, too, interpret their lines differently, depending on their director's vision and the co-stars with whom they share a given scene.

PART 2. PLAYS ARE FOR THE STAGE

Michael Kahn has served as the Artistic Director of the Shakespeare Theatre Company in Washington, D.C. since 1986. After his first rehearsal of *Hamlet* in 2007, he wrote, "I'm interested in exploring completely, carefully, and deeply what happens in this play line by line. I think I do my best work that way . . . when I try to expand my thinking into the myriad possibilities that the text offers. The exciting thing about this play is that the characters develop and change based on what happens. They don't seem to arrive with fixed identities . . . I think Shakespeare still appeals to us because of the ambiguity of his characters."

Asides Magazine, Volume 5, 2006–2007

Unlike modern play scripts, directors must also be aware that most of Shakespeare's great plays were published in more than one edition before they appeared in his 1623 First Folio. A director of *Hamlet*, for example, can base his or her production on the 1603, 1604, or 1623 edition, or some combination thereof!

Shakespeare in Live Performance

If you are studying or acting Shakespeare, or if you want to see a live performance of your favorite play, visit the World Wide Web to find the Shakespeare festival nearest you. Approximately 120 producers of Shakespeare's plays belong to the Shakespeare Theatre Association of America. Their venues, institutional affiliation, and budgets vary considerably. Top-tier festivals devoting a significant portion of their multimillion dollar budgets to staging Shakespeare include the Stratford Festival of Canada, Oregon Shakespeare Festival, and Utah Shakespeare Festival. The Shakespeare Theatre Company D.C., New York Shakespeare Festival, Chicago Shakespeare Festival, and Alabama Shakespeare Festival are also nationally renowned. High-budget and notable regional festivals include the Texas Shakespeare Festival, New Jersey Shakespeare Festival, Great Lakes Theatre Festival/Idaho Shakespeare Festival, and Colorado Shakespeare Festival, among others.

FACTS TO REMEMBER
- To Elizabethan audiences, Shakespeare's plays were rich entertainment for the ear and had none of the visual spectacle found in today's more elaborately staged plays.
- Remember, Shakespeare wrote his plays as scripts for public playhouse and court performances, not for publication.
- Like today's stage and TV writers, Shakespeare adapted his romantic comedies and revenge tragedies to entertain audiences and sell tickets.
- There is no single way to approach a Shakespeare script. The director bases decisions about blocking scenes and cutting lines on his budget, his performance space, and his cast.

Chapter 5

Shakespeare's Music

> **INTRODUCTION**
> - An introduction to Shakespeare's verse line and how it is composed
> - A look at rhetorical devices such as repetition, rhyme, alliteration, antithesis, and punning
> - Common Shakespearean expressions in everyday English
> - The elaborate wordplay and wit of *Love's Labor's Lost*
> - Tips about Shakespeare's use of verse and prose

Recall once again that each Shakespeare play is a script. With this orientation, you can begin to think about the words and lines of your favorite plays in terms of spoken language, just as an actor would. To fully appreciate *Romeo and Juliet*, for example, you need to unlock the secrets of Shakespeare's sound garden.

Let's look closely at the artistry of Shakespeare's dramatic language. What do we mean when we say the plays are written in blank verse? Why the inverted syntax? Why do some plays have more rhyme than others? Why do some characters speak in verse and others in prose? Why does Shakespeare's verse sound so much richer when spoken out loud? How does Shakespeare use rhyme, antithesis, and other rhetorical tools? Let's explore a few answers to these questions. Then we'll talk about performing Shakespeare's verse from the actor's perspective.

The Artistry of Shakespeare's Verse Line

Just for a moment, forget about trying to keep the Montagues and Capulets straight in *Romeo and Juliet* and listen to the rhythm of the Prologue: "Two households, both alike in dignity,/In fair Verona, where we lay our scene." Notice how each line consists of ten syllables. Listen further: "From forth the fatal loins of these two foes/A pair of star-crossed lovers take their life." Do you hear the alliterative use of words beginning in *f* and *l*? In each of these lines, you can hear the beat and notes of Shakespeare's music.

Blank Verse and Rhyme, Repetition, and Syntax

Let's recite the entire Prologue quoted below. Try saying each of the lines out loud.

> Two households, both alike in dignity,
> In fair Verona, where we lay our scene,
> From ancient grudge break to new mutiny,
> Where civil blood makes civil hands unclean.
> From forth the fatal loins of these two foes
> A pair of star-cross'd lovers take their life;
> Whose misadventur'd piteous overthrows
> Doth with their death bury their parents' strife.
> The fearful passage of their death-mark'd love,
> And the continuance of their parents' rage,
> Which, but their children's end, nought could remove,
> Is now the two hours' traffic of our stage;
> (Prologue.1-12)

Notice that each one has ten syllables and conforms to a predictable rhythmic pattern. You'll find deviations and exceptions, but for the most part, much of Shakespeare's verse consists of a rhythmic pattern known as *blank verse*.

CHAPTER 5. SHAKESPEARE'S MUSIC

Shakespeare makes full use of his sound garden by repeating words in a given line of the Prologue—"Where *civil* blood makes *civil* hands unclean." You find *alliteration* in the words "forth," "fatal," and "foes" in line five, as well as "Doth" and "death" in line eight. Next, notice the alternating rhyme within the final word of each verse line. When spoken, the meaning in this musical speech comes across clearly. Try reading it silently, and then have a friend read it to you out loud—notice the difference?

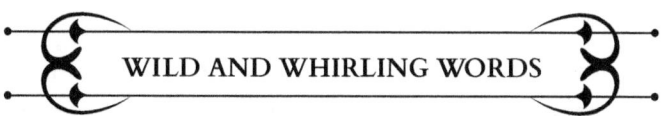

WILD AND WHIRLING WORDS

Blank verse is defined as unrhymed iambic pentameter, which refers to a line consisting of five "meters" or feet. Each foot is made up of an iamb, that is, two syllables, consisting of one unstressed syllable and one stressed syllable. Drama written in blank verse sounds pleasant to our ears because it approximates the natural rhythms of English prose. Realize that Shakespeare didn't invent this verse form. We credit Christopher Marlowe, author of *Dr. Faustus*, for his trendsetting use of blank verse in English drama.

We use the term **alliteration** to refer to the recurrence of an initial consonant sound in one or many verse lines or phrases, as in Mercutio's label of Tybalt as the *courageous captain of compliments*. The term **assonance** refers to the recurrence of the same or similar vowel sounds across one or more verse lines, as in Mercutio's quip to Romeo: *Thy wit is a very bitter sweeting, it is a most sharp sauce.*

Elsewhere in the play, notice how Shakespeare frequently inverts the normal "subject–verb–object" syntax of spoken prose. Listen when Mercutio describes how Queen Mab "gallops night by night/ . . . O'er ladies' lips, who *straight on kisses dream,*/Which oft the angry Mab *with blisters plagues,*/Because their breath *with sweetmeats tainted are.*" The inverted syntax shown in the italicized phrases allows the playwright to retain the rhythmic stress of the iambic pentameter.

The Dramatic Power of Antithesis

Shakespeare often infuses his verse with conflicting ideas to enrich the ambiguity of emotion or situation. This technique, called **antithesis,** was one of Shakespeare's favorite poetic and rhetorical devices. The term refers to the use of contrasting images or ideas within one or more verse lines. Using antithesis, Shakespeare creates oxymoronic images that combine adjectives and nouns that sound contradictory. Images that we classify as antithetical make sense metaphorically.

When actors are presented with *antithesis*, they work hard to inject the line (or lines) with the right pace and tone. Unhappy because he's getting nowhere with Rosaline, Romeo uses antithesis, or paradox, over and over to great emotional effect:

> Here's much to do with hate, but more with love.
> Why, then, O brawling love! O loving hate!
> O any thing, of nothing first [create]!
> O heavy lightness, serious vanity,
> Misshapen chaos of well[-seeming] forms,
> Feather of lead, bright smoke, cold fire, sick health,
> Still-waking sleep, that is not what it is!
> (I.1.175-181)

Later, Romeo's complaint about Rosaline's insistence on remaining chaste employs antithesis: "O, she is rich in beauty, only poor/That, when she dies, with beauty dies her store."

Punning, Figures of Speech, and Elaborate Wordplay

One rich source of Shakespeare's verbal genius lies in his zeal for figurative language and puns. The use of puns in the plays is limitless. *Romeo and Juliet* offers many good examples. After Tybalt fatally stabs Mercutio, Romeo rushes to his side, and the dying man quips: "Ask for me tomorrow, and you shall find me a *grave* man," punning darkly on his imminent burial.

In other moments Mercutio's speech is chock full of alliteration, sexual puns, word repetition, and deliciously bawdy overtones. When Romeo whines over his misfortune with the aloof Rosaline in Act one, Mercutio riffs: "If love be rough with you, be rough with love./Prick love for pricking, and you beat love down." "Prick love for pricking"—in other words, relieve your sexual appetite by having sex! In general, Shakespeare's plays are heavily laced with metaphor and hyperbole. The latter is found in Juliet's "A thousand times good night!" followed by Romeo's "A thousand times the worse, to want thy light."

In the following passage from *The Tempest*, Sebastian begins with a simile and introduces a diatribe of puns and counter-puns:

Alonso: Prithee peace.

Sebastian (to Antonio): He receives comfort like cold porridge . . .

Sebastian: Look, he's winding up the watch of his wit, by and by it will strike. (II.1.9-12)

Gonzalo: When every grief is entertain'd that's offer'd,
Comes to th'entertainer—

Sebastian: A *dollar*.

Gonzalo: *Dolor* comes to him indeed, you have spoken truer than you purpos'd. (II.1.16-21)

Antonio: Which, of he or Adrian, for a good wager, first begins to crow?

Sebastian: The old cock.

Antonio: The cock'rel. (II.1.28-31)

In the last two lines, Adrian is compared to a younger rooster and Gonzalo to an old one.

Talking Verse and Prose

Shakespeare's use of verse and prose varies from play to play. *Richard II* and *King John* are written exclusively in verse. *The Merry Wives of Windsor*, on the other hand, is almost entirely in prose, and two-thirds of *Twelfth Night*'s lines are classified as prose. Both parts of *Henry IV* and *As You Like It* are roughly equal parts verse and prose. Most plays combine the two modes, and if you study your favorite play closely, you'll notice that nobles and highborn characters often speak in verse, while clowns and lowborn people speak in prose. This generalization is overly simplistic, though. In *As You Like It*, for example, topics having to do with love and romance are explored in verse by all classes of people. If you study the plays closely, you'll notice how key moments of drama can provoke a character to switch from verse to prose, or from prose to verse.

TIMELESS SOLILOQUIES

It is difficult to assess Shakespeare's impact on our English vocabulary. He coined countless words and expressions that are fixtures of our English lexicon. We give Shakespeare credit for coining colorful words such as *bedazzle, assassination, cold-blooded, zany, puke, rant, mewling, jaded, foppish, eyeball, shooting star,* and *madcap*. The first documented use of common words such as *monumental, successful, pious, priceless, upstairs, well-bred, soft-hearted, uneducated, tranquil, invitation,* and *grime* came from Shakespeare's plays. By the same token, Shakespeare is often credited for coining words that began circulating decades before he was composing plays. Manuscript scholars are turning up usages of words that Shakespeare must have stumbled upon in his myriad reading and research.

Here are a few sayings that are original to Shakespeare's plays. Most have come to sound hackneyed because they're so familiar. From *Hamlet*, we get *To thine own self be true, Sweets to the sweet,* and *The lady doth protest too much.* From *King Lear,* we get *I am more sinned against than sinning.* From *Romeo and Juliet,* recall *A rose by any other word would smell as sweet* and *Parting is such sweet sorrow.*

Other Patterns and the Wit Combat of *Love's Labor's Lost*

Shakespeare has enriched his verse with a variety of rhetorical patterns commonly used by sonneteers, epic poets, and other dramatists of his day. Two such patterns are rhymed couplets and *anaphora*, the repetition of an initial word or phrase for several consecutive lines. In planning to trick Claudius by staging a play, Hamlet utters a famous rhymed couplet: "The play's the thing/ Wherein I'll catch the conscience of the king." Look at a copy of *A Midsummer Night's Dream* and notice that it's made up of nothing but rhymed couplets!

> No Shakespearean play is richer in self-conscious, verbal artistry than *Love's Labor's Lost*. (Read more about the story in Appendix A.) Note Berowne's very famous line: "Light seeking light doth light of light beguile." Here the word *light*, by turns, means *intellect*, *wisdom*, *eyesight*, and *daylight*, according to Harold Bloom's observation in *Shakespeare: The Invention of the Human*. The play is so rich in poetry, punning, and verbal word games that you wonder if Shakespeare deliberately set out to charm an early private audience with his verbal gifts.

Pick any scene of *Love's Labor's Lost* and you'll be dazzled by the brilliance of its repartee. Throughout the play Shakespeare uses numerous examples of civil jesting or merry scoffing—formally known as *asteismus*. This kind of jesting involves interplay among two or more characters using facetious or mocking answers. Rosaline and Katherine's play on the words *light* and *dark* in the verbal fencing match below sounds highly complex!

> Kath: He made her melancholy, sad, and heavy,
> And so she died. Had she been light, like you,
> Of such a merry, nimble, stirring spirit,
> She might 'a' been [a] grandam ere she died;
> And so may you; for a light heart lives long.

Rosaline:	What's your dark meaning, mouse, of this light word?
Kath:	A light condition in a beauty dark.
Rosaline:	We need more light to find your meaning out.
Kath:	You'll mar the light by taking it in snuff, Therefore I'll darkly end the argument.
Rosaline:	Look what you do, you do it still i' th' dark.
Kath:	So do not you, for you are a light wench.
Rosaline:	Indeed I weigh not you, and therefore light.
Kath:	You weigh me not? O, that's you care not for me.
Rosaline:	Great reason: for past care is still past cure. (V.2.14-28)

Love's Labor's Lost is performed less often than other comedies, but if you happen to be in a city where it's being performed, don't miss it. When the Houston Shakespeare Festival staged *Love's Labor's Lost* in 2007, it provided subtitles of the actual script for audiences at Miller Outdoor Theatre.

Chapter 5. Shakespeare's Music

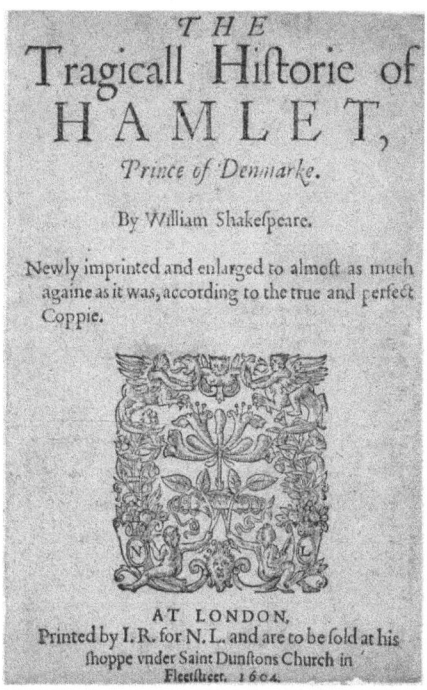

Pictured is the title page of the 1604 quarto edition of Hamlet, *a version of the play that is believed to have come from Shakespeare's original manuscript. Hamlet's advice to the players while staging the* Mousetrap *for the court offers a clue about how Shakespeare meant for his lines to be interpreted.*

(Public domain image obtained via Wikimedia Commons.)

> **FACTS TO REMEMBER**
> - Shakespeare's principal verse form in the plays is blank verse, or unrhymed iambic pentameter.
> - In varying his rhetorical technique, Shakespeare creates a rich sound garden. Some of his favorite devices include rhyme, puns, alliteration, assonance, and antithesis.
> - Shakespeare's plays contain countless words and expressions that are fixtures of the English language.
> - Shakespeare's balance of verse and prose varies greatly from play to play, often corresponding to a character's class or topic of conversation.

Chapter 6
How Shakespeare's Plays Were Published

> **INTRODUCTION**
> - Renaissance attitudes toward writing and publishing plays
> - The differences among early quarto editions, prompt-books, and the 1623 First Folio
> - Mysteries surrounding what happened to Shakespeare's original scripts
> - How do scholars arrive at the order in which Shakespeare wrote his plays?
> - Relating your notions about genre to Shakespeare's plays

In previous chapters, we've talked about the theatre business that employed Shakespeare and how he became known as a highly renowned dramatist for London's playhouses and the royal courts of England. We've looked at the heady world of London playhouses, their shape and popular atmosphere, and their rowdy suburban locale on the Bankside. You've gotten tips about the importance of thinking about the plays as scripts that can be freely interpreted by the actor and director. Most importantly, you've gotten a sense of how important it is to watch the plays in performance to truly appreciate them.

Despite the availability of centuries of written opinions by esteemed scholars, there is no substitute for judging the plays on your own.

But what if you genuinely want to read the plays and make some sense of what Shakespeare wrote? You might wonder exactly where the original scripts of Shakespeare's plays are. What shape are they in, and where can you find them? When you go to the library or bookstore, why are there so many different editions of Shakespeare's plays? These are excellent questions, but the answers to them are a bit more complicated than you'd imagine.

Playwriting—A Less Noble Profession

The first three books of Edmund Spenser's epic poem *The Faerie Queen* were published in 1590. Sir Philip Sidney's *Arcadia*, a pastoral romance written in prose, appeared in print that same year. Shakespeare's great narrative poems *Venus and Adonis* and *The Rape of Lucrece* were published in 1593 and 1594, respectively, and a collection of his sonnets was printed in 1609. But oddly enough, Shakespeare published no collection of his plays during his lifetime.

To understand exactly why, realize that being a poet and man of letters was highly esteemed in Shakespeare's day. Poets often depended on noble patrons to support their work. Shakespeare dedicated *Venus and Adonis* and *The Rape of Lucrece* to his patron Henry Wriothesley, the third Earl of Southampton. Writing plays, on the other hand, was considered less reputable because it was more commercial, because the playhouses had a bad reputation, and because plays were written by low-paid freelance dramatists who collaborated freely to keep their companies supplied with scripts.

During the early 1590s, before he attracted acclaim from his peers for writing great plays like *Romeo and Juliet*, Shakespeare was a great poet, a writer of beautiful sonnets, who also made a living by writing plays. However, during the mid to late 1590s and beginning in 1599 when he wrote plays acted by the Lord Chamberlain's Men at The Globe, there is no evidence that he cared about printing his plays. (Unlike today, authors didn't own the copyright to their works. We'll say more about this later.) Many quarto editions of the plays appeared that were not sanctioned by Shakespeare. Like fellow poet and rival Christopher Marlowe, who also earned money by writing plays, Shakespeare

Chapter 6. How Shakespeare's Plays Were Published

may have held the view that his plays were not worthy of being published in an expensive anthology.

VERSE BY VERSE

Before and during Shakespeare's time, books were relatively expensive and crafted with better quality materials than they are today. The Folger Shakespeare Library has the third-largest collection of English books published between 1475 and 1640, after the British Library and the Bodleian Library at Oxford University. Thanks in large part to the efforts of the Folger's founder and benefactor Henry Clay Folger, the Folger possesses 82 copies of the 1623 First Folio (about one-third of the world's copies) along with Folio fragments and over 200 early quarto editions. These rare treasures are stored inside a locked, low-temperature vault and are restricted, even to most scholars. They lie on their sides in short stacks and live only a few feet away from rare fifteenth-century editions of *The Canterbury Tales*, Sidney's *Arcadia*, and many others. Most of the Folger's First Folio editions were "re-backed, mended, and re-bound from the eighteenth to the twentieth centuries to keep them intact," says Georgianna Ziegler, Head of Reference at the Folger.

Ben Jonson, Shakespeare's friend and rival with the pen, was the first playwright to publish a collection of his own plays. This edition, titled *Works*, was published in 1616. The fact that Jonson would take an active part in publishing his own plays was seen by some as highly irregular and thought to be downright ridiculous by many who repudiated drama! But Jonson's *Works* may have ultimately paved the way for events that led Shakespeare's friends John Heminges and Henry Condell to preserve Shakespeare's works for posterity. Read a little further and you'll understand why.

The First Folio of 1623

So, how did Shakespeare's plays come to be published? Recall for a moment that Shakespeare died in 1616. About five or six years later, Shakespeare's fellow actors Heminges and Condell—both of whom are named in Shakespeare's will—approached a printer about publishing all the plays that Shakespeare wrote and co-wrote.

Pictured is the title page of Titus Andronicus *from the only known quarto edition in existence.* Titus Andronicus *was published in 1594 and is one of the first Shakespeare plays to appear in print. Discovered in Sweden in 1904, this rare book is held by the Folger Shakespeare Library. The* Titus *quarto edition would probably sell for more than several original First Folio editions, says Georgianna Ziegler, Head of Reference at the Folger.*

(Public domain image obtained via Wikimedia Commons by Folger Shakespeare Library photographer)

In 1623 William and Isaac Jaggard published the First Folio titled "Mr. William Shakespeares Comedies, Histories, & Tragedies." It was a large volume, with pages that were approximately 11 x 16 inches in size. It took about nine *compositors*—the clerks who had the cumbersome job of setting type—18 months to finish! The volume contained 36 of the author's plays. Each copy sold for 1 pound apiece. Out of the estimated 750 First Folio editions printed in 1623, 233 are known to have survived. Eighty-two of these volumes are owned by the Folger Shakespeare Library in Washington, D.C. In 2001, a single First Folio original sold for over six million dollars!

"WILD AND WHIRLING WORDS"

A **quarto** (Latin for "four") refers to a book in which the printer's sheet was folded twice, creating four leaves, or eight pages, for each sheet. By contrast, the printer's pages in the First Folio were folded only once, which created two separate leaves and four total pages. The **compositors** who manually arranged, or "composed," the individual letters or type used certain editing and spelling practices that scholars have scrutinized to make sense of many quirks and misspellings in Shakespeare's plays.

The publication of the First Folio is interesting and important for a number of reasons. Of the 36 plays amassed in this book, 18 had never been published before. This group included masterworks like *The Tempest*, *As You Like It*, *Twelfth Night*, *The Winter's Tale*, *Macbeth*, *Julius Caesar*, and *Antony and Cleopatra*. Without the effort of Heminges and Condell, the world may have never known these great works! The First Folio's other 18 plays, including *A Midsummer Night's Dream*; *Henry IV, Part I*; and *Romeo and Juliet*, had each been published in an earlier, single-play edition known as a *quarto*.

Nowadays, if you need to study Shakespeare's plays in an English class, you purchase a modern edition with modern spelling. The visual differences between the First Folio texts and a twenty-first century edition of Shakespeare's complete works are amazing. In the original Folio, the sixth comedy is titled "Much adoe about Nothing (*Much Ado About Nothing*);" the third history play is called "The First part of Henry the Fourth, with the Life and Death of Henry Sirnamed Hot-spurre," known to us as *Henry IV, Part I*. In the First Folio you'll notice the quaint Elizabethan English spelling, the curly antique calligraphy, odd punctuation quirks, and multiple spellings of the same word characteristic of a period when spelling wasn't standardized.

The introductory pages of the First Folio also contain vital testimonials to the brilliance of Shakespeare's dramatic works. Addressing "the great Variety of Readers" after their letter of dedication to William, Earl of Pembroke and Philip, Earl of Montgomery, Heminges and Condell wrote these words about Shakespeare:

> "Who, as he was a happy imitator of Nature, was a most gentle expresser of it. His mind and hand went together: And what he thought, he uttered with that easiness, that we have scarce received from him a blot in his papers. But it is not our province, who only gather his works, and give them you, to praise him. It is yours that read him. And there we hope, to your diverse capacities, you will find enough, both to draw, and hold you: for his wit can no more lie hid, then it could be lost."

Ben Jonson's two-page verse dedication refers to Shakespeare as the "Sweet Swan of Avon!" This elegant moniker gives the lie to ages of conspiracy theorists who claim that the Stratford-born actor William Shakespeare did not write the plays in the First Folio. Jonson also gives us proof of the respect that Shakespeare had earned from a fellow dramatist, suggesting how his plays had continued to liven the English stage long after his death:

> I, therefore will begin. Soul of the Age!
> The applause! delight! the wonder of our Stage!
> My Shakespeare, rise; I will not lodge thee by
> Chaucer, or Spenser, or bid Beaumont lye
> A little further, to make thee a roome:
> Thou art a Moniment, without a tombe,
> And art alive still, while thy Booke doth live,
> And we have wits to read, and praise to give.

What Source Was Used to Create the First Folio?

Today textual experts grapple with the million-dollar question: what manuscripts and sources did Blount and Jaggard's staff use as the texts for the First Folio? This is a key question because no decent fragments or complete play manuscripts survive in Shakespeare's handwriting. (The only surviving partial manuscript believed to be in Shakespeare's own handwriting is a 147-line scene in *Sir Thomas More*, a play whose authorship is disputed. The entire play manuscript is held in the British Library.) Over the last century, scientific scrutiny has yielded a few answers, much speculation, and a host of fascinating theories.

The First Folio collection comes from a variety of sources. They include Shakespeare's now-lost original manuscripts, known as *foul papers* because they contain scratch-outs and margin notes and were generally difficult to read. They also include "fair" copies of the plays, which were cleaner versions copied by scribes from the "foul" papers, and they include the prompt-book copies of the plays used by the theatre company during the actual stage productions.

The prompt-book, or "book of the play," was a special dramatic version of Shakespeare's more literary manuscript. It was usually prepared by the acting company's bookkeeper, a person charged with duties similar to a modern stage manager. The prompt-book was created to suit the needs of the acting company, incorporating specific stage directions for cueing actors about their exits, entrances, gestures, and other dramatic action not readily inferred from the verse.

Multiple Script Versions Put Scholars in a Muddle

Many critics believe the first printed editions (or quartos) of some plays were pirated. How did this happen? Various explanations have been presented but one seems to make the most sense. Actors who performed minor roles were known to recall the play from memory, transcribe their recollection, and sell the transcript to a printer. Such activity was wholly unsanctioned by Shakespeare or his acting company, but there was little they could do about it until they supervised the printing of a new edition. These pirated versions are often labeled "bad quartos." Critics call them bad because they are often incomplete, are missing whole sections, or contain badly corrupted speeches.

TIMELESS SOLILOQUIES

The debate about how early quarto editions of *Hamlet* differ from the First Folio text would make your eyes glaze over. (Read more about key issues surrounding *Hamlet* in Chapter 21.) Today directors who stage *Hamlet* are struck by profound differences between Hamlet's famous third-act suicide speech in the 1603 "bad quarto" and the 1604 second quarto. Which passage do you recognize?

Hamlet (1603Q): To be or not to be, I there's the point,
To die, to sleep, is that all? I all:
No, to sleep, to dream, I mary there it goes,
For in that dream of death, when we awake,
And borne before an everlasting Judge,
From whence no passenger ever retur'nd,
. . .

Hamlet (1604Q): To be, or not to be, that is the question:
Whether 'tis nobler in the mind to suffer
The slings and arrows of outrageous fortune,
Or to take arms against a sea of troubles,
And by opposing, end them.

The first quarto of *Romeo and Juliet*, issued in 1597, is known as a bad quarto because it is half as long as the second edition, which appeared in 1599. Many faulty passages were revised in this and subsequent editions, and some feel that odd stage directions and quirks in this version are evidence that it was based on Shakespeare's foul papers. Bad quartos are not useless for scholars, though. Generally they contain useful stage directions that lend insight into how the play was performed early on.

Chapter 6. How Shakespeare's Plays Were Published

VERSE BY VERSE

Shakespeare scholars have gained innumerable insights from closely studying the texts of the First Folio. We know, for example, from a slip of the pen by Shakespeare himself, or from a scribe who recopied *Much Ado About Nothing*, that Will Kempe was the first actor to perform the role of Dogberry.

Nowadays, editors of Shakespeare's plays are generally the select few allowed to consult the First Folio editions in the Folger Shakespeare Library. But today through computer technology, anyone can turn the pages of this magnificent text inside the Folger Shakespeare Library museum or online using the digital facsimile on the Folger website. (See for yourself by visiting www.folger.edu.) You can also view and compare digitized versions of 107 copies of Shakespeare's quartos on the British Library website. Numerous modern facsimiles such as *The Applause First Folio of Shakespeare in Modern Type* are also available.

Why Didn't Shakespeare Publish His Own Plays?

You might be asking yourself why Shakespeare didn't just do what Jonson did and supervise the publication of his own plays. To understand why, you might imagine that Shakespeare was writing in a commercial environment not unlike a writer or team of writers working for television. Movie and TV scripts undergo numerous changes before we see the show on the air. It matters less what gets into print, and more what the camera shows us, the viewers.

In Shakespeare's day dramatists wrote plays for the sole purpose of being performed, not for publication. Yes, a play by Shakespeare is a literary document, but because he wrote it to be performed, it was amended into a useful prompt-book, an actor-friendly script that was seen as a commodity owned by the acting company.

The Second, Third, and Fourth Folios

The 1623 First Folio was reprinted in 1632, reissued in 1664, and reprinted again in 1685, and these editions are known as the Second Folio, Third Folio, and Fourth Folio, respectively. The Folger Shakespeare Library owns one of the most unusual editions of the Second Folio. The volume was owned by the English college in Valladolid, Spain, and was censored by the Spanish Inquisition! The book is inscribed with the name of official censor Guillermo Sanchez, of the Holy Office. The Spanish Catholics didn't like Queen Elizabeth at all, and many of the book's passages, perceived as heretical, have been blotted out. One comes from the final scene in *Henry VIII*, in which Cranmer praises the infant Princess Elizabeth, who became Queen Elizabeth I, using language containing specific echoes of the Virgin Mary and reminiscent of biblical passages. Interestingly, the entire play of *Measure for Measure* has been torn out, probably because it involves a duke who disguises himself as a holy friar, as well as a young woman about to become a nun who is asked to have sex and sacrifice her virginity.

The Modern Editions

Remember that modern editors of Shakespeare's plays still rely on the edited works of literary icons like Alexander Pope and Samuel Johnson. But seriously, why are there so many modern editions of Shakespeare's collected works? You'd think that scholars who edit his works could agree on a text with minor variations. Nothing could be further from the truth. To read the plays just as literature and/or stories, perhaps no more than a modern text would be needed. But the First Folio is not just poetry and literature. It's a reflection of the greatest era of Western theatre, of the genesis of the Elizabethan playhouse, which gave rise to modern theatre. It is not simply a theatrical document; it is a magnificent cultural and historical treasure.

How Many Plays Did Shakespeare Actually Write?

Another controversy that persists among Shakespeare scholars concerns the exact number of plays that Shakespeare should get credit for. If you're wondering how many plays Shakespeare actually wrote, there is no easy answer. Thirty years ago, it was 37. Today, there is solid evidence that he co-wrote *The Two Noble Kinsmen* with John Fletcher, so the total has risen to 38. Others believe he definitely wrote *Edward III* and *Sir Thomas More*, bringing the total to 40. Most recently, the *New Oxford Shakespeare* (2016) credits Shakespeare as being a co-author of *Arden of Faversham* alongside an anonymous playwright. (See Chapter 2 and Appendix B for more details about Shakespeare's practice of collaborating with his peers.)

By the way, the only significant manuscript excerpt that we have in Shakespeare's own writing comes from a play titled *Sir Thomas More*. Some believe that Shakespeare wrote the entire play; others reject this idea, saying that the play was probably written by an inferior dramatist and Shakespeare merely contributed a section in his own handwriting.

Can Anyone Agree on Chronology?

Without so much as one partial or complete play manuscript in Shakespeare's own handwriting, how can we know when a given play was written? This is a good question without an easy answer. We are fortunate to have a document summarizing the works of prominent poets and writers of the 1590s, written by Francis Meres, called *Palladis Tamia: Wit's Treasury*. In it Meres praises Shakespeare as the best English dramatist, listing several comedies such as *Two Gentlemen of Verona*, *The Comedy of Errors*, and *A Midsummer Night's Dream* and tragedies like *Richard III* and *Romeo and Juliet*. Meres's work appeared in 1598, which tells us for certain that Shakespeare wrote the plays named in it by that year.

Dating the composition of plays written earlier and later than these works is painstaking. Scholars rely on documents such as Henslowe's *Diary* and other theatrical records, written evidence of the performances, and letters from individuals who may have seen an early performance. On rare occasions, there are topical references inside the plays that help scholars determine Shakespeare's possible composition date.

Part 2. Plays Are for the Stage

The following table indicates one view of the order in which Shakespeare composed his plays.

Order of Composition

Title of Play	Proposed Date Written
Henry VI, Part 1	1589-1590
Henry VI, Part 2	1590-1591
Henry VI, Part 3	1590-1591
Richard III	1592-1593
The Comedy of Errors	1592-1594
Edward III (the play's authorship is disputed)	1592-1595
Titus Andronicus	1593-1594
The Taming of the Shrew	1593-1594
The Two Gentlemen of Verona	1594
Love's Labor's Lost	1594-1595
King John	1594-1596
Richard II	1595
Romeo and Juliet	1595-1596
A Midsummer Night's Dream	1595-1596
The Merchant of Venice	1596-1597
Henry IV, Part 1	1596-1597
The Merry Wives of Windsor	1597
Henry IV, Part 2	1598
Much Ado About Nothing	1598-1599
Henry V	1599
Julius Caesar	1599
As You Like It	1599
Hamlet	1600-1601
Twelfth Night	1601-1602
Troilus and Cressida	1601-1602
All's Well That Ends Well	1602-1603
Measure for Measure	1604
Othello	1604

Title of Play	Proposed Date Written
King Lear	1605
Macbeth	1606
Antony and Cleopatra	1606-1607
Coriolanus	1607-1608
Timon of Athens	1607-1608
Pericles	1607-1608
Cymbeline	1609-1610
The Winter's Tale	1610-1611
The Tempest	1611
Henry VIII	1612-1613
Cardenio (this play has been lost)	1612-1613
The Two Noble Kinsmen	1613

Taken from The Riverside Shakespeare, Second Edition: Complete Works, Eds. G. Blakemore Evans and J.J.M. Tobin.

Trust Me: Hamlet Is Funny—A Mini-Lesson in Genre

Consider taking a look inside the table of contents of a First Folio facsimile. You'll notice that there are 36 plays and that each falls into one of only three genres: The Comedies, The Histories, and The Tragedies. Look closely at the list of Comedies and you'll see that *The Tempest* and *The Winter's Tale* are lumped in with the comedies. Editors of Shakespeare now classify these two plays as Romances or Late Romances.

Some critics will tell you that *Richard III*, one of Shakespeare's earliest history plays, was actually his first tragedy. (In the First Folio it is titled "The Tragedy of Richard the Third" . . .) Critics will never agree on where to put *Troilus and Cressida*—it's labeled as a tragedy in the First Folio, a problem comedy by some, and a history by other modern critics!

Don't waste time trying to fit Shakespeare's plays into neat categories of genre either. Like analysis of character and theme, genre classification is an academic exercise. Trust me—despite any impression to the contrary, there is plenty of comedy in *Hamlet* and *King Lear*. Those of you who've studied the plays are probably saying, "But wait a minute! Shakespeare understood Aristotle's precepts of comedy and tragedy when writing many of his plays!" True. Shakespeare actually patterned some comedies on works by Plautus, the ancient Roman dramatist. Shakespeare's tragedies show influences of Seneca, the ancient Roman tragedian and statesman. But in his own day, Shakespeare was considered a respectable rebel who broke many rules of classical drama and forged his own way.

"A KINGDOM FOR A STAGE!"

When you're ready to get serious about Shakespeare, grab a good edition of *Hamlet* and rent Kenneth Branagh's ground-breaking 1996 film. Thanks to Branagh, the world has a brilliant rendering of Shakespeare's most philosophical play, with none of the cuts in dialogue that we've come to expect from the typical live showing. (Branagh's film, which is based on the second quarto or published edition of 1604, lasts 238 minutes; that's nearly four hours!) Without hearing every scene and every speech, you miss the build-up to key moments like Hamlet's accidental slaying of Polonius. Scenes like this make less sense in Franco Zeffirelli's highly cut 1990 film.

Like commercial writers who pen scripts for the stage and movies, Shakespeare wrote plays, in part, to entertain his audiences. And the more he wrote, the richer and more complex his plays became. *The Comedy of Errors*, a satirical farce that closely hews to the classical unities of time, place, and action, is not nearly as rich and profound as *Twelfth Night*, written much later. Comparisons based on genre are meaningless inside the theatre. Look at Shakespeare's revenge tragedies, as an example. There's a world of difference between the B-movie slasher quality of *Titus Andronicus*, Shakespeare's first revenge tragedy, and the subtle artistry of *Hamlet*. If you get too hung up on definitions of genre, you're liable to get confused when you read *Measure for Measure*, which is neither comedy nor tragedy!

Chapter 6. How Shakespeare's Plays Were Published

FACTS TO REMEMBER
- It was customary for Renaissance dramatists to sell their plays to an acting company. They did not own or copyright their works as modern playwrights do.
- Shakespeare's fellow actors John Heminges and Henry Condell ensured that his plays were published in the First Folio of 1623.
- The 1623 First Folio contained 18 plays performed while Shakespeare lived but that were never published before in a quarto edition. These 18 plays included masterworks like *Julius Caesar*, *Twelfth Night*, *Macbeth*, and *The Tempest*.
- The first printed versions of *Romeo and Juliet* and *Hamlet* were labeled as "bad quartos." Many scholars believe such editions are poor reconstructions of the true original by an actor who re-created the play from memory.
- As far as we know, no manuscript of a play undisputedly attributed to Shakespeare has survived. When modern scholars edit the plays, they compare various scripts of a single play that originally appeared in a quarto edition and the 1623 First Folio edition.
- Inside the theatre, don't take fixed notions about genre too seriously. In writing the script of *Hamlet*, Shakespeare cared more about entertaining you than writing a "textbook" revenge tragedy.

Part 3
The Comedies

Part 3. The Comedies

*I*f you're not sure what to expect from a 400-year-old comedy, Shakespeare will surprise you. Here you'll find plenty of humor, but it's presented differently from the one-liners in laugh-track–driven sitcoms or short stand-up routines of today. Besides the jokes and occasional cheap laughs, the Elizabethan style of comedy centers on romantic intrigue and courtship rituals between men and women and the crazy obstacles that come between them, before things get happily resolved.

The basic tales will sound familiar—boy meets girl and something inevitably gets in the way. Rather than invent new plots, Shakespeare took the stuff of familiar folktales and ancient narrative poems and transformed it using his own artistic powers. There's something here to entertain everyone. Shakespeare keeps you guessing with lots of tricks of mistaken identity, disguises, mysterious letters, and other ruses. And don't despair—there are plenty of puns and bawdy jokes to keep you watching.

All told, Shakespeare wrote 15 comedies. Not all are instantly recognizable, though, and several, like *Love's Labor's Lost*, are rarely performed today. Here we limit the selection primarily to the *festive comedies*—masterworks that Shakespeare created before he began his great tragedies.

Chapter 7
The Taming of the Shrew

> **INTRODUCTION**
> - A reminder that *The Taming of the Shrew* is a farce
> - A look at the play's main characters
> - Stories that comprise the framing plot, the taming plot, and the subplot
> - Devices and disguises that make for lively diversions
> - Is *The Taming of the Shrew* a sexist, brutal play?
> - Why *The Taming of the Shrew* stumps modern directors

Despite its rip-roaring popularity in Shakespeare's day, *The Taming of the Shrew* is one of the most controversial plays in the canon. It's impossible to know for certain, but scholars believe Shakespeare wrote the play around 1593-94. Some say it was written earlier for an acting company known as the Queen's Men, but it remains one of Shakespeare's earliest comedies.

Having said that, you need to remember that *Shrew* is a farce. Simply put, farce is a form of stage entertainment that's as old as the ancient Romans. In *Shrew*, Shakespeare aimed to entertain his audiences with lots of horseplay and bawdy humor. Many directors and viewers believe some of the play's action borders on cruelty, which isn't softened by the end of the story. Is *Shrew* blatantly misogynistic? We'll address this question later in the chapter.

Alleged misogyny aside, there are pitfalls to reading this play without experiencing it in the theatre. It is full of burlesque, wordplay, jokes, puns, and off-color jokes that are liable to fall flat on the page. Don't get me wrong, *Shrew* has serious meaning, but you'll miss its comic effects if you deprive yourself of seeing a live performance.

The Characters

Baptista—A very rich man from Padua who has a real problem on his hands. He's got two daughters of marriageable age, but all the available suitors are after the younger one! Marrying the younger daughter off first just won't do. Remember, the Elizabethans were old-fashioned in this regard. So Baptista creates an incentive for Bianca's many suitors to find a husband for Katherina.

Katherina—Baptista's oldest daughter, also called "Kate" and one of the star characters in this play. When the play opens, Katherina is miserable and utterly incorrigible. She scolds and strikes anyone who speaks to her or crosses her, including her own sister.

Bianca—Baptista's younger daughter. She's easy to sympathize with because her sister abuses her terribly. She's eligible to marry and is desired by three suitors who engage in trickery and deceit to win her hand in marriage.

Petruchio—A gentleman from Verona who is determined to marry to improve his financial situation. When he learns of Baptista's plan to find a husband for Katherina, he's intrigued. In a series of tests that are psychologically astute, Petruchio takes on the challenge of wooing a shrew as if he were taming a wild hawk. (Don't miss the metaphorical language to this effect.)

OTHER CHARACTERS IN THE TAMING PLOT

Grumio and Curtis—Servants of Petruchio.

A tailor, a haberdasher, and servants who wait on Baptista and Petruchio

"A KINGDOM FOR A STAGE!"

We can't be sure exactly when and where *Shrew* was first performed, but here is a clue about the size of the company that first performed it. By doubling up, or taking on more than one role, ten male actors and four boys could have covered the 20 or so main parts. The supernumeraries could cover the remaining minor roles.

THE SUBPLOT

Gremio—An older citizen of Padua who is Bianca's suitor.

Hortensio—Another suitor of Bianca who pretends to be a music teacher.

Lucentio—A young man who loves Bianca, who pretends to be Cambio, a tutor; he is also Vincentio's son.

Tranio and Biondello—Lucentio's personal servants.

Vincentio—A rich, older gentleman from Pisa.

Merchant from Mantua who pretends to be Vincentio.

Widow—A woman in love with Hortensio.

THE INDUCTION SCENE

Christopher Sly—A tinker.

Lord

Alehouse hostess

Page

Players

Huntsmen

Servants

Setting: The town of Padua, Italy, and Petruchio's country home

Part 3. The Comedies

Sly's Dream—The Play-Within-the-Play

Before Shakespeare begins his story, he introduces a brief vignette about Christopher Sly, a tinker who falls asleep in a drunken stupor. Meanwhile a lord and his huntsmen happen upon Sly inside a country alehouse and the aristocrat carries him into his home and treats him luxuriously. The nobleman tricks Sly into thinking he's really an aristocrat who's gone mad. The lord orders some vagabond actors to perform for Sly's entertainment, continuing the charade by having his own page parade as Sly's wife.

During the entertainment Sly falls asleep, which makes us wonder if *The Taming of the Shrew* is just a conceit that Sly has dreamed. In any case, this mini-plot is known as The Induction. Think of the main plot that I'm about to describe as entertainment for Sly, or the *play-within-the-play*.

The Main Plot—Wooing a "Wildcat"

Grumio: Katherine the curst!
          A title for a maid of all titles the worst.
          (I.2.129-130)

Baptista Minola has two daughters named Katherina and Bianca, and both are old enough to be married. But according to Renaissance tradition, Katherina has to marry first because she's the oldest. In the opening of the main plot (called the *taming plot*), Baptista finds himself in a tricky position. Two suitors have declared their interest in Bianca, and a third is in love with her.

Either girl would be a good catch for these gentlemen. After all, Baptista is a wealthy, respected citizen of Padua, but there's a problem, of course. Baptista insists that nobody can get close to Bianca until Katherina is married off. But poor Kate isn't likely to get much attention from any of these guys.

You're thinking she's a dog, right? No; she's . . . difficult, shall we say. Seriously, she has a reputation as a royal shrew, a real bitch, if you will. She's a man-eater! Any man who gets near her runs shrieking to escape her scolding and beating fists. So you can see why Baptista is distraught. Predictably, the hungry suitors swarm around the lovely Bianca, leaving poor Kate in the cold.

CHAPTER 7. THE TAMING OF THE SHREW

Conquering Kate

Enter Petruchio, a Verona-based chap in search of a wife. He isn't deterred by the harsh reports about Kate's temperament. After all, Baptista is a wealthy man and his daughter would come with a hefty dowry! Here's an inkling of how he reacts to the scuttlebutt about Kate's awful temperament:

Petruchio:
>Think you a little din can daunt mine ears?
>Have I not in my time heard lions roar?
>Have I not heard the sea, puff'd up with winds,
>Rage like an angry boar chafed with sweat?
>Have I not heard great ordnance in the field,
>And heaven's artillery thunder in the skies?
>Have I not in a pitched battle heard
>Loud 'larums, neighing steeds and trumpets' clang?
>And do you tell me of a woman's tongue,
>That gives not half so great a blow to hear
>As will a chestnut in a farmer's fire?
>Tush, tush, fear boys with bugs!
>(I.2.201-210)

You're not the only one who thinks this man is nuts. But Petruchio surprises everybody. It's obvious that Kate has met her match when Petruchio first lays eyes on her. He's not cowed like all the other men who've crossed her path. In fact, during this first meeting, this cheeky gentleman completely disarms her. Matching wits every step of the way, Petruchio and Kate parry and thrust in a rapid, ear-pleasing display of puns, poetry, and metaphor.

To heighten the rapid-fire quality of their talk, Shakespeare has Petruchio and Kate speak in shared or split lines (read more about this in Chapter 5). Here's a naughty illustration from their first meeting:

Petruchio:	Who knows not where a wasp does wear his sting? In his tail.
Katherina:	In his tongue.
Petruchio:	Whose tongue?
Katherina:	Yours, if you talk of tales, and so farewell.
Petruchio:	What, with my tongue in your tail? Nay, come again. Good Kate; I am a gentleman— (II.1.213-219)

After this juicy exchange, Kate even strikes Petruchio, but, as you can imagine, she doesn't get very far with her fists. Bit by bit, Petruchio woos this wildcat with clever words before bluntly declaring that he intends to share her bed and be her husband. Things go according to plan, the shrewd suitor from Verona gets his way, and the couple get married. Petruchio displays some nerve when he shows up late for the wedding without wearing the appropriate clothing. At this point, things begin to get interesting.

Besides his interest in having Kate's dowry, Petruchio has a plan to bring his new wife under control. He enacts a series of tests to subvert Kate's every want, need, and expectation. In the ensuing scenes, he succeeds in breaking his wild bride by denying her food, drink, nice clothing, and even sex. As Kate is forced into submission with each new challenge, she calms down and learns a few lessons about how her behavior affects others.

Chapter 7. The Taming of the Shrew

Elizabeth Taylor (as Kate) and Richard Burton (as Petruchio) in the 1966 film directed by Franco Zeffirelli.
(Photo Courtesy of Photofest.)

Before you get indignant over the sexist and inhumane overtones of what's happening here, keep the Elizabethan context in mind (and keep on reading). In our modern era, we've lost the ability to pick up on the play's artful connections between taming a wild hawk and taming Kate. Elizabethan audiences would have readily picked up on this and laughed aloud at these nuances.

Shakespeare also knew his audience would laugh at centuries of folk tales about the shrewish wife. She was a stock character, the long-standing butt of centuries of jokes. (And don't forget that Shakespeare was writing for a cross section of playgoers who also got their kicks out of seeing bears baited by dogs until they bled profusely.)

But wait a minute, you're saying—this Petruchio guy is a real jerk and his behavior is inexcusable! No woman deserves to be treated that way. But think about old and recent TV comedies beloved by many for their rough sight gags. Shows like *Laurel and Hardy*, *The Simpsons,* and Saturday morning cartoons. These shows are literally brutal, but many of us laugh at them anyway. There's brutality throughout the tradition of English and American farce that's hard to deny.

The Subplot—Rival Suitors Plot to Win Bianca

While Petruchio is busy taming his new wife, Bianca's suitors embroil themselves in silly tricks and disguises to get close to her and gain her favor. Old Gremio has designs on Bianca, and Hortensio and young Lucentio also vie to win her love. The carefully laid plans of all three men make for an entertaining subplot.

In developing this angle of the story, Shakespeare plays up the zany device of masquerade, which allows for a series of mistaken identities. Here are a few examples.

To secure entrance into Baptista's house to see Bianca, the suitor Hortensio pretends to be a music teacher. In another twist, Lucentio falsely represents himself to Baptista as a tutor as well, by taking the identity of someone named Cambio. (To extend this masquerade, Lucentio even orders his servant Tranio to assume his own identity!) Other similar impersonations keep this subplot lively and interesting.

The Wager

Both the taming plot and the subplot dovetail nicely after Lucentio marries Bianca and Hortensio marries a rich widow. At a feast celebrating all three marriages, the husbands agree to an interesting wager after the wives have left the room. Petruchio bets the others that if Kate is summoned to return, she'll return without giving him any lip. Confident that their new brides are more obedient than Kate, Lucentio and Hortensio eagerly accept the bet.

When summoned by their husbands, the widow and Bianca are surprisingly obstinate, and flout their new husbands' authority. But when Kate is summoned, she returns unexpectedly and without delay. Here's an excerpt from her famous, or should I say now-infamous, "submission" speech.

> Thy husband is thy lord, thy life, thy keeper,
> Thy head, thy sovereign; one that cares for thee
> And for thy maintenance; commits his body
> To painful labor both by sea and land;
> To watch the night in storms, the day in cold,
> Whilst thou li'st warm at home, secure and safe;
> And craves no other tribute at thy hands
> But love, fair looks, and true obedience—
> Too little payment for so great a debt.
> Such duty as the subject owes the prince,
> Even such a woman oweth to her husband;
> And when she is forward, peevish, sullen, sour,
> And not obedient to his honest will,
> What is she but a foul contending rebel,
> And graceless traitor to her loving lord?
> (I.5.146-160)

I know what you're thinking. So, Petruchio has won his precious bet, but how could Kate say such a thing? How could any woman subordinate herself to a man in this fashion? Indeed, you haven't been alone over the past three centuries. This speech, along with Petruchio's jovial reply—"Come on and kiss me, Kate"—have provoked a raft of hostility, surprise, and critical second-guessing about the significance of Kate's expression and what Shakespeare meant by it.

"WILD AND WHIRLING WORDS"

In *Shrew* and other early comedies, Shakespeare's verse took the form of couplets in which the last two syllables rhymed with one another. The play's final couplet gives us a clue about how differently Elizabethans pronounced words that we still use. During the 1590s, the word *shrew* most likely was pronounced like *shrow*.

Hortensio:	Now, go thy ways, thou hast tamed a curst shrew.
Lucentio:	'Tis a wonder, by your leave, she will be tam'd so. (V.2.188-189)

Making Sense of the Shrew and Bully Farce

Though *Shrew* is an engaging, classic farce, many theatergoers still regard Petruchio's taming of Kate as highly sexist. Today directors and scholars find the play very difficult to stage and interpret in ways that satisfy audiences and students. Without forgetting that Shakespeare wrote the play to entertain us, let's look at precisely why this play deserves to be studied and appreciated.

Not Your Stereotypical Shrew

First of all, Shakespeare's audiences would have recognized Kate's shrewish temperament from folktale and medieval mystery drama. The wife of the biblical Noah and Chaucer's wife of Bath from *The Canterbury Tales* were similar overbearing types. But Shakespeare doesn't simply take these sources and ham up Kate's stereotypical antics to get a few cheap laughs onstage. He goes beyond his literary predecessors. He artfully introduces Kate to a sophisticated suitor who shows her, subtly and not so subtly, a better way to act.

Shakespeare makes Petruchio out to be more than just a money-hungry suitor. His motives are altruistic—he wants to ensure that Kate has a promising future and a better life. So contrary to what the Petruchio-haters say, his (and Shakespeare's) strategy is benevolent and psychologically astute.

In turn, Kate passes Petruchio's tests and learns how to love and accommodate him within the confines of Elizabethan marriage conventions. One prominent Shakespeare director suggests another way to make sense of the interactions between Kate and Petruchio.

One Director's Perspective

Today, Shakespeare directors can't ignore the play's sexist overtones when they stage *The Taming of the Shrew*. Sidney Berger, the late veteran producing director of the Houston Shakespeare Festival, said *Shrew* had become a real problem play for directors.

"Most people think the play is a lighthearted soufflé or a light romantic comedy, which isn't true at all. I've done three productions of this play, and for the last two productions, I've been unable to solve the problem. That is, until recently, when Shakespeare himself gave me a way to solve the dilemma.

"One day I counted the syllables of each metric line in Kate's final submission speech and discovered that every line in that speech has a feminine ending [i.e., a final weak syllable indicating indecision or insecurity]—which would indirectly suggest to perceptive listeners that the speaker is equivocating in some way. After that discovery I reviewed the ideas of Shakespeare scholar and feminist Germaine Greer after hearing her speak on the University of Houston campus.

"Here's a way to read that speech: When the tamed Kate submits to Petruchio in the end, these are two people making a deal with each other. When Kate submits in that final scene, she's saying, 'I will give you what you need to save face with your peers. The world is a tough place, so if you protect me, I'll give you what you need.' His reply—'Come and kiss me, Kate'—acknowledges that they are essentially agreeing to an unspoken verbal contract to ensure a healthy marriage.

"Unfortunately, I still haven't found a way to articulate this to an audience. People don't just walk into the theatre knowing the information implied in Shakespeare's verse. Whenever I direct the play, women in the audience start booing after Kate's submission speech, while the men are cheering. I don't believe in presenting the play like Zeffirelli's charming film romance, nor do I agree with having Kate undercut her speech by winking at the audience, like many directors do.

"There's an integrity to Petruchio. His hard lesson to Kate during their first meeting is simple—'I don't get hit. If you hit me, I hit you.' Shakespeare's whole point is to show how a wild animal must be tamed so she can contribute to society and be a vital part of human commerce. She's gifted, Shakespeare is saying, and you want her to keep every gift she's got."

Consider the Context of Elizabethan Marriage

Consider the Elizabethan patriarchal context for a moment—audiences would have taken it for granted that a woman's duty is to submit to her husband. This form of obedience was a given and challenging it was unheard of because it was part of the accepted social order. Also, such a norm conformed to the dictates of the Bible and would have been part of the Elizabethan cultural and social fabric. So try to make sense of the play that Shakespeare gave us within this very specific context, *not* our own modern context.

Today, practically anyone interested in Shakespeare can appreciate the feminist viewpoint. The idea of any man forcing a woman into submissive obedience today is repugnant. No question. But it is important to remember that our contemporary views of marriage are based on radically different laws and accepted social norms. If you interpret this play solely in a twenty-first-century context, you're making a big mistake.

TIMELESS SOLILOQUIES

Actors playing Petruchio and Kate can take a variety of approaches to the all-important moment when these two first meet. When John Cleese played Petruchio in 1981 for BBC-TV, he infused the role with his wry, Monty Pythonesque bluster. In Zeffirelli's 1967 film version, on the other hand, Richard Burton's Petruchio came across as a sexy, virile, woman-handling macho man. Ladies, watch this film and you'll see why Liz Taylor just couldn't resist him.

CHAPTER 7. THE TAMING OF THE SHREW

Shakespeare's Artifice—Illusion and Irony

Shakespeare also enriches the play with multilayered illusion, offering persistent contrasts between appearances and reality. There are numerous, hilarious examples of mistaken identity. Bianca's suitors disguise their real identities; a servant Tranio impersonates his master; several characters exploit a false connection with Vincentio, Lucentio's father, to improve their standing with Baptista.

While Petruchio tames Kate in a wholly unconventional fashion, he ends up in a mutually satisfying match. How ironic is that? By contrast, you have multiple suitors who court Bianca according to the highly conventional norms of Paduan society. One of them wins out, of course; in this case, it's Lucentio.

But in the end, which husband gets the better wife? Petruchio or Lucentio? Even though Lucentio plays by all of the social rules and courts his bride according to social expectations, Bianca flouts him at her first opportunity. She's not the obedient wife Lucentio bargained for after all. Don't lose sight of these ironies because they are part and parcel of this play's wisdom and foresight. These are insights that Shakespeare artfully conveys through the play's structure.

Let's briefly carry the appearance/reality theme one step further. If you imagine for a moment that the entire drama is just a dream or a figment of Sly's imagination, the whole play is an illusion.

The Taming of the Shrew—A Chronology of Notable Screen Productions

Despite the controversy that *Shrew* provokes among academics, the play remains one of Shakespeare's most popular on the stage and screen. Following are noteworthy film and TV adaptations since the 1929 silent movie.

- 1929: Sam Taylor directed this United Artists/Pickford Corporation production, which starred Mary Pickford and Douglas Fairbanks Sr.
- 1948: Metro-Goldwyn-Mayer's adaptation, known as *Kiss Me Kate*, featured music and lyrics by Cole Porter. The show starred Kathryn Grayson and Howard Keel.

- 1950: Paul Nickell directed the Westinghouse Studio One/CBS film featuring Lisa Kirk and Charlton Heston.
- 1967: Franco Zeffirelli's version for Royal Films International is the best-known rendering of *Shrew*. This is largely because superstars Elizabeth Taylor and Richard Burton perform the lead roles.
- 1981: Jonathan Miller's well-regarded production for BBC/Time-Life Television stars Sarah Badel and John Cleese.

FACTS TO REMEMBER

- On the stage, the play's use of farce and ingenious punning and wordplay make it highly effective.
- Shakespeare frames the story of Petruchio and Kate within a tale of Christopher Sly to heighten his motif of illusion versus reality.
- Shakespeare inserts tricks of disguise and mistaken identity to enrich the subplot about three rival suitors.
- Sidney Berger and other modern directors have had a devil of a time staging *Shrew* because its premise seems downright sexist, and audiences often react with hostility.
- *Shrew* is *not* a modern romantic comedy; it's an Elizabethan farce and can be understood as Petruchio's attempt to help Kate become a constructive member of society.

Chapter 8

A Midsummer Night's Dream

> **INTRODUCTION**
> - The mystery and complexity of *A Midsummer Night's Dream*
> - The play's main characters and multilayered setting
> - The mini-dramas and agonies surrounding many pairs of lovers
> - Some thoughts on Puck, Bottom, and Shakespeare's play-within-the-play
> - A look at *Dream*'s intriguing patterns and themes
> - An actor's viewpoint: F. Murray Abraham's Bottom

When people talk about Shakespeare's greatest plays, they mention the mature plays—*Hamlet*, *King Lear*, *As You Like It*, and *Twelfth Night*. But *A Midsummer Night's Dream* has been more difficult for some experts to love. Throughout centuries of being performed and adapted since the theatres reopened in 1660, *A Midsummer Night's Dream* has been woefully misunderstood.

Dream's checkered reputation began when Samuel Pepys, the famous diarist, saw the play in 1662, not long after the theatres reopened. In his diary he wrote that it was "the most insipid, ridiculous play I ever saw in my life." For centuries, Shakespeare's actual script was buried as producers presented the play onstage as a song-and-dance spectacle or opera. Until the early 1900s, *Dream* was regarded much as Pepys saw it.

PART 3. THE COMEDIES

You'll see that beneath the surface of potions and spells, it's a clever drama with lovely verse, recognizable quotations, and intoxicating meaning. Look closely at how Shakespeare weaves a labyrinth of irony out of multiple plots, and you'll see what I mean. Many believe Shakespeare wrote *Dream* around 1595-96 for a private wedding because Shakespeare may have alluded in the second act to rough summers during this period. Nobody knows for sure. The title refers to Midsummer Eve (also known as St. John's Eve), the eve of the summer solstice. Though it was deeply frowned upon, it was all the rage for "young persons of both sexes to withdraw to the woods for their pleasure," writes Frank Kermode in *The Age of Shakespeare*.

The Characters

THE COURT OF ATHENS

Theseus—The Duke of Athens takes his name from a mythical character who slew monsters alongside Hercules. He has won Hippolyta as part of his war spoils, but he means to treat her well as he makes her his wife. He is a dignified ruler, compassionate, sensitive, and generous toward the Mechanicals when they prepare to stage *Pyramus and Thisbe*.

Hippolyta—The Queen of the Amazons is engaged to Theseus. When the play opens, there are four days left before her wedding. She has very few lines until the latter half of the play. In scenes involving the four lovers and the Mechanicals' stage play, she shows the dignity and compassion befitting a duchess. (According to Greek myth, the Amazons were female warriors from Scythia.)

Egeus—The father of Hermia insists that his daughter marry Demetrius, so he is not happy when she has a different idea. In performance, Egeus comes across as stern and authoritarian.

Hermia—The pretty daughter of Egeus is dead-set against marrying Demetrius, the man chosen by her father. She is in love with Lysander, who returns her affections. Hermia isn't afraid to flout her father either. She appears unruffled when Duke Theseus warns her that going against her father could lead to her death. This poor girl is about to have her romance turned completely upside-down.

Lysander—The young man who loves Hermia utters some of the play's most memorable lines about love. As the story develops, Puck, Oberon's attendant, mistakenly casts a spell on him, making him love Helena instead.

Demetrius—The young man who courts Hermia and hopes to marry her, with her father's approval. His life is complicated because Hermia doesn't love him, but her friend Helena is crazy about him. Like Lysander, he is also bewitched by Oberon and falls in love with Helena. Be forewarned—he is often hard to distinguish from Lysander because Shakespeare didn't give him much of an identity of his own.

Helena—A young woman who worships Demetrius, but he has no eyes for her unfortunately. When Lysander and Demetrius fall under their magical spells, this girl is in for a shock. Both guys are suddenly after her!

Philostrate—A lord who serves Theseus.

Other lords of Theseus

THE MECHANICALS WHO STAGE *PYRAMUS AND THISBE*

Nick Bottom—A weaver whose name literally referred to the "bottom," a part of yarn making up the skein. He's the innocent victim of Oberon's mean trick on Titania and is turned into an ass. Bottom is Shakespeare's uniquely multidimensional character because he appears in three realms—that of the court, the fairies, and the play-within-the-play. See if you can figure out why he becomes more enlightened and self-aware than any other character in the play. When Bottom is chosen to play the part of Pyramus, he lets out a goofy rant from a classic play about Hercules. He wants to be a star of the stage, but he's big on ambition and low on talent. Seen *American Idol* lately?

Peter Quince—A carpenter, who speaks the Prologue.

Francis Flute—A bellows-mender, who plays Thisbe.

Tom Snout—A tinker, who plays a Wall (You got it; he literally personifies that thing that holds up your house.)

Snug—A joiner, who plays the Lion.

Robin Starveling—A tailor, who plays Moonshine.

THE FAIRY REALM

Oberon—The king of the fairy realm is a formidable figure. He speaks lovely lines of lyrical poetry, but as king, he doesn't measure up to Theseus' standards. When he doesn't get his way with Titania, he punishes her by making her fall in love with a donkey.

Titania—The queen of the fairies is regal and has an independent mind. She doesn't budge when Oberon demands that she hand over the changeling child she wants to raise as her own.

Puck—Also named Robin Goodfellow, he is a goblin or spirit who waits on Oberon. A complex character, he is mischievous and a bit cruel, and mistakenly targets Lysander for Oberon's spell, instead of Demetrius. He is given key lines in the play that have made him the object of much talk and symbolic speculation through the ages. (According to ancient superstition, a puck referred to an evil spirit.) Shakespeare's audiences would have seen Oberon's Puck as a hobgoblin by the name of Robin Goodfellow.

Peaseblossom, Cobweb, Moth, and Mustardseed—Titania's fairies

Fairies who serve Titania

Fairies who serve Oberon

Setting: Athens—a city that seems to mix elements of the ancient, medieval, and Elizabethan worlds—and a nearby forest

Chapter 8. A Midsummer Night's Dream

Let's Get to Know the Lovers and the Plots

The play begins on a dark note. Duke Theseus and Hippolyta look ahead to their upcoming wedding day. The duke acknowledges having captured his fiancée during a military fight, but he promises to marry her in a mode of celebration. But Theseus is soon distracted with a problem in his court.

A Father-Daughter Dilemma

Egeus is very unhappy with his daughter Hermia and wants Theseus to help him out. Egeus expects Hermia to marry Demetrius, but she doesn't want to because she loves Lysander instead. She boldly asks Theseus what's the worst that can happen if she refuses to obey her father. Under Athenian law, he tells her she'll die or be forced into a nunnery.

Pretty strict, huh? When Hermia and Lysander are alone again, you feel their pain and distress as Lysander waxes poetic:

> Ay me! For aught that I could ever read,
> Could ever hear by tale or history,
> The course of true love never did run smooth;
> (I.1.132-134)

But the clever lad realizes that if he takes his girl outside of town to where a rich aunt lives, Athenian law doesn't apply. So they agree to elope. Hermia confides her plan to her friend Helena, who complains because Demetrius hardly notices her. Here Shakespeare gives the lovelorn girl one of his great speeches about love.

TIMELESS SOLILOQUIES

In the following speech, Helena speaks with envy and alarm about Hermia's luck in turning men's heads and Demetrius' lack of awareness of her plans:

> Love looks not with the eyes, but with the mind;
> And therefore is wing'd Cupid painted blind.

Nor hath Love's mind of any judgment taste;
Wings, and no eyes, figure unheedy haste;
And therefore is Love said to be a child,
Because in choice he is so oft beguil'd.
(I.1.234-239)

Here, Helena speaks about love, one of the play's central concerns. In this excerpt Love is compared to Cupid, a child lacking good judgment or taste in his choice of whom to love.

Helena soon plans to let Demetrius in on her friend's secret.

The "Mechanicals" Rehearse *Pyramus and Thisbe*

We leave the young lovers and cut to Shakespeare's comic subplot involving the Mechanicals. This motley crew of tradesmen, led by Quince and Bottom, prepare to work up entertainment for Duke Theseus' wedding day. Their play's title is *The Most Lamentable Comedy and Most Cruel Death of Pyramus and Thisbe*. From the get-go this silly troupe is a farce, a hilarious parody of the work of professional actors.

The Mechanicals are a group of working-class tradesmen who work with their hands. Note how Shakespeare gives each one a last name that literally refers to his trade—Quince comes from "Quoins," a carpenter's wedge. Flute refers to the shape of the bellows to be mended. Snout stands for a kettle's spout, something this tinker would fix. Snug makes sense if you consider what this guy does to piece together furniture. Starveling suggests "starving" or thin, an apt adjective for many Elizabethan tailors. Their play's treatment of *Pyramus and Thisbe* is based on a tale from Ovid's *Metamorphosis*.

CHAPTER 8. A MIDSUMMER NIGHT'S DREAM

But through this side plot, Shakespeare offers interesting clues to the actual methods of Elizabethan acting troupes. For example, as Quince assigns the parts to each actor, he distributes a scroll containing each assigned part and the line cues that precede and follow each line. (Read more about these scrolls in Chapter 3.) Needless to say, this group of actors will make you laugh.

Titania Defies Oberon

Let's leave the amateur actors and cut to the fairy realm. We meet Oberon and Titania, the fair king and queen. Their world is no paradise of total harmony, though. These two have a few problems of their own. Titania has something that Oberon wants. A young changeling has come into her possession and Oberon wants the boy for himself. But Titania refuses to hand him over.

The Rough Hands of Nature

As we're about to see, these spirits shouldn't be dismissed. They are powerful and capable of serious misdeeds. Puck is full of his own guile and mischief. When Titania flouts Oberon's authority, Oberon has Puck fetch an herb potion that will make the fairy queen fall in love with the first creature she lays eyes on. When we meet her again she is smitten with a donkey (who is actually Bottom after he is transformed by jealous Oberon).

F. Murray Abraham played Bottom in A. J. Antoon's 1987 production of *Dream* at the New York Shakespeare Festival. He described what it felt like to share the bed of a fairy queen (played by actress Lorraine Toussaint) in *Actors on Shakespeare: A Midsummer Night's Dream*:

> I promise you, when I put on that ass's head, I felt instantly potent, randy, and very, very attractive. You should try it sometime with your sweetheart. It doesn't have to be an ass's head particularly, just any old beast that appeals.

In the following excerpt from Titania's very famous speech, she casts the fairies' immortal powers in a darker light:

> These are the forgeries of jealousy. . .
> But with thy brawls thou hast disturb'd our sport.
> Therefore the winds, piping to us in vain,
> As in revenge, have suck'd up from the sea
> Contagious fogs; which, falling in the land,
> Hath every pelting river made so proud
> That they have overborne their continents.
> The ox hath therefore stretch'd his yoke in vain,
> The ploughman lost his sweat, and the green corn
> Hath rotted ere his youth attain'd a beard;
> . . . the moon (the governess of floods),
> Pale in her anger, washes all the air,
> That rheumatic diseases do abound.
> And thorough this distemperature, we see
> The seasons alter: hoary-headed frosts
> Fall in the fresh lap of the crimson rose, . . .
> And this same progeny of evils comes
> From our debate, from our dissension;
> We are their parents and original.
> (II.1.81; 87-95; 103-08; 115-17)

Pay particular attention to her last three lines. She is saying that when she and Oberon fight, nature destroys without compunction, and there's hell to pay on earth.

Oberon Toys with Mortals

Puck:
> Helena is here at hand,
> And the youth, mistook by me,
> Pleading for a lover's fee.
> Shall we their fond pageant see?
> Lord, what fools these mortals be!
> (III.2.111-115)

After squeezing the love juice on Titania's eyes, Oberon casts his spell over the mortals. He spies Helena following Demetrius and when the boy rebuffs her,

Oberon orders Puck to "anoint his eyes" and make him love her. But silly Puck puts a spell on the wrong man and causes Lysander to leave Hermia in their forest camp and chase after Helena!

A Season of Transformation

At this juncture Oberon and Puck have wreaked havoc on the lovers. While Lysander pursues Helena, Demetrius abandons Hermia altogether and goes after Helena. Helena is so confused and suspicious of this sudden burst of amorous attention, she lashes out at both men. (Now that she and Hermia are rivals in love, the two bicker and fight. Sound familiar to some of you?) And there's poor Bottom, who's transformed into an ass. In a shocking twist, the elegant Titania is now sharing her bed with him!

Bottom is never more eloquent than when he awakens from his dream. Though he speaks in prose, you can hear the music in Bottom's verse. Here is a short excerpt, but read the entire passage for yourself. Elizabethans would have heard the echoes of St. Paul in his words:

"I have had a most rare vision. I have had a dream, past the wit of man to say what dream it was. Man is but an ass, if he go about t' expound this dream . . . The eye of man hath not heard, the ear of man hath not seen, man's hand is not able to taste, his tongue to conceive, nor his heart to report, what my dream was." (IV.1.204-207; 211-214)

In the midst of these shenanigans, Oberon realizes Puck has bewitched Lysander by mistake. Puck was supposed to manipulate Demetrius into falling in love with Helena (instead of Hermia). (Are you following this?) Chastised by Oberon, Puck reverses his error and ensures that Lysander will love Hermia again.

Three Weddings

Eventually all the spells are broken and Theseus sanctions the marriage of Hermia and Lysander. As his wedding day festivities get underway at court, Duke Theseus makes a notable comparison among lovers, madmen, and poets, speaking directly to key concerns in the play—love, irrationality, and the powers of the imagination.

> Lovers and madmen have such seething brains
> Such shaping fantasies, that apprehend
> More than cool reason ever comprehends.
> Are of imagination all compact.
> The lunatic, the lover, and the poet
> One sees more devils than vast hell can hold;
> That is the madman. The love, all as frantic,
> Sees Helen's beauty in a brow of Egypt.
> The poet's eye, in a fine frenzy rolling,
> Doth glance from heaven to earth, from earth to heaven;
> And as imagination bodies forth
> The forms of things unknown, the poet's pen
> Turns them to shapes, and gives to aery nothing
> A local habitation and a name.
> (V.1.4-17)

The Play-Within-the-Play

During the wedding feast, Bottom and company give Theseus, Hippolyta, and the other newlyweds a show that ranges from mediocre to horrible! This interlude is an example of Shakespeare's trademark play-within-the-play. So why does Shakespeare use this device, and what does it mean? Imagine watching the play in the theatre or a televised adaptation—you (the audience) are watching Theseus' court audience in Athens as they, in turn, are watching Bottom's performance. Using this device, Shakespeare can't help but remind you that the world of Athens—which looks a lot like England, remember—is itself a stage, and the members of the court go through life like actors in a comedy or tragedy. The play-within-the-play makes us self-conscious about the difference between illusion and reality.

Scholars also feel sure that through Quince and Bottom's staging of *Pyramus and Thisbe*, Shakespeare is winking at his contemporary audiences by making fun of plays often performed by boys' troupes around London.

Are We the Stuff of Dreams or Reality?

In the end the lovers get their way and Hermia's violation of the law of Athens goes unpunished. So we ask the question—which is stronger, the law of humans or the law of the human heart?

By contrasting the two sets of rulers in this play, Theseus and Hippolyta (royals of the Athenian court) and Oberon and Titania (immortals of the forest), Shakespeare invites us to contrast these overseers and the different realms they control. Theseus is associated with Athens, a highly advanced society that governs itself using reason and order, by placing faith in justice and law. Oberon, on the other hand, seems to govern by whim and personal impulse, holding a tight grip on his universe of fairies and mortals.

After Oberon plays his games of transforming the four lovers, Titania, and Bottom, everyone is left feeling confused, amazed, and convinced they've experienced a dream. By subjecting the lovers to Oberon's irrational influence, the play suggests that lovers cannot choose with whom or when they will fall in love any more than they can choose whether they'll be born a blond or brunette.

The four lovers and Bottom inhabit both worlds in this play, and their movement from one to the other invites us to ponder what is real and what is illusion. Theseus, however, seems rooted in the real world. After the play, however, he tells his wedding party "'tis almost fairy time," the twilight hour when the newlyweds will succumb to passion's embrace. But it is Puck who has the last word in this mysterious play.

Puck's Last Word on the Grave

After a festive triple wedding in the court and a benign entertainment, we expect that the newlywed couples will live on, be happy, fruitful, and multiply. But Puck quickly creates a different image of the hungry lion and the howling wolf amid dead mortals:

> Now the hungry lion roars,
>   And the wolf behowls the moon;
> Whilst the heavy ploughman snores,
>   All with weary task foredone.
> Now the wasted brands do glow,
>   Whilst the screech-owl, screeching loud,
> Puts the wretch that lies in woe
>   In remembrance of a shroud.
> Now is the time of night
>   That the graves, all gaping wide,
> Every one lets forth his sprite,
>   In the church-way paths to glide.
> (V.1.371-382)

It's interesting that Shakespeare gives our devious goblin the play's last word. Here, Puck utters a jarring reminder that every romance, every wedding, every new birth will end in death.

Staging *A Midsummer Night's Dream*

As I mentioned earlier, until the early twentieth century, the original script of *Dream* had been reinvented as musical or operatic versions. Harley Granville Barker's 1914 production at the Savoy in London—which reached Broadway a year later—finally deep-sixed much of the song and spectacle that had been grafted onto Shakespeare's original script since the seventeenth century. Since then *Dream* has been produced in Britain and North America on numerous occasions.

Young John Gielgud played Oberon in a 1929 staging at the Old Vic, and in 1937 Tyrone Guthrie and Vivien Leigh created Oberon and Titania in a lavish Victorian-era staging at London's Old Vic. Two American productions of *Dream* occurred in 1961—Joseph Papp's version at the New York Shakespeare Festival and one directed by Douglas Campbell in Stratford, Ontario. In 1977 Robin Phillips directed Maggie Smith as Titania and Hippolyta at Stratford-upon-Avon.

Chapter 8. A Midsummer Night's Dream

"A Kingdom for a Stage"

In 1970 Peter Brook's production of *Dream* at Stratford-upon-Avon had a huge impact on the theatre world. Critics were impressed by its careful attention to the basic rhythms of Shakespeare's language. In that show the actors who played Theseus and Hippolyta doubled as Oberon and Titania, respectively. When a single actor doubles as Theseus, a duke who embodies reason, and Oberon, a selfish, impulsive king who is less rational, it makes for a meaningful contrast. Based on the narrative, which one has the last word?

The Royal Shakespeare Company produced a 1986 version in which Janet McTeer doubled as Titania and Hippolyta, directed by Bill Alexander. Kenneth Branagh directed the Renaissance Theatre Company in a production in New York and Los Angeles, starring Emma Thompson as Puck. The British TV comedienne Dawn French, who stars in *The Vicar of Dibley*, performed as Mrs. Bottom in a 2001 production in London's West End. In 2003 Edward Hall directed an all-male cast in a touring production that opened at Watermill, Newbury.

F. Murray Abraham as Bottom

In *Actors on Shakespeare: A Midsummer Night's Dream*, F. Murray Abraham gives us a fascinating memoir about his experience in director A.J. Antoon's 1987–1988 production for the New York Shakespeare Festival. Antoon changed the setting from Shakespeare's Athens to Bahia, Brazil, around 1900. The all-American cast felt an implicit connection to this New World setting, Abraham wrote, since many were understandably uneasy about doing Shakespeare. Many critics raved about this production.

Playing Bottom changed Abraham's life. He writes about how difficult it was for his fellow actor/Mechanicals to perform bad acting convincingly: "Try singing a familiar song slightly off key, as though you truly believe you are perfect. Being 'bad' is not good enough. It must be done artfully."

Part 3. The Comedies

Kevin Kline artfully executed the bad acting required of Nick Bottom and his team of Mechanicals during their staging of Pyramus and Thisbe, *the play-within-the-play that occurs within Michael Hoffman's 1999 film version of* A Midsummer Night's Dream. *Michelle Pfeiffer performed the lead role of Titania.*
(Photo Courtesy of Photofest)

Elijah Mohinsky's 1980 adaptation of *Dream* for television is extremely worthwhile. Few lines are cut, and it's almost as good as seeing the play onstage. Peter McEnery stars as Oberon, Helen Mirren is stunning as Titania, and Phil Daniel portrays Puck as a pretty rough, malicious spirit. If you're after a fluffier, less faithful version, see Michael Hoffman's glitzy 1999 film starring Rupert Everett as Oberon, Michelle Pfeiffer as Titania, and Stanley Tucci as a more benign Puck. It's no substitute for good theatre, but it will introduce you to the intricacies of the plot.

Chapter 8. A Midsummer Night's Dream

FACTS TO REMEMBER

- *A Midsummer Night's Dream* occupies the worlds of Duke Theseus' Athenian court, the supernatural fairy realm of a nearby forest, and the Mechanicals' play-within-the-play.
- Inspired by Ovid, the ancient Roman poet, Shakespeare goes a bit wild with love potions and his transformation motif.
- Puck and Oberon's mischief and Titania's famous speech suggest there's a destructive side to God and nature.
- Among many themes, *Dream* explores the irrationality of love and the powers of the imagination.

Chapter 9
The Merchant of Venice

> **INTRODUCTION**
> - A word about Shakespeare's most controversial play and its anti-Semitic overtones
> - Insights into the roles of Portia, Shylock, Antonio, Bassanio, and other characters
> - The double plot in *The Merchant of Venice* and how to interpret the play intelligently, in a modern context
> - An experienced Shakespearean actor talks about Antonio
> - A Jewish-American director talks about his experience directing *The Merchant of Venice*

From a twenty-first century moral, political, and cultural standpoint, *The Merchant of Venice* is undoubtedly Shakespeare's most controversial play. Shakespeare developed the play as a romantic comedy, using bits of a fairytale plot from a medieval Italian prose tale. The Belmont story explores tensions stemming from love and friendship, and Shakespeare tries to resolve these tensions in a lighthearted fashion.

More disturbing is *Merchant's* parallel plot, set in Venice, about a Christian merchant and a Jewish moneylender. This story explores questions about the taking of oaths, justice, mercy, and accumulating wealth against Venice's sixteenth-century religious and cultural landscape. When Shakespeare introduces Shylock, the Jew, an inspired but complex role, he seems to get in the way of his own storytelling.

Many critics believe Shakespeare created Shylock to improve upon Barabas, Marlowe's comic villain in *The Jew of Malta* (1589). But in today's cultural context, it is impossible to view Shylock as an absurd comic stereotype, as the Elizabethans probably did. Shylock is a highly spirited portrait whose cruel and selfish qualities are regarded today as negative Jewish stereotypes. By forcing Shylock to convert to Christianity late in Act four, Shakespeare unwittingly ensured that post-Holocaust audiences would see his Jew as a sympathetic character. The way the Venetians mistreat him—in spite of his being a cruel miser—seems downright tragic.

The Characters

THE WORLD OF VENICE

Antonio—The merchant of Venice is burdened by a peculiar melancholy, and everyone talks about it as the play opens. It seems farfetched, but one possible explanation for this sadness is the love he feels for his friend Bassanio. He should run for the hills when this guy enters the picture! Bassanio's wish to wed Portia provides the catalyst for Antonio's fateful decision to enter into a bond with Shylock that gives him 3,000 ducats in exchange for a pound of flesh. If there is a flaw in the play, it seems to lie in Shakespeare's limited development of Antonio's obvious dark qualities. Antonio sees nothing wrong with spitting on the man he would later ask for money. The merchant seems to embody the intolerance of sixteenth-century Christians toward Jews, many of whom practiced usury because they were forbidden to own property.

Shylock—The Jewish moneylender has scarcely more than 300 lines in the play, but Shakespeare infused him with a dramatic richness irresistible to great actors like Olivier. He is a miser who values his money too much. He also disappoints his daughter Jessica, who runs away from him, steals his money, and vows to become a Christian. Despite his small number of lines, next to Portia, he strikes some modern playgoers as the play's most memorable character. He agrees to lend 3,000 ducats to Antonio in exchange for a pound of flesh.

Shakespeare created Shylock as part comic villain, part greedy miser of ancient myth, and part seer who astutely stands for the Old Testament principle of strict justice, as well as strict obedience to Venetian law.

Bassanio—Nerissa clues us in to the fact that Bassanio is "a scholar and a soldier." We first encounter him when he visits Antonio, down on his luck, without money or prospects. He sees an opportunity to turn bad fortune into good by playing the casket game required of Portia's suitors. A man of no means, his motives are questionable. But in the idyllic realm of Portia's Belmont, this Venetian's speeches suggest he has an integrity and substance that didn't come forth when he negotiates Antonio's bond with Shylock. When he chooses the lead casket during Portia's game, we glimpse Bassanio's penchant for honesty.

Jessica—Shylock's daughter disappoints modern audiences because she abandons her religion and her father, stealing his precious money and jewelry. Shakespeare's audiences probably wouldn't have judged her as harshly as we do. Her union with Lorenzo is part of the play's examination of the virtues of love.

Gratiano—A friend of Antonio and Bassanio who marries Nerissa

Lorenzo—A man who loves Jessica; he is a Christian

Solanio, Salerio—Friends of Antonio and Bassanio

Tubal—A loyal friend of Shylock who is also a Jew

Launcelot Gobbo—A servant of Shylock who becomes Bassanio's servant

Old Gobbo—Launcelot's father

Leonardo—A servant to Bassanio

Stephano—A messenger

Magnificoes of Venice, court officials, a jailer, and attendants

THE WORLD OF BELMONT

Portia—Portia is a rich heiress bound by a strange dictate in her father's will. Any man who wants to marry her must submit to a guessing game reminiscent of ancient folktales, in which he selects the best of three caskets made of gold, silver, and lead. Inside the "winning" casket is a likeness of Portia. The suitor who chooses the right box will have her for his wife. There is nothing to guide the suitors in their selections except a cryptic inscription on each casket. Throughout this odd ritual, Portia displays a wise and patient attitude that is admirable. You quickly see that she's no heroine of fairy lore; Shakespeare grants her a more expansive role, as she figures in both plots. Unfortunately, her image as Shakespeare's astute heroine has become tainted by the play's overtones of anti-Semitism. She intervenes in the Venetian trial involving the merchant Antonio's forfeiture of his bond with Shylock, the Jewish moneylender. Disguised as a male lawyer named Balthazar, she involves herself in Antonio's case, carefully articulating Antonio's legal duty toward the Jew. She urges Shylock to show mercy toward the merchant. Sadly, she shows little mercy toward him, arguing that his guilt should be punished by death.

Nerissa—Portia's gentlewoman is an amiable companion to her mistress. She benefits from Bassanio's good fortune in choosing the right casket. She is eyed by Gratiano, Bassanio's friend, and soon becomes his wife.

Prince of Morocco—Portia's first suitor

Prince of Aragon—Portia's second suitor

Balthazar—A servant of Portia

A servant and messenger

Setting: Venice and Portia's rich estate near Belmont

CHAPTER 9. THE MERCHANT OF VENICE

Bassanio's Expensive Wish

The play's opening dialogue focuses on the sadness of Antonio, the Venetian merchant of the play's title. Although his friends Salerio and Solanio are trying to make him feel better, Antonio's melancholy sets the tone for the next few scenes. Bassanio, Antonio's dear friend, is in financial trouble but plans to court a rich heiress from Belmont named Portia. He asks Antonio to stake him so he can travel there to woo her.

Antonio is the kind who would do anything to help his friend. He says, "My purse, my person, my extremest means,/Lie all unlock'd to your occasions." The relationship between Antonio and Bassanio seems to be very close. (Some modern directors go so far as to assume a homosexual attraction between the two men.) Scott Wentworth, a veteran stage and TV actor who played Antonio in the Stratford Festival of Canada's 2007 production of *Merchant*, believes Antonio's choice of imagery in these lines reveals a deep, mysterious devotion to Bassanio. (Wentworth will say a lot more about Antonio later.) But there's a problem. All of Antonio's wealth is tied up in various trading ships that are away at sea and presumably bound for home. So he can help, he tells Bassanio to find someone in Venice who will extend Antonio credit.

3,000 Ducats and a Bond of Blood

The story gets interesting when Bassanio approaches Shylock, a Jewish moneylender, and asks if Antonio can borrow 3,000 *ducats*. When Antonio arrives, Shylock points out the irony that Antonio, a Christian who hates him because he practices usury, now needs him for something.

"WILD AND WHIRLING WORDS"

A *ducat* is a gold or silver coin of varying value. Most European countries used the ducat from the early twelfth century, when Roger II of Sicily, the Duke of Apulia, first issued it. According to "The Ducat," an online article in the World Internet Numismatic Society (WINS) newsletter by Doug Prather, the gold ducat was highly popular across Europe because each

109

> coin weighed 3.5 grams and was "struck in .986 gold. These specifications for the ducat would remain the same for the next 700 plus years," Prather writes.

Shylock agrees to lend Antonio 3,000 ducats for three months without interest. He half-humorously proposes, however, that if the merchant forfeits his bond, Shylock will be entitled to a pound of Antonio's flesh. No way, Bassanio thinks! But Antonio seems unfazed by these terms, confident that his cash flow will increase before the bond comes due. So he signs the contract.

Intrigue at Belmont—The Trial of Three Caskets

We leave Venice and find ourselves inside rich Portia's estate near Belmont. She welcomes a suitor, the Prince of Morocco, who takes part in an intriguing game involving three caskets. In contemplating these gold, silver, and lead boxes, he must choose the correct one or he cannot ever marry. While Morocco is pondering his decision, we cut back to Venice where we learn that Launcelot is planning to leave Shylock's service. What's more, Jessica, the Jew's daughter, is plotting to elope with Lorenzo. She also intends to renounce Judaism and become a Christian:

> Jessica: Alack, what heinous sin is it in me
> To be ashamed to be my father's child!
> But though I am a daughter to his blood,
> I am not to his manners. O Lorenzo,
> If thou keep promise, I shall end this strife,
> Become a Christian and thy loving wife.
> (II.3.16-21)

When she escapes, this horrible girl steals her father's ducats and precious rings. (Later, this act seems to destroy her father, but his cry of "My daughter! O my ducats! O my daughter!" leaves us wondering. Which does he love more? His ducats or his child?)

Chapter 9. The Merchant of Venice

~ TIMELESS SOLILOQUIES ~

In one of the most famous scenes of Act three, Salerio asks Shylock about what he would do with Antonio's flesh should the merchant default on his loan. Insistent on forcing Antonio to honor his contract, Shylock claims that keeping the bond will "feed [his] revenge." He bitterly rails against Antonio's cruel and bigoted treatment of him, simply because he is a Jew:

Shylock: I am a Jew.
Hath not a Jew eyes? Hath not a Jew hands, organs, dimensions, senses, affections, passions; fed with the same food, hurt with the same weapons, subject to the same diseases, heal'd by the same means, warm'd and cool'd by the same winter and summer, as a Christian is? If you prick us, do we not bleed? If you tickle us, do we not laugh? If you poison us, do we not die? And if you wrong us, shall we not revenge? If we are like you in the rest, we will resemble you in that.
(III.1.58-68)

In giving Shylock this speech, Shakespeare humanized and vindicated a persecuted man and his entire downtrodden race. Shakespeare is often accused of being anti-Semitic because his Jew embodies negative stereotypes. Directors and scholars who disagree often point to this speech as evidence that the playwright empathized with the plight of the Jew in his time.

Cutting back to Belmont, Morocco chooses the gold casket, hoping to win Portia's hand in marriage, but he gets no prize; after him, the Prince of Aragon fusses over the silver one, picks it, and is similarly disappointed. When it is Bassanio's turn, he stands in front of the lead casket and says, "So may the outward shows be least themselves—/The world is still deceiv'd with ornament."

His words and his choice speak sagely about the deception of appearances. He opens the casket, finds Portia's picture, and wins her hand in marriage. While Portia humbly bestows half of what she owns to her future husband, she gives Bassanio her ring and expects him to keep it on as long as he loves her. He accepts the oath, promising never to remove it. (In a comic Shakespearean stroke, Gratiano has made a play for Nerissa, Portia's gentlewoman, and snagged her for his wife!)

Shylock Calls in His Pound of Flesh

By the time Bassanio wins Portia in a merry moment, the mood in Venice has darkened. We've already learned that Antonio's ships are not going to arrive in time for him to repay Shylock. The bad news finally makes its way to Belmont in the form of Antonio's letter to Bassanio. When Portia hears the story of Antonio's bad fortune, she wants to help. She concocts a plan so that she and Nerissa can secretly disguise themselves and intervene in the Venetian courtroom on Antonio's behalf.

Antonio's Trial—Harsh Justice from a "Learned Judge"

At Antonio's trial, the Duke expresses disbelief that Shylock would demand a pound of Antonio's flesh, exhorting him to show mercy. You have to admire Shylock's sage arguments during these thrilling moments. He refuses, eloquently warning against the danger of violating the letter of Venetian law.

During Shakespeare's day, the Venetian Republic was greatly admired as a powerful republic with an enviable system of law. Jews were considered foreigners or *aliens* and were forbidden to own property. In the *New Cambridge Shakespeare* edition of *The Merchant of Venice*, M. M. Mahood reviews some facts and myths that influenced the plot of *Merchant* and works by other Renaissance authors. First, Venice allowed its citizens to borrow money from, or enter into a bond with, foreigners. Venice also "gave foreigners full access to its courts," Mahood says. When

Chapter 9. The Merchant of Venice

Antonio forfeits his bond with Shylock, Venetian law similarly allows Shylock redress in the courts. Because this period predated commercial banking, Venetians depended on some Jewish moneylenders to bankroll their investments. One myth about Venetian Jews, Mahood notes, was that they were privileged because of their legal rights, their ability to practice their religion, and their freedom to practice *usury* (the lending of money with interest). Contrary to what many believed, "Jews were tolerated in Venice, not out of humanitarian feelings, but because their moneylending was an essential service to the poor and saved the authorities the trouble of setting up the state loan banks. . ."

Hearing this, Bassanio offers Shylock 6,000 ducats (a gift from Portia), twice the value of the loan. But the Jew won't take it. When the Duke implies Shylock might incur a punishment because he won't be merciful, Shylock resists this logic by pointing up the hypocritical practice of slavery among Christians.

Following Nerissa, who pretends to be her clerk, Portia enters the courtroom, impersonating a lawyer named Balthazar. Her opening salvo is presented as a noble discourse on the "law" of Christian mercy:

Portia:	Do you confess the bond?
Antonio:	I do.
Portia:	Then must the Jew be merciful.
Shylock:	On what compulsion must I? tell me that.
Portia:	The quality of mercy is not strain'd,
	It droppeth as the gentle rain from heaven
	Upon the place beneath. It is twice blest:
	It blesseth him that gives and him that takes.
	'Tis mightiest in the mightiest, it becomes
	The throned monarch better than his crown.
	(IV.1.181-189)

Undoubtedly, we are meant to contrast Shylock's fervid advocacy for obeying the law with Portia's praise of Christian virtue. Portia fails to convince Shylock to tear up the bond or take the additional money offered to him. Shylock is poised to win his case when Portia plays a trump card in their game of legal reasoning:

> Shylock: Most learned judge, a sentence! Come prepare!
>
> Portia: Tarry a little, there is something else.
> This bond doth give thee here no jot of blood;
> The words expressly are "a pound of flesh."
> (IV.1.304-07)

Upon hearing that he can't have his pound of flesh if he sheds any of Antonio's blood, a dejected Shylock settles for the offer of 6,000 ducats. But it's too late for that. Portia asserts that he is guilty of violating a different law, which makes it illegal for an alien to "seek the life of any citizen." His punishment? The death penalty. Next, he must give up half of his wealth to the one he conspired against and half to the state. Showing mercy, the Duke erases his death sentence. Antonio, in turn, mercifully allows Shylock to keep half of his fortune if he promises to convert to Christianity. On top of that, he must give half of his fortune to his daughter and her husband, while also leaving his portion to them when he dies. In the end, Shylock is destroyed by the code of law he worked so strongly to uphold. In spite of Shylock's cruel insistence on having Antonio's flesh, his forced conversion is deeply disturbing.

Rings and Merry Revelations

The Merchant of Venice continues to puzzle viewers and critics because the courtroom climax hangs over the merry mood of the entire fifth act. (This problem is a great challenge for the director.) In fine comedic fashion, Shakespeare reunites the three couples and resolves all conflicts. After the court scene, "Balthazar" (Portia) talks Bassanio out of the ring he promised Portia he would never give up. The disguised Nerissa manages to get Gratiano's ring. Back in Belmont, Portia and Nerissa taunt their husbands for breaking their oaths and being unfaithful. Then they reveal their disguises. Both men promise to do better; Jessica and Lorenzo learn they will inherit Shylock's wealth; Antonio's ships magically materialize. And the lovers look forward to a tranquil life in marriage.

Attending to the Language—An Actor Inhabits Antonio

The title role of *The Merchant of Venice* is Antonio. Students and theatregoers often forget this detail. To arrive at a deep understanding of Antonio's part for his role in a 2007 production of *Merchant* at the Stratford Festival of Canada, Scott Wentworth avoided approaching the play with extraneous ideas. "I try to let the language and poetry go into me and lead me a little bit," he said. "If we start with the language and always return to that, it seems to bear more fruit."

For centuries critics have questioned the negative stereotype implicit in Shylock's baleful cry "My daughter! O my ducats! O my daughter!" after Jessica has fled with his money and jewels. Shakespearean actor Scott Wentworth notes that Antonio equates himself to a purse during an early scene with Bassanio. "Shylock equates his daughter to the contents of a purse, which, of course, we cringe at because it stereotypes Jewish behavior. But we don't cringe when Antonio compares himself to a purse, partly because the ruling class doesn't have to cringe; the persecuted do. However, implicit in Antonio's metaphor is a criticism of a superficial, social aspect of Christian culture—the accumulation of wealth."

Antonio is nothing if not mysterious. "It's a role that audiences and actors come to understand by inference," Wentworth said. "Antonio is not as verbal as a lot of the other characters, even when he takes center stage. His speech isn't idiosyncratic like Shylock's prose, nor does he have a large, imagistic view of things like Portia's suitors, for example.

"The first thing I noticed in working on this role was Antonio's remoteness, a guardedness, which is never fully explained.

"When Antonio and Bassanio are alone, Antonio links Bassanio's quest for Portia to a pilgrimage. Bassanio's quest for a woman seems heightened because of the way Antonio describes it. When he says, 'My purse, my person, my extremest means,/Lie all unlock'd to your occasions,' I was taken with a man who identifies himself with a purse. Here, Antonio's language and rhythm get emotional, direct, and very heightened, as though he's saying to Bassanio, 'You essentially wrong me by questioning whether I'll give money to you.' So by financing this quite extravagant quest, Antonio finds himself in a triangular relationship with Bassanio and Portia."

While performing Antonio, Wentworth felt this triangular connection acutely in the final scene. "When I show up at Belmont, I feel like I'm looking for something to do. She gives me this mysterious letter telling me three of my ships have magically returned, which allows her to remove me from her marriage. It's as if Portia is saying to us, 'Bassanio, when we're married, you can't be as close to Antonio.'"

In Michael Radford's 2004 film adaptation of The Merchant of Venice, *Al Pacino's vision of Shylock, the Jewish moneylender who insists on collecting his pound of flesh when Antonio forfeits his bond, was acclaimed by critics. Pictured to Pacino's left is Allan Corduner, playing the role of Tubal, Shylock's loyal friend.*

(Photo courtesy of Sony/Photofest.)

During his performance, Wentworth also experienced the key conflict between the merchant and Shylock. "The first time Shylock and Antonio are placed together, both say their essential conflict is business, not Christian," Wentworth said. "They have a business dispute, a philosophical dispute—Shylock doesn't appreciate Antonio's name-calling. For both of these men, their religious difference is a jumping-off place for a professional way of dealing with the world, between venturing capital and saving money. I found that surprising. I expected there to be more substantive religious conflict between them, but there isn't."

Our Modern Empathy for Shylock—A Problem for Directors

Although John Heminges and Henry Condell lumped *The Merchant of Venice* in with the comedies in the First Folio (1623), the play is rich in contrasting moods, ideas, themes, and tragic impulses that complicate how we respond to it. Shakespeare wrote *Merchant* around 1596-1597. Serious scholars remind us that Elizabethans would have viewed Shylock as a comic villain, as a stock allegorical figure familiar from medieval drama. Somehow, Shylock seems better rounded than a stock villain. He turns Christian hypocrisy on its ear, and we excuse his cruel insistence on "having his bond" because he reminds us that he learned this behavior from the Christians. He is also the means by which Shakespeare offers us a dramatic discourse between the merits of following the letter of Venetian law and tempering "strict justice" with mercy, a New Testament leaning.

"A KINGDOM FOR A STAGE"

While performing Antonio in *The Merchant of Venice* at the 2007 Stratford Festival of Canada, Scott Wentworth learned that whether one chooses to play Shylock as "victim, villain, or in between," one scene is extremely important to the play's action and resolution. "In the short scene 7 in Act two, after Jessica has escaped, Shylock has the Duke search Bassanio's ship and is given to believe Lorenzo and Jessica are on it; Antonio assures the Duke they are not, but at that moment Antonio is implicated through his association with Bassanio. Had Jessica not been stolen by the Christian, would Shylock have reacted as harshly when Antonio forfeited the bond?"

In the Wordsworth edition of *The Merchant of Venice*, Cedric Watts suggests why we still value such a controversial play.

> Though Shylock's vengeful malice is evident, he can be engaging because of it as well as in spite of it: we know him so fully that our knowledge veers toward complicity. His gamut of moods and tones make him one of the most interesting characters in Shakespeare for an audience to watch.

Sidney Berger Talks About Staging *The Merchant of Venice*

Sidney Berger, the late founder and producing director of the Houston Shakespeare Festival, staged *The Merchant of Venice* twice at Miller Outdoor Theatre in Hermann Park. The director also addressed the play in his doctoral dissertation *The Theme of Persecution in Selected Plays of the Yiddish Art Theatre*. He was no stranger to the controversy that *Merchant* provokes for today's playgoers.

When Berger directed *Merchant* for the Houston Shakespeare Festival in 1991, he wanted to redress the imbalance between our own sympathy for Shylock after his forced conversion and the play's lighthearted, comic ending. "Once that forced conversion happens in Act four, there's not one reference to Shylock; the two couples run off to their marriage beds and the conversion seems meaningless in light of their actions. In our production, as everyone ran off to bed, Antonio was left onstage, remembering what happened to Shylock." Like Berger, modern directors are inclined to adjust *Merchant*'s ending to keep Shylock's suffering at the forefront of our imaginations when the play is over.

"Shakespeare was writing this play in a society largely devoid of Jews," Berger said. "What Shakespeare does by virtue of his genius is humanize the Jew. Shylock is not a nice man, but Shakespeare has him clearly impart to us, 'You can't destroy me because of what I believe.' Even though Shylock isn't admirable, his Judaism is part of the fabric of this man. When you destroy a man's religion, you destroy the man. At the same time, there is not one admirable character in the play. They're all bigoted. Portia destroys him by forcing him to convert. She's not the heroine that centuries of critics make her out to be. She's the opposite. Here's a bright woman who has a great speech about mercy, and she shows none."

Berger was convinced that Shakespeare's development of Antonio's portrait lends further insight into the playwright's genius. "In the play's opening lines, we feel Antonio's sadness, and it's important to see how his mood follows along the spine of the play. Antonio is not comfortable being an anti-Semite simply by virtue of the fact that he's been raised as one. In the world of the play, England is a society in which anti-Semitism is so deeply rooted that it's a natural part of life. This is why Antonio can ask Shylock to lend him money without compunction. It's also why he doesn't feel remorse when Shylock points up the hypocrisy in the fact that Antonio will borrow money from him one day and spit on him the next."

Berger believed that when Shakespeare created Shylock, he created a complex portrait that went contrary to Marlowe's despicable caricature of Barabas, as well as to his own country's deeply rooted anti-Semitism. "For Shakespeare to write Shylock's great 'Hath not a Jew eyes' speech, which suggests persons of all religions should be treated equally, was incredibly courageous. How brave of Shakespeare to get away with it and give a Jew empathy as a Jew."

FACTS TO REMEMBER

- *The Merchant of Venice* offers striking contrasts between merry Belmont and the cold world of Venetian commerce.
- *The Merchant of Venice* is highly controversial because the play's ostensible villain, Shylock, is an inspired dramatic role, evoking sympathy in today's viewers.
- Shakespeare's Elizabethan audiences would have viewed Shylock as a stock figure of allegory, a comic villain, rather than a sympathetic victim of Christian persecution.
- One critic notes that sixteenth-century myths about Venetian Jews influenced Shakespeare's plays and other European literature.
- In performing Antonio at the Stratford Festival of Canada in 2007, Scott Wentworth discovered that the character is guarded and difficult to know except by inference.
- In spite of its anti-Semitic overtones, the play remains highly popular onstage because Shylock's negative attributes are offset by the cruelty of his Christian persecutors.

Chapter 10
Much Ado About Nothing

> **INTRODUCTION**
> - What makes *Much Ado About Nothing* so popular?
> - A look at the characters and story of *Much Ado* and Shakespearean tricks that complicate the plot
> - What directors say about *Much Ado* when it's performed
> - The juicy puns in *Much Ado's* title
> - What we can learn from two relationship styles
> - An actor muses about Benedick and Beatrice's relationship and Shakespeare's purpose

Imagine what makes for a good romantic comedy on TV. On the sitcom *Cheers*, remember how Sam and Diane bickered all the time? He was a handsome, regular guy who liked being single. She was smart and sophisticated and reveled in putting him down. Sitting around that cozy Boston bar, Sam and Diane spent hours matching wits and hurling insults at each another. But ultimately, it was an act. The sexual attraction was always there.

In *Much Ado About Nothing*, Shakespeare invented the prototype of Sam and Diane. Beatrice and Benedick are two people who'd rather pummel each other with insults than admit their true feelings. Like other festive comedies that make up Shakespeare's mature work, *Much Ado* centers on a love intrigue and the obstacles that lovers overcome. Onstage, Beatrice and Benedick are so lifelike that *Much Ado* continues to be as wildly popular today as it was four centuries ago.

Written around 1598-99, *Much Ado About Nothing* was performed several times for the court of King James and originally printed in 1600. The play's huge popularity during Shakespeare's lifetime enhanced his appeal as one of London's finest playwrights.

The Characters

Don Pedro—The Prince of Aragon is a good noble and a good warrior. He's also the perfect foil to his evil brother, Don John. Though he thrives on high-stakes heroics in battle, he has no trouble taking on the role of Cupid and the matchmaker in this play. He woos Hero on Claudio's behalf and engineers the plan to make Benedick think Beatrice is in love with him.

Benedick—The young lord of Padua has a big ego and is dead set against getting married. His attraction to Beatrice sparks the play's central love story. As others do their best to bring him and Beatrice together, he stays hopelessly—and hilariously—in denial.

Claudio—This immature squire from Florence has a lot to learn about love. When he falls for the young and lovely Hero, he follows all the Elizabethan social mores surrounding arranged marriage. Don't be fooled, though, by his old-fashioned sense of courtesy. He's the type who may care more about appearances than genuine virtue.

Beatrice—The niece of Governor Leonato is a sharp-tongued lady full of the signature wit and wisdom Shakespeare reserved for his greatest heroines. But she's so stubborn and determined to be independent that she's as blind as Benedick. So Hero and Margaret deceive her into thinking that Benedick loves her.

Hero—Leonato's daughter is innocent and even childlike compared to her cousin Beatrice. She has an old-fashioned sense of duty and is perfectly willing to marry any man chosen by her father. Despite being the victim of a horrendously evil plot, she survives and overcomes the harm done to her reputation.

Leonato—The Governor of Messina wants what's best for his daughter. When he becomes one of the victims in Don John's plot to smear his daughter's name, he is shamed and does what any father would have done four centuries ago. He disowns her.

Margaret and Ursula—Hero's maids.

Don John—Don Pedro's bastard brother.

Borachio and Conrad—Don John's evil cohorts.

Dogberry—The constable of Messina.

Verges—A petty constable.

Antonio—Leonato's brother.

Balthasar—Attendant of Don Pedro

Friar Francis

Attendants, Boy, Messenger, Sexton, Watchmen

To help you make sense of the various communities that inhabit the play's main plot and subplot, take note of the groupings in the following chart.

Don Pedro and Company: Don Pedro, Signior Benedick, Count Claudio, Balthasar, and two Messengers

The House of Leonato: Leonato, Beatrice, Hero, Margaret, and Ursula

Don John and Cohorts: Don John (a.k.a. the Bastard), Borachio, and Conrad

Community of Messina: Constable Dogberry, Verges (Dogberry's partner), Friar Francis, a Sexton, and Attendants

Two Lovers Fight a "Merry War"

The play opens amid a lively bustle in the small Sicilian town of Messina. A messenger brings word to Governor Leonato, Hero, and Beatrice that Don Pedro—the young Prince of Aragon—is coming to town on horseback with the young lords Claudio and Benedick.

The prince is a handsome, congenial sort of guy. Dragging behind him, though, is a sour-faced Don John, the bastard brother he has just defeated in battle. Be forewarned. This guy is so bitter that the moment he walks onstage, he spews words full of hate and spite. This black prince is up to no good.

Before these nobles walk onstage, Beatrice lets out a rip-roaring tirade of witty abuse against Benedick, her old friend from Padua. She takes such delight in hurling insults at him that you have to wonder what, in fact, is *really* going on between these two. When Benedick eventually appears during the homecoming scene, the couple's witty sparring escalates into high-pitched word-combat.

Beatrice is proud, clever, and self-possessed and she's determined to stay single. Benedick, who has a hard time holding his ego in check, is an impressive talker. He isn't looking to get married either. There's no denying the sexual tension between these two. During their verbal fencing, emotions fly high and they persist in waging a "merry war" throughout the play. Beginning with *The Taming of the Shrew*, Shakespeare loved to stage this kind of battle between the sexes in his lively festive comedies.

Over the last few decades, seasoned actors from both sides of the Atlantic have performed the roles of Beatrice and Benedick onstage and on the screen. Stars such as Katharine Hepburn, Judi Dench, and Emma Thompson have shined as Beatrice. As Benedick, John Gielgud, Derek Jacobi, Jimmy Smits, Kevin Kline, and Kenneth Branagh have earned kudos from the critics.

Chapter 10. Much Ado About Nothing

Alexis Denisof and Amy Acker performed the roles of Benedick and Beatrice in the modern-dress adaptation of Much Ado About Nothing *(2012), shot in black-and-white by director Josh Whedon.*

(Photo Courtesy of Photofest)

Under Cover—Romancing Hero by Proxy

All skirmishing aside, the plot of *Much Ado* is set in motion when shy Claudio first lays eyes on Hero. She's modest and respectable; he's reserved and respectful. His long stint at war makes him go a little soft when he lays eyes on this fair young maiden. He says, "In mine eye, she is the sweetest lady that ever I looked on."

Realize, young lords like Claudio and other Elizabethan aristocrats believed in arranged marriage, so Claudio is bound to move carefully to obey social rules of courtship. Being circumspect, he decides to play it safe and have Don Pedro test the waters for him. But don't be misled by this picture. It's likely that Claudio may be *only* attracted to Hero's good looks and social position.

Being a magnanimous sort, Don Pedro is happy to play the intermediary on Claudio's behalf. He has a brainstorm. Why not pretend to be Claudio by putting on a mask at the upcoming dress ball and court Hero in Claudio's name? Claudio likes the idea, especially because it allows him to stand on the sidelines while someone else sticks his neck out for him. During these opening scenes, the atmosphere onstage has been festive and slightly frenetic as the villagers look forward to an evening of partying and revels.

"A KINGDOM FOR A STAGE"

As the play's title suggests, there is "much ado" onstage the minute the curtain rises. John Russell Brown notes in *Discovering Shakespeare* that when you see *Much Ado* performed, you'll be amazed at how quickly the actors move about the stage during the opening scenes. One moment the stage is filled with people, and the next moment the players disappear. Lively parties, dances, and songs also fuel this play's quick tempo. A flurry of abrupt scene changes complement the many mood changes that occur in the play.

But the romantic mood created by Claudio's attraction to Hero suddenly darkens when the villain Don John learns about his brother's plan to go under cover. He's so bitter that he concocts a plan to sabotage Don Pedro's efforts. This is his chance, he thinks, to get even with his brother and settle the score over his recent military defeat.

Don John plants the first seeds of distrust when he tells an unsuspecting Claudio that Don Pedro actually wants Hero for himself. And Claudio falls for it! But indeed the bastard is proved false when the good prince proposes marriage to Hero on Claudio's behalf. The mischief doesn't end there. This is just the first of the black prince's many attempts to hurt Claudio. Early on, he reveals his true colors in a conversation with Borachio:

> I had rather be a canker in a hedge than a rose
> in his grace, and it better fits my blood to be disdain'd
> of all than to fashion a carriage to rob love from
> any. In this, though I cannot be said to be a flattering
> honest man, it must not be denied but I am a plain-dealing
> villain.
> (I.3.27-32)

> ### "WILD AND WHIRLING WORDS"
>
> The masquerade party, or *masque*, was a popular form of entertainment during the Renaissance. Guests were treated to amateur singing and dancing by masked performers. The masque is actually a cross between a fancy dress ball and an elegant costume party. Shakespeare used the masque so his characters could hide their real identities and trick one another.

Meanwhile, dancing and merrymaking create a lively backdrop for Don John's dastardly deeds against his brother. At the same party Beatrice and Benedick are busy with their own arguing, but in this scene, of course, they do it in disguise.

Don Pedro Plays Cupid, the Matchmaker

Hero is won over by Don Pedro's suave courtship-by-proxy and agrees to marry Claudio. Thus far, Don Pedro seems to be reveling in his new role as matchmaker, but now he's ready for a bigger challenge. As the wedding preparations get underway, Don Pedro suggests that he and his friends take on the Herculean task of making Beatrice and Benedick fall in love.

Finding a way to unite these two won't be easy. Both are dead set against matrimony. In a brilliant maneuver—and a clever trick Shakespeare likes to use—Don Pedro, Claudio, and Leonato play-act a conversation designed to be overheard by Benedick and make him think Beatrice has fallen for him. Confident that Benedick is eavesdropping, Don Pedro, Claudio, and Leonato loudly marvel at how Beatrice has suddenly fallen for "Signior Benedick."

Hero and her two maids use a similar strategy on Beatrice. By making it possible for the unsuspecting girl to overhear a conversation they stage to trick her, they dupe her as well. In this scene she is easily gulled into believing that Benedick "is sick in love with [her]".

VERSE BY VERSE

Though the title of this comedy may sound trite, there's a lot more to it. The word "nothing" was pronounced n-o-t-i-n-g (or more like "noht'n"). With this in mind, you realize Shakespeare has slipped in a multilayered pun on "noting." To Elizabethans the word brought to mind "eavesdropping," "overhearing," or even "observing." (Recall, there's lots of this sort of thing going on in *Much Ado.*) There's also a sexier pun. Shakespeare knew his audiences would have caught "nothing's" bawdy pun on the vagina. "Something" was slang for a man's penis.

When this gullible pair ponders the gossip that has been leaked to them, the real fun begins. Benedick, who loves his freedom, is completely surprised. But he soon mellows and determines to "requite" Beatrice's affections. Beatrice, who's given to hiding her true feelings beneath big doses of sarcasm, says goodbye to her "maiden pride."

Shaming Hero (For Shame, Claudio!)

As the news of Beatrice's "true" feelings softens the way Benedick looks at her, Don John gets even more diabolical. This time, he tricks Claudio by luring him into watching a staged scene where Hero appears to be making out with another man. The dastardly scheme works—Claudio and Don Pedro are deceived into believing she's a morally loose girl who has given up her virginity. Poor Hero has been framed and her fate is sealed. Or so it seems . . .

On the big wedding day, Claudio shows up at the altar to take his bride. Only, instead of saying "I do" when the friar prompts him, he flings the innocent girl right back to her father and insults her honor:

> . . . Would you not swear,
> All you that see her, that she were a maid,
> By these exterior shows? But she is none:
> She knows the heat of a luxurious bed;

> Her blush is guiltiness, not modesty.
> (IV.1.38-42)

When Leonato and Hero press him for the proof, Claudio pulls no punches:

> You seem to me as Dian in her orb,
> As chaste as is the bud ere it be blown;
> But you are more intemperate n your blood
> Than Venus, or those pamp'red animals
> That rage in savage sensuality.
> (IV.4.57-61)

These are fighting words. In Shakespeare's time, railing against a woman's honor had a powerful, irreversible effect. Accusations like these would have clouded a woman's family in shame. But wait—when Leonato first hears Claudio accuse and insult his daughter, wouldn't you think he'd give her a chance to explain? No way—he jumps to his own conclusions and assumes the worst. Sadly, Hero is so shocked by Claudio's public humiliation, she faints.

Faking Death to Reclaim Virtue

Leonato may have doubts about his daughter's virtue, but Beatrice knows good and well her cousin has been slandered. Friar Francis also believes she is innocent. He sees that "in her eye there hath appear'd a fire/To burn the errors that these princes hold/Against her maiden truth."

The friar has an idea. He convinces Leonato to report his daughter's death and go ahead with plans to bury her. When the others mourn the loss of her, they'll forget all the bad gossip and start to pity the poor girl. Then Claudio will feel true remorse and begin seeing her in a virtuous light.

In the middle of this calamity, Benedick tells Beatrice he loves her and invites her to let him prove it. With signature dexterity, she retorts, "Kill Claudio." Now Benedick is on the hook—does he forsake his best friend to please Beatrice, or does he put loyalty to his friends first? Seeing the courage of Beatrice's convictions, Benedick promises to challenge Claudio to a duel.

Leonato's Challenge

Don John's cruel plot unravels when the buffoonish Constable Dogberry has the henchman Borachio arrested. A watchman testifies that he heard Borachio brag about his involvement in Don John's villainous scheme: "Marry, that he had receiv'd a thousand ducats of Don John for accusing the Lady Hero wrongfully."

Stung by Hero's loss and determined to prove her innocence, Leonato—who is far too old for swordfights, by the way—ventures a pathetic challenge:

> . . . Know, Claudio, to thy head,
> Thou hast so wrong'd mine innocent child and me
> That I am forc'd to lay my reverence by,
> And with grey hairs and bruise of many days,
> Do challenge thee to trial of a man.
> I say thou hast belied mine innocent child!
> Thy slander hath gone through and through her heart,
> And she lies buried with her ancestors—
> (V.1.62-69)

In spite of Leonato's defense, the prince and Claudio insist there is truth behind Hero's infidelity. Up until now Benedick has been slow to defend Hero. But finally he challenges Claudio to fight, saying, "You have among you kill'd a sweet and innocent lady."

Saved by Fools in Uniform

The truth eventually dawns upon Don Pedro and Claudio after they learn Don John has fled Messina. In Constable Dogberry's hilarious scene, Claudio and Don Pedro finally hear Borachio confess his evil role in Don John's plot:

> I have deceiv'd even your very eyes. What your wisdoms
> could not discover, these shallow fools have
> brought to light, who in the night overheard me con-
> fessing to this man how Don John your brother in-
> cens'd me to slander the Lady Hero, how you were
> brought into the orchard, and saw me court Margaret

in Hero's garments, how you disgrac'd her when you
should marry her . . .
(V.1.232-239)

Shakespeare's portrait of the bumbling, dull-witted Dogberry is legendary. He longs to sound respectable, but his silly speeches are riddled with malapropisms. These scenes are some of the best examples of farce ever written for the theatre or movies. Needless to say, he looks pretty ridiculous onstage.

When he created the figure of Dogberry, there's no doubt that Shakespeare was inspired by the clownish personality of William Kempe, the very first actor to play the role. More recently, actor Michael Keaton cashed in on playing the notorious clown in Kenneth Branagh's well-directed film version of *Much Ado*.

"WILD AND WHIRLING WORDS"

We create *malapropisms* when we misuse a word in a certain context and the effect is laughable. Dogberry's frequent malapropisms transform him into a delightful caricature. He says silly things like "auspicious" when he means "suspicious," "vigitant" instead of "vigilant," and even "blunt" when he means "sharp." At one point he blurts out, "When the age is in, the wit is out," perverting the proverb: "When ale is in, wit is out." The word "malapropism" was coined when playwright Richard Brinsley Sheridan created Mrs. Malaprop for his 1775 comedy *The Rivals*.

A Bride in Disguise

Hearing the truth, the prince and Claudio humble themselves before Leonato. First, the governor demands that they hang an epitaph on Hero's tomb. Then he tells Claudio to come to the church the next morning and marry his niece. (When you see the play, you'll notice that this girl happens to be the spitting image of Hero.)

When Claudio arrives at the church, he encounters a masked bride. When she raises her veil, he gazes in shock at his beloved Hero. (Hero wasn't really dead after all! The friar's plan definitely fooled Claudio.) She tells him, "One hero died defil'd, but I do live,/And surely as I live, I am a maid." This uplifting scene is capped by wry exchanges between Beatrice and Benedick. Getting them to admit they love each other has taken some doing, but in the end, they come around and the dancing starts up again.

Two Kinds of Relationships

Shakespeare drew his plot about Claudio and Hero from an Italian story that dates back to 1554. The Beatrice and Benedick tale could be his own concoction, though, and a change from his habit of borrowing plots from his sources.

From the start, Shakespeare places the two couples in striking contrast. The two different relationships provide an enduring commentary on love.

 TIMELESS SOLILOQUIES

> As Shakespeare became an expert at writing comedies, he abandoned a tendency to have his characters speak largely in verse. To our ears, verse sounds very artificial and prose sounds much more natural. Claudio, a conventional type of guy, often speaks in verse. But Beatrice and Benedick often speak in prose. To Elizabethans, this kind of talk would have sounded like a spoken conversation, sermon, or political speech. (It wasn't exactly the same, though, because dramatic language was more artificial than ordinary speech.) Shakespeare hoped this verse/prose contrast would teach his audiences about how genuine lovers actually speak. In *Much Ado*, nearly three-quarters of the lines are in prose.

Claudio and Hero pursue a conventional courtship. From the moment they fall in love, each depends on an authority figure to advance their relationship. Claudio is shy and also believes in following traditional courtship rituals, so he depends on his close friend, the prince. Hero is quiet, modest, and obviously dependent on her father to screen her choice of husband. Because he barely knows Hero and puts greater faith in what others say over what he genuinely sees and knows, Claudio is easily duped into rejecting her.

Though Beatrice and Benedick fiercely guard their independence, each is more open to honest communication. As the others conspire to bring them together, both are open to changing their ways. While Beatrice's candor seems jarringly modern for a woman of Shakespeare's day, she is still respected by her uncle and her cousin. As her constant bickering with Benedick gives way to empathy and trust during Hero's trial, their mutual respect grows.

Actor Jeffrey Bean Muses About Benedick and the "Smartest Guy in the Room"

Jeffrey Bean has been a resident member of Houston's Alley Theatre since 1989. He's no stranger to Shakespeare. During a five-year stint on Broadway, he worked with the eminent Shakespearean director Peter Hall while appearing in Peter Shaffer's *Amadeus*. A few months after finishing the role of Benedick in the Alley's 2006 staging of *Much Ado*, Bean offered his own ideas about Benedick's motivations and why this complicated play thrills modern audiences.

Bean feels Benedick is an "arrested adolescent," someone who's "stuck in youth, and the persona has worn him out by the time we see him." But Benedick changes after he sees Claudio shun Hero in the chapel scene. "There we see the imminent marriage between Benedick and Beatrice because he refuses to defend Claudio's actions," he says. "At the moment when Benedick and Beatrice witness Hero's humiliation, the two are coupled as though they are married. They become comfortable with one another after that."

Bean finds Beatrice's defense of Hero's honor illuminating for Benedick, allowing him to empathize with feminine suffering. When Benedick agrees to challenge Claudio at Beatrice's request, "he leaves adolescence and becomes a man," Bean says.

"You've got this sense that Shakespeare must have started out writing the play reluctantly and he can't help but make it more serious. In doing the part,

I came to feel there was a long history between Beatrice and Benedick by the time the play opens. Everyone in Messina can't wait for these two to get together to watch the verbal fireworks."

Bean adds that *Much Ado* starts out being kind of "frothy" and then suddenly becomes "deadly serious." Though critics and scholars often see this as a flaw, Bean disagrees. "Shakespeare is always going to be the smartest guy in the room," he says. The tone of the play shifts because Benedick becomes somebody different, he says. "He's entered a union with the opposite sex." In Bean's view, this is when the play transcends genre and becomes a play that says something very real about gender politics and the relationship between men and women. "The play is so popular today because Shakespeare hits on something so universal here. He was so modern in his viewpoint."

Much Ado: Four Notable Versions on Stage and Screen

Much Ado has been so popular through the ages that it's impossible to list every major production. Here are a few notable versions and details about what made them unusual:

- 1972—The setting was the United States during the 1920s. Scenes with Dogberry and Company were played as the Keystone Kops, made famous during the silent film era. The show featured ragtime music and an oompah band. The Broadway production starred Sam Waterston, Kathleen Widdoes, and Bernard Hughes and was directed by A. J. Antoon.
- 1984—In a Royal Shakespeare production, Derek Jacobi won a Tony award for his role as Benedick. For many Americans, Jacobi became a household name playing Brother Cadfael in the TV series *Cadfael*.
- 1988—In a New York Shakespeare Festival production directed by Gerald Freedman, Kevin Kline's Benedick and Blythe Danner's Beatrice made an impression on critics.
- 1993—Four years after Kenneth Branagh made his mark as the director of *Henry V* on film, he directed a star-studded cast in a lush adaptation of *Much Ado*, filmed in Florence and Tuscany's sun-drenched Chianti region. The show featured Denzel

CHAPTER 10. MUCH ADO ABOUT NOTHING

Washington (a very handsome Don Pedro), Keanu Reeves (a bad Don John!), Branagh himself (impeccable as Benedick), Robert Sean Leonard (as Claudio—oh, baby!), Emma Thompson (as a very sexy Beatrice), and Kate Beckinsale (well cast as chaste Hero).

FACTS TO REMEMBER
- *Much Ado About Nothing*, one of Shakespeare's festive comedies, was performed several times at King James's court.
- Through Beatrice and Benedick's barbed repartee, Shakespeare revisits a favorite "battle of the sexes" theme, also used in *The Taming of the Shrew*.
- Disguises and eavesdropping complicate the plot of this action-filled comedy.
- Beatrice and Benedick are foils for Claudio and Hero, who carry on a more formal, traditional courtship.
- Shakespeare juxtaposes the two couples' actions and speaking styles to show audiences what love was all about.
- Alley Theatre actor Jeffrey Bean believes *Much Ado* changes from a "frothy" comedy to a serious play at the moment Benedick empathizes with Beatrice's belief that Hero has been treated unjustly.

Chapter 11

The Merry Wives of Windsor

> **INTRODUCTION**
> - How *The Merry Wives of Windsor* came to be written
> - A look at the play's main characters
> - How *Merry Wives'* bourgeois focus differs from other Shakespearean comedies
> - The two principal plots of *Merry Wives*
> - Interesting facts about dialect in this play
> - A director's views about staging *Merry Wives*

Critics have often dismissed *The Merry Wives of Windsor* as nothing more than a romp. But the play seems to stand apart from other Shakespearean comedies for several reasons. For one thing, Shakespeare reportedly wrote it very quickly after Queen Elizabeth commissioned it in 1597.

As the legend goes, the queen wanted Shakespeare to write a new play in which Falstaff falls in love, to be performed at the Garter Feast on April 23. Falstaff was the popular knight featured in Shakespeare's *Henry IV* history series.

Perhaps with the exception of Falstaff, *Merry Wives* is not filled with characters who leave a lasting impression. There are no squabbling lovers like Kate and Petruchio from *Shrew* or Beatrice and Benedick from *Much Ado*. No wise heroines that we greatly admire, like Portia (*The Merchant of Venice*) or Rosalind (*As You Like It*). Even Falstaff, who's delightfully despicable in this play, is easily forgettable.

But this doesn't mean *Merry Wives* isn't a play worth getting to know. Here's an introduction to characters from the play's two main plots.

The Characters

THE PLOT INVOLVING THE MERRY WIVES AND FALSTAFF

Sir John Falstaff—The mischievous knight, staying at the Garter Inn, is strapped for cash and down on his luck. Shakespeare immortalized him as a keenly self-aware comic figure who is so verbally dexterous, audiences find him irresistible. In this play he is definitely funny, but without any kind of moral upper hand. He is a poor aristocrat among several well-to-do bourgeois families. When he sets his sights upon wooing Mistresses Page and Ford to get to their husbands' money, Falstaff meets his match.

Mistress Alice Ford—This mature, wise woman wasn't born yesterday. She sets up Falstaff after he propositions her in a letter, conspiring with Mistress Page to get even with the lascivious knight. And rightly so, she has to watch her back because her husband is the jealous type.

Mistress Margaret Page—She and Alice Ford are the merry wives referred to in the play's title. Mistress Page is equally offended by the silly knight's epistolary overtures and schemes with her cohort to best Falstaff at his own game. In the subplot involving the choice of husband for her daughter, she pushes for the silly-spoken Dr. Caius to be her son-in-law.

Francis Ford—Ford is an upright, prominent member of Windsor's middle class. He is Alice Ford's overly jealous husband who disguises himself as Master Brook, Alice Ford's lover, to bribe Falstaff into wooing her in order to underhandedly test her fidelity to him. He is fooled twice by the ladies' scheme to swift Falstaff away using a laundry basket and a disguise. What a jerk!

George Page—Page is similar in social position to Francis Ford, although he's not the suspicious type at all. As a matter of fact, his positive, cheerful outlook is in striking contrast to Ford's brooding jealousy. Page seems strongly opposed to his daughter's desire to marry Fenton. He wants her to marry the shy Slender instead. But this congenial sort comes around to accepting her decision in the end.

Mistress Quickly—The servant to the French-accented Dr. Caius who delivers the merry wives' letters to Falstaff. She is also involved in the comings and goings of suitors fighting for Anne Page. She talks a lot and is delightful to watch.

William Page—George Page's young son.

Bardolph, Pistol, and Nym—Falstaff's followers.

Robin—Falstaff's page.

John and Robert—Ford's servants.

Host of the Garter Inn

THE PLOT TO WIN ANNE PAGE

Anne Page—The somewhat shy daughter of Mistress Page is under 17 years old and courted by three suitors who want to marry her. She is the center of a mini-drama that raises questions about how much say a daughter has in her choice of husband and her destiny.

Master Fenton—A young gentleman of aristocratic background and noble birth who has squandered his fortune. Early on, he obviously is attracted to Anne for the dowry her family can provide him, but eventually he falls in love with her.

Abraham Slender—An aristocrat who is well off and interested in courting Anne Page. He is also Robert Shallow's cousin. But as you'll see during one of his scenes with Anne, Slender isn't very skilled at the game of courtship and would rather leave the wooing to Hugh Evans.

Doctor Caius—A rich French physician with a quick temper and a unique way with the English language.

Robert Shallow—An over-eighty justice of the peace and country gentleman from Gloucestershire.

Peter Simple—Slender's servant.

Sir Hugh Evans—The Welsh parson who mediates a conflict between Falstaff and Shallow, which ultimately leads to a duel with Dr. Caius. These actions make up another mini-plot in the play, but don't be too concerned about it.

John Rugby—Dr. Caius' servant.

Scene: The area of Windsor, a town north of London, during Elizabethan times.

No Royals Here! A True English, Middle-Class Comedy

The Merry Wives of Windsor is the only Shakespearean play set in a small English town. Set in Windsor, the town where the queen once resided and home of the famous Windsor Castle, the play is a lively, light comedy about the middle class. Literary historians find this interesting because the First Folio version of the play has specific place names and references from Windsor that we know were familiar to an Elizabethan audience.

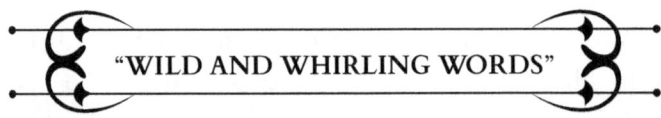

In the final act of *Merry Wives*, the Queen of Fairies (who is Mistress Quickly in disguise) appears to order the elves involved in the merry wives' scheme to prepare Windsor Castle for the Order of the Garter ceremony. In real life, a regular feast connected with this ceremony took place in Whitehall Palace in the city of Westminster (London) and honored knights about to be initiated into the Order of the Garter. Some scholars show evidence that *Merry Wives* was first performed for Elizabeth's court during the Garter Feast on April 23, 1597 (St. George's Day), which occurred a few weeks before the new knights were formally installed at Windsor.

Although *Merry Wives* has its fair share of slamming doors, silly pranks, and elements common to farce, it's not a play we would pigeonhole as farce. The story's basic plot comes from the tradition of *fabliau*, a funny and bawdy kind of tale that goes back to twelfth-century France. *Merry Wives* is so full of action, it's best to enjoy it in the theatre.

The play has two distinct plots that revolve around marriage and married couples who live in small-town Windsor. The main plot generates much of the play's lively action and conflict. It stars Falstaff, the aristocratic knight who is desperate for money and willing to do whatever it takes to get some action!

Falstaff Plays the Lecher for Easy Cash

As the play opens we learn that Falstaff and his followers, Bardolph, Nym, and Pistol, are making lots of enemies. Shallow comes to Windsor to sue Falstaff, irate because his men have been attacked by Falstaff's men and his deer have been stolen! Slender also complains of being robbed.

Falstaff's Self-Serving Ruse

Falstaff has a plan. He gets the weird notion that Mistress Ford finds him irresistible:

> No quips now, Pistol. Indeed I am in the waist two yards
> about, but I am now about no waste; I am about thrift.
> Briefly—I do mean to make love to Ford's wife. I spy
> entertainment in her. She discourses, she carves, she
> gives the leer of invitation.
> (1.3.41-46)

Based on his own impressions, Falstaff feels he has an opportunity to take advantage of his personal popularity with two respected and purse string-wielding matrons. After all, he's strapped for cash and each one could be a source of ready money! So he orders Robin, his page, to deliver a love letter to each lady after his two sidekicks, Pistol and Nym, refuse to help him.

Both women read Falstaff's letters, and both, of course, are highly offended. Mistress Ford is especially miffed—For God's sake, what if her husband had seen the letter? Both women agree that the old cuss shouldn't be allowed to get away with making such risky overtures. So they concoct a plan they hope will bankrupt him. They plot to arrange secret meetings with him to lead him on.

After Mistress Quickly gives Falstaff the reply letters from Mistress Page and Mistress Ford, Shakespeare kinks up the plot even more. Meanwhile, Pistol and Nym, who are feeling put upon by Falstaff, you recall, tell the two women's husbands about Falstaff's plan and their invitation to have him come to their houses.

Faithless Ford Goes Under Cover

Ford, a dangerously jealous sort, has gotten his dander up when he learns the two wives have invited Falstaff to visit them by letter. He seems to be one of those husbands who doesn't trust his wife, but we're not really told why. Here's an inkling of what's going on inside his head:

> What a damn'd Epicurean rascal is this! My heart is ready to crack with impatience. Who says this is improvident jealousy? My wife hath sent to him, the hour is fix'd, the match is made. Would any man have thought this? See the hell of having a false woman! . . . I will prevent this, detect my wife, be reveng'd on Falstaff, and laugh at Page. I will about it; better three hours too soon than a minute too late. Fie, fie, fie! cuckold, cuckold, cuckold!
> (II.2.287-292; 310-314)

Bear in mind, in the Elizabethan culture, a man cuckolded by his wife brought terrible dishonor and personal shame. By the same token, cuckolding and social responses to it offered scenarios to dramatists that were ripe for humorous exploitation and literary satire. (Here's a factoid—there is no Elizabethan or modern English word for what happens when a man cheats on his wife. There's a shock, ladies.)

"WILD AND WHIRLING WORDS"

Although Shakespeare included elements of farce in *The Merry Wives of Windsor*, the play is best described as a *fabliau*. The *fabliau* is a French verse poem that originated in the twelfth century. In the *fabliau*, the plot is comic, maybe even a little bawdy, and usually dwells on what happens when a man gets cuckolded (cheated on by his wife). "The Miller's Tale" and "The Reeve's Tale" in Chaucer's *The Canterbury Tales* are outstanding examples of *fabliaux*.

Getting back to our jealous husband . . . Ford's plan to avoid being a cuckold is to disguise himself as someone named "Master Brook." As "Brook," Ford visits Falstaff and tells him that he is Mistress Ford's lover. (Getting confused?) At this point he bribes the sleazy knight and asks him to trick Mistress Ford into cheating on her husband in order to give him (i.e., "Brook," who is really Ford in disguise, remember) a legitimate pretext to go after her.

The Buck-Basket and Old Woman of Brainford

The housewives busily plan the details of Falstaff's first meeting at Mistress Ford's house. Then Ford runs into Mistress Page and Falstaff's young page, which stifles any faith the jealous guy had in either wife's fidelity.

Falstaff makes his rendezvous at the Ford household, and true to form, he makes a pass at her. But then Mrs. Page, who has been hiding behind the curtain, bursts into the room unannounced. Before she sees him, Falstaff dashes behind the curtain, overhearing the news that Ford is about to come home any minute, steamed and ready for a fight. Whoops! Can you guess what happens next? Falstaff climbs into a laundry basket of dirty clothes, which the wives have put in place, and is swiftly hoisted outside by household servants and dumped in the river.

Soon afterward, these merry wives dupe Falstaff a second time. This time they issue him an apology—after all, he ended up in the river—as well as an invitation from Mrs. Ford. Falstaff shows up again and the same thing happens. Mrs. Page interrupts him while he woos Mrs. Ford. So how does he get out of the pickle he's in? Barely—the two ladies dress him up in old women's clothes, as a witch known as the old woman of Brainford, and Ford runs him out of his house with his fists!

Courting Anne Page

While these clever matrons are duping the silly knight, Shakespeare's subplot gets interesting. The story revolves around Anne Page and the attention of three rival suitors: Slender, Dr. Caius, and Fenton. The painfully shy Slender, who is well bred and well financed, is the first choice of Anne's parents. This is not surprising, as Mr. and Mrs. Page are typical bourgeois parents of Windsor who want their daughter to marry into the right class. Anne's first suitor is Slender, who is quickly exposed as a silly, unsuitable prospect.

Anne's second suitor is the pitiful Dr. Caius. He's aware of Slender's interest, but he's determined to have Anne Page for himself. The poor twit's grasp of English leaves a lot to be desired. When Page invites Ford and Evans to go birding with him, here's what he says:

Evans:	If there is one, I shall make two in the company.
Caius:	If there be one or two, I shall make-a the turd. (III.3.234-237)

Because *Merry Wives* is set in the playwright's own rural English culture, he delights in including a huge variety of dialects and *double entendres*. Here are a few examples of Windsor country speech:

Mistress Quickly:	Go; and we'll have a posset for't soon at night; in faith, at the latter end of a sea-coal fire. (I.4.7-8)

Pistol:	O base Hungarian wight! wilt thou the spigot wield? (I.3.20-21) Why then the world's mine oyster, Which I with sword will open. (II.2.3-4)
Evans:	[Jeshu] pless my soul! how full of chollors I am and trempling of mind! (III.1.11-12)

But Anne doesn't love Slender or Dr. Caius. She loves Fenton, who we learn is a highborn gentleman and cash-poor, with properties he can't afford to maintain. He urges Anne to decide for herself who her husband will be, without her father's interference:

Fenton:	I see I cannot get thy father's love; Therefore no more turn me to him, sweet Nan.
Anne:	Alas, how then?
Fenton:	Why, thou must be thyself. He doth object I am too great of birth, And that, my state being galled with my expense I seek to heal it only by his wealth. (III.4.1-6)

What we learn from the rest of this exchange is important. Fenton tells her that Page believes he can only be after Anne because of her property. When she asks him if that is true, he makes an important confession:

Fenton:	Albeit I will confess thy father's wealth Was the first motive that I woo'd thee, Anne, Yet wooing thee, I found thee of more value Than stamps in gold, or sums in sealed bags; And 'tis the very riches of thyself That I now aim at. (III.4.13-18)

Hinting at one of the play's overriding visions, Fenton's overtures suggest that marrying for romantic love is more important than making a match of expedience.

A Tryst with Herne the Hunter

After the merry wives foil Falstaff's plan twice, their husbands are let in on the joke and Ford asks his wife to pardon him. Both men are eager for the women to outwit the knight a third time. Here the play builds toward a boffo ending.

Falstaff's Comeuppance

The wives propose to get Falstaff to dress up like Herne the Hunter, a fairytale beast believed to stalk the forest during winter nights, blasting oak trees and poaching cattle. Then, as Mistress Ford explains, Falstaff will meet her at the legendary oak trees in his get-up, where Anne and her son, William, and other children will spring out of the forest disguised as elves and rush at him, demanding why he would trespass on their "sacred paths" at such an auspicious time of night.

All goes according to plan, but at this juncture, Page makes a plan for Slender to carry his daughter away disguised as Queen of the Fairies. Separately, Mistress Page plans for Dr. Caius to capture her and then get married. In the end, both parents' motives are thwarted when Anne and Fenton manage to elope.

TIMELESS SOLILOQUIES

Following the mayhem created when the cruel elves descend on Falstaff, Fenton and Anne elope, despite their parents' scheming to the contrary. Fenton's final speech to Anne's parents gives voice to the value of marrying for love, despite the expectations of family and society:

Fenton: You would have married her most shamefully,
Where there was no proportion held in love.
The truth is, she and I (long since contracted)
Are now so sure that nothing can dissolve us.

> Th' offense is holy that she hath committed,
> And this deceit loses the name of craft,
> Of disobedience, or unduteous title,
> Since therein she doth evitate and shun
> A thousand irreligious cursed hours
> Which forced marriage would have brought upon her.
> (V.5.221-230)
>
> The idea that daughters should have a say in their choice of husbands is a familiar theme in Shakespearean comedy. Shakespeare revisits this theme in *A Midsummer Night's Dream* (Chapter 8) and *As You Like It* (Chapter 12), as well as many tragedies and romances.

In the end, Falstaff is pinched and burned by the dancing fairies who make him look ridiculous in their scornful song about the evils of lust.

The Merry Wives Triumph

It's hard to take a play about Falstaff's folly too seriously because the farce plays so well in the theatre. But scholars and critics like to find meaning in everything. Some believe Shakespeare had a motive for allowing the merry wives to be on the side of right. By lampooning Falstaff, the play suggests the declining power and influence of the aristocracy and the rise of a growing class of middle-class merchants. It's an interesting theory, considering that *Merry Wives* is the only play explicitly set in a small English town.

A Director's View

Veteran actor/director Rutherford Cravens has directed two productions of *Merry Wives* for the Houston Shakespeare Festival. "It's not a great play," he says, "but it is a great portrait of Elizabethan village life. There are no princes, no kings, but still, you feel how specific it was to the time when Shakespeare grew up. And the picture of the small Windsor community is relevant for any small community."

In both productions, he wanted to change the Elizabethan context but retain the diverse dialects among the characters. He set the 1978 show in the South, in rural Louisiana. "In that show the hazing scene at the end had a dark Mardi Gras flavor. The 2000 production was set in a small Mississippi town in the 1940s. We cast an actor of African-Caribbean origin as Ford. It was interesting to have a black actor playing a leader in a small white town.

"In this play, Falstaff is an utter con man. It's a shame that W. C. Fields never got the chance to play him. Falstaff always tries to put one over on the rubes and the rubes always win. The women are, by far, the smartest ones in the play."

Mistress Alice Ford (Vanessa Sterling on left) and Mistress Margaret Page (Alice Sherman) merrily conspire in this scene from the Texas Shakespeare Festival's (2012) production of The Merry Wives of Windsor, *directed by John Neville-Andrews.*

(Photo Courtesy of the Texas Shakespeare Festival)

Other Notable Productions

Between 1660 and 1667 the famous author and diarist Samuel Pepys saw *Merry Wives* on three different occasions. One was among the first performances seen by anyone at the start of the Restoration, a period when the theatres were opened again after being shut down for 18 years.

Chapter II. The Merry Wives of Windsor

Interestingly, the Yale School of Drama staged the play in 1954 and aimed to render the wide array of dialects exactly as Shakespeare's acting company would have pronounced them. To do this, they consulted Helge Kökeritz, a Yale professor of English who specialized in Elizabethan pronunciation.

More than two centuries after Shakespeare wrote *Merry Wives*, Giuseppe Verdi immortalized one of the playwright's greatest comic characters in his last opera, *Falstaff*. If anyone should be credited with improving on Shakespeare's portrait of English country life, Verdi should. His opera libretto, written by Arrigo Boito, adapts *Merry Wives* and adds material from *Henry IV, Parts 1 and 2*. The 1893 premiere of *Falstaff* pleased audiences, and David Kimbell explains in the *Penguin Opera Guide* how Verdi's aim for authenticity (through scenery, costumes, and sensual interaction between the sexes) took some stodgy operagoers by surprise.

FACTS TO REMEMBER
- The English setting, absence of kings and noble characters, and bourgeois class focus of *The Merry Wives of Windsor* make it unique among Shakespeare's comedies.
- While some believe *Merry Wives* has elements of farce, it is more accurate to describe it as a *fabliau*.
- *Merry Wives*' main plot pits Falstaff against Mistress Page and Mistress Ford, as the carousing knight takes steps to compromise their virtue.
- By allowing Anne Page to marry Fenton, the man she loves, Shakespeare raises questions about the traditional Renaissance view that daughters should marry someone chosen by their parents.
- Though *Merry Wives* is considered the lightest of all Shakespeare's plays, one director believes it gives us a window into the country life of Warwickshire, the county where Shakespeare grew up.

Chapter 12
As You Like It

INTRODUCTION
- An introduction to Shakespeare's great pastoral comedy
- Key roles in the play and a few tips about the ideas represented by major characters
- The play's principal story and conflicts
- Making sense of conversations about court and country life and the Forest of Arden
- Famous actresses who made their mark as Rosalind
- One hundred years of *As You Like It* on film and TV

As You Like It is an unusually rich, festive comedy written in 1599, the same year the Globe theatre opened. In creating it, Shakespeare took his knack for romantic comedy to a new level. In writing the play, he was inspired by the conventions of the pastoral poetry of his day, which featured shepherds and rustics in bucolic settings.

On the surface, *As You Like It* seems to be very thin on dramatic action, which can be death to a play. But Shakespeare knew what he was doing. Using the style of pastoral poems as his point of departure, he creates two dramatic landscapes—a duchy, representing a "civilized court," and the Forest of Arden, an emblem of a natural life in the country. Early on in the story, several victims find themselves exiled from the court and are forced to make new lives in their primitive surroundings. Beyond telling us their basic stories of survival, Shakespeare has the banished ones and their newfound country friends engage in conversations about the merits of "country" life versus "court" life. Their lively disagreements will get you thinking—which lifestyle has more to recommend it?

The play has a talky quality, but you won't lose interest. Rosalind's sparkling passion and powers of manipulation are a pleasure to watch. The reflections of Jaques, a melancholy wise man, and Touchstone, a cynical Fool (both original to Shakespeare) definitely boost the entertainment value. *As You Like It* also pokes fun at the conventions of pastoral poetry. This classical genre had been popular for centuries before Shakespeare was born. In writing the play, Shakespeare's primary source was Thomas Lodge's prose romance *Rosalynde* (1590).

The Characters

THE GOOD DUKE-IN-EXILE AND HIS FOLLOWERS

Duke Senior—The good duke has been exiled after his kingdom was usurped by his brother. When we first meet him in Act two, he extols the virtues of living in the forest, compared to the court. Early on, he finds value in nature and freedom from an oppressive court.

Rosalind—The daughter of Duke Senior is one of Shakespeare's best-loved heroines. Her wit and intelligence are unsurpassed by any other Shakespearean woman. She masquerades as Ganymede (named after the page of the Greek god Jove) after she is banished by her uncle, Duke Frederick. Rosalind is unprecedented in her ability to understand her own emotions. She knows that humans are silly creatures when they fall in love; she also has a keen sense of her own mortality. She can laugh at herself and recognizes that life isn't perfect. She is a wily actress, using the guise of a boy to role-play with Orlando as "Rosalind," the girl he loves. Without Rosalind, Shakespeare's talky, thinly plotted intrigue would leave us yawning in our seats.

Jaques—This melancholy lord of the banished Duke Senior is a real misanthrope. He is the fly in the ointment, quick to contradict the views of others. He tells Amiens, "I can suck melancholy out of a song, as a weasel sucks eggs." A genuine contrarian, he is a type the Elizabethans would have recognized from contemporary satire. He delivers the now-familiar lines "All the world's a stage, and all the men and women merely players." These lines precede his often-quoted speech about the seven stages of human life, which suggest that we basically live, ripen, rot, and turn into helpless children in old age.

Amiens—A lord of Duke Senior.

Two Pages

THE BAD DUKE AND HIS FOLLOWERS

Duke Frederick—The grasping, unsavory brother of Duke Senior, who has usurped his brother's control. In the end he gets religion and gives back the kingdom he took away.

Celia—The daughter of Duke Frederick is the cousin and bosom friend of Rosalind. She, too, decides to leave the court after her father banishes her friend. She assumes the identity of Aliena (Latin for "stranger"). Courageous and loyal, she is Rosalind's foil and falls quickly in love with Oliver.

Le Beau—A courtier.

Touchstone—This clown or court jester is physically attracted to Audrey. His entire view of love doesn't go much beyond this. In Act three he tells Audrey, "We must be married, or we must live in bawdry," implying that, when it comes to women, a guy has to follow his appetite! He is the opposite of Orlando, who tends to idealize the woman he loves. More important, though, Touchstone is one of Shakespeare's witty fools, a man who gives us different views to help us consider the merits of each person's perspective.

Charles—Duke Frederick's wrestler

THE FAMILY OF SIR ROWLAND DE BOYS

Orlando—The youngest son of Sir Rowland de Boys falls in love with Rosalind at first sight. His head is full of artificial and unrealistic notions about love and what happens when it's one-sided. He gets these ideas from love poetry written by the likes of Petrarch (a medieval poet whose sonnet form Shakespeare improved upon with brilliance). Orlando's rhymed odes to Rosalind are lame attempts at poetry. Emotionally, he is less mature than Rosalind, but through his friendship with "Ganymede," he gains a better understanding about women and love, free of the distractions of sexual attraction.

Oliver—The oldest son of Sir Rowland de Boys cruelly disobeys his dead father's wish that he take care of his younger brother Orlando. As lovers, he and Celia are foils for Orlando and Rosalind.

Jaques—The second son of Sir Rowland de Boys.

Adam—An old servant of Sir Rowland, a part that Shakespeare is said to have played himself.

Dennis—Oliver's servant.

INHABITANTS OF THE FOREST OF ARDEN

Corin—An old shepherd who is something of an armchair philosopher of the forest. He waxes philosophical about the virtues of rural life and is frequently contradicted by Touchstone. He works hard and is not ashamed of how he makes a living.

Scholars are tempted to connect the Forest of Arden to the forest near Shakespeare's native Warwickshire, where Stratford-upon-Avon is situated. If you've read about Shakespeare's life, you may also wonder if he named the forest after his mother, Mary Arden.

> Silvius—This young shepherd is crazy about Phoebe, and though she is reluctant, he gets her in the end, thanks to Rosalind. His conventional style of wooing Phoebe looks ridiculous and artificial compared to the natural ease of Orlando. His courtship style is meant to look silly, compared to Orlando or the vulgar Touchstone.
>
> Phoebe—This dainty shepherdess rejects Silvius' attentions and falls in love with Ganymede (Rosalind). She utters an allusion from Christopher Marlowe's poem *Hero and Leander*, believed to be Shakespeare's homage to his brilliant rival: "Dead shepherd/Now I find thy saw of might/'Whoever lov'd that lov'd not at first sight?'"
>
> Audrey—A homely goatherd who is courted by Touchstone and ends up marrying him.
>
> William—A country person in love with Audrey.
>
> Sir Oliver Martext—A country clergyman.
>
> Hymen—The god of marriage.
>
> Lords, pages, and attendants
>
> *Setting: Oliver's house; Duke Frederick's court; and the Forest of Arden (the name may be a shortened form of the French "Ardennes" region).*

Court Intrigue—A Duke Usurps His Brother

To make sense of the various threads of *As You Like It*, it helps to distinguish the world of the court from the Forest of Arden. At court, Duke Frederick has taken control of the duchy and exiled his brother, Duke Senior. Even though the brothers are estranged, Frederick allows his brother's daughter Rosalind to continue living under his roof. After all, Rosalind is his own daughter Celia's cousin and best friend.

Let's look for a moment at the family of the dead Sir Rowland de Boys. Poor Orlando, Sir Rowland's youngest son, has been cursed with an older brother (Oliver) who has treated him shabbily. Tired of being mistreated, Orlando leaves his home and joins the exiled Duke Senior. Meanwhile, Orlando engages in a wrestling match with a formidable opponent in Duke Frederick's realm. He takes one look at Rosalind, who is present, and falls in love.

Duke Frederick Banishes Rosalind

Out of nowhere, Frederick loses his temper after learning Orlando is the son of his brother's good friend. Fearing that it's too risky to keep the virtuous Rosalind under his roof, he banishes his niece from the court. But Celia can't bear to be apart from her cousin, so the two young women make plans to escape the court together. Rosalind disguises herself as a countryman named Ganymede and Celia pretends to be Aliena (Latin for "stranger"), his sister. Touchstone, a court jester, goes with them.

The Forest of Arden

In the Forest of Arden, the banished Duke Senior lives with his followers, including Jaques, a melancholy sort who's in a class by himself. Orlando and his servant Adam have joined the duke, and "Ganymede" and "Aliena" soon arrive. These two get some sheep and pretend to be shepherds. Rosalind learns that Orlando has been pinning love poems to her on trees, so, passing herself off as Ganymede, she encounters him and gives him a hard time about his love poetry. She makes him a proposition. Since he can't have Rosalind, she offers to give him advice about dealing with his passions. She offers to pretend to be Rosalind, allowing the two of them to act out their love affair. (This is a little confusing, I agree, but onstage it makes sense.)

TIMELESS SOLILOQUIES

As You Like It is packed with undercurrents satirizing the literary fashions of Shakespeare's day. In a huge jab at the clichés of Renaissance love poetry, Rosalind wisely affirms that unrequited love is a fate that *never* leads to death:

No, faith, die by attorney. The poor world
is almost six thousand years old, and in all this
time there was not any man died in his own

> person, *videlicet*, in a love-cause. Troilus had his
> brains dash'd out with a Grecian club, yet he did
> what he could to die before, and he is one of the
> patterns of love . . .
> But these are all lies: men have died
> from time to time, and worms have eaten them,
> but not for love.
> (IV.1.95-100; 106-108)

Here is some clever, bawdy banter that demonstrates the down-to-earth style of Shakespeare's heroine:

Orlando: Then love me, Rosalind.

Rosalind: Yes, faith, will I, Fridays and Saturdays and all.

Orlando: And wilt thou have me?

Rosalind: Ay, and twenty such.

Orlando: What sayest thou?

Rosalind: Are you not good?

Orlando: I hope so.

Rosalind: Why then, can one desire too much of a good thing?
(IV.1.115-124)

What's indecent about this exchange? Shakespeare's audiences would have known that "thing" referred then to one's genitalia. Keep in mind that during this scene, Orlando thinks he's talking to a boy (Ganymede) and thus incognito, Rosalind is pretending to be Rosalind in order to teach Orlando a thing or two about women.

One day, as Orlando makes his way to visit Ganymede, he spots a man asleep with a snake coiled around his neck. Seeing a hungry lioness poised to kill him, he realizes the man is Oliver, his brother. Orlando hesitates a little—he's still chapped over how badly his brother treated him—but decides to do the right thing. So he kills the snake and lioness with his sword. Saved by his brother, Oliver shows remorse for his past misdeeds and the brothers are reconciled.

Not long afterward, Oliver encounters Aliena (Celia in disguise, remember?) while on an errand to visit Ganymede. He is carrying a bloody handkerchief to show Ganymede that Orlando is too weak to meet her because of his wounds. Aliena is impressed by Oliver's generosity on his brother's behalf, so she falls in love with him. The couple make plans to get married the next day.

The Rustics

At this point, the love intrigue gets complicated. Silvius, a young shepherd, has fallen in love with Phoebe, but does she reciprocate his feelings? No! She has already fallen in love with Ganymede, for heaven's sake, but he has basically ignored her. (Remember, Ganymede is not actually a boy, and this irony, hidden from the characters onstage, is very funny to those of us in the audience.) Touchstone, the fool, has already fallen for Audrey, an empty-headed girl who herds goats. (He even tries to marry her, but Jaques stops him.)

Ganymede Plays Magician

Eventually, these frustrating sexual entanglements must be resolved. Ganymede, Orlando, Phoebe, and Silvius begin tussling over how they will be paired off. To solve this dilemma, Ganymede has Orlando promise to marry Rosalind. To satisfy the other couple, he tells Phoebe that she must commit to marrying Silvius if Ganymede won't be her husband. (While all this is going on, Duke Frederick leaves his court to search for his missing daughter Celia. He's determined to find Duke Senior and his followers and have them killed. But he meets a hermit in the forest who puts the evil thoughts out of his head.)

VERSE BY VERSE

By the way, *As You Like It* includes more songs than any other Shakespeare play. They include Amiens' lyric "Under the greenwood tree" (II.5) and the Page's ditty "It was a lover and his lass" (V.3).

Resolution occurs the next day when Ganymede throws off his disguise and reveals his/her true identity as Rosalind. (Phoebe, of course, is no longer game to marry Ganymede when she finds out she's not a man . . .)

Pop! A Quadruple Wedding!

After two couples are paired off, other conflicts are reconciled. In a quintessential Shakespearean resolution, four pairs of lovers are joined in marriage—Rosalind and Orlando, Celia and Oliver, Phoebe and Silvius, and Audrey and Touchstone. In the end, the group gets word that the two estranged dukes have made peace when Frederick realizes his evil ways. Having reformed after his spiritual encounter with the hermit, he returns the dukedom back to its rightful ruler, Duke Senior.

Court Versus Country? Is There Life After the Forest of Arden?

Jaques: . . . All the world's a stage,
And all the men and women merely players;
They have their exits and their entrances,
And one man in his time plays many parts,
His acts being seven ages . . .
(II.7.139-143)

The Forest of Arden is a safe haven for everyone—for those in exile, such as Duke Senior and Rosalind (Ganymede), and those who escape voluntarily, such as Orlando and Celia. Like the Garden of Eden, Arden has mythical significance. It's a natural world where men and women can escape injustice, mistreatment, and misguided pursuits. Duke Senior extols the forest's virtues early on:

Duke Senior: Hath not old custom made this life more sweet
Than that of painted pomp? Are not these woods
More free from peril than the envious court?
. . . And this our life, exempt from public haunt,
Finds tongues in trees, books in the running brooks,
Sermons in stones, and good in every thing.
(II.1.2-4; 15-17)

By "public haunt" the duke refers to human society, the root of cruelty and corruption embodied by the usurping Duke Frederick. The forest, however, is free from the taint of human institutions. Although Touchstone accuses him of being shallow, Corin also reminds us that the forest's rural existence offers a clean, honest way to make a living:

Corin: Sir, I am a true laborer: I earn that I eat,
get that I wear, owe no man hate, envy no man's
happiness, glad of other men's good, content with my
harm, and the greatest of my pride is to see my ewes
graze and my lambs suck.
(III.2.73-77)

By contrast, the court offers luxuries, but it also succumbs to decadence.

"A KINGDOM FOR A STAGE"

Touchstone is one in a line of fools or comic court jesters that Shakespeare created for ironic effect. Shakespeare liked to cloak his wise men in a fool's clothing and give them pithy sayings:

Why, thou sayst well. I do now remember a
saying: 'The fool doth think he is wise, but the wise
man knows himself to be a fool.'
(V.1.30-32)

Theatre historians believe Shakespeare wrote the part of Touchstone for Robert Armin. Armin performed comic roles for the Lord Chamberlain's Men and is believed to have replaced Will Kempe. Armin may have inspired Shakespeare to create sage clowns like Feste in *Twelfth Night* and the Fool in *King Lear*.

Besides the magic and madness of the complex love plot, the characters' incessant talking about truth and manners reflects universal tensions between what civilization and bucolic life each has to offer us. When the characters leave the court and enter the world of the forest, they are changed forever. In a sense, they can never go back. In the end, of course, all the courtiers will go back to their noble way of life, presumably changed for the better by their experience in the forest.

As You Like It at the Oregon Shakespeare Festival

Penny Metropulos, former associate artistic director at the Oregon Shakespeare Festival, talked about her experience directing *As You Like It* inside the company's Elizabethan theatre in 2002. *As You Like It* lends itself to being outside, Metropulos said, because so much of it takes place in the Forest of Arden. The director discusses how she re-created the play's intimate quality, using the palette of the American West and a diverse cast:

"*As You Like It* is a play about relationships. Most of the scenes are very intimate. They often consist of two characters talking to one another—you have Celia talking to Rosalind or Jaques talking to the duke, or Ganymede with Orlando, etc. As a director I wanted to capture that intimacy despite the challenge of our large, open-air Elizabethan theatre. Scenic designer Michael Ganio designed a simple set consisting of a slightly raked circular floor surrounded by an eight-foot wall—a sort of wooden O that focused the action for the audience.

"Next, I wanted the show to have a good American feel instead of an English one. In *As You Like It*, every character goes into the forest, and that's where they will go through some sort of transformation. So the early American West became our palette and our pattern. If Duke Frederick's court had a feeling of the upscale East Coast, then where does Duke Senior escape to? Out West, of course, where he can experience losing all the accoutrements of the city. That was our Arden. And we depicted the period through beautiful costumes, designed by Deborah Dryden, and wonderful music by Aleric Jans.

"At the Oregon Shakespeare Festival we honor diversity in all our casting. We've led the country in this effort. At first our audiences were somewhat resistant to what they saw as nontraditional casting, but over the years they've embraced this. This *As You Like It* was the first time OSF had an African-American Rosalind (Deidre Henry) and Orlando (Kevin Kenerly). We also

PART 3. THE COMEDIES

cast Latino actors Jos Viramontes and Vilma Silva as Oliver and Celia. Another unusual choice was that Adam became "Adda," played by Dee Maaske, who at the end of the play bestowed Hymen's blessing. As a director, this casting was surprisingly useful because most of the actors of color had never thought much about being cast in this play. So they didn't come to rehearsal with preconceived notions about their roles."

For Metropulos, Shakespeare's events, situations, and thoughts are universal, and can be translated by actors of all backgrounds to any culture or time period. "Shakespeare's characters are us; he was writing about all of us."

Alfred Molina (performing Touchstone, the Fool) and Romola Garai (as Celia) are looking a bit wary in the Forest of Arden in Kenneth Branagh's 2006 film adaptation of As You Like It.

(Photo Courtesy of Photofest)

Chapter 12. As You Like It

Rosalind—An Actress for All Time

It is likely that Shakespeare created the part of Rosalind for an exceptionally gifted boy actor. Myriad North American and British actresses have made their mark playing Rosalind in the twentieth century. Before 1950 they included Mary Anderson, Ada Rehan, Athene Seyler, Fabia Drake, Margaretta Scott, Edith Evans, Margaret Leighton, and Peggy Ashcroft. After 1950 there were Katharine Hepburn, Irene Worth, Nancy Wickwire, Vanessa Redgrave, Dorothy Tutin, Carole Shelley, Janet Suzman, Maggie Smith, Susan Fleetwood, Eileen Atkins, Juliet Stevenson, Sophie Thompson, Fiona Shaw, and Adrian Lester in the all-male Cheek by Jowl production.

"A KINGDOM FOR A STAGE"

Rosalind stands apart from other Shakespearean heroines. Look at the sheer number of lines Shakespeare has given her. There are 2,810 lines in *As You Like It*, according to the *Oxford Dictionary of Shakespeare*, by Stanley Wells. Rosalind has 721 of these! The sound of her voice consumes one-quarter of the play. Not to mention her wit, her wisdom, and her uncanny self-awareness.

In many ways Rosalind is the guiding light of *As You Like It*. As you watch a performance, notice that it's Rosalind who recites the Epilogue. Unusual? Well, yes, because Shakespeare generally cast a male as the Prologue and Epilogue. Line 18 of Rosalind's Epilogue reminds us that her part was originally played by a boy:

> ... I charge you, O women,
> for the love you bear to men, to like as much of
> this play as please you; and I charge you, O men,
> for the love you bear to women (as I perceive
> by your simp'ring, none of you hates them), that
> between you and the women the play may please.
> If I were a woman I would kiss as many of you as
> had beards that pleas'd me, complexions that lik'd

me, and breaths that I defied not; and I am
sure, as many as have good beards, or good faces, or
sweet breaths, will for my kind offer, when I make
curtsy, bid me farewell.
(V.Epilogue.12-23)

A Century of *As You Like It* on Film

Since Laurence Olivier made his Shakespearean screen debut in the 1936 film version of *As You Like It*, a handful of movie and TV adaptations have appeared. Some are more memorable than others:

- Paul Czinner directed this British film in 1936, starring Elisabeth Bergner as a poor-spoken Rosalind and Laurence Olivier as Orlando. This was Olivier's Shakespearean film debut.
- Jonathan Miller directed *As You Like It* for the BBC Television Shakespeare series in 1979. Helen Mirren shined as the cross-dressing heroine. It was filmed at Glamis Castle, Scotland.
- John Hirsch directed a production for the Stratford Festival of Canada in Stratford, Ontario, in 1983. The show was later filmed.
- In 1992, Christine Edzard directed a movie rendition set in London's East End, starring Emma Croft as Rosalind and Andrew Tiernan as Orlando and Oliver.
- Kenneth Branagh's film adaptation of *As You Like It* was distributed in Italy in 2006 and released in the United States on HBO in 2007. The setting is inspired by nineteenth-century Japan. It stars Bryce Dallas Howard as Rosalind and Kevin Kline as Jaques.

Chapter 12. As You Like It

FACTS TO REMEMBER

- *As You Like It* is a sophisticated romantic comedy based on pastoral conventions, in which four pairs of lovers eventually get married.
- Rosalind's part dominates *As You Like It*—she is Shakespeare's wisest heroine and commands more than 25 percent of the play's lines.
- Through lots of lively talk, Shakespeare's characters debate the merits and drawbacks of urban and rural lifestyles.
- An Oregon Shakespeare Festival director transformed the Forest of Arden setting into the early American West in a 2002 production. Like many Shakespearean settings, the Forest of Arden's symbolic associations offer freedom of interpretation to both reader and director.

Chapter 13
Twelfth Night, or What You Will

> **INTRODUCTION**
> - Tips about Shakespeare's comic masterwork and what makes it stand apart
> - The festive comedy's many-sided characters
> - The plot and subplot of *Twelfth Night*
> - The realism, symbolism, and paradox that pervade the play
> - Viewpoints of two actors on Shakespeare's Fools
> - An American director explains two ways of interpreting *Twelfth Night* for the stage

Twelfth Night or *What You Will* is unique among Shakespeare's mature romantic comedies because it begins and ends with a song. The play is full of music, cross-dressing and ambiguity, mistaken identity, love delusions and intrigues, and general carnival madness. These fairytale qualities are keenly offset by the play's elegant look at class, love, death, misfortune, and the passage of time. Deepening the play are Malvolio, the dour, puritanical steward, and Feste, Olivia's wise fool.

This ingeniously paradoxical work is the pinnacle of Shakespeare's comedy. Shakespeare probably wrote *Twelfth Night* around 1600-1601; many believe the play was first performed at the Globe theatre, although there is no record of it. We have lawyer John Manningham's diary reference to a performance of *Twelfth Night* at Middle Temple Hall within London's Inns of Court on February 2, 1602.

It is possible that Shakespeare was writing *Hamlet*, his great tragedy, when he composed *Twelfth Night*. This twilight comedy moves away from the neat resolution found in *Much Ado About Nothing* and *The Merry Wives of Windsor*. Like these comedies, confusion and disarray are ultimately resolved in the familiar celebration of marriage, but the melancholy Feste and cruel treatment of Malvolio cast a pall. Though love and lunacy are joyously presented in earlier comedies like *As You Like It*, *Twelfth Night*'s love plots are laced with a poignant melancholy that alludes to our darker motives.

The Characters

Viola (disguised as a male, she is Cesario)—The twin sister of Sebastian is originally from Messaline. Less willful and in control of her destiny compared to Rosalind (*As You Like It*) or Beatrice (*Much Ado About Nothing*), she is one of Shakespeare's most captivating heroines. After the twin sister of Sebastian is washed up on the shores of Illyria, she puts on a man's clothing and assumes the identity of Cesario to serve as a page to Duke Orsino. In describing her to his friend Antonio, her twin Sebastian says, "she bore a mind that envy could not but call fair."

Sebastian—Viola's twin brother has a much smaller part than she does.

Antonio—A sea captain and friend of Sebastian

Sea Captain—A man who befriends Viola after they are shipwrecked. When they are washed ashore, he tells her about Illyria, Duke Orsino's frustrations in love, and Countess Olivia's loss of family and her excessive grief.

Chapter 13. Twelfth Night, or What You Will

THE DUKE OF ILLYRIA AND HIS COURT

Duke Orsino—The Duke of Illyria is young and infatuated with the eligible but unapproachable Countess Olivia. Almost deliriously, he fixates on his unrequited love and how her denial makes him feel. When we first meet him, he is a man in love with the idea of love and lacks self-knowledge. But all of this changes when "Cesario" comes into his life.

Valentine and Curio—The Duke's attendants

COUNTESS OLIVIA AND HER HOUSEHOLD

Sir Toby Belch—He is Olivia's uncle (often referred to as her kinsman) who plays a key role beyond a comic figure in a Shakespearean romantic subplot. To start, Toby Belch has more lines than any other character. His situation would have been familiar to Elizabethans—a knight who is down in the world, who has to sponge off a richer (and younger) relative such as Countess Olivia. He controls his own "court" and followers in Maria, Sir Andrew Aguecheek, and Fabian. In the play he is associated with the good and bad of unbridled merrymaking under her roof. He utters the famous lines to Malvolio, his foil: "Out o'time, sir? Ye lie! Art any more than a steward? Dost thou think because thou art virtuous there shall be no more cakes and ale?"

Sir Andrew Aguecheek—Sir Toby's foolish drinking companion courts Olivia. He gets involved in the plot to trick Malvolio.

Malvolio—Olivia's steward, who held the highest position among servants in her household. The Latin roots of Malvolio's name are translated as "ill will" or "ill wish." For Sir Toby Belch and Sir Andrew Aguecheek, he is a real killjoy. When asked by the others about him, Maria says, "Marry, sir, sometimes he is a kind of puritan."

PART 3. THE COMEDIES

✥ TIMELESS SOLILOQUIES ✥

"I'll be reveng'd on the whole pack of you." Malvolio, seething with rage and bitterness, delivers this threat and stomps off at the end of the play. The implications of this threat have provoked centuries of questions about Shakespeare's ability to accurately predict the Puritan revolution that led to civil war and the end of the monarchy in 1649.

Maria—Olivia's gentlewoman and the one who conceives the plan to trick the pompous Malvolio

Fabian—A gentleman in Olivia's household

Feste—The clown or jester in Olivia's household is also known as a Fool. Feste is one of Shakespeare's ingeniously conceived comic roles comparable to other great fools like Touchstone (in *As You Like It*) and the Fool in *King Lear*. (See more about Shakespeare's Fools later in this chapter.) Feste, whose Latin name suggests 'party' or 'celebration,' is somewhat mysterious. His sardonic commentary and tone infuse *Twelfth Night* with the dark realism that counterbalances the play's fantasy. Some have suggested he is romantically attracted to Olivia, his mistress. Robert Armin created the role of Feste when the play was first performed at the Globe theatre around 1600-01.

Priest

Musicians, Lords, Sailors, Officers, Attendants

Setting: A city in Illyria, situated along the east coast of the Adriatic Sea around modern Croatia, and the nearby coast

CHAPTER 13. TWELFTH NIGHT, OR WHAT YOU WILL

Royal Houses of Sentiment and Mourning

As the play opens, we glimpse two nobles stifled in their separate realms—the young Duke of Illyria pines away among his courtiers and servants, unable to get the mournful Countess Olivia to return his love. Olivia has no interest in him, however. Wrapped up in grieving her dead father and brother, she has decided to perpetuate her mourning by wearing a black veil for seven years!

When you hear Orsino make his first speech, you'll see that there's something else at work in this man's heart.

> Orsino: If music be the food of love, play on,
>   Give me excess of it; that surfeiting,
>   The appetite may sicken, and so die.
>   That strain again, it had a dying fall;
>   O, it came o'er my ear like the sweet sound
>   That breathes upon a bank of violets,
>   Stealing and giving odor.
>   (I.1.1-7)

Sound a bit overly sentimental? You'll soon see that this duke is more in love with the idea of love than he is with young Olivia. And Olivia has fallen in love with the rituals of mourning at the expense of living a full life.

Shipwrecked and Washed Ashore, Viola Goes Undercover

Viola believes her twin brother Sebastian is lost at sea after their ship is wrecked off the coast of Illyria. Surviving, she is washed ashore in this new land with a friendly sea captain. In trying to find a way to survive in her new home, she determines to disguise herself as a servant and serve Duke Orsino. As we shall soon see, the masculine-clad Viola (a.k.a. "Cesario") is about to shake the self-absorbed Duke and the morose Olivia out of their suffocating shells of sentimentality.

In the meantime, we meet Olivia's impecunious uncle, Sir Toby Belch, a carousing noble who lives off his niece's hospitality. We also meet Sir Toby's upwardly mobile cohort and knight, Sir Andrew Aguecheek, who plans to woo Olivia for himself. Maria, Olivia's gentlewoman, warns this guy to put limits on his drunken behavior.

Girls Will Be Boys—Shakespeare's Brilliant Dramatic Irony

As you might guess, the Duke quickly takes a shine to "Cesario." He soon sends "him" to court Olivia on his behalf. Here's where the fun really begins! In a soliloquy Viola confesses she has fallen in love with Orsino. Oh, what's a girl disguised as a boy to do?

In his 1996 screen version of *Twelfth Night*, Trevor Nunn deftly captures the play's mood of frustrated love and comic pranks. He supplements Shakespeare's plot with an opening scene showing Viola and Sebastian in women's veils, singing "O mistress mine" for dining passengers on the doomed ship. When they remove their veils, the twins are wearing moustaches. Shakespeare's gender-bending and cross-dressing is well explored in the film.

Though inspired by *Romeo and Juliet* when they created Viola de Lesseps' character for *Shakespeare in Love*, scenarists Marc Norman and Tom Stoppard also borrowed from *Twelfth Night*. When Viola (Gwyneth Paltrow) decides to impersonate the boy actor who plays Romeo for the Lord Admiral's Men, we're reminded of Viola's similar action in *Twelfth Night*. Queen Elizabeth commands Will to write a comedy for the occasion of Twelfth Night, and we see him pen Viola's first words as he fantasizes about Viola de Lesseps' shipwreck off the Virginia coast.

Shakespeare is famous for exploiting the homoerotic implications of women disguised as boys in his late comedies. Keep in mind that when his Elizabethan audience watched *Twelfth Night*, they saw a boy actor playing Viola, who in turn, masqueraded as a male page named Cesario. The layers of irony must have kept their heads spinning!

Chapter 13. Twelfth Night, or What You Will

For the next four acts, Shakespeare mines the rich possibilities of these layers of dramatic irony. Shakespeare creates dramatic irony when he allows those of us in the theatre audience to know a lot more than Orsino, Olivia, and the rest of the gang bamboozled by "Cesario's" disguise.

The Countess Reveals Her Passion

Back on Olivia's estate we meet Feste, Olivia's household clown, or Fool. He has returned to service and the countess is not too happy about his absence. Feste works on cheering her up, and during this encounter, we witness the friction between this wise, sardonic jester and the dour, disapproving steward Malvolio. Olivia clearly sees that Malvolio haughtily disapproves of Feste because the Fool's manner contradicts the steward's melancholy disposition.

The plot thickens. Persisting on Orsino's behalf, "Cesario" is granted permission to see Olivia. She makes a few advances on the Duke's behalf:

> Viola: Lady, you are the cruell'st she alive
> If you will lead these graces to the grave,
> And leave the world no copy.
> (I.5.241-243)

Oops! Instead of falling for "Cesario's" courtship by proxy, Olivia falls irresistibly in love with the cross-dressing Viola!

> Olivia: Methinks I feel this youth's perfections
> With an invisible and subtle stealth
> To creep in at mine eyes. Well, let it be.
> (I.5.296-298)

So what have we here? In the play's jewel of a main plot, we have Viola playing a man, secretly smitten with her master; we have an unsuspecting duke, determined to win over a funereal woman in love with the rituals of her grief; and in a new twist, we are surprised by Olivia's lusty cravings for "Cesario," who's actually a female!

PART 3. THE COMEDIES

"WILD AND WHIRLING WORDS"

Critics spend a lot of energy dissecting the symbolism in this comedy's two titles. *Twelfth Night* refers to January 6, the Feast of the Epiphany and the last day of the Christmas feast. Make no mistake—in the Renaissance it was one of those holidays that was a great excuse for some hearty celebrating before you began your ritual Lenten sacrifice.

To get at the meaning of *What You Will*, focus on the word "will" and its late sixteenth-century connotation of "wish." Shakespeare could be pointing up the tendency for deluded lovers such as Orsino, Olivia, and Malvolio to wish or create the illusions their imaginations require. "What You Will" also suggests that the theatre audience has the power to "will" or create their own reality.

Plotting Against Malvolio

Before the rich subplot gets underway, we learn that Viola's twin brother Sebastian has survived the shipwreck and is also in Illyria. He, of course, grieves for the sister he presumes dead and plans to visit Orsino's court. "Cesario" manages to resist Olivia's bold advances, but the smitten countess tries different ways to get the young page to return. Back with Orsino, Viola's love deepens.

A Forged Letter

As Olivia's man in charge of the servants, Malvolio is also the epitome of restraint and abstinence. The sour-faced steward is not happy at all with the drinking and debauchery of Sir Toby, Sir Andrew, and Feste. But this poor puritan is in for a shock. Fed up with Malvolio's pompous ways, Maria devises a plan to lure the unsuspecting fool into reading a letter, ostensibly written by his mistress Olivia.

Chapter 13. Twelfth Night, or What You Will

Malvolio: . . . [Reads] 'If this fall into thy hand, revolve. In my stars I am above thee, but be not afraid of greatness. Some are born great, some achieve greatness, and some have greatness thrust upon 'em. Thy Fates open their hands, let thy blood and spirit embrace them, and to inure thyself to what thou art like to be, cast thy humble slough and appear fresh . . .
She thus advises thee that sighs for thee. Remember who commended thy yellow stockings, and wish'd to see thee ever cross-garter'd: I say, remember.
(II.5.143-149; 152-155)

The plan works! In reading the letter, Malvolio convinces himself that it is intended for his eyes. So the self-absorbed steward resolves to smile and dress in yellow stockings to please a highborn lady he'd like for himself. As you can imagine, this willful folly and pie-in-the-sky wishing will soon backfire on Malvolio.

Malvolio Makes an Idiot of Himself

"Cesario" rebuffs Olivia's outpourings of love; Sir Andrew gets jealous of the young page's ability to sway the woman he wants for himself; then Sir Toby urges him to challenge "Cesario" to a duel. (All the while, Sebastian's friend Antonio risks his life following Sebastian to town. The Illyrians want his hide over a past sea battle he won over them.)

Then, in the subplot's coup de grâce that edges the play into a darker realm, Malvolio shamelessly parades before Olivia, completely out of character, grinning and graced in yellow stockings. At first, she's nonplussed by his extremely odd behavior. When he continues to make advances toward her, she realizes he must be out of his head. So she gives her own staff license to deal with him. Sir Toby sees that he is locked up.

PART 3. THE COMEDIES

Viola's Twin Creates Chaos and Confusion

As soon as Sebastian enters "Cesario's" realm, violent dueling and Malvolio's torment overshadow the lovers' frustrated love and the play's general carnival atmosphere. Antonio believes Sebastian has abandoned him because, of course, he doesn't realize he's looking at "Cesario," Sebastian's twin. To top off the confusion, Sir Andrew takes a strike at Sebastian, thinking it's "Cesario," and gets soundly beaten by this twin. Countess Olivia interrupts the fight and mistakes Sebastian for her beloved "Cesario." Sebastian is no dummy. He knows a good thing when it drops in his lap. Without any persuasion at all, he agrees to marry Olivia, a woman he's barely laid eyes on!

Voilà! Viola Is Unmasked

As everyone ends up at Olivia's house, the various disguises are eventually revealed. The Duke is angered by "Cesario's" engagement to Olivia without his knowledge. Olivia is furious because "Cesario" seems not to remember that he promised to marry her. The unveiling of Viola is prompted by Antonio, who is furious because "Cesario," whom he's mistaken for Sebastian, seems to have forgotten the three-month period the two have spent together since the shipwreck.

All is resolved in that pleasant Shakespearean fashion when Orsino realizes that he actually loves Viola (formerly "Cesario"), not Olivia. Olivia gets Sebastian, of course, the very picture of the "man" she originally fell in love with. Sir Toby has married Maria. In the midst of these revelations, Malvolio confronts Olivia about her so-called letter, and she acknowledges that Maria, not herself, was the epistle's author. The only fly in the ointment is the parting admonition we get from Malvolio for being so cruelly tricked and mistreated.

Witty Fools and Buffoons—Two Actors Talk About Shakespeare's Clowns

In Shakespeare there are clowns and there are great clowns. In the playwright's early comedies, the clown is a boisterous figure of fun whose job is to make the audience laugh. Dromio (*The Comedy of Errors*) and Launce (*The Two Gentlemen of Verona*) are two such roles. In the festive comedies, figures like Dogberry, the pompous cop in *Much Ado About Nothing*, are the idiots we love to laugh at.

Chapter 13. Twelfth Night, or What You Will

Rutherford Cravens, a director and veteran stage, movie, and TV actor, has performed with the Houston Shakespeare Festival, Alley Theatre, Stages, and many other companies. He serves as executive director of The Shakespeare Globe Center of the Southwest. He has played a dozen or more comic roles in more than 30 Shakespeare productions. As one who often plays the Fool, Cravens offered this perspective: "Shakespeare's clowns are very often the anarchic spirit in his plays. The great clowns seem to be the descendants of the entitled Fool who can speak the truth to power with some kind of impunity. They are protected and are allowed to say and do what they want."

The great Shakespearean clowns, who are often wiser than the masters they serve, include Touchstone (*As You Like It*), Feste (*Twelfth Night*), and the Fool in *King Lear*. Viola's speech below nicely sums up the role of Shakespeare's wise fool, not only in *Twelfth Night*'s fantasy about lovers, but in other great plays like *As You Like It* and *King Lear*.

> This fellow is wise enough to play the fool,
> And to do that well craves a kind of wit.
> He must observe their mood on whom he jests,
> The quality of persons, and the time; . . .
>   . . . This is a practice,
> As full of labor as a wise man's art;
> For folly that he wisely shows is fit,
> But wise men, folly-fall'n, quite taint their wit.
> *Viola to Feste* (III.1.60-63; 65-68)

In *Twelfth Night*, Olivia gives us insight into the power her own Fool is afforded under her own roof:

> There is no slander in an allow'd fool, though he do nothing but rail;
> *Olivia to Feste* (I.5.94-95)

"I loved playing Feste," Cravens said. "He seems to be one, if not the *only*, character in *Twelfth Night* who tells the truth and can also see the truth surrounding Olivia's infatuation with Viola. Before anyone else, Feste realizes that Cesario is a woman, not a boy."

PART 3. THE COMEDIES

Actor Jeffrey Bean Talks About Witty Fools and Natural Fools

"Better a witty fool than a foolish wit."
Feste to Olivia (I.5.36)

Jeffrey Bean has been a resident company member of Houston's Alley Theatre since 1989 and a Broadway actor. He has performed in many Shakespeare productions. He admitted he was reluctant to play Feste when the Alley staged *Twelfth Night* in 2004. Like all experienced actors, Bean looks into himself to understand a part, but he also examines what theatrical history can teach him.

When Bean first learned he would play Feste, he assumed the role resembled that of buffoonish clowns like Dogberry. For the modern actor, these parts are full of arcane language and comedy that ceased being funny at the passing of the Elizabethan era. Bean, of course, was mistaken. "In Shakespeare there are witty fools, and there are natural fools. Feste is a witty fool. At one point when Orsino is in a mangle over his feelings for 'Cesario,' Feste paints him as a complete idiot. I realized that Shakespeare had made this Fool the smartest guy. The rest were just fools in love. So I went from being afraid to play Feste to a place of respect."

One turning point for Bean came when he did research on Robert Armin, the first actor who played Feste for the Lord Chamberlain's Men. He recalled: "The witty fool seems to make his appearance in Shakespeare's plays when Robert Armin arrived in his company. Armin wrote a play called 'Tutch the Clown' in which he played a witty and natural fool. You see the offshoot of this play in Touchstone (the clown in *As You Like It*). Shakespeare apparently let Armin do some of his own writing when he created the part of Feste."

Bean's understanding of the part deepened when he paid close attention to the words in Feste's songs. "They're almost always about unrequited love. This got me to thinking that Feste could be in love with Olivia. As a fairly young actor playing Feste, I created a back-story, using the idea that Olivia relies on him and uses him to give her perspective. When Feste chastises Olivia for staying in mourning, she listens to him. But Feste can never have Olivia and that is why he is so melancholy."

In playing Feste, Bean also discovered that *Twelfth Night* is essentially Buddhist. Buddhists believe that life is about suffering. Bean feels that through Feste's songs, Shakespeare reminds us of that suffering. "It's not for nothing that Feste owns the stage at the end of the play. His last song goes, 'With hey ho, the wind and the rain . . . it raineth every day,' reminding us that suffering is an inevitable part of life. In the midst of this topsy-turvy world, you have Feste, centered and calm, like the center of a pinwheel. His centeredness comes from his long suffering over Olivia, whom he can never love because of his inferior social status."

Robert Hupp Interprets *Twelfth Night* for the Stage

Robert Hupp, artistic director at Syracuse Stage and the former producing artistic director at the Arkansas Repertory Theatre, has participated in the *Shakespeare in American Communities* project since it began. His production of *Romeo and Juliet* was one of seven plays chosen to launch the national program, which is supported by the National Endowment for the Arts (NEA). Hupp's experiences producing and directing *Twelfth Night* have taught him that its balance of comedy and melancholy presents some challenges to directors of Shakespeare.

The director of *Twelfth Night* has the option to emphasize the play's low comedy or its darker side, Hupp said. "The emphasis that you take determines how you cast the various key roles. You have to consider the questions: Are you telling the romantic story of Olivia and the Duke and how it unfolds? Or are you telling the story of Sir Toby Belch? Are we going to urge the audience to laugh at Malvolio or feel sad for him?"

"A KINGDOM FOR A STAGE"

When directing *Twelfth Night* at Dickinson College in Carlisle, Pennsylvania (1998), director Robert Hupp set the play in a nineteenth-century European, one-ring circus. "The circus-like atmosphere helped us capture the play's absurdity and romanticism. Malvolio's affections, Orsino's affections, Olivia's affections—these were illusions and masks. When we finally strip away these masks, we can get at who these people really are."

Part 3. The Comedies

Certain characters offer casting challenges, Hupp continued. "Casting Malvolio can be difficult because his role has comedic and dark moments. You need an actor who can bring out the many facets of Malvolio. While touring with the Arkansas repertory, I worked with an actor who played Hamlet and Malvolio well. To do this, an actor has to be able to capture the depth of pathos that's in Malvolio. Casting Feste is not easy either. In the wrong hands, Feste can come across as mean and unlikable. He has to be handled with kid gloves so his torment of Malvolio seems justified."

Viola is a wonderful role for a young woman, Hupp said. He explained: "In casting the twins Viola and Sebastian, it's less important to find two actors who look alike and more important to find a young woman who can play the role. In general, you have to decide what age actor you want to work with. If you have an older Duke and Olivia, the play can seem darker. And if you want a darker play, you need to go with older actors."

Viola's disguise as a boy starts to get her in trouble when her twin brother arrives in Illyria. Trevor Nunn's 1996 film stars (from left) Helena Bonham Carter (Olivia), Steven Mackintosh (Sebastian), Imogen Stubbs (Viola), and Toby Stephens (Duke Orsino).

(Photo courtesy of Fine Line Features/Photofest.)

Chapter 13. Twelfth Night, or What You Will

FACTS TO REMEMBER
- The title *Twelfth Night or What You Will* invites you to connect the Feast of Epiphany and the play's pre-Lenten carnival mood.
- Shakespeare's late comedy is rich in the kind of mistaken identity and homoerotic attraction that emerges from Viola's masculine disguise.
- Malvolio's final promise of revenge uncannily foreshadows the Puritan revolution and civil war that caused the monarchy's demise in 1649.
- One actor notes that Shakespeare's fools are entitled clowns who can speak the truth to power with impunity.
- Before casting *Twelfth Night*, a director has to decide whether he or she wants to emphasize the play's low comedy or darker overtones.

Chapter 14
Measure for Measure

INTRODUCTION
- Why *Measure for Measure* is labeled as a tragicomedy or problem comedy
- Tips and insights into the play's major characters
- A synopsis of the main plot in *Measure for Measure*
- The play's focus on abuse of authority, justice, and mercy, and a few words about its Christian overtones
- Prominent revivals of *Measure for Measure* on stage and TV

Although we refer to it as a comedy, *Measure for Measure* is one of Shakespeare's most pessimistic dramas. It is the last comedy he wrote and one of three late comedies composed between 1601 and 1604, after he had finished the festive comedies and began writing tragedies. Today critics refer to these final comedies as *problem comedies* or *problem plays*. In part, this name evokes the challenges they present to the modern stage director. They include *Troilus and Cressida* (1601-02), *All's Well That Ends Well* (1602-03), and *Measure for Measure* (1604). At one time we called these dramas *tragicomedies* because they combined comedic themes of love and marriage with a darker vision.

In all Shakespearean comedy, from early plays like *The Comedy of Errors* to the later *Much Ado About Nothing*, conflict disrupts the order of things, but harmony ultimately prevails in spite of villainy or immoral acts. In Shakespearean tragedy, murder and evil triumph, but the moral order is violated in a way we can accept because the villainy is discovered or punished.

But in a *problem comedy* such as *Measure for Measure*, Shakespeare takes away our moral compass. There is no neat resolution, as in comedy, nor is the moral order shattered, as in tragedy. When you watch a performance of *Measure for Measure*, you'll leave the theatre with many questions and few answers. Prepare to be shocked by the long final scene when we learn who is forgiven, who gets punished and why, and who ends up married to whom. Let's review the characters and the story first; we'll revisit the play's issues later.

The Characters

THE MAIN PLOT

Vincentio—The Duke of Vienna may be the most complex character in the play. He seems to have nothing but good intentions when he puts his deputy in charge while legal reforms are put in place. While he is away, though, Angelo turns tyrant and the Duke returns *incognito*, masquerading as a friar. He sneaks around, intervening to help Angelo's victims, but the more people who suffer, the more you begin to question his motives. Duke Vincentio has 858 lines and the seventh-longest male role in a Shakespearean play, according to the *Oxford Dictionary of Shakespeare*'s ranking of the lengthiest Shakespearean roles.

Angelo—The Duke's deputy governor is the guy you love to hate in this play. When the Duke leaves Vienna while instituting new reforms against fornication and immoral behavior, Angelo enforces the law stringently, showing no mercy for violators. He embodies a Puritanical extreme condemning immoral behavior.

Escalus—An ancient lord, the Duke's brother is a warm soul who serves as an advisor to Angelo while the Duke is on his leave of absence. Acting as magistrate, he is more just and reasonable than the extremist Angelo.

Claudio—He is a young gentleman who is betrothed to Juliet. Had the Duke not decided to enforce an old law against immorality, Claudio's premarital affair with Juliet would not have been an issue.

Isabella—Claudio's sister is a young novice, preparing to take the oath of the Order of Saint Clare. She is highly virtuous, so much so that when Angelo blackmails her with an offer to save her brother's life in exchange for sex, she tells Claudio that she will not compromise her virtue. The disguised Duke tests her, however, by refusing to reveal that her brother was never executed, contrary to appearances. By the end of the play, Isabella becomes less absolutist in upholding her ideals and pleads for Angelo's pardon.

Mariana—She is the woman once betrothed to Angelo, but she was thrown over by him years ago because her dowry was lost at sea when her brother drowned. Mariana agrees to take on Isabella's identity and visit Angelo's bed in order to satisfy his lust, a condition for saving Claudio's life.

Juliet—She is Claudio's lover, who gets pregnant before she is married. As discussed later, her premarital sex probably did not seem as disgraceful to Shakespeare's audiences as it may seem to some moderns because she and Claudio were *betrothed* and were taking steps to cement their marital bond. Claudio is punished for getting Juliet pregnant, largely because the Duke had begun to enforce a strict law against fornication.

Francisca—A nun

Lucio—A *fantastic*, a person with wild and fanciful notions

Two gentlemen

Provost

Thomas and Peter—Two friars

> **SUBPLOT**
>
> Mistress Overdone—A bawd
>
> Elbow—A simple constable
>
> Froth—A foolish gentleman
>
> Pompey—A clown and servant to Mistress Overdone
>
> Abhorson—An executioner
>
> Barnardine—A prisoner
>
> Servant
>
> *Setting: Vienna and its surrounding neighborhood*

To Reform Vienna, a Duke Relinquishes Power

Duke Vincentio is troubled because the Viennese people under his authority have grown morally lax and unscrupulous. Although he admits he is at fault for not enforcing some laws, he decides he must crack down by instituting certain reforms. Among them is a little-enforced law that prohibits fornication. Fearing that such change may come across as too harsh under his rule, he decides to take a leave of absence. He appoints Angelo to take his place and carry out the reforms.

Cracking Down on Fornication

Soon after the Duke leaves and Angelo begins his rule, Angelo goes on a vigorous rampage to punish anyone who disobeys an old, unenforced statute that prohibits fornication and immorality. First, he closes down the brothels. Next, he arrests Claudio, a nobleman, for impregnating Juliet and then condemns him to death.

Chapter 14. Measure for Measure

"Wild and Whirling Words"

Editors Barbara A. Mowat and Paul Werstine of The New Folger Library edition of *Measure for Measure* credit Victoria Hayne in their discussion of certain private and public customs taken by English couples to cement their marriage bond. (These customs are grafted onto the world of Vienna in the play.) If you know something about these steps, the conflicts centered on Claudio and Juliet and Angelo and Mariana, respectively, will make a lot more sense.

"Marriage began in courtship, which was usually brief in Shakespeare's day . . . Then would come a private exchange of a promise to marry, followed by a more or less public betrothal in a ceremony called 'handfasting,' in which the couple joined hands and exchanged vows, usually before witnesses." At this point some couples considered themselves married and "free to begin their sexual relationship." The church, however, did not view their marriage as official until the banns were read and a wedding took place inside the church.

Whoa! It appears the Duke's wishes are being thwarted from the get-go. The puritanical Angelo appears completely intolerant of any mitigating circumstances that would excuse Claudio and Juliet's premarital sex. In fact, the two are "betrothed" and may have considered themselves already married, a fact that Shakespeare's audiences would have understood. But under the new laws that strictly prohibit fornication, Claudio has committed an offense for which he must die.

Pleading for Claudio's Life

His life hanging in the balance, Claudio gets his friend Lucio, who's a real sexual sleaze, to convince his sister Isabella to visit Angelo to try to save his life. Meanwhile, Escalus tries to convince Angelo to spare Claudio. (Claudio happens to be the son of Escalus' good friend.) Not long afterwards, the Duke comes back into the picture, disguised, of course, in the modest garb of a friar. He gets the scoop about what really happened to Claudio from Juliet, who assures him that Claudio did not seduce her; rather, the two were engaged and were deeply in love. Problems with her dowry had held up the progress of their marriage.

As you know, Isabella is preparing to take her vows to enter the convent. When you see her onstage, she'll strike you as a paragon of virtue. Pleading with Angelo to save Claudio's life, her passionate discourse on mercy might remind you of Portia's famous words to Shylock during the trial in *The Merchant of Venice* (refer to Chapter 9).

> Isabella: . . . Merciful heaven,
> Thou rather with thy sharp and sulphurous bolt
> Splits the unwedgeable and gnarled oak
> Than the soft myrtle; but man, proud man,
> Dress'd in a little brief authority,
> Most ignorant of what he's most assur'd
> (His glassy essence), like an angry ape
> Plays such fantastic tricks before high heaven
> As makes the angels weep; who, with our spleens,
> Would all themselves laugh mortal.
> (II.2.114-123)

The icy Angelo starts to melt from her eloquence and seems to warm up even more toward her the second time she visits. As a matter of fact, this zealous civil authority seems to completely forget who he is and what he stands for!

VERSE BY VERSE

In *Shakespeare's Advice to the Players*, eminent director Peter Hall pinpoints the patterns in the pausing, rhythm, and pace within Angelo's self-questioning soliloquy, which follows Isabella's plea for Claudio's life. Poor fellow is upset because he has been turned on by a chaste girl who's about to go into the convent!

> What's this? what's this? Is this her fault, or mine?
> The tempter, or the tempted, who sins most, ha?
> Not she; nor doth she tempt; but it is I
> That, lying by the violet in the sun,
> Do as the carrion does, not as the flow'r,
> Corrupt with virtuous season. Can it be
> That modesty may more betray our sense
> Than woman's lightness? . . .
> What dost thou? or what art thou, Angelo?
> Dost thou desire her foully for those things
> That make her good? O, let her brother live!
> (II.2.162-169; 172-174)

Note which lines contain a break or pause, known as a *caesura*. Hall says, "once the caesura line is over, a new tempo is established with the next full line—a new beat. All these caesura changes are a perfect framework for a string of agonized questions that spring from a neurotic mind."

Out of the blue, Angelo makes Isabella a proposition—if she will go to bed with him, he will release her brother from his death sentence. (Angelo, you've got to be kidding! Isn't that rich! The paragon of justice can't resist the allure of the paragon of virtue. This is Shakespearean irony at its best.)

A Plan with a Bed Trick

Stunned and powerless to overcome Angelo's blackmail, Isabella visits Claudio in prison. It takes her a while to tell him what Angelo wants from her. When she does, Claudio is momentarily disgusted by the prospect that Angelo is effectively raping his sister in exchange for his own life. But Claudio is a mere mortal who likes his life. He briefly empathizes with his sister but then comes to his senses. Not surprisingly, he tells Isabella he'd rather live and allow her to lose her virginity than be executed. Incensed, Isabella derides Claudio for being a coward and expecting her to compromise her principles.

An impossible moral dilemma? Enter the Duke masked as friar with a possible solution. He's aware of the score between Juliet and Claudio. He advises

Isabella to trick Angelo by arranging to meet with him and then sending another woman to lie with Angelo in her place. That surrogate would be Mariana, a woman once betrothed to Angelo but eventually thrown over by him when her dowry disappeared.

"WILD AND WHIRLING WORDS"

When Shakespeare has the Duke engineer a plan for Mariana to take Isabella's place in bed with Angelo, he's using a very old device known as the *bed trick*. Long before Shakespeare wrote his plays, characters were switching places in the marital bed in some of the early prose romances he used for inspiration. *All's Well That Ends Well*, another Shakespearean tragicomedy, employs the bed trick (see Appendix A).

As they watched the play, Shakespeare's audience may have realized that Angelo's *betrothal* to Mariana was similar to Claudio and Juliet's betrothal. Using the bed trick, Isabella gets to keep her virginity and her religious vows, Angelo gets to satisfy his lust, and Mariana might succeed in forcing the cad to fulfill his original marriage promise.

The bed trick goes according to plan. Isabella gives Angelo what he wants. But sadly, the cruel coward reneges on his promise to save her brother. Angelo refuses to withdraw his orders to execute Claudio. Claudio is saved at the last minute, though, when the friar goes behind the scenes and plots to have the provost fool Angelo by substituting the head of a prisoner who was already dead for Claudio's. Mysteriously, the Duke hides the fact that Claudio's life has been spared from Isabella.

The Duke Returns and Justice Yields to Mercy

At this point, it appears the friar has had enough of his pretend hiatus. So he sends Angelo a letter telling him to expect him back, saying he expects the red-carpet treatment at his homecoming. Making sure there's a crowd present at the city gates, the Duke makes his entrance. Wearing a veil, Isabella accuses

Chapter 14. Measure for Measure

Angelo of being a traitor and a rapist. The Duke doesn't believe her and orders her arrest. Then Mariana, who is veiled, publicly reports that Angelo has refused to acknowledge her as his lawful wife, but Angelo denies any recent contact with her.

But the Duke's charade isn't over. Feigning anger, he demands to see the friar, instructing Angelo and Escalus to figure out what's going on. (Sound silly? Yes! You remember correctly that the Duke *is* the friar.) The Duke leaves the stage and suddenly the "friar" reappears, talks about Angelo's crime, and rails against the incompetence of the Viennese rulers. Escalus is about to have him arrested for his outburst when Lucio, in support of Escalus, exposes the friar's disguise by ripping off his hood. In front of an amazed crowd, Angelo wastes no time in acknowledging his guilt. He asks the Duke to sentence him to death and forget the trial.

The rest of the scene unfolds in a flurry of resolution and pardon. The Duke orders Angelo to marry Mariana, but he hasn't let him off the hook for his misdeeds. The couple leave with Friar Peter and return as husband and wife.

TIMELESS SOLILOQUIES

In the Duke's judgment upon Angelo during the long and climactic final scene, he invokes Christ's Sermon on the Mount. Here is the New Testament chapter 7:1-2 from the Bible's gospel of Matthew, which Shakespeare obviously recalled: "Judge not, that ye be not judged. For with what judgment ye judge, ye shall be judged: and with what measure ye mete, it shall be measured to you again" (*King James Version*). The Duke's message to Angelo, Isabella, and the Viennese crowd is that when you judge others, you are guaranteed to bring judgment upon yourself.

Duke: . . . but as he adjudg'd your brother—
        Being criminal, in double violation
        Of sacred chastity and of promise-breach,
        Thereon dependent, for your brother's life—
        The very mercy of the law cries out

> Most audible, even from his proper tongue,
> "An Angelo for Claudio, death for death!"
> Haste still pays haste, and leisure answers leisure;
> Like doth quit like, and *Measure* still *for Measure.*
> Then, Angelo, thy fault's thus manifested;
> Which though thou wouldst deny, denies thee vantage.
> We do condemn thee to the very block
> Where Claudio stoop'd to death, . . .
> (V.1.403-415)

The truism above, of course, is echoed in the title of the play. Paradoxically, the Duke appears to flout the New Testament command to show mercy in order to provoke Isabella and Mariana to beg for Angelo's life. Another object lesson from the Duke?

When the Duke sentences Angelo to death for killing Claudio, Mariana asks the Duke to pardon him. It is Isabella, though, who tips the scales of justice that would harshly punish Angelo for his sins. When she begs the Duke to free Angelo, we see a grief-stricken, merciful girl who is no longer the principled young novice who was quick to sacrifice her brother to guard her virtue. To many viewers, she seems less wedded to her ideals, but more human, nonetheless.

When the Duke sends for Barnardine, a prisoner whose life has been spared, he comes onstage with Claudio. Both men are then pardoned. Then the Duke gives in and pardons Angelo, but not before he asks for Isabella's hand in marriage! (This proposal seems farfetched in the theatre.) The Duke orders Lucio to marry his mistress, sentencing him to harsh punishment and jail. Later, he lets him off the hook. Claudio is now free to happily wed Juliet with the Duke's blessing. Once again, the Duke asks for Isabella's hand in marriage. She can only respond with silence. No one is more surprised by this turn of events than modern audiences and critics.

CHAPTER 14. MEASURE FOR MEASURE

A pregnant Juliet (Erika Peckhardt) is seated next to Duke Vincentio masquerading as a friar (Arthur Lazalde) in director Chuck Ney's 2012 production of Measure for Measure *at the Texas Shakespeare Festival.*

(Photo Courtesy of Texas Shakespeare Festival)

Justice and Mercy in *Measure for Measure*

On its face, *Measure for Measure* seems to be a play about how a ruler uses his authority. In the story, we are invited to compare how Angelo rules Vienna compared to the more temperate Duke. If we allow ourselves to admire the Duke in *Measure for Measure*, the play explores the problems that result when the Duke appoints his Deputy to enforce the letter of a strict law. Claudio's death sentence is overly rigid, of course, and the Duke ensures that one of his citizens is not unfairly punished for having sex with a woman willing to marry him. For the most part, the Duke seems to embody a willingness to choose mercy or instigate the quality of mercy in others, like Isabella and Mariana.

The play becomes a problem, though, when you consider closely the behavior of the Duke. Is he really so honorable, masquerading as a false friar? On the one hand, he seems to be semi-omnipotent and able to manipulate events so that no one suffers or dies. But if he truly loved his citizens, why would he abandon them to the harsh rule of Angelo?

The Energy of *Measure for Measure* Onstage

Measure for Measure's performance history has been uneven. Onstage, it has never been one of Shakespeare's most popular plays. It was first performed at the court of King James at Whitehall Palace on December 26, 1604. (Shakespeare probably wrote the play that same year.) Although it was well received in the eighteenth century, the presenters who adapted it severely cut the subplot because it was considered unsavory! Nineteenth-century audiences saw Shakespeare's original script restored, but they weren't too keen on the play either, possibly because the Victorians found its moral overtones questionable.

"A KINGDOM FOR A STAGE"

BBC-TV's 1978 production of *Measure for Measure* offered a penetrating vision of the lascivious Vienna of Shakespeare's imagination. Kenneth Colley's Duke and Duke-disguised-as-friar offers a plausible portrait of a benign ruler trying to clean up an immoral kingdom. Kate Nelligan (Isabella) is an engaging virtuous novice, and Tim Pigott-Smith (as Angelo) gives us insight into how extremist rulers can fall prey to the weaknesses they can't tolerate in their own subjects. Actor John McEnery pegged the licentious Lucio to a tee. When you watch this version, notice the funny Oliver Cromwell-style, Puritan hats sported by the Duke and Escalus. Typical of Shakespeare, the world of Vienna is simply a microcosm of early seventeenth-century London.

Though *Measure for Measure* isn't a crowd puller like *Much Ado About Nothing* or the other festive comedies, its dark tone and moral ambiguities strike a chord among modern audiences. Here are some high-profile productions for stage and TV over the last century.

- 1933: Tyrone Guthrie directed this show at the Old Vic in London, with Charles Laughton (Angelo), Flora Robson (Isabella), and James Mason (Claudio).
- 1950: Peter Brook directed John Gielgud (Angelo) for the Royal Shakespeare Company (Stratford-upon-Avon).
- 1962: Judi Dench performed as Isabella, with Marius Goring in the role of Angelo (Stratford-upon-Avon).
- 1978: In the BBC-TV/Time Life production, Kate Nelligan starred as Isabella and Tim Pigott-Smith played Angelo.
- 1994: David Thacker directed another adaptation for BBC-TV, featuring Corin Redgrave (Angelo), Juliet Aubrey (Isabella), and Tom Wilkinson (Duke).
- 2012: Chuck Ney directed the stage production at the Texas Shakespeare Festival, starring Nick Henderson (Angelo), Vanessa Sterling (Isabella), and Arthur Lazalde (Duke).

FACTS TO REMEMBER

- *Measure for Measure* is Shakespeare's last comedy, often referred to as a *problem comedy* or *problem play* because it contains dark, morally ambiguous meanings that present challenges for the modern director.
- Angelo's strict enforcement of the law and Isabella's insistence on maintaining her virtue are often compared as similarly absolutist.
- To prevent Angelo from forcing sex on a chaste Isabella, Shakespeare has the Duke propose the *bed trick*, which allows Mariana to lie with Angelo in her place.
- The last scene of the play is confusing, implausible, and outrageous, especially when the Duke proposes to Isabella without ever having revealed a hint of being in love with her.
- *Measure for Measure* explores what happens when a ruler exercises strict justice or tempers justice with mercy. The play is considered flawed, though, by those who believe the Duke is less than honorable.

Part 4
The Histories

Part 4. The Histories

Shakespeare actually invented the history or chronicle play. He wrote 10 histories to be exact. I warn you—unlike his lighthearted comedies, the histories can get a little heavy because they spotlight the English dynastic wars and other political conflicts during the fourteenth through sixteenth centuries.

Though many of the best histories are still produced by companies worldwide, three are especially well known and liked by playgoers—*Richard III; Henry IV, Part I;* and *Henry V.*

Richard III is the last play in Shakespeare's *minor tetralogy*, which covers an internal political conflict known as the Wars of the Roses. These plays take a hard look at the use and abuse of power. (Read more about the *Henry VI* plays in this saga in Appendix B.)

Henry IV, Part I and *Henry V* are the second and fourth parts of Shakespeare's best-known history saga, or *major tetralogy*. These two plays feature Prince Hal, a very engaging, complex noble. In both plays, you'll be amazed at how well the characters are developed. In *Henry IV, Part I* you'll also meet Falstaff, the bumptious noble found in *The Merry Wives of Windsor*, a later comedy. (Read more about *Richard II* and *Henry IV, Part II*, other plays in this tetralogy, in Appendix A.)

Chapter 15
Richard III

> **INTRODUCTION**
> - Who was Shakespeare's arch-villain, and what did he have to do with the historical Richard III?
> - The main characters in *Richard III*
> - The play's bloody sequence of events
> - How *Richard III's* language and rhetorical structure will mesmerize you
> - Shakespeare's theme, sources, and mythmaking
> - How producers and actors have re-created Richard in their own image over the centuries

In *Richard III* Shakespeare invented a Machiavellian anti-hero who never wavers along his bloody path of villainy and betrayal. The story of this monster, told as a juicy melodrama, has captivated audiences since it was first performed. In fact, the play must have been terribly popular because six quarto editions were published between 1597 and 1622, before it was included in the 1623 First Folio.

The story of this wicked royal is loosely based on the life of Richard, Duke of Gloucester, who became king and ruled England from 1483 until 1485. Historically, Richard was the last of the Plantagenet line, a Yorkist king who followed a line of Lancastrian kings who ruled in the fifteenth century. In writing his tale about this cruel tyrant, Shakespeare exaggerates the vices of the historical Richard and plays up his physical deformities, creating a villain for the ages.

Although *Richard III* is classified as a history play, it's the playwright's first crack at writing a sweeping tragedy centered on the motives and actions of one powerful individual. To the world, his experiment worked. But historians aren't too crazy about the fact that the Richard Shakespeare invented has become legendary. Today he overshadows any notion we may have about the real Richard III.

The Chief Characters

Richard, Duke of Gloucester (later King Richard III)—This cruel king, who is Shakespeare's creation, will stop at nothing short of treachery and murder to get what he wants. Born with a hunchback and withered arm, he connives against his families, his enemies, and his closest friends in order to assume the throne after the death of King Edward IV, his elder brother. After the king dies, Richard is named Lord Protector of the two young princes, his brother's heirs. When the play begins, Richard has already murdered the English King Henry VI, Lady Anne's father-in-law.

George, Duke of Clarence—Just call him "Clarence," for our purposes. He is Richard's older brother and King Edward IV's younger brother. As the play opens, King Edward has put Clarence in the Tower prison because he suspects some sort of treachery. (The details about this are a little fuzzy in the play.) Don't worry too much about the king's motives for doing so. Clarence is Richard's first victim and is executed early on in the first act.

King Edward IV—His full name is Edward Plantagenet, and he's on the throne when this play opens. You don't need to know much about him either. He doesn't have many lines in this play.

Chapter 15. Richard III

"A Kingdom for a Stage"

Be careful not to confuse King Edward with the many other Edwards mentioned in this play. There is the Earl of Warwick, Lady Anne's father; Edward, the former Prince of Wales, who is Lady Anne's dead husband; and the young Prince Edward, the *current* Prince of Wales, who is only a child when taken to the Tower under Richard's care.

Lady Anne—Anne Neville is the daughter of the Earl of Warwick (who does not figure in this play, by the way). Richard courts her even though she still mourns the death of her husband, Edward, Prince of Wales, and father-in-law, Henry VI. Lady Anne marries Richard and is crowned queen for a brief period, until the villain gets rid of her to court Princess Elizabeth, the young princes' sister.

Buckingham—Until Act four, the Duke of Buckingham appears as an unscrupulous noble who allies himself with Richard. Richard uses him to justify killing Hastings and to smear the princes' names so he can convince the people that he should become king. Buckingham will surprise you, though, because he eventually turns the tables on Richard.

Hastings—Lord Hastings is a chamberlain in King Edward's household. He miscalculates Richard's ability to consolidate his power while King Edward is still alive. Richard has him beheaded without so much as a trial.

Earl of Richmond—Actually, Richmond is not a very well-developed hero, as Shakespearean heroes go. Right off the bat, Elizabethan audiences would have recognized him as the grandfather of their own queen, Elizabeth I. Most important, Richmond is the good guy who puts an end to the evil king's villainy.

Margaret—Margaret is the widow of the respected King Henry VI, whose reign is the focus of the three history plays that precede

Richard III. She berates Queen Elizabeth and her family throughout the play because of her own suffering and personal loss. Margaret, who does a lot of moaning and complaining, makes several prophecies in this play that come true.

Elizabeth—Wife of Edward IV, Elizabeth is queen when this play opens. Traditionally and in this play, Richard and others aligned with the Yorkists looked upon her Lancastrian family with suspicion. Before her husband dies, she fears that the influence of her powerful family is about to be lost. Sure enough, after King Edward becomes ill and dies, Richard forbids her to see her sons, the two princes.

Duchess of York—The mother of Edward IV, Richard, and Clarence. She does her fair share of whining, too!

Beware! There are more than 50 characters in this play! Refer to the character diagram for a more complete list.

Scene: London and other locations in England

Chapter 15. Richard III

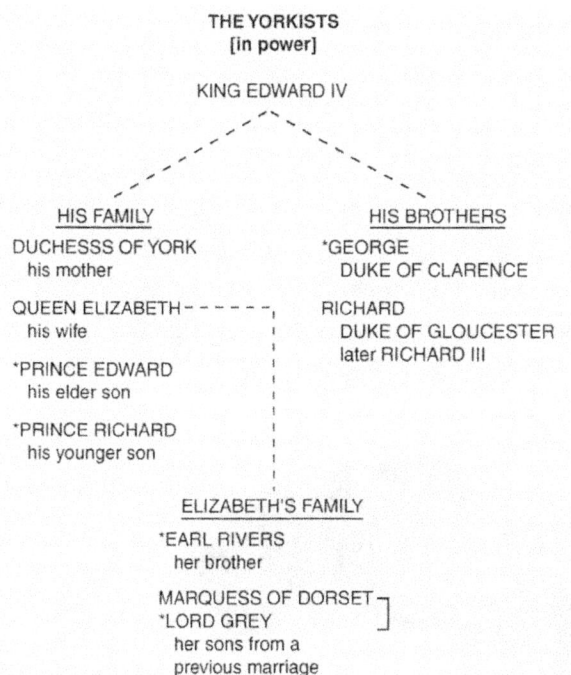

Character relationship diagram.

The Yorkist and Lancastrian sides of the royal family tree and the political alliances in Richard III.

A Cruel and Charming Tyrant

Shakespeare drew upon a variety of influences in creating his tyrant-king. First, he was indebted to character portraits created for medieval morality plays, which were especially popular before he was born. Despite being rather two-dimensional, "Vice" was a stock character of evil from morality drama and was always a crowd favorite. Shakespeare's Richard is a richer and more attractive "Vice" figure, but he manipulates the audience in a similar way. Going further, this fictional monarch is more diabolical than the real Richard III, whose reputation has suffered largely because of Shakespeare!

The real Richard III's reputation suffered during Shakespeare's lifetime. Elizabethans blamed him for the death of his two young nephews—Prince Edward and Prince Richard—who disappeared under his watch.

(Illustration by Robert Molder.)

Chapter 15. Richard III

Shakespeare's Take on the Wars of the Roses

Shakespeare probably wrote *King Richard III* in 1592 or 1593 as a sequel to his first trilogy of history plays that chronicle the English dynastic wars between the powerful Lancastrian and Yorkist families. These three plays recount clashing that began after the death of Henry V in 1422, lasting until Richard III was defeated in battle in 1485. This four-part history cycle covers the 32-year conflict known as the Wars of the Roses. (Henry V's death coincides with the culmination of England's conflict with France, known as the Hundred Years War.) (See Appendix A for more background on *Henry VI, Parts 1, 2, and 3*.)

Even though Shakespeare wrote *King Richard III* shortly after he finished the *Henry VI* trilogy, it is a superior play in many respects. It shouldn't surprise you that, as Shakespeare wrote more plays, his genius for blending history with drama got better and better. Bear one thing in mind as you read *Richard III* or any other history play: Shakespeare was a dramatist, not a historian in the modern sense. As you'll see later in this chapter, he collapsed time and adapted historical fact and circumstance to suit his own inventive and ingenious aims.

A Villain Gets to Work

In Richard's opening soliloquy, he observes that England is finally at peace after a long period of civil war. But peace doesn't really agree with Richard. Though he serves as the powerful Duke of Gloucester and is brother to King Edward IV, he realizes deep down he is a freak of nature. He is one dissatisfied individual. Elaborating on his physical abnormalities, Richard justifies his decision to pursue a life of villainy.

> I, that am curtail'd of this fair proportion,
> Cheated of feature by dissembling nature,
> Deform'd, unfinish'd, sent before my time
> Into this breathing world, scarce half made up,
> And that so lamely and unfashionable
> That dogs bark at me as I halt by them—
> Why, I, in this weak piping time of peace,
> Have no delight to pass way the time,
> Unless to see my shadow in the sun

> And descant on mine own deformity.
> And therefore, since I cannot prove a lover
> To entertain these fair well-spoken days,
> I am determined to prove a villain
> [I.1.18-30]

He's just walked onstage and already he's got you hooked, doesn't he? In this opening scene Richard has made you, the spectator, his closest confidante. From this moment forward, he will continue to seduce you with the subtle intimacy of his asides. His ongoing commentary to you and me makes him an irresistible villain from beginning to end.

Richard wastes no time perpetuating the evil deeds he started before the curtain rises. First off, he's the cause of the ill will between his two brothers, King Edward IV and Clarence. When Clarence is being escorted to the Tower of London to be locked up, the mongrel Richard acts sympathetic and leads his brother to believe that the queen and her Lancastrian family—enemies of the Yorkists—are to blame for the king's current suspicion. (To worsen everyone's fears, King Edward has fallen ill.)

Not long afterward, Richard meets Lady Anne walking in a funeral procession for her father-in-law, Henry VI. She has just lost her husband, Edward, the late Prince of Wales. (Not to confuse you, but according to historian John Julius Norwich, the real Anne Neville was only engaged to Prince Edward, not married to him.)

Calling Richard a "lump of foul deformity," Lady Anne's speech is full of venom and hatred. But before she even has time to see her father-in-law buried, Richard begins wooing this grief-stricken lady. Admitting that he murdered King Henry *and* Prince Edward, he convinces Anne he did so out of love for her. At first she spits in his face. But he's such a master manipulator that he manages to win her over.

Right now you must be thinking, "Oh, please! Is this guy for real?" I know it sounds far-fetched, but Lady Anne really falls for him! You really have to wonder what's up with her. What makes this scene so fascinating onstage is

Chapter 15. Richard III

Richard's clever performance. He lies, pretends, and manipulates Anne and anyone else who would resist his rise to power, and one by one, they each fall victim to his plots. When you see this smooth operator in action on the stage or screen, you, too, will fall under his spell. (By the way, the real Richard, Duke of Gloucester wasn't really all that bad looking.)

Old Queen Margaret Curses and Prophesies

Queen Elizabeth, King Edward's wife, has reason to worry. (Don't confuse her with Elizabeth I, who ruled a century later.) Richard is in line to become the protector of her young sons, the two princes who stand to inherit the throne. During this scene Richard strategically casts doubt on the queen's motives to make the rest of the court believe that she and her family are responsible for having Clarence locked up.

Enter Margaret of Anjou, the widow of dead Henry VI. A former queen herself, Margaret has her own ax to grind. In a series of bitter asides, she accuses the murderous Richard, calling him a "devil" and "murth'rous villain." Then, mindful that she would still be queen had Richard not murdered her husband, she angrily accuses the court of depriving her of her rightful crown. Then she curses Queen Elizabeth and her family:

> Can curses pierce the clouds and enter heaven?
> Why then give way, dull clouds, to my quick curses!
> Though not by war, by surfeit die your king,
> As ours by murther, to make him a king!
> Edward thy son, that now is Prince of Wales,
> For Edward our son, that was Prince of Wales,
> Die in his youth by like untimely violence!
> (I.3.194-200)

Fighting words! Old Queen Margaret is the only female character who is given depth as Richard's spiritual nemesis. After her prophecies, she locks horns with Richard himself in verbal combat. He calls her a "hateful with'red hag" and she offers a withering retort, referring to him as a "dog," "traitor," and "worm of conscience."

TIMELESS SOLILOQUIES

As in many of Shakespeare's early plays, a stylized form of rhetoric inspired by Greek tragedy heightens the characters' speeches. Notice the poetic effect of the initial-word repetition in Margaret's invective below, a rhetorical technique known as *anaphora*:

> Thou elvish-mark'd, abortive, rooting hog!
> Thou that wast seal'd in thy nativity
> The slave of nature and the son of hell!
> Thou slander of thy heavy mother's womb!
> Thou loathed issue of thy father's loins!
> Thou rag of honor! Thou detested—
> (I.3.227-232)

The image "elvish-mark'd" suggests, according to an Elizabethan notion, that Richard has been marked by elves because he has birth defects. Margaret ends this taunting speech by calling him a "bottled spider" and a "poisonous bunch-back'd toad."

Never underestimate Margaret. Pay close attention to what she says and how she says it. Directors have cut and minimized her role in productions since the seventeenth century, but today's scholars remind us that Shakespeare would have considered her part to be vital to the play's structure and meaning.

On a Murder Rampage

Fear hangs in the air now. For the next three acts, Richard climbs his way to power, stepping on every royal and obstacle in his path. The death knell sounds once again when Richard secretly meets with two murderers he hired to kill his brother Clarence.

Clarence's Dream

Flash to Clarence, who is locked up in the Tower. After he wakes up, he tells his Keeper about a dream involving him and his brother Richard. Clarence imagines that he has escaped from the Tower and he and Richard are walking

Chapter 15. Richard III

along an unstable pier above the moat. Richard stumbles toward the water, and as Clarence tries to steady him, Richard pulls them both in the drink. Clarence imagines he is drowning in a vision of the underworld. Not long after the dream, two murderers hired by Richard get access to his cell and put Clarence to sleep for good.

King Edward Falls Out of the Picture

The next obstacle to Richard's upward climb is the king himself. As a gravely ill Edward IV attempts to stop his fractured court from being at odds with one another, Richard brings news that Clarence is dead. Elizabeth and King Edward are stunned, of course, and don't even suspect Richard of foul play. (Of course, we know better . . .) As Edward's health declines, he is overcome with guilt and remorse at not being able to safeguard his own brother.

VERSE BY VERSE

Critics and scholars have made much of Shakespeare's infusing of formal rhetoric into many characters' speeches. After Elizabeth, her children, and the Duchess of York learn about Clarence's death in the second act, they express grief for all of their murdered loved ones in a litany of one-line laments reminiscent of a Greek chorus.

Q. Elizabeth:	Ah for my husband, for my dear Lord Edward!
Children:	Ah for our father, for our dear Lord Clarence!
Duchess:	Alas for both, both mine, Edward and Clarence!
Q. Elizabeth:	What stay had I but Edward? and he's gone.
Children:	What stay had we but Clarence? and he's gone.
Duchess:	What stays had I but they? and they are gone. (II.2.71-76)

Richard further pollutes the court's atmosphere by blaming the queen and her family for Clarence's death. Now the court must look to the new king, the very young Prince Edward, who's not even old enough to govern. At this point Richard puts his next plot in motion—to control the movements of the heir apparent and his young brother, Prince Richard. To support Richard's power play, Buckingham summons Prince Edward to London and sets about isolating him and his brother Richard from their mother and her allies.

Lock 'Em Up! Chop Off Their Heads!

It's not hard to guess what happens next. Being the Lord Protector of the crown prince and his brother, Richard has his nephews right where he wants them. Meanwhile across London, people are feeling the shake-up of the court and speculating about England's future. But Richard continues plotting behind the scenes. Rivers, Grey, and Vaughan, three of the queen's relatives, are put in prison in the Tower of London. These three are doomed, of course, and not long afterward, all lose their heads. When this happens, Elizabeth realizes her family's hold on the throne is tenuous.

Richard has been plotting the fate of his next victims. Pretending to look after his nephews' well-being, he has them safely ensconced in the residential rooms in the Tower. To keep Buckingham loyal to him, he promises to appoint him as Earl of Hereford. To help cast doubt on the prince's divine right to the throne, he gets Buckingham to spread rumors that his nephews are Edward's bastard sons.

A Final Grab for the Throne

Next, Richard accuses Lord Hastings, his ally thus far, of being a traitor after he hesitates to support Richard's bid for the throne. He then wastes no time ordering Hastings' execution. Then he and Buckingham use some play-acting of their own to justify this vile deed. They bamboozle the mayor and citizens into believing that Hastings has plotted against them and Richard deserves to be king.

Chapter 15. Richard III

"A Kingdom for a Stage"

Strictly speaking, *Richard III* is one of Shakespeare's bloodiest plays. The number of victims mounts with each passing scene—Clarence, Rivers, Grey, Vaughan, Hastings, the two princes, Lady Anne, and, finally, Richard himself. But Shakespeare portrays only one of these murders onstage. Do you remember which one?

After he is king, Richard carries out perhaps his worst and most evil maneuver. He hires Tyrrel to murder the princes. When Buckingham first gets wind of it, he cannot even abide such an act. Not surprisingly, the hump-backed villain retaliates by refusing to grant his sidekick the earldom that he's promised.

By this time Richard has become so bloodthirsty that we're not shocked to discover he has ordered that rumors be spread about Lady Anne's death so he can marry Queen Elizabeth's daughter.

"My Kingdom for a Horse"

Buckingham realizes he will end up like Hastings if he doesn't get out of Dodge. So he escapes and joins the Earl of Richmond's rebellion against Richard. (Eventually Buckingham is captured, and after the war between Richard and Richmond is underway, he is beheaded.)

The play's fifth act concerns Richard's military conflict with Richmond. By this time Richmond's army and navy are strong and a formidable threat to the bad tyrant. On the night before the famous battle of Bosworth, Richard has a nightmare that is strangely reminiscent of Clarence's earlier dream. In it, the ghosts of each of his victims foretell the villain's doom and impending defeat. Richmond sees the same ghosts in his dream, but for him they promise victory the next day.

Richard awakens, his conscience wracked with guilt and fear. During the battle of Bosworth, he and Richmond go head to head and Richmond prevails. At one point Richard loses his horse and is reduced to uttering the now-famous line, "My horse. My horse. My kingdom for a horse!" Richmond triumphs and becomes the next king, known as Henry VII.

The Play's Lessons and Sources

One of the play's persistent themes is the tension that Shakespeare builds inside every audience member between that perverse side of us that loves to be seduced by the devil and the side that wants good to triumph in the end. In contrast to the demon Richard, Margaret, Elizabeth, and the Duchess embody all that is just and good. The three acts in which these women appear are meant to balance all of Richard's wrongs with conscientious protests, reminding us of what is right.

As we see in Richard's opening speech, he chooses to be a villain from the get-go. Scholars believe that since Richard appears to determine his own destiny, this play has a "humanist" bent that radically departs from the religiously centered medieval dramas that preceded it.

As he was accustomed to doing, the dramatist borrowed background from several sources: Sir Thomas More's *History of King Richard the Third* (1513), Raphael Holinshed's *Chronicles of England* (1587), and Edward Hall's *Union of the Two Noble and Illustre Families of Lancaster and York* (1548). He also drew upon the later portrait of Richard III contained in *A Mirror for Magistrates*, a collection of verse tragedies by different authors, licensed for publication in 1559.

How Big-Time Actors Have Re-created Richard

Richard Burbage, the Elizabethan actor who popularized many of Shakespeare's heroes on stage, played the villain in an early *Richard III* production before the play was printed in 1597. Beginning in the seventeenth century, though, writer Colley Cibber created an entirely new version by cutting scenes and adding new ones of his own for easier staging. Thankfully, modern scholars and directors have reclaimed Shakespeare's original, using a simplified performance version from one of the many quarto versions that circulated before the 1623 First Folio.

Chapter 15. Richard III

Benedict Cumberbatch (center) is shown as the Yorkist King Richard III in a scene from the Battle of Bosworth Field during the BBC-TV's 2016 production of Shakespeare's Richard III. *BBC produced the play as part of its four-part film cycle,* The Hollow Crown—The Wars of the Roses.

(Photo courtesy of Photofest.)

Today all stage and film productions of *Richard III* are compared to Laurence Olivier's captivating 1955 film. Though Olivier drastically cut pivotal scenes of the women lamenting their lost loved ones, his performance is unforgettable. He understates Richard's physical deformity—a nice touch.

Since 1945, actors have mined the part of Richard in a variety of ways. Some have emphasized his political machinations while others have delved into psychological causes of his deviance. In Gillian Day's analysis of *Richard III* productions at Stratford-upon-Avon, actors and producers differ tremendously in how they approach the play. Some focus on Richard's political rise and fall. Others revel in turning Richard inside out and dwell on his "psycho-social" dimensions.

Other, more avant-garde versions have milked the play to show ways in which it is self-consciously commenting on the very nature of theatre. All in all, since Olivier came along, directors have dispensed with too much melodrama, the norm in pre-Olivier era. Since Olivier reinvented Richard's persona around 1945, many others have taken on this gigantic role, including Alec Guinness, George C. Scott, Christopher Plummer, and John Wood.

There are some interesting adaptations of Richard III on film. You've got Olivier's 1955 classic; the haunting 1995 version featuring Ian McKellan and set in Nazi Germany, directed by McKellan and Richard Loncraine; and Al Pacino's half movie/half documentary *Looking for Richard*, released in 1993.

Richard III in the Late Twentieth Century

Although *Richard III* was one of the earliest plays Shakespeare wrote, it's unclear who first performed in it and when. In The Arden Shakespeare edition of *Richard III*, Antony Hammond suggests that actors from the Admiral's Men and Lord Strange's Men performed the play in 1591. Elizabethan playgoers would have immediately connected the heroic Richmond with Henry Tudor, their beloved Queen Elizabeth's grandfather. Also, they would have been predisposed to adopt Shakespeare's bias against the real-life Richard III because of widespread propaganda that the Tudor kings (remember the likes of Henry VIII and his six wives?) should take credit for ending the Wars of the Roses.

Here are some notable productions of Richard III in North America and Britain:

- 1945—Laurence Olivier created quite a stir with his highly original take on Shakespeare's bad guy. What was so original about it? Before this era, producers tended to ham up the play's melodrama.
- 1949—Richard Whorf revived a 1946 show performed for G.I.'s after World War II ended. William Windom's Richard had severely deformed legs.
- 1953—Tyrone Guthrie directed *Richard III*, starring Alec Guinness, in the Canadian Stratford Festival debut production.
- 1956—Olivier's film version capitalized on his success in playing Richard on the English stage. Olivier directed the movie and played Richard, of course. Very entertaining.
- 1957—George C. Scott played Richard at the New York Shakespeare Festival, directed by Stuart Vaughan. This was Scott's first crack at doing Shakespeare and the critics really liked him.

Chapter 15. Richard III

- 1963—Ian Holm played Richard in a show directed by Peter Hall, John Barton, and Frank Evans. They staged the play in a four-part series called *The Wars of the Roses*, probing how Richard's political corruption grew out of preexisting evil in the earlier courts of Henry VI. In 1970, Barton's script was adapted into a BBC-TV version.
- 1973—Al Pacino began to make his mark doing Richard. He did the role for the Theatre Company of Boston at the Church of the Covenant, for director David Wheeler.
- 1984—In a memorable Royal Shakespeare Theatre production at Stratford-upon-Avon, Anthony Sher took the description of Richard as a "bottled spider" to heart. His monster had scoliosis and was hunched over on crutches. A pretty scary crippled guy! Directed by Bill Alexander.
- 1990—Stacy Keach's take on Richard at The Lansburgh Theatre in Washington, D.C. got mixed reviews. That same year, Denzel Washington took on the role in New York's Central Park.
- 1995—Jennifer Ehle played Lady Anne and David Troughton was Richard in this Royal Shakespeare Company production at Stratford-upon-Avon, directed by Steven Pimlott.
- 2016—Benedict Cumberbatch performed the role of Richard in the BBC-TV's 2016 production, a single installment in its four-part film cycle, *The Hollow Crown—The Wars of the Roses*.

FACTS TO REMEMBER

- Richard, Duke of Gloucester is a well-rounded anti-hero and a facile actor who manipulates audiences into identifying with him, even though he is evil.
- Remember, this diabolical Richard is a fiction! Modern historians believe the real Richard III was not such a bad sort.
- *Richard III* has distinctive rhetorical patterns resembling those found in ancient Greek tragedy.
- Margaret, Queen Elizabeth, and the Duchess of York are believed to be the moral center of the play.
- Starting with Colley Cibber's slashed-up, readapted version, *Richard III* has been cut and adapted variously over the centuries as producers try to capture the mythical tyrant from different political and psychological points of view.

Chapter 16
Henry IV, Part I

INTRODUCTION
- Tips about how to approach *Henry IV, Part I* as an ensemble play
- The principal characters of *Henry IV, Part I*
- The three "worlds" of *King Henry IV, Part I*, and tips about how Shakespeare cleverly juxtaposes these subplots
- How the play's narrative structure offers richly varied points of view
- Actor/director Mark Mineart muses about playing King Henry in a combined staging of *Henry IV, Parts I and II*
- Notable twentieth-century stage and film productions

Henry IV, Part I is considered Shakespeare's most brilliant history play. Its clever, ironic juxtaposition of court and tavern scenes makes for an entertaining story of political rebellion and one king's disillusionment with his son and heir. It is likely that Shakespeare wrote *Henry IV, Part I* between 1596 and 1597, a few years before he wrote his great festive comedies.

Some critics feel that *Henry IV, Part I* is a showpiece for the debauched Sir John Falstaff. Modern audiences usually favor the comic knight, but there's a lot more to this play than Falstaff. Its four key parts—Prince Hal, King Henry, Falstaff, and Hotspur—are rich and colorful and require the strong support of an acting company or "ensemble." The play chronicles events that actually occurred from 1402-03. Shakespeare's history is fiction, loosely based on English history; it conflates actual events and combines real and fictional characters.

Though it lacks the towering presence of a deliciously evil Richard or a tormented Lear, *Henry IV, Part I* is an ensemble play as finely constructed as a Bach concerto. *Henry IV, Part I* strikes a different tone from *Richard III*, an earlier melodramatic play. Unlike King Richard, the title role of King Henry doesn't hijack our hearts and minds with an alluring presence. Using cleverly juxtaposed scenes, the play raises profound questions about what it takes to be an effective king.

The Characters

KING HENRY'S FACTION

King Henry IV—Before he was crowned, King Henry was known as Henry Bolingbroke (pronounced "Bullingbrook"), the son of John of Gaunt. (The actual King Henry IV ruled from 1399-1418, by the way.) It has been three years since King Henry instigated the deposition and death of King Richard II. King Henry is guilt-ridden and weary when this play opens. He feels like God may be punishing him for overthrowing Richard. He bemoans the domestic burdens he faces, believing fortune has turned against him for usurping the throne. To compound his troubles, his former allies are plotting to overthrow him. What's worse, his son (and heir) refuses to give up a debauched lifestyle.

Henry, Prince of Wales—He is the king's oldest son, known as "Prince Hal." Hal is at the heart of this play. The play centers upon how he acts, what he learns about himself and his potential, and his duty. Pinpointing Hal's motives can be tricky. For starters, his buddy Falstaff thinks he is a hedonistic practical joker just like himself, whose position as heir to the throne is meaningless. When Hal is with Falstaff and other drinking buddies, he pretends to be just that. But Hal has many faces. By role-playing, Hal manages to fool Falstaff and his own father. We learn how the prince actually views himself in an early soliloquy. (Here's a factoid—in Shakespeare's play Hal is roughly the same age as Hotspur, but historically they were 20 years apart.)

"WILD AND WHIRLING WORDS"

Not to confuse you, but there are four Henrys in this play, and Shakespeare has given them each a key role. They include King Henry IV; Henry, Prince of Wales (Prince Hal); Henry Percy (a.k.a. Hotspur or Harry); and Henry Percy, Sr.(the Earl of Northumberland and Hotspur's dad).

Prince John of Lancaster—A younger son of King Henry IV

Earl of Westmerland—A kinsman of Henry IV

Sir Walter Blunt

THE REBELS

Henry Percy (Hotspur)—Hotspur, also called Harry, is the son of Henry Percy, the Earl of Northumberland. He is an important rebel who plots the overthrow of King Henry. Hotspur is an old-fashioned aristocrat who worships the early Renaissance ideals of honor and chivalry that were fast becoming obsolete during Shakespeare's day. King Henry holds Hotspur up as an example of model behavior. If you scrutinize Hotspur's actions, though, you'll see that he lacks maturity and makes rash decisions. This young rebel reacts too harshly and offends people. On the surface, he seems more kingly than Prince Hal, but there is more to Hal than meets the eye.

Henry Percy, Earl of Northumberland—He is the father of Hotspur, known as "Northumberland." Northumberland once allied himself with King Henry during the overthrow of Richard II, but in this play he has joined the rebel camp against King Henry.

Part 4. The Histories

Thomas Percy, Earl of Worcester—Part of the rebels, known as Worcester.

Edmund, Lord Mortimer (Earl of March)—The brother-in-law of Hotspur and part of the rebels. Known as Mortimer.

Owen Glendower—An elderly Welshman who is part of the rebel camp. Though they are few and far between, Glendower's speeches are colorful and memorable. His daughter, Lady Mortimer, is married to Lord Mortimer, the Earl of March.

Lady Percy (Kate)—Hotspur's wife and Mortimer's sister.

Lady Mortimer—Glendower's daughter and Mortimer's wife.

Richard Scroop—Archbishop of York.

Archibald—Earl of Douglas.

Sir Richard Vernon.

Sir Michael—A friend to the Archbishop of York, in his household.

PRINCE HAL'S COHORTS

Sir John Falstaff—The rotund, extremely hedonistic knight may be Shakespeare's most famous comic character. But this guy is more than a drunken bum. He is a wise aristocrat and the sort of witty, ingenious anarchist we all love. The first time *Henry IV, Part I* was performed, probably around 1597, Shakespeare had named his famous knight "Oldcastle" instead of Falstaff. It is speculated that he replaced the name Oldcastle with Falstaff because a descendant of the actual Oldcastle—Lord Cobham—took offense. Around this time Lord Cobham was Queen Elizabeth's esteemed Lord Chamberlain.

Edward Poins—A gentleman-in-waiting to Prince Henry.

Bardolph

Peto

Mistress Quickly—Hostess of the Boar's Head Tavern in Eastcheap.

Chapter 16. Henry IV, Part I

> Francis—A drawer (a bartender).
>
> Vintner
>
> At Rochester: Gadshill, First Carrier, Second Carrier, Chamberlain, Ostler, First Traveler, Second Traveler
>
> Servant, Sheriff, and Officers; Messengers, Lords, Attendants, Soldiers
>
> *Scene: England and Wales*

King Henry Is Tired and Disillusioned

Henry: Uneasy lies the head that wears a crown.
(III.1.31)

When our story begins, King Henry IV has been on the throne for three years. But a group of disgruntled men feel that Henry doesn't deserve the crown because he usurped it from Richard II, an anointed king, and caused his deposition and murder. (Read more about this in the Appendix A summary of *Richard II*.)

VERSE BY VERSE

To get your historical bearings before watching the play, consider this. When you hear King Henry's opening speeches you might surmise he is something of a wimp because he is uneasy about how he came by the throne. Understand that, to the Elizabethans, what Henry did was radical. Until Richard II was deposed, all English royals who stood to inherit the throne were believed entitled by virtue of the laws of *primogeniture*. The practice held that the throne must pass to the oldest son of an anointed king. Primogeniture was rooted in the faith that heirs to the English throne were divinely inspired.

Part 4. The Histories

Things aren't going so well for King Henry. He wears his crown uneasily, believing he came by his position immorally. He hopes things will be easier for his son Hal, who will accede to the throne legitimately, through inheritance. Four men who supported his overthrow of Richard II are plotting to overthrow him. These rebels include Glendower, from Wales; Harry Percy (known as Hotspur); Worcester, Hotspur's uncle; and Northumberland, Hotspur's father.

> Hotspur: Shall it for shame be spoken in these days,
> . . .
> That men of your nobility and power
> Did gage them both in an unjust behalf
> . . .
> To put down Richard, that sweet lovely rose,
> And plant this thorn, this canker, Bullingbrook?
> (I.3.170; 172-73; 175-76)

In this speech Hotspur expresses his dissatisfaction with King Henry's rule and abuse of power. Although he supported Henry Bolingbroke's rise to power, he now feels the king has turned against him and other supporters.

To compound matters, King Henry is seriously disappointed in his son's dissolute behavior. What's a sitting king to do when his heir acts like a deadbeat? Prince Hal's choice of friends is questionable, and this is his biggest problem. He likes to hang out at the Boar's Head Tavern in Eastcheap and drink with men of questionable reputation. Hal's best friend, Sir John Falstaff, enjoys his hedonistic lifestyle more than being a good knight, and this has King Henry terribly worried.

Unbeknownst to dear old Dad, Hal vows in the following soliloquy to mend his ways at the appropriate time:

> Prince Hal: So when this loose behavior I throw off
> And pay the debt I never promised,
> By how much better than my word I am
> By so much shall I falsify men's hopes,

Chapter 16. Henry IV, Part I

> And like bright metal on a sullen ground,
> My reformation, glitt'ring o'er my fault
> Shall show more goodly and attract more eyes
> Than that which hath no foil to set it off.
> (I.2.208-15)

Falstaff Stages a Robbery and Gives His Version of Events

While four men plot treachery outside of London, liquor flows and mischief brews at the Boar's Head Tavern in Eastcheap. As Prince Hal and Poins eavesdrop, Falstaff and Bardolph conspire to rob some wealthy travelers on their way to London. Then Hal and Poins make a secret plot to don disguises and foil the robbery. The plan works, and after Falstaff and company steal from the travelers, Hal and Poins, in turn, steal from them and manage to scare Falstaff and Bardolph away from the scene.

Back at the tavern, Falstaff tells a false story of what took place, lying and bragging (at Hal and Poins' prodding) about his courageous conduct. Eventually, though, the Prince brings him up short and reveals the truth about what happened. Being exposed as a liar doesn't sit well with the curmudgeon. So Falstaff hedges and backtracks, claiming he recognized Hal all along and opted to leave the scene rather than do anything to harm Hal.

There are few scenes in Shakespeare that are more colorful than these tavern scenes. The sparring between the garrulous Prince Hal and the liquor-loving Falstaff offers an intimate glimpse into the soul of England's people. These sketches, interspersed among scenes about the rebellion against King Henry, help transform Hotspur's rebel plot into a political conflict that feels much more plausible than the Earl of Richmond's plot to overthrow King Richard in *Richard III* (see Chapter 15).

In the midst of the sparring and merrymaking, Prince Hal gets word that his father wants to see him the following morning. Hotspur has started his rebellion and Falstaff encourages Hal to practice what he will say to his father. During the rest of this now-famous scene, Falstaff and Prince Hal act out a charade, both pretending to be King Henry. In this play-acting, the behavior of Falstaff and Hal is severely criticized.

The role-playing between these two has given birth to the idea that Falstaff is Hal's surrogate father and moral advisor. It's an interesting notion. All is interrupted, though, when they learn the Sheriff has arrived to arrest Falstaff for robbery. He questions Hal about the whereabouts of a "gross fat man" and Prince Hal denies he is at the tavern, to protect the knight.

Rebellion Is Brewing

As the rebels convene in Wales, they talk and argue about how they might divide up England when they triumph over the king. The group consists of Hotspur, Glendower, Mortimer (Hotspur's brother-in-law who was once Glendower's prisoner), and Worcester. The meeting gets heated when Hotspur and Glendower scuffle over the size of Hotspur's portion of land, and Glendower is offended by the exchange.

On the eve of the rebellion, King Henry chastises the prince for his irresponsible behavior and choice of friends.

 TIMELESS SOLILOQUIES

> Hotspur and Falstaff's speeches about honor are in striking counterpoint. Both present highly unrealistic perspectives on the ideal—Hotspur is so ambitious, he will chase any opportunity to demonstrate honor in battle, even before his own rebel army is ready. Ironically, the irresponsible knight Falstaff, by contrast, would do anything to avoid risking his life for a military cause. Here are excerpts to illustrate their views:
>
> Hotspur: (while ranting about King Henry's ingratitude for his family's support of his overthrow of Richard II)
> By heave, methinks it were an easy leap,
> To pluck bright honor from the pale-fac'd moon,
> Or dive into the bottom of the deep,
> Where fadom-line could never touch the ground,
> And pluck up drowned honor by the locks,
> So he that doth redeem her thence might wear

Chapter 16. Henry IV, Part I

> Without corrival all her dignities;
> But out upon this half-fac'd fellowship!
> (I.3.201-207)

Falstaff: (during the Battle at Shrewsbury)
> Though I could scape shot-free at London, I
> Fear the shot here, here's no scoring but upon the pate.
> Soft, who are you? Sir Walter Blunt. There's honor
> For you! Here's no vanity! I am as hot as molten lead,
> And as heavy too. God keep lead out of me!
> . . .
> I like not
> Such grinning honor as Sir Walter hath. Give me life,
> Which if I can save, so; if not, honor comes unlook'd
> For, and there's an end.
> [Exit]
> (V.3.30-34; 58-61)

By the end of the play, Prince Hal falls somewhere in the middle, don't you think? He abandons his dissolute ways, leads his father's army, kills Hotspur, and conquers the rebels.

The king is deeply concerned that Hal won't fulfill his duty as prince and help defend the kingdom. He denounces Hal's unreadiness for battle and the throne, holding up Hotspur's military leadership as an example:

King:
> Now by my scepter, and my soul to boot,
> He hath more worthy interest to the state
> Than thou the shadow of succession.
> For of no right, nor color like to right,
> He doth fill fields with harness in the realm,
> Turns head against the lion's armed jaws,
> And being no more in debt to years than thou,
> Leads ancient lords and reverend bishops on
> To bloody battles and to bruising arms.
> (III.2. 97-105)

When he hears his own behavior contrasted with Hotspur's impressive military success, Prince Hal apologizes for his irresponsible, unprincely behavior and promises to do better.

In the Rebel Camp

Let's cut away to the rebel camp where Hotspur, Worcester, and Douglas are lying in wait. We get the first signs that the offensive may be compromised, though, when these three get word that Mortimer is ill and Glendower's troops will be delayed another two weeks. But in spite of this news, the heady Hotspur is eager to move forward and fight. Worcester would prefer to wait for more military support.

When King Henry sends a message offering to negotiate for peace, Hotspur lambastes his character and questionable right to the throne. Still, Worcester and Vernon are sent to discuss a possible peace. When the king offers to pardon all the rebels if they will give up the fight, Worcester opts not to tell Hotspur about the offer. He's afraid Hotspur will give in, and he doesn't trust the king anyway.

The Battle of Shrewsbury gets underway. Prince Hal leads King Henry's army and bravely kills Hotspur in hand-to-hand combat. He even offers a touching eulogy for his enemy. In a final twist, Falstaff (whom Hal has presumed dead on the battlefield) grabs his sword, stabs the dead Hotspur, and insists on getting credit for it!

Chapter 16. Henry IV, Part I

Keanu Reeves (foreground), performed Scott Favor and River Phoenix played Mike Waters in My Own Private Idaho *(1991), Gus Van Sant's reimagining of* Henry IV, Parts I and II *and* Henry V.
(Photo Courtesy of Photofest)

Concerns About Kingship and the Growth of a King

What does it take to be a good king? How does a conscientious monarch like King Henry reconcile past sins, which he sees as personally immoral but for the good of England? At the root of *Henry IV, Parts I and II* and *Henry V* is a basic question—can a person be a just and able ruler and retain personal integrity? We infer from King Henry's self-doubt and self-blame that kings must, by nature, operate somewhere outside the moral framework of ordinary individuals.

Shakespeare develops this theme even further in the drama surrounding Prince Hal, showing how he puts away bad ways and influences and lives up to King Henry's expectations. In presenting Prince Hal's personal journey, Shakespeare wanted us to compare Prince Hal to Hotspur, who is eager for power, and Falstaff, who greatly influences Hal and believes the pleasures of life are as important as a knight's honorable service to his country.

Weighing the virtues and vices of Hal, Hotspur, and Falstaff, you should draw your own conclusions about which combination makes for the best king. Ultimately, Hotspur's rash decision to attack Henry's army before his ranks fully convene proves fatal to his campaign and his men. And for all of Falstaff's brilliant speech about the overrated virtue of honor, would you want to live in a world ruled by the likes of him? Just who would keep the order and the peace? Falstaff rejects responsibility and feels beholden to no one. He is a witty anarchist. Bottom line—Prince Hal can straddle the worlds of Hotspur and Falstaff. But to become like his father, he has to take on Hotspur in the Battle of Shrewsbury. To prove himself worthy, he cleans up his act and leaves his Boar's Head Tavern life and cronies for good.

"A KINGDOM FOR A STAGE"

In 1981, actor John Goodman played Falstaff at the New York Shakespeare Festival in Central Park. Other prominent film productions of *Henry IV, Part I* include Orson Welles's highly acclaimed *Chimes at Midnight* (1965), a conflation of *Henry IV, Parts 1 and 2*; a 1979 BBC-TV version featuring Anthony Quayle as Falstaff; the 1991 film *My Own Private Idaho*, directed by Gus Van Sant, a modern tale about two gay men whose characters are inspired by Shakespeare's; and a 2005 production at the National Theatre in London directed by Nicholas Hytner.

Onstage, the story of Hotspur's rebellion against King Henry's court has often been overshadowed by the raucous, drunken merrymaking of Jack Falstaff and his hilarious sidekicks.

Actors on Acting: How to Play a Plausible King Henry

Mark Mineart is a veteran director and theatre educator, as well as a classically trained actor who has performed Shakespeare on Broadway and throughout the country. He has performed in numerous Shakespearean productions and could once recite the entire scripts of *King Lear* and *Macbeth* from memory!

Chapter 16. Henry IV, Part I

When Mineart played King Henry in a conflated version of *Henry IV, Parts I and II* for the University of Delaware's Professional Theatre Training Program in 1992, he learned that playing a king presents unique challenges to the modern actor. He offered a few acting fundamentals for emerging performers of Shakespeare.

"A KINGDOM FOR A STAGE"

Next to Falstaff, actors love playing the role of Hotspur, according to John Russell Brown in *Shakespeare in Performance: An Introduction Through Six Major Plays*. He recalls various takes on the overeager rebel: In 1930, John Gielgud made him seem as noble as Prince Hal. In 1945, Laurence Olivier affected a stutter to make him appear mentally overly hurried. In 1951, Michael Redgrave's Hotspur spoke impatiently in a Northumbrian (northern English) accent to appear perpetually ready for action.

"First of all, it's the crowd on the stage that truly makes a person seem kingly," Mineart said. "If the people onstage don't treat you like a king, you won't appear kingly." This requirement places certain demands on the acting company. "When actors play people in power, they make the mistake of moving around too much, and they overdo. This makes their actions appear too extreme to the audience," Mineart said. "A king doesn't need to move much. The world revolves around him because he's powerful. When they perform a role with power, actors today need to learn to be still and just speak, and move the world without words."

FACTS TO REMEMBER

- *Henry IV, Part I* offers rich contrasts between characters that inhabit the court, the military, and the raucous tavern.
- Through his friendship with Falstaff, Prince Hal learns about the person he is and his future role as king.
- Hotspur, Falstaff, and Hal represent different views about honor, an important theme.
- How Prince Hal grows and readies himself for kingship is a key concern in the play.
- On the stage, the play showcases the towering knight Jack Falstaff, the star of the minor plot.
- Broadway actor Mark Mineart maintains that "less is more" in word and gesture when an actor plays a king or a powerful personage.

Chapter 17
Henry V

> **INTRODUCTION**
> - The play's focus on war and a synopsis of the main plot
> - Tips about King Henry and other key characters in *Henry V*
> - The important function of the Chorus
> - Shakespeare's vision of kingship and other themes
> - Olivier, Branagh, and Hiddleston re-create *Henry V* on film

If you're just getting acquainted with Shakespeare's major history plays, *Henry V* may be a tough play to love. Unlike *Henry IV, Parts I and II*, which feature Falstaff and Prince Hal, *Henry V* is an epic about war. It is loosely based on the experience of the English king who invaded France during the Hundred Years War. The play is full of memorable lines, offering a patriotic drama about kingship and the vagaries of military conflict. (Critics opposed to this view feel Shakespeare is satirizing the hypocrisy of Henry V as he prosecutes the war. But here we'll take the play and the king at face value.)

Shakespeare relied on Raphael Holinshed's *Chronicles of England, Scotland, and Ireland* as a primary source. King Henry displays very little psychological development in *Henry V*, but his tactical and verbal skills are definitely on display. War itself and how the English and French prosecute their campaigns are the real stories here. And to ensure that the spotlight stays on Henry,

Part 4. The Histories

Shakespeare opted to kill off Falstaff, his legendary comedian and anarchist, early in the story.

Henry V was one of the first plays performed by the Lord Chamberlain's Men in 1599 at the Globe theatre. The play's stirring speeches make for good war propaganda. (The Act five allusion to Lord Essex and his 1599 campaign to quell the Irish rebellion wasn't lost on Shakespeare's audiences.) The strong rhetoric partly accounts for the play's popularity on the English stage since the eighteenth century. *Henry V* is staged less often in North America. Directors often re-fashion the play to suit a national mood during wartime.

The Characters

Note: *Henry V* is not a strict sequel to *Henry IV, Parts I and II* (refer to Chapters 16 and Appendix A). The lineup of key characters is inconsistent with the previous histories.

Chorus (or Epilogue)—Unlike the Chorus in *Romeo and Juliet*, which foreshadows the sad tale's outcome, *Henry V*'s Chorus asks us to make an imaginative leap to place ourselves in the heart of the play's far-flung landscape of southern England and northern France.

THE ENGLISH COURT

King Henry V—This more mature version of Prince Hal bears little resemblance to the dissolute tavern buddy of Falstaff in *Henry IV, Parts I and II*. In this play Henry is a patriotic, forthright, and resolute monarch who is single-minded in grabbing the French throne. Shakespeare appears interested in probing the king's motives as much as he did the prince's in earlier histories. Now that he is king, Henry possesses none of the ambivalence of Hal, his former self. Though the French nobles take Henry for a dissolute merrymaker unfit to be king, Exeter reminds the Dauphin, "You'll find Harry different from his greener days."

Humphrey, Duke of Gloucester—A brother of King Henry V.

Chapter 17. Henry V

John, Duke of Bedford—A brother of King Henry V (formerly Duke of Lancaster).

Thomas, Duke of Clarence—A brother of King Henry V.

Duke of Exeter—Uncle of King Henry V.

English Noblemen and Commanders

Duke of York—Cousin of Henry V.

Earl of Salisbury

Earl of Warwick

Earl of Westmerland

Sir Thomas Erpingham

THE FRENCH COURT

The French King (Charles VI)—Actors have injected different levels of fortitude and resolve into the role of the French king.

Lewis (the Dauphin)—The heir to the French throne is a much more warlike, aggressive version of his father. The French king's son and heir to the French throne sends a gift of tennis balls to the English king, as a veiled warning to stop trying to forge an alliance with the discontented dukes who are at odds with the French king. The gift is a calculated, witty jab, however, designed to remind Henry of his youthful, irresponsible past. The gesture insults King Henry and makes him that much more determined to invade France.

Princess Katherine—Daughter of King Charles VI and Isabel. Though her part is not a large one, Katherine's two big scenes are critical to providing comic relief and showing a softer side to the warrior King Henry.

Queen Isabel—Queen of France and mother of Katherine.

Dukes of Burgundy, Orleance, Britain, Bourbon, Berri, and Beaumont.

The Constable of France

Lords Rambures and Grandpré—Two French lords.

Governor of Harfleur

Montjoy—The French herald.

French Ambassadors to England

OFFICERS IN KING HENRY'S ARMY

Gower—The Englishman.

Fluellen—The Welshman.

Jamy—The Scot.

Macmorris—The Irishman.

SOLDIERS IN KING HENRY'S ARMY

John Bates

Alexander Court

Michael Williams

THE TRAITORS

Richard, Earl of Cambridge

Henry, Lord Scroop of Masham

Sir Thomas Grey

FALSTAFF'S FORMER COMPANIONS

Pistol

Nym

Bardolf

Hostess Quickly—Pistol's wife, hostess of the Boar's Head Tavern in Eastcheap; called Mistress Quickly in *Henry IV*.

Boy

Archbishop of Canterbury

Bishop of Ely

Duke of Burgundy

Alice—Lady-in-Waiting to Princess Katherine.

French Ambassadors to England

French Messengers

English Herald

Lords, Ladies, Officers, Soldiers, Citizens, and Attendants

Setting: England and France (specifically Normandy)

"O for a Muse of Fire"—Gentles, Let Your Imaginations Run Wild!

In the first two acts, the Prologue and Chorus warn us that the stage is woefully inadequate for representing a tale set in England and northern France. The Chorus persists in reminding us to re-create the play's vast landscape in our minds.

> . . .   Follow! Follow!
> Grapple your minds to sternage of this navy,
> And leave your England as dead midnight, still, . . .
> . . .
> Work, work your thoughts, and therein see a siege;
> Behold the ordinance on their carriages,
> With fatal mouths gaping on girded Harflew.
> . . .   Still be kind,
> And eche out our performance with your mind.
> (III.Chorus.17-20; 25-27; 34-35)

"A KINGDOM FOR A STAGE"

Laurence Olivier's 1944 film cleverly captures the self-referential message in the Chorus' opening address. By splicing scenes of actors dressing backstage and a flurry of activity in the wings, we never forget we are watching a stage play about war. Released while World War II was still raging, Olivier's *Henry V* is highly patriotic but also serio-comic, particularly in its silly send-up of the Bishop's dry lecture on the origin and merit of the Salic Law in France.

When you hear the Chorus speak before each act, you'll be struck by its self-reflexive tone, as if Shakespeare himself is talking to you directly from the page, apologizing for the inadequacy of his stage.

Henry Gets Down to Business—Contemplating War and Catching Traitors

While the French ambassador waits to speak with King Henry, we are treated to an unusual scene. The king wants to know if he has a legal and moral justification for ruling France. The Bishop of Canterbury offers a long and terribly dry explanation of the Salic Law. Based on his interpretation of the centuries-old document, the Bishop assures Henry that he has a valid claim to the French throne.

A Laid-Back Prince Hal Takes on a New Identity

Take note that King Henry carries the weight of all of England on his shoulders. And personally, this king bears little resemblance to the onetime ne'er-do-well prince who helped his father win the Battle of Shrewsbury (refer to Chapter 16 and Appendix A). We quickly surmise that the young King Henry has come a long way from his youthful, careless days. Early on, there is ample evidence that the young King Henry is well respected by his court, religious leaders, and people. In the play's first scene, in which the Archbishop of Canterbury and Bishop of Ely converse, the archbishop credits King Henry

Chapter 17. Henry V

with becoming a "sudden scholar" and reforming his conduct after his father died. Here, we get the sense that the king is considered knowledgeable about religion, politics, oratory, and how to put those skills into action.

King Henry shows his strength in his delightful response to the French ambassador, who has just delivered a warning from the Dauphin (heir to the French throne). The ambassador orders the king to cease his bargaining with disgruntled French dukes and cheekily presents him with a mysterious gift of tennis balls. Henry is stung by the veiled insult implied in such a frivolous gift, intended to remind him of his reckless youth. In a poetic show of wit, Henry promises to "play a set" that will overshadow the Dauphin's insulting gesture. Next King Henry orders his nobles to prepare for war and promises to "chide this Dolphin at his father's door." Dauphin, beware!

In Southampton, on the southern English coast, Henry's fleet must wait for him to deal with a treacherous plot by three once-loyal friends—Cambridge, Scroop, and Gray. The three have been plotting to have him killed in a deal they worked out with some unnamed French nobles. Henry publicly exposes their crime and arrests them. Then he orders his fleet to sail to Harfleur, a town that is overshadowed today by the populous city of Le Havre on the Normandy coast.

Revisiting the Boar's Head Tavern Crew from Eastcheap

Though their role is greatly diminished in *Henry V*, several of Henry's former drinking companions from *Henry IV, Parts I and II*, figure in this play. They include Pistol, Nym, Bardolf, and Hostess Quickly (who has become Pistol's wife). In one important scene, Falstaff has just died and Hostess Quickly retells the story of his death in a sad lament. These characters are but a shadow of their lively portraits in the earlier histories, but they play an important role. As Henry dazzles us with his rhetoric and looms large as king, the Eastcheap crowd represents the real people of England. They remind us that the little guys do the fighting and dying, that their families suffer the most, and that war is never as dignified as Henry's pomp and oratory.

Rallying the Troops at Harfleur and Agincourt

For the remaining three acts, Shakespeare transplants us from the English coast to the shores and soil of Normandy. At the start of Act three, the Chorus directs us to imagine the English ships setting sail for France: "Play with your fancies, and in them behold/ Upon the hempen tackle ship-boys, climbing." We are spirited along dramatically as Henry engages in three key conquests—a plan to besiege Harfleur, the Battle of Agincourt in the vast fields south of Calais, and a proposal of marriage to the French princess!

Four army captains from different British regions lighten the grave tone of Henry's attack on France. Shakespeare has fun with the interplay of their contrasting dialects. The men include Gower (English), Fluellen (Welsh), Jamy (Scottish), and Macmorris (Irish). Two of them speak below, offering different pronunciations of a common English greeting:

Jamy:	I say gud day, Captain Fluellen.
Fluellen:	God-den to your worship, good Captain James. (III.2.3-85)

At Harfleur Henry rouses his troops with a speech that still has a familiar ring:

> Once more unto the breach, dear friends, once more;
> Or close the wall up with our English dead.
> In peace there's nothing so becomes a man
> As modest stillness and humility;
> (III.1.1-4)

When the army arrives at the city gates, Henry warns the citizens about the calamity they're about to face. Frightened by the prospect of being annihilated, the governor of Harfleur surrenders.

Chapter 17. Henry V

A Bloody Victory at Agincourt

After taking Harfleur easily, Henry takes on the superior French army near the medieval castle of Agincourt. During these scenes Shakespeare allows us to peek into the minds and souls of men in both camps. The French nobles seem overconfident, but that's not surprising because they have at least five times more men than the English! The English, of course, are aware of the disparity and are understandably concerned.

Two scenes in Act four, imbued with Henry's rhetoric, continue to inspire audiences. These moments give Henry (and the theatre audience) good reason for pause, to weigh the personal sacrifice of the common soldier against the "higher duty" of a Christian king.

TIMELESS SOLILOQUIES

On the eve of the Battle of Agincourt (in Act four), Henry visits his troops disguised as a soldier under Captain Thomas Erpingham. His conversations with soldiers John Bates and Michael Williams raise questions about whether a soldier can be blamed if his king wages an unjust war.

Bates: ... If his cause be wrong, our obedience to the King wipes the crime of it out of us.
(IV.1.132-133)

Williams: ... I am afeared there are few die well that die in a battle; for how can they charitably dispose of any thing, when blood is their argument? Now, if these men do not die well, it will be a black matter for the King that led them to it; who to disobey were against all proportion of subjection.
(IV.1.141-146)

In the second of these moments, Henry delivers his now-famous battle cry (known as the "St. Crispin's Day speech"), rallying his troops to meet the much-larger enemy on the field. (By the way, St. Crispian was an early Christian martyr.)

King Henry: This day is call'd the feast of Crispian:
He that outlives this day, and comes safe home,
Will stand a' tiptoe when this day is named,
And rouse him at the name of Crispian.
He that shall see this day, and live old age,
Will yearly on the vigil feast his neighbors,
And say, "To-morrow is Saint Crispian." . . .
We few, we happy few, we band of brothers;
For he to-day that sheds his blood with me
Shall be my brother; . . .
(IV.3.40-46; 60-62)

By the way, you're probably wondering how the French managed to lose despite such odds. In the early fifteenth century, they thought it honorable for the noble ranks of the cavalry to ride up front. During this battle, when the band of English archers fired their first rash of arrows from their longbows, they disabled the horses of the French cavalry. The nobles fell to the ground, crushed and debilitated by their armor, while the infantry charged from behind.

Chapter 17. Henry V

BBC-TV produced Shakespeare's Henry V *in 2012 as part of its first* Hollow Crown *film cycle, which recreates Shakespeare's major historical tetralogy (that also includes* Richard II *and* Henry IV, Parts I and II*). Pictured are Tom Hiddleston (center) in the title role of Henry V, flanked from left by Joseph Paterson (Duke of York), Richard Clothier (Earl of Salisbury), and James Laurenson (Westmoreland).*

(Photo Courtesy of Photofest)

The Salic Law, King Henry, and Thoughts About Kingship

King Henry takes careful steps before he decides to wage war against the French. To justify his invasion, Henry had to learn whether an ancient law that required the throne to pass through the female line applied in France. The French nobles maintained that it did apply, but Henry had knowledge of how the French themselves had violated that law. Satisfying himself that it didn't apply, he could wage his war in good conscience.

Although *Henry V* often takes a hit by critics who prefer King Henry in his colorful youth, the play and its protagonist deserve to be judged on their own terms. In King Henry, Shakespeare shows us a confident young king willing to take a huge political risk, not unlike his historical namesake. He shows courage in taking this risk, and it pays off. Against huge odds, the outnumbered English army defeats the overconfident French, winning the right to rule France. That is, until Henry VI, King Henry's son, loses it again in 1453. (The real Henry V took the throne in 1413 and won the Battle of Agincourt in 1415.)

Beginning with *Henry IV, Parts I and II*, Shakespeare uses his multipart chronicle to probe the issue of kingship in Britain. What does it take for a person to be a good monarch, and how does the position of king or queen compromise the individual's personal and moral duties to his subjects? Shakespeare probes these issues in *Henry V*. Through the words of Bates and Williams, Shakespeare forces us to consider disparities between a king's duty to his subjects and a lone soldier's moral duty to his nation, especially when his king engages in an unjust war. For elegantly raising such questions, Shakespeare is credited by Harold Bloom for ushering in humanism, the Renaissance prism of perspective that moderns take for granted when we write plays, novels, and movie scripts.

To Seal His Conquest, Henry Proposes to Princess Katherine

> Is it possible dat I sould love de ennemie of France?
> (V.II.170)

In contrast to Shakespeare's other histories, *Henry V* is concluded with a marriage proposal and a royal wedding. In the 1944 film that he directed and starred in, Laurence Olivier manages to appear suave, sexy, and maybe a little too sophisticated when the triumphant Henry is wooing the French princess. (Still, when the debonair actor produces awkward French, he seems to come across as a plain king.) Renee Asherson's performance as Princess Katherine is, by turns, demur, stubborn, and coy, forcing the English king to work hard for his prize.

Chapter 17. Henry V

VERSE BY VERSE

As Henry's troops move toward Harfleur, Shakespeare interjects a comical scene involving Princess Katherine as she tries to learn a few words of English from Alice, her gentlewoman. She gets on a roll and her French-accented pronunciation of English starts to sound a bit filthy! Here's what happens after she masters "d'hand, de fingers, de nails . . ."

Katherine:	Comment appelez-vous le pied et la robe? *(How do you say 'foot' and 'gown'?)*
Alice:	Le foot, madame, et le count.
Katherine:	Le foot et le count? O Seigneur Dieu! ils sont les mots de son mauvais, corruptible, gros, et impudique, et non pour les dames de honneur d'user. *(Oh, my God, these words are bad, corrupt, ugly, and shameless, and not for honorable ladies to use.)* (III.4.50-54)

Oops! To Katherine's delicate ears, "foot" sounds like the French word "foutre," meaning "to fuck." Her mispronunciation of "gown" as "count" sounds like "cunt"!

Branagh got plenty of flack from highbrow stage critics when he caved in to the TV-weaned masses in making *Henry V*. But don't pay attention to that. At age 27, after having performed the role of King Henry starting at age 24, Branagh created a heroic film that continues to inspire. The young director drew his own inspiration from contemporary war movies like *Platoon*. In the scene when Henry (Branagh) woos Princess Katherine (Emma Thompson), the young director/actor transfers the magic of his stage charisma to the screen. With the understated, youthful impatience that Branagh did so well, the young English king comes off more like Shakespeare intended—as a plain warrior king who is less sophisticated than the lady he pursues.

Henry V in Performance

Henry V lends itself to productions that emphasize its patriotic strains and glorify a king and hero. Before World War II, showings at London's Old Vic and Drury Lane theatres must have been particularly inspiring. Laurence Olivier's 1944 film offered a poignant message about heroism to the Western allies. When Michael Bogdanov and Michael Pennington directed *Henry V* for the English Shakespeare Company in the late 1980s, there were allusions to the 1982 Falkland Islands war between the U.K. and Argentina. Kenneth Branagh's star-studded movie in 1989 also invited easy parallels between Shakespeare's King Henry and the British government.

> **FACTS TO REMEMBER**
> - Before each act begins, Shakespeare's Chorus reminds us that the stage cannot technically do justice to a cross-continental dramatization of war.
> - *Henry V* is a play that explores the nature of war and how an ambitious warrior king tries to regain French lands ruled by English kings in the eleventh through thirteenth centuries.
> - Scenes featuring Prince Hal's old Boar's Head tavern drinking companions and French Princess Katherine provide refreshing comic relief.
> - When he visits his troops incognito, King Henry hears hard questions about warrior kings and morality.

Part 5
The Tragedies

Part 5. The Tragedies

Many of Shakespeare's greatest plays are tragedies. But when we speak of *tragedy* inside the theatre, the meaning is different from the significance of a monumental human tragedy such as the grievous events of September 11th.

Shakespearean tragedy focuses on what happens when a larger-than-life figure—a king or a noble—is subjected to an intensive moral and psychological crisis and fails to overcome the adversity he faces. Often this character's downfall occurs as a result of some inherent tragic flaw.

You've heard of the legends, or *protagonists*, of Shakespearean tragedy—highborn men and women such as Hamlet, King Lear, Macbeth, and Cleopatra. Their flawed actions and decision-making have an irreversible, fatal effect on everyone around them.

In a Shakespearean tragedy, the body count can be as high as the main character's precipitous fall from power! And someone's always getting maligned, betrayed, stabbed, or poisoned. Watching these plays will remind you a little of watching an old-style shoot 'em up Western or a Quentin Tarantino movie. The following great tragedies represent Shakespearean theatre at its best.

Chapter 18

Romeo and Juliet

> **INTRODUCTION**
> - The poetry and breathless pace of one of Shakespeare's most romantic plays
> - A look at the major characters in *Romeo and Juliet*
> - The story of the two lovers and famous speeches you already know
> - Brilliant puns, bawdy wordplay, and what makes this blockbuster tragedy so sexy
> - How Shakespeare adapted his source in *Romeo and Juliet*
> - Notable performances of this tragedy on the stage and screen

Romeo and Juliet—it has a familiar ring, doesn't it? You probably read the play in high school. Written around 1595-96, it's the story of a young girl and boy who fall in love, in spite of the festering hate between their families that threatens to destroy Verona, Italy. The play ends when Romeo and Juliet kill themselves—he takes poison and she stabs herself. You may also remember seeing *West Side Story*, Leonard Bernstein's popular musical adaptation of the tale set in Spanish Harlem.

Romeo and Juliet is the best of Shakespeare's early tragedies. Its poetry, pace, and mood have more in common with festive comedies like *A Midsummer*

PART 5. THE TRAGEDIES

Night's Dream than they do with late, psychological tragedies like *King Lear* and *Macbeth*. The play has a higher percentage of rhymed lines than all of Shakespeare's tragedies and all but three comedies. Attune your ear to Shakespeare's sound garden, and you'll hear the beauty of the blank verse and the rhymed couplets and octets. These characters even speak in sonnets!

Romeo and Juliet is distinctive because it moves at an incredibly fast pace. The lovers meet, marry, and die, all in less than a week. Unlike the late tragedies, the story is not *tragic* in a classic sense—as a result of an individual's flawed nature or behavior—but because of circumstances beyond the couple's control.

The Characters

Escalus—The Prince of Verona warns both families to stop their fighting, but like any of us who come from small communities, the prince is probably related to the Montagues and Capulets both.

THE MONTAGUES

Romeo—The only son of old Montague and his wife appears to be something of a dreamer. In Verona, Romeo has a good reputation, even among the Capulet family. When Romeo speaks about his love for Rosaline, a woman he can't have, his speech is formal and eloquent. But when he meets Juliet, Romeo falls in love at first sight and discovers what love is all about. She stirs him with authentic passion, not some dreamy notion about love that fools him into thinking he loves Rosaline. His love for Juliet is both precious and forbidden.

Mercutio—This kinsman of the prince and a friend of Romeo has a character that is true to his mythical namesake, Mercury, the god with a changeable, "mercurial" nature. Mercutio is aggressive and seems to be arrogant and hotheaded, until he is stabbed. His jest at this moment lends insight into the wise and thinking individual he is. As a foil (or contrast) to Romeo, his verbal sparring and speeches dwell on the carnal attractions between men and women.

Chapter 18. Romeo and Juliet

Benvolio—Romeo's cousin and friend, the nephew of Montague, is mild-mannered and good-hearted. He poses a striking contrast to Mercutio. In Italian his name is translated as "ben volio" or good will, which suggests his role as peacemaker among the warring families.

Montague and Lady Montague—Romeo's parents, whose kinsmen engage in constant feuding with the Capulet family.

THE CAPULETS

Juliet—The Capulet's only child is under 14, but after she meets Romeo she seems of an age beyond her years. She has no interest in marrying Paris, a man her father has chosen for her, and determines to escape the fate they have in store the same day she is supposed to marry Paris. If you get to know the play, you'll see that Juliet is one of Shakespeare's most sublime heroines. She is the heart of the play's wisdom and lyricism. In talking of love, she is also the most eloquent.

Nurse—Juliet's nurse has been with her from the time she was born. She is religious, but quite down-to-earth. We meet her onstage before we meet Juliet and discover that she can be quite funny and quite bawdy. The nurse helps set the tone for many scenes in the play, keeping the mood lighthearted when it might seem more serious.

Tybalt—Juliet's cousin, the nephew of Lady Capulet, can be rash, high-minded, brave, and a loyal defender of the Capulet family.

Old Capulet and Lady Capulet—Juliet's parents.

Petruchio—A follower of Tybalt.

OTHERS

Friar Lawrence—A Franciscan friar who helps Romeo and Juliet make the necessary arrangements to get married.

Paris—This young aristocrat is referred to by Juliet's father as County Paris. He is considered a suitable husband for Juliet—according to her parents, that is. He is the prince's kinsman.

Friar John—Also a Franciscan.

Balthasar—A servant of Romeo.

Abram—A servant of old Montague.

Sampson, Gregory, Clown—Capulet servants.

An Old Man—Part of the Capulet family.

Peter

Page—Belonging to Paris.

Apothecary

Three Musicians

Citizens of Verona

Gentlemen and Gentlewomen of both houses

Maskers, Torch-bearers, Pages, Guards, Watchmen, Servants, and Attendants

Setting: Verona and Mantua, in northern Italy

Family Feud in "Fair Verona"

When you have an opportunity to see *Romeo and Juliet* in the theatre, notice that a single actor recites the opening prologue. This lyrical sonnet, attributed in the script to the Chorus, puts you squarely in the world of two rival families of Verona. Interestingly, the prologue sums up the action of the entire play and warns you to expect the demise of the two stars!

> Two households, both alike in dignity,
> In fair Verona where we lay our scene,
> From ancient grudge break to new mutiny,

Chapter 18. Romeo and Juliet

> Where civil blood makes civil hands unclean.
> From forth the fatal loins of these two foes,
> A pair of star-cross'd lovers take their life;
> (I.Prologue.1-6)

But "fair Verona" doesn't seem so fair according to this description. Servants and feisty young men toting swords, who belong to the rival Montague and Capulet families, scuffle regularly. When Prince Escalus appears on the scene, he's had enough of the chaos and bloodshed.

When the prince addresses the Montague and Capulet heads of household, he rails against those who disrupt the community with constant brawls. Hoping to stop the never-ending family feuding, he issues an ultimatum: if anyone from either side disturbs the peace again, the perpetrator will die.

Young Love Amid Bloody Swordfights

Meanwhile, Romeo's family is a bit worried about him. He's acting strangely. His cousin Benvolio—a Montague, remember—tries to figure out what his problem is. It turns out that Romeo is heartsick over Rosaline, but she won't have anything to do with him. (By the way, Rosaline is a Capulet, but Romeo keeps this little fact to himself.)

Now, cut to the Capulet household for a moment. Juliet, who's not yet 14, has caught the eye of Paris, a nobleman. Though her father thinks she's a little too young to marry, he permits Paris to court her at the dance, or "masque," he is planning to throw that same evening. Romeo manages to learn about the party from a Capulet servant, so he makes plans to crash the party in disguise, just to get a closer look at Rosaline.

Mercutio Teases Romeo

Romeo, Benvolio, and their friend Mercutio arrive at the Capulets' masked ball. But seeing that Romeo is feeling rather moody, Mercutio begins to spar with his good friend. On stage, the wit combat Shakespeare wrote for these two is some of his best of all time. And it's not G-rated either, a fact that your high school teachers may conveniently overlook (particularly if you didn't bother to read the explanatory footnotes)!

TIMELESS SOLILOQUIES

The musical wordplay and combative wit of Mercutio and Romeo in Act two is electric. It's enough to make you want to take acting lessons and audition for one of these parts. Notice the alliteration in this bold talk.

Mercutio: (before Romeo enters)
    Alas, poor Romeo, he is already dead, stabb'd with a white wench's black eye, run through the ear with a love-song, the very pin of his heart cleft with the blind bow-boy's butt-shaft;
    (II.4.13-16)

Romeo: O single-sol'd jest, soly singular for the singleness!
    (II.4.66)

The verbal dueling in this scene climaxes with Mercutio's "Queen Mab" speech. In it, Romeo's friend lets out a fantastical diatribe—a riff of sorts—in response to the lovelorn Romeo's self-indulgent preoccupation with his love for the aloof Rosaline. This is Mercutio's tour de force, where he commands the attention of the nearby partygoers. In *Shakespeare in Performance*, John Russell Brown reminds us that the Queen Mab speech allows the actor playing Mercutio to give us insight into Mercutio's true personality.

Mercutio: O then I see Queen Mab hath been with you.
               She is the fairies' midwife, and she comes
               In shape no bigger than an agot-stone
               On the forefinger of an alderman,
               Drawn with a team of little atomi
               Over men's noses as they lie asleep.
               . . .

Chapter 18. Romeo and Juliet

> And in this state she gallops night by night
> Through lovers' brains, and then they dream of love;
> [O'er] courtiers' knees, that dream on cur'sies straight;
> O'er lawyers' fingers, who straight dream on fees;
> O'er ladies' lips, who straight on kisses dream,
> Which oft the angry Mab with blisters plagues,
> Because their breath with sweetmeats tainted are.
> ...
> This is the hag, when maids lie on their backs,
> That presses them and learns them first to bear,
> Making them women of good carriage.
> This is she—
> (I.4.53-58; 70-76; 92-94)

Who is Queen Mab anyway? She's no "queen" at all in the modern sense. She's a Celtic fairy creature of Shakespeare's imagination. In Mercutio's vision she's the immortal who puts crazy notions about love into our heads, influencing our dreams. But Mab is also a dark spirit who makes virgins pregnant—not a pretty picture. This incubus visits the dreams of a parson, a soldier, and a virgin, and Mercutio gives us a bawdy take on what each of them learns from her. (Even her name is a double pun—"Quean" and "Mab" were also slang terms for a slut.)

Part 5. The Tragedies

Carlo Carlei directs Christian Cooke (as Mercutio), Douglas Booth (Romeo), and Ed Westwick (Tybalt) in a fight scene from the 2013 production of Romeo and Juliet. *Scriptwriter Julian Fellowes has been roundly criticized for rewriting Shakespeare's original script, having assumed that the average moviegoer lacks the training to follow Elizabethan English.*

(Photo Courtesy of Photofest.)

Instant Love and a Sonnet

After Mercutio is interrupted by Romeo and cools down, the boys venture inside the Capulet household where the party is going strong. When Romeo lays eyes on Juliet, it's love at first sight. (You'll have to suspend your disbelief when you watch this scene. You would think that Romeo would know Juliet is a Capulet and off-limits.) In a stroke of genius, Shakespeare allows them to share a 14-line sonnet.

Chapter 18. Romeo and Juliet

VERSE BY VERSE

When you read *Romeo and Juliet*, see if you can count how many lines they share. And take note when you watch the play. You'll see how Shakespeare's clever use of the *shared line* (or *split line*) reinforces how much this passionate pair identify with and love each other. The shared line is one 10-syllable line of iambic pentameter spoken by two actors instead of one.

Romeo: [To Juliet.] If I profane with my unworthiest hand
This holy shrine, the gentle sin is this,
My lips, two blushing pilgrims, ready stand
To smooth that rough touch with a tender kiss.

Juliet: Good pilgrim, you do wrong your hand too much,
Which mannerly devotion shows in this:
For saints have hands that pilgrims' hands do touch,
And palm to palm is holy palmers' kiss.

Romeo: Have not saints lips, and holy palmers too?

Juliet: Ay, pilgrim, lips that they must use in pray'r.

Romeo: O then, dear saint, let lips do what hands do,
They pray—grant thou, lest faith turn to despair.

Juliet: Saints do not move, though grant for prayers' sake.

Romeo: Then move not while my prayer's effect I take.
[Kissing her.]
(I.5.93-106)

Juliet's cousin Tybalt gets predictably furious when he discovers that a rival Montague gang member has crashed his uncle's party. But Romeo has a solid, upright reputation, so the elder Capulet refuses to allow Tybalt to start a row over Romeo's presence. Still, Romeo is playing a dangerous game. In this highly charged atmosphere, the young lovers make their acquaintance. From this point, the suspense continues to build.

A Secret Wedding

Romeo and Juliet have fallen in love, but in the Prologue (Act two) we're reminded of the difficulty of their situation. Juliet ponders her quandary in a famous speech from this play:

Juliet: O Romeo, Romeo, wherefore art thou Romeo?
Deny thy father and refuse thy name;
Or, if thou wilt not, be but sworn my love,
And I'll no longer be a Capulet.

Romeo: [Aside.] Shall I hear more, or shall I speak at this?

Juliet: 'Tis but thy name that is my enemy;
Thou art thyself, though not a Montague.
What's Montague? It is nor hand nor foot,
Nor arm nor face, [nor any other part]
Belonging to a man. O, be some other name!
What's in a name? That which we call a rose
By any other word would smell as sweet;
So Romeo would, were he not Romeo call'd,
Retain that dear perfection which he owes
Without that title. Romeo, doff thy name,
And for thy name, which is no part of thee,
Take all myself.
(II.2.33-49)

In Juliet's now-familiar lines she asks why Romeo has the same name as her family's enemy. She questions the value of names in general, implying that Romeo would be just as perfect with any other name. In other words, his name cannot possibly sully her view of him, even if the name is Montague. While Juliet speaks these thoughts, Romeo is listening intently in her garden. Eventually he makes himself known and they discuss how they feel about each other in honest, straightforward terms. When the nurse begins calling Juliet from inside the house, the young girl speaks plainly. She tells Romeo that if his intentions are honorable and he wants marriage, to send word the next day about "Where and what time thou wilt perform the rite."

Romeo is eager to marry Juliet. It is daybreak and he visits Friar Lawrence in the hermitage where he lives. There he tells all and gets surprising support from this man of the cloth. Maybe if Romeo and Juliet marry, the Montagues and Capulets will stop killing one another.

As Romeo and Juliet take destiny into their own hands, the cruel hand of Fortune is plotting to lay waste to their future happiness. Back on the street we learn that Tybalt has challenged Romeo to a duel in a letter. Mercutio spouts off in great detail again, this time about Tybalt, a formidable Capulet opponent. Another street fight is brewing; Romeo has joined Mercutio; the Nurse gives Romeo Juliet's message; and, in turn, she gets word about his plan for a secret ceremony to be performed by the Friar. Juliet sneaks out of her house and meets up with Romeo, and the Friar whisks them off to church and marries them.

Romeo Avenges Mercutio's Death

From this moment, which begins Act three, things happen swiftly. We're back on the streets and Tybalt is spoiling for a fight. Romeo doesn't take the bait, apparently trying to finesse his way out of the conflict. This enrages Mercutio. With tempers flaring and testosterone seething, things get heated. Mercutio draws his sword and in the scuffle, Tybalt fatally stabs him.

As Mercutio is dying, he jokes while also delivering his famous curse, "A plague a' both your houses!" Watching his friend die, Romeo issues a retort using his sword and slays Tybalt to avenge his friend's death. The unthinkable has happened—Romeo has murdered Juliet's cousin. He quickly escapes the scene, knowing well that the Prince's punishment now hangs on his head. When the Prince appears and hears conflicting sides of the story, he exiles Romeo to enforce the law and keep the peace.

PART 5. THE TRAGEDIES

In the 1998 movie Shakespeare in Love, *the famed sixteenth-century actor Edward "Ned" Alleyn (Ben Affleck) plays a wise, imperious Mercutio in the film's imagining of Philip Henslowe's (Geoffrey Rush) production of* Romeo and Juliet *at the Curtain theatre.*

(Photo Courtesy of Photofest.)

A Ruse, a Letter, and a Sleeping Potion

Juliet's passionate yearning for Romeo is interrupted when the Nurse gives her the bad news about Tybalt. The girl tells the Nurse to summon Romeo, who is hiding out with the Friar. Meanwhile, the Friar tells Romeo things could be worse—he could have been sentenced to death! Romeo becomes upset when the Nurse tells him about Juliet's distress. The Friar takes matters into his own hands and orders Romeo to visit Juliet and consummate the marriage to cement the union. (Ironically, in the next scene, Old Capulet puts a plan in motion for Juliet to marry Paris in three days!)

Romeo and Juliet make love in her bedroom, but the rendezvous is all too short. At the first sign of light, Romeo flees to Mantua. When Juliet learns that the planned celebration centers on her wedding to Paris, she is shocked. She refuses to go through with the ceremony. As you might guess, it was unacceptable for a young girl to flout her parents this way. Amid curses from her father, both parents disown her. She doesn't even get sympathy from her Nurse.

The Poison of Despair

Paris's attempt to enlist the Friar's help comes to naught. The Friar has a plan: he gives Juliet a potion that will put her into a coma and make her appear dead. After her family buries her in the vault, she will lie asleep and Romeo will later come to her rescue.

Knowing she will escape from her predicament, Juliet makes peace with her parents. Fearful, she drinks the drug, lapses into a coma, and is later found "dead" by the Nurse.

Exiled, Romeo learns of Juliet's death, and here's where the Friar's plan goes awry. (In the next scene we learn that Friar John was supposed to give Romeo a letter telling him that Juliet was to fake her own death. A classic Shakespearean twist!) Thinking that all is lost, Romeo buys real poison from an apothecary in Mantua and sets off for Verona to kill himself at Juliet's tomb. Paris, who is already near the tomb, senses someone approaching and promptly steals out of sight. As Romeo opens Juliet's tomb, Paris recognizes him as Tybalt's murderer and insists that he must die. Provoked into a swordfight, Romeo slays Paris.

With Paris lying dead in the mausoleum, Romeo looks at the "dead" Juliet, who is actually still drugged. So he decides that it's time for him to join her. Lying at Juliet's side, he drinks poison and dies. All of this happens moments before the Friar rushes in, hoping to greet Juliet before she awakens. Juliet does awaken, but not soon enough to prevent Romeo's suicide, and not in time for the Friar to save her.

At the sight of her dead Romeo, Juliet is determined to join her lover in the grave. Taking Romeo's weapon, she stabs herself in the heart and says, "Oh happy dagger,/This is thy sheath."

When everyone convenes at the vault, the Friar confesses his guilt and the full story is known. Learning that their children are married, the foes vow to make a permanent peace. In a ringing epilogue, *Romeo and Juliet* ends with the Prince's elegant note of gloom:

> A glooming peace this morning with it brings,
> The sun for sorrow will not show his head.
> Go hence to have more talk of these sad things;
> Some shall be pardon'd, and some punished:
> For never was a story of more woe
> Than this of Juliet and her Romeo.
> (V.3.305-310)

How Shakespeare Transforms His Source

What do we make of this poetic tale of love, hate, and violence? Remember how the Chorus summed up the story in the Prologue? In that speech we were promised a tale about "star-cross'd lovers" who sacrifice their lives and whose deaths force a "gloomy reconciliation" between the Montagues and Capulets.

VERSE BY VERSE

Based on its style and unique wordplay, Shakespeare probably wrote *Romeo and Juliet* between 1595 and 1596. Some scholars believe this date is supported by an allusion by the Nurse—"It's since the earthquake now 11 years"—to an actual earthquake that happened in 1584. A pirated version of the play appeared in 1597, but the respected, "good quarto" edition was published in 1599.

Scholars tell us that Shakespeare borrowed the story of Romeo and Juliet from a moralistic narrative poem by Arthur Brooke, called *The Tragicall Historye of Romeus and Juliet*, published in 1562. Unlike his source, though, Shakespeare refused to cast aspersions on Romeo and Juliet's behavior. He sees them as victims of bad fortune and their deaths as a tragic culmination of a series of random events. Ironically, the couple's families learn to find peace after their children are dead.

Chapter 18. Romeo and Juliet

In *Shakespeare: The Invention of the Human*, Harold Bloom notes, "Shakespeare stands back from assigning blame, whether to the feuding older generation, or to the lovers, or to fate, time, chance, and the cosmological contraries." Bloom believes the play is a unique drama about romantic love; he calls it "unmatched in Shakespeare and the world's literature as a vision of uncompromising mutual love that perishes of its own idealism and intensity."

Romeo and Juliet on Stage and Screen

"Can a play show us the very truth and nature of love?"
Shakespeare in Love, by film director John Madden
(Spoken by Judi Dench as Queen Elizabeth I)

On the stage, *Romeo and Juliet* has remained highly popular since the eighteenth century. Here are some notable actors who've played Romeo and Juliet in top-notch productions:

- 1960—John Stride and Judi Dench at the Old Vic (London)
- 1968—Christopher Walken as Romeo at Stratford, Ontario
- 1976—Ian McKellan and Francesca Annis at Stratford-upon-Avon (Royal Shakespeare Company)
- 1986—Sean Bean and Niamh Cusak, a Royal Shakespeare Company production at Stratford-upon-Avon, featuring a bright red Alfa Romeo on the set

"A KINGDOM FOR A STAGE"

Roseann Sheridan, a professional director and former associate artistic director of the American Players Theatre, recently directed a young cast in *Romeo and Juliet* at Edgewood College in Madison, Wisconsin. When she talks about the play, she is struck by how fully the energy of adolescent males and females colors *Romeo and Juliet*. "Fundamentally, there's a sexual energy here that can't be denied," she said. "When Juliet looks forward to seeing Romeo early in Act three, she's looking forward to the night when she'll lose her virginity."

That energy can also be developed through some unusual casting choices. For this production, Sheridan cast a young woman as Benvolio. "By casting Benvolio as a female, there was a subtextual hint of attraction between her and Romeo, which reinforced the play's youthful energy."

In 1956, Jerome Robbins, Stephen Sondheim, and Leonard Bernstein adapted *Romeo and Juliet* into a musical known as *West Side Story*, set in New York City's Spanish Harlem. Instead of feuding Italian families, the tuneful tale featured the clash between the white-skinned Jets and the Puerto Rican Sharks.

On the screen Italian director Franco Zeffirelli impressed the world with his highly realistic 1968 film. Breaking with a long stage tradition of using older, experienced actors in the leads, Zeffirelli cast the young, unknown Olivia Hussey and Leonard Whiting in the leads. The film works well because Hussey and Whiting look as young as they're supposed to be. More important, Zeffirelli translates the lyric poetry in the love scenes into the teens' palpable embracing on screen.

The 1978 BBC-TV production, directed by Alvin Rakoff, has an impressive cast. But it can let you down if you like the realism of Zeffirelli's movie. As the Chorus, John Gielgud offers a stately opening prologue. Alan Rickman (Tybalt), Michael Hordern (Capulet), Anthony Andrews (Mercutio), and Celia Johnson (Nurse) perform extremely well. But the chemistry between Patrick Ryecart's Romeo and Rebecca Saire's Juliet is practically nonexistent.

In his frenetic 1996 film, Baz Luhrman transplants the lovers into modern-day Verona Beach, California, with intriguing effects. You get plenty of clues about who's who and what's going on. Despite lots of cutting, the film stays true to the verse and rhyme, although the playwright's mellifluous iambic pentameter goes out the window. Lots of clever visual puns here!

Chapter 18. Romeo and Juliet

FACTS TO REMEMBER
- Pay close attention to Shakespeare's language or you'll miss the play's bawdy puns and poetry.
- Unlike most of the play's narrowly drawn characters, Romeo and Juliet grow much wiser throughout the play.
- Romeo is unaware that Juliet has faked her death by taking a sleeping potion; he takes her for dead and drinks poison, provoking her suicide.
- Watching a play that celebrates authentic rather than ideal love was novel to Shakespeare's audiences.

Chapter 19
Julius Caesar

> **INTRODUCTION**
> - An introduction to Shakespeare's first great Roman tragedy and what makes it fascinating to watch
> - The characters in *Julius Caesar*, with some key motives and beliefs of Brutus, Cassius, and Julius Caesar
> - The story and main dramatic action of *Julius Caesar*
> - A word about Plutarch and Shakespeare's other sources

Shakespeare's *Julius Caesar* is commonplace in the curricula of North American English classes. Most Americans are exposed to "Et tu, Bruté" and the play's other catchy speeches while slogging through it in high school. Still, there are good reasons for the solid position it holds in the Western canon.

Shakespeare's re-creation of the Roman conspiracy to murder Caesar has captivated people for a variety of reasons. From ancient times until the present, Caesar's rise and fall has mystified and fascinated historians and ordinary people. This mighty ruler was the most powerful leader of the ancient world, and his death led to the creation of the first empire. How he rose to such a position has mystified and fascinated men and women from the Renaissance to the present. The Elizabethans were no exception. One psychological speech by

Brutus seems to show us Shakespeare's first step in creating his more brooding, self-aware protagonists like Hamlet and Macbeth.

Shakespeare probably wrote *Julius Caesar* in 1599, around the time that he wrote *As You Like It* and *Henry V*. It was his third tragedy, per se, and his first great Roman tragedy. But strictly speaking, it's a history play, despite the belief by some that Brutus is an underdeveloped tragic figure. When the Globe theatre opened on the Bankside in 1599, *Julius Caesar* may have been one of the first Shakespeare plays performed there by the Lord Chamberlain's Men. But the play did not appear in print until the First Folio. *Julius Caesar*'s popularity onstage has persisted since the sixteenth century.

The Characters

Julius Caesar—He is Rome's highest ruler, who is suspected of seeking even more power in our story. Shakespeare portrays him less vividly than he does Brutus or Cassius, but this may work in his favor. He has been called arrogant and even cowardly, but Shakespeare grants us little insight into the workings of Caesar's mind. Focusing away from Caesar himself allowed Shakespeare to cast a bright light on the Roman people, particularly the motives of the mob and the conspirators.

Mark Antony (or Marcus Antonius)—Caesar's close friend has unusual instincts and oratorical skill. He puts these talents to use when speaking to the mob during Caesar's funeral. He deftly pushes the crowd into an angry frenzy over the murder of Caesar, subtly undercutting Brutus' considered justification for ending Caesar's life and protecting the Republic. He is allied with Octavius and Lepidus after Caesar's death.

Octavius Caesar—Ally of Mark Antony; historically, Caesar's great-nephew, adopted son and heir.

M. Aemilius Lepidus—Ally of Antony and Octavius.

Cicero, Publius, Popilius Lena—Senators.

Chapter 19. Julius Caesar

CONSPIRATORS

Marcus Brutus—Brutus helps lead the conspiracy against Julius Caesar. Compared to the other conspirators, his motives for doing so aren't personal or self-serving. He disdains the prospect that a Caesar might become the supreme ruler who would hold himself higher than the Roman Republic. Ironically, Caesar has already reached that pinnacle.

Cassius—He is perhaps the most ambitious and self-serving conspirator. He influences Brutus and the others to end Caesar's life. Unlike Brutus, he is obviously jealous of Caesar's growing power among the people. Brutus' wife is his sister.

Casca

Trebonius

Caius Ligarius

Decius Brutus

Metellus Cimber

Cinna

Flavius and Murellus—Tribunes who address the crowd.

Artemidorus of Cnidos—A teacher of rhetoric.

Soothsayer

Cinna—A poet.

Another poet

FRIENDS TO BRUTUS AND CASSIUS

Lucilius

Titinius

Messala

Young Cato

Volumnius

Flavius

BRUTUS' SERVANTS

Varrus

Clitus

Claudio

Strato

Lucius

Dardanius

OTHER CHARACTERS

Pindarus—Servant to Cassius.

Calpurnia—The wife of Caesar is unable to bear children. She dreams of Caesar's death and pleads with him not to leave the house and visit the Senate on the day he is supposed to be crowned in the Capitol.

Portia—The wife of Brutus whose fears for his safety cause her to despair. She is Cassius' sister. She kills herself by swallowing hot coals.

Senators, Citizens, Guards, Attendants, etc.

Setting: Rome; near Sardis; near Philippi

Chapter 19. Julius Caesar

Rome Is Dissatisfied on the Feast of Lupercal

The play opens amid the bustle of Rome's city streets. At the feast of Lupercal, the citizens celebrate Julius Caesar's most recent military victory against Pompey's sons. The Roman Republic is plagued by civil war, and the memory of Caesar's defeat of Pompey (who once ruled Rome with Caesar) still hangs in the air. But for all those who laud Caesar's accomplishment with optimism, this mighty ruler provokes an equal amount of dissatisfaction in others. Marullus, for one, cannot abide the merrymakers' disregard for Pompey, the dead leader conquered by Caesar in battle: "You blocks, you stones, you worse than senseless things!/ Oh you hard hearts, you cruel men of Rome,/Knew you not Pompey?"

On this day, something is definitely amiss. A group of noble Romans are unhappy with Rome's political state of affairs. Julius Caesar is their supreme commander in military and domestic matters; he also leads the Roman senate. But many aristocrats feel that Caesar may have too much power. There is a growing fear that the people look up to him more as a god or king, instead of Rome's highest leader.

TIMELESS SOLILOQUIES

Julius Caesar pays interesting attention to omens and portents, suggesting the play's concern with fate and a destiny beyond our control. Recall the scene when Caesar himself wants his wife Calpurnia to be touched by Mark Antony, who has participated in a fertility ritual, so that she might bear children? And remember Calpurnia's bad dream, in which he is imagined spouting rivers of blood? Don't forget how she despairs of experiencing bad omens before she begs him to stay home instead of visiting the Senate. What if Caesar had paid attention to the following warning? Would he still be alive today?

Caesar:	Who is it in the press that calls on me?
	I hear a tongue shriller than all the music
	Cry "Caesar!" Speak, Caesar is turn'd to hear.

Soothsayer:	Beware the ides of March.
Caesar:	What man is that?
Brutus:	A soothsayer bids you beware the ides of March. (I.2.15-19)

In Caesar's first scene, he is surrounded by other nobles, his friend Mark Antony, and his wife Calpurnia. He is approached by a soothsayer who warns him to "beware the Ides of March." (The Ides of March is the fifteenth, by the way.) Such a portent so early in the play is not gratuitous on Shakespeare's part. By the way, if Shakespeare knows one thing, it's how to build suspense. You'll see that in this play he is at the height of his dramatic powers.

Brutus Is Lured into a Conspiracy

> And therefore think him as a serpent's egg,
> Which, hatch'd, would as his kind grow mischievous,
> And kill him in the shell.
> (II.1.32-34)

Caesar and his followers exit the stage, leaving Brutus and Cassius alone. Brutus acknowledges, "I do fear that the people/ Choose Caesar as their king." Brutus is prepared to accept this fact, however, until Cassius points out his own misgivings about bowing down to another mortal, who is no better than himself. Cassius also reminds Brutus that the common Romans expect him to set an example of leadership. They remember that Brutus' own ancestor (also named Brutus) drove out the evil Tarquin kings. Then Brutus indicates that a revolt similar to his ancestor's isn't far from his mind. When Brutus is gone, Cassius confesses alone that he plans to manipulate Brutus into his own way of thinking using letters from disgruntled Romans interested in revolt.

Chapter 19. Julius Caesar

VERSE BY VERSE

Take a moment to mull over Brutus' thoughts in the following speech. You can almost hear the indecision of Hamlet (see Chapter 20) or the resignation of Macbeth after he puts his faith in the idle prophecy of the weird sisters (see Chapter 23):

> Since Cassius first did whet me against Caesar,
> I have not slept.
> Between the acting of a dreadful thing
> And the first motion, all the interim is
> Like a phantasma or a hideous dream.
> The Genius and the mortal instruments
> Are then in council; and the state of a man,
> Like to a little kingdom, suffers then
> The nature of an insurrection.
> (II.1.61-69)

In the midst of this important conversation, Caesar confides to his close friend Mark Antony that Cassius spells trouble.

Caesar:	Antonio!
Mark Antony:	Caesar?
Caesar:	Let me have men about me that are fat,
	Sleek-headed men and such as sleep a-nights.
	Yond Cassius has a lean and hungry look,
	He thinks too much; such men are dangerous.
	(I.2.190-95)

A conspiracy against Caesar is born when Cassius convinces Casca to join him in a plot. Cinna is also recruited to win over Brutus. The next morning Cassius sends an anonymous letter to Brutus asking him to be Rome's protector. Brutus is convinced the cause is right. At this moment he decides to lead a conspiracy to assassinate Caesar for the good of Rome.

Murder on the Ides of March

The conspirators meet and make a plan to murder Caesar on that day, when he arrives at the Senate. Decius will invent a pretext to get Caesar to leave his house, in case he decides not to come to the Senate. Even though Calpurnia begs Caesar not to leave the house that day, he gives up on pacifying her, refusing to bow to fears of ill omens. Caesar, somewhat glibly, also rebuffs Artemidorus' plea outside the Senate for him to read a message containing the names of the conspirators. (Oh, Caesar, what were you thinking?)

Caesar gets ready for the day's business, and Mark Antony is conveniently called away from the room. At that point Caesar receives a petition, which he rejects. That is the cue for the murderers to strike. They stab Caesar repeatedly; he dies, but only after realizing that Brutus is one of his killers. "Et tu, Bruté!" he says. These murderers even wash their hands in their victim's blood! Soon afterwards, Mark Antony sends word that he will support the conspiracy, but he'd like an explanation. Brutus says it's okay because he wants Antony's support.

Mark Antony Incites the Rabble

The scenes that occur next are some of the most memorable in Shakespeare. If you see *Julius Caesar* in the theatre or see a movie adaptation, you'll see what I mean. Mark Antony requests to speak at Caesar's funeral. After the conspirators depart, we learn from his soliloquy that he will undercut Brutus and his lot and turn the mob against them. A new civil war is imminent, and Octavius' legions are moving closer to Rome.

At Caesar's funeral, Brutus delivers a highly logical rationale for the murder, assuring everyone that he and his followers did it out of love for Rome, in order to save the republic. Though the mob seems to accept Brutus' speech, they seem a little restless. Brutus leaves and Mark Antony takes the podium. Here is where magic happens. Antony, who is a more gifted orator, emulates the style and even the wording of Brutus' speech, only he veils his own diatribe in enough irony and passion to plant doubt in the minds of the mob.

Mark Antony:	Friends, Romans, countrymen, lend me your ears!
	I come to bury Caesar, not to praise him.
	The evil that men do lives after them,
	The good is oft interred with their bones;
	So let it be with Caesar.
	. . .
	When that the poor have cried, Caesar hath wept;
	Ambition should be made of sterner stuff:
	Yet Brutus says he was ambitious,
	And Brutus is an honorable man.
	(III.2.73-77; 91-94)

And though Antony's words denigrate Caesar and sing Brutus' praises, the net effect of his rhetoric skillfully turns the mob against the conspiracy. The play reaches its climax at the moment when the mob works itself into a frenzy.

Antony and Octavius Get Even

Caesar's foul murder prompts Antony, Octavius (Caesar's great-nephew), and Lepidus to form the triumvirate that will fight the conspirators. Meanwhile, Brutus, Cassius, and the others have fled Rome and are raising an army. Antony and Octavius decide to go on the offensive militarily against the rebels.

In the rebel camp, Brutus questions Cassius' loyalty as a friend. The two begin to quarrel as each expresses his misgivings about the other's behavior. But the two eventually reconcile after Cassius offers to let Brutus kill him with his own dagger. Then Brutus informs Cassius that his wife Portia has committed suicide by swallowing hot, fiery coals. She had grown desperate and fearful that her husband was doomed to defeat. Then Brutus and Cassius agree to fight the army of Antony and Octavius' at Philippi. On the eve of the battle, Caesar's ghost appears before Brutus and warns him that the two shall meet again at Philippi.

In the 2005 hit Broadway production of Julius Caesar, *Daniel Sullivan directed Denzel Washington (center) as Marcus Brutus and Colm Feore (second from left) as Cassius. (Not pictured is actor William Sadler, in the role of Caesar).*

(Photo Courtesy of Photofest.)

Brutus Falls on His Sword

Brutus: There is a tide in the affairs of men,
Which, taken at the flood, leads on to fortune;
Omitted, all the voyage of their life
Is bound in shallows and in miseries.
On such a full sea are we now afloat,
And we must take the current when it serves,
Or lose our ventures.
(IV.3.218-224)

On the day of the battle, Brutus' army is stronger against that of Octavius, but Cassius' men are weak against Antony. Things turn sour for the killers of Caesar. Cassius mistakenly assumes that Brutus' troops have been overcome and feels that his side has lost the war. So, he orders Pindarus, his servant to slay him. Ironically, the battle had been going well for Brutus and Cassius, but when Brutus' troops find Cassius dead, they become discouraged. Demoralized over his soldiers' recent defeat by Antony, Brutus makes more than one attempt to die. With the help of his servant, he falls on his sword.

Mark Antony utters Brutus' epitaph, which reinforces the idea that Shakespeare may have cared more about Brutus than anyone else in the play. He painted him as a man divided—a noble leader and an idealist who believed in the principles of the Roman republic. But he was also a man who was too easily led by lesser men, someone who made a wrong decision and couldn't escape its consequences:

> This was the noblest Roman of them all:
> All the conspirators, save only he,
> Did that they did in envy of great Caesar;
> He, only in a general honest thought
> And common good to all, made one of them.
> (V.5.68-72)

A Word About Roman History and Shakespeare's Fascination

Two millennia have elapsed since a group of radical conspirators murdered Julius Caesar in A.D. 44. Caesar's death was the first incident that moved Rome from a republic to an empire whose reach and power were far-flung. When Caesar died, three leaders ruled Rome until Octavius (known as Caesar Augustus) became the first emperor.

Questions about how Shakespeare may have adapted his main source for *Julius Caesar* are an endless source of fascination to critics of the play. The playwright relied heavily on Plutarch's *Lives of the Noble Grecians and Romans*, leaning specifically on the Greek author's biographies of Brutus, Caesar, and Mark Antony. In parts of the play, Shakespeare seems to lift some of Plutarch's entire speeches! Elsewhere, however, he draws upon small details and expands them into vivid scenes of huge dramatic importance. Scholars who take pains to dissect the motives of the characters and Shakespeare himself would do well to remember the gaping distance between the playwright and his original source. In *The Age of Shakespeare*, Frank Kermode writes, "Shakespeare read [Plutarch] in an English translation of a French translation of the Greek original, which imposed a little more distance."

But time hasn't erased the swirl of political, moral, and historical questions surrounding his possible tyranny and untimely death. Even Dante, the great medieval poet, creates his own vision of Caesar in the *Inferno*. The Elizabethans were equally captivated, and Shakespeare took full dramatic advantage of the popularity of this subject. In the twenty-first century, literary scholars are still poking around, trying to turn up new evidence of Shakespeare's own political views about monarchy, tyranny, and the motives of Brutus.

Julius Caesar Onstage

Julius Caesar's popularity in the theatre never seems to wane. This may have something to do with its stature among directors and actors as an ensemble play that places unique demands on an entire company. Directors often allow their productions to be colored by profound political concerns of the day. In 1937, in particular, Orson Welles revived the play in New York, dressed his characters in modern dress, and grafted the imminent threat of Fascism onto the play's atmosphere. Caesar was even dressed up as the Italian leader Benito Mussolini!

"A KINGDOM FOR A STAGE"

Scholars surmise that the Lord Chamberlain's Men tested the success of their new digs at the Globe theatre by performing *Julius Caesar*. How do they know this? From a letter that still exists, written by Thomas Platter, a Swiss doctor. In the letter, Platter describes his visit to a London theatre south of the Thames on

September 21, 1599, which had a thatched roof. He reports seeing a "tragedy of the first Emperor Julius Caesar with about fifteen characters," followed by a four-person dance with "two dressed in men's clothes, and two in women's." (Letter quoted in *The New Penguin Shakespeare*, edited by Norman Sanders.)

Famous stage and screen productions of *Julius Caesar* include:

- 1864—In New York, the famous Booth brothers (Edwin; Junius; and John Wilkes, who killed President Lincoln) played Brutus, Cassius, and Antony, respectively.
- 1953—Joseph L. Mankiewicz directed the film starring Marlon Brando (Mark Antony) and John Gielgud (Cassius).
- 1978—BBC-TV's complete Shakespeare series featured Richard Pasco (Brutus) and Keith Michell (Cassius).
- 2004—Edward Hall directed a version at Stratford-upon Avon featuring Greg Hicks (Brutus) and Tim Pigott-Smith (Cassius).
- 2017-Director Oskar Eustis caused an international stir (and outrage among some critics and corporate sponsors) when his New York Public Theatre production featured an actor portraying Julius Caesar (Gregg Henry), who was dressed up to resemble President Donald Trump.

FACTS TO REMEMBER

- *Julius Caesar* is Shakespeare's first great Roman tragedy.
- Several omens suggest Caesar's life may be in danger, including the soothsayer's caution, Calpurnia's dream, and Artemidoris' paper that names the conspirators.
- Brutus, though honorable, makes a wrong decision and receives a punishment that fits his error in judgment.
- Critics cannot agree on whether Shakespeare personally felt a greater loyalty toward Caesar, a kind of monarch, or Brutus, who fiercely guarded the Roman Republic.

Chapter 20

Hamlet, Prince of Denmark

> **INTRODUCTION**
> - An introduction to *Hamlet*, Shakespeare's ultimate revenge tragedy and the most famous play in the world
> - Who's who in *Hamlet*, illuminating key characters
> - The story and meaning of *Hamlet*, and the added dimension of *The Mousetrap*, its play-within-the-play
> - *Hamlet's* themes, patterns, theatricality, and fights
> - Acclaimed director Michael Kahn talks about the challenges of staging *Hamlet* and Shakespeare's ambiguity

Hamlet, the Prince of Denmark is Shakespeare's most famous tragedy. For good or ill, we seem to know it best through sound bites. Expressions like "To be or not to be" and "Brevity is the soul of wit" are a few of the countless expressions we take for granted. While you probably have a passing familiarity with the story—a young prince sets out to avenge his father's death after his mother hastily marries his uncle—the plot of *Hamlet* seems to pale next to Hamlet himself, the titan of all Western protagonists. "When we attend a performance of *Hamlet*, or read the play for ourselves, it does not take us long to discover that the prince transcends his play," says Harold Bloom.

It is ironic that this towering dramatic figure often fails to satisfy us in the theatre. Hamlet always seems poised on the brink of action. His pensive nature and subtle soliloquizing are not easy to portray well, even for skillful classical actors. *Hamlet* also poses unusual challenges for directors. The lines are so familiar, they ring in our ears like clichés.

As Frank Kermode reminds us, "Hamlet himself theorizes constantly—about the Ghost, about passion, about action; about manners and acting and suicide and custom." The prince's contemplation keeps us, as well as other characters, guessing about the kind of hero he will become. Hamlet forces his family, his court, and us to wait and doubt throughout the play. In this context Kermode contends that "we are always conscious that we are being offered not so much a man, but a play, or a world, that delays and doubts."

The Characters

THE DANISH COURT

Hamlet—He is the young prince of Denmark, the deceased king's son and the nephew of Claudius, the present king. From the moment Hamlet addresses the spirit claiming to be his dead father, we know that their relationship was sincere, based on love and trust. Even before King Hamlet's ghost tells Hamlet the story of how he was murdered, this brooding university student is deeply hurt and melancholy after his mother's hasty marriage to his uncle. The prince senses that her marriage and his uncle's rise to power are symptoms of disorder in the Danish court. He says, "To me Denmark is a prison." Highly introspective, Hamlet philosophizes on every imaginable subject to make sense of the chaos and absurdity inside and outside the court. (Critics often fault Hamlet because he thinks more than he acts.) He's an idealistic, sensitive soul, a poet, a thinker, a student of theology, an actor, and a theatre lover who delights in human mask-making. Through Hamlet's soliloquies and speeches, we see a reflection of our own moral dilemmas and despair. We identify with Hamlet's familial distress, the disorder in the Danish court, and the impending doom of his revenge plot. "The time is out of joint," Hamlet tells us, and he "was born to set it right!"

Claudius—He is the king of Denmark who is newly married to Gertrude, the widow of his deceased brother, King Hamlet. Hamlet has a hard time accepting Claudius as his stepfather, given that his uncle has married his mother only two months after King Hamlet's death. When Hamlet is addressed by his father's ghost, he is convinced that Claudius murdered his father. Though Claudius' conscience plagues him after the murder, he doesn't dare repent. He loves his kingdom and his wife too much! Claudius is a realist, as indicated by his decision to banish Hamlet to England when he suspects that Hamlet's madness may actually be the act of one who plans to get even. He is Hamlet's antagonist.

Gertrude—She is the queen of Denmark and Hamlet's mother. Gertrude is warm-hearted and loving, but somewhat inscrutable because she is often silent. She appears to be ignorant of her second husband's treachery and murder. In the first act she tells Hamlet that his willingness to wear black and fulfill "mourning duties" are "sweet and commendable," but she tells him that his "obstinate condolement" is "unmanly grief" and contrary to God's wishes. She also appears skeptical of Polonius' belief that Hamlet's love for Ophelia has caused his melancholy. Although she becomes convinced Hamlet is truly mad after the closet scene, she tells Claudius early on that her son's behavior is a result of their hasty marriage.

Ghost of Hamlet's father—He is the spirit of King Hamlet, who has a fond place in his son's heart. His speech to Hamlet after he appears on the castle battlements in Act one suggests that the bond between them was very strong. He tells Hamlet that Claudius took his life through evil treachery, which shocks the prince. He exhorts his son to "revenge his [father's] foul and most unnatural murder."

Polonius—He is the king's Lord Chamberlain and the father of Laertes and Ophelia. Polonius is rather strict and imperious with both of his children. He trusts neither of them. Sending Reynaldo to spy on his son, Polonius cautions Laertes about his conduct. Fearing that Ophelia may give her affections too freely to Hamlet, he warns her of the importance of guarding her chastity to preserve the family honor. When Ophelia witnesses Hamlet's mad behavior, Polonius takes steps to distance his daughter from Hamlet. This action backfires and possibly fuels Hamlet's frustrations over his mother's hasty marriage. Ultimately, Polonius' interference in Hamlet's game leads to his own undoing. While eavesdropping, he is killed when the prince mistakes him for Claudius. (Actors often render Polonius as little more than a bumbling fool. Richard Briers offers a more nuanced Polonius in Kenneth Branagh's film.)

Laertes—He is Polonius' son and the brother of Ophelia. There are hints that Laertes is a rake and a bit of a libertine. He adores Ophelia but is concerned that Hamlet may lead her on with amorous advances but refuse to marry her. Realizing that Laertes is a good swordfighter, Claudius conspires with him to kill Hamlet in a duel using a poisoned sword.

Ophelia—She is Polonius' daughter and sister of Laertes. She is in love with Hamlet and we can be fairly certain that he loves her. She is obedient, much like Hero in *Much Ado About Nothing*. Like most unmarried Elizabethan women, she has little choice but to obey her father regarding her choice of husband. So when Polonius demands that she stop returning Hamlet's affections and return his letters, she obeys. Mortified when her father is killed by the man who loved her, she goes mad. She is found drowned in a stream. Whether she caused her own death has been debated endlessly.

Horatio—He is Hamlet's friend, former schoolmate, a scholar, and loyal to the prince until his death. Before Hamlet dies, Horatio threatens to drink poison, to end his life honorably like an "antique Roman." But Hamlet stops him, insisting that he tell the truth about Hamlet.

Chapter 20. Hamlet, Prince of Denmark

> Rosencrantz and Guildenstern—Hardly distinguishable from one another, these two courtiers are old school friends of Hamlet. Claudius summons them to the Danish court to spy on Hamlet. When the king suspects that Hamlet has dark intentions, he sends Rosencrantz and Guildenstern on a mission to kill Hamlet in England. In the end, they end up dead. Tom Stoppard immortalized these two in his funny, absurdist play *Rosencrantz and Guildenstern are Dead* (1966).
>
> Fortinbras—He is the prince of Norway, nephew of the present king and son of Norway's former king, old Fortinbras. He tries to invade Denmark to requite King Hamlet's conquest and killing of his father. But his uncle, the Norwegian king, negotiates with Claudius to prevent military conflict. The dying Hamlet hopes Fortinbras will be elected as the future Danish king.
>
> Voltemand and Cornelius—Two courtiers; ambassadors to Norway
>
> Marcellus, Bernardo—Officers
>
> Francisco—A soldier
>
> Osric—A courtier
>
> Reynaldo—A servant of Polonius
>
> A gentleman, priest, players, two gravediggers/clowns, a Norwegian captain, Doctor of Divinity, English ambassadors
>
> Lords, Ladies, Officers, Soldiers, Sailors, Messengers, Attendants
>
> *Setting: The royal castle of Elsinore in Denmark*

A Specter Stalks

Ah, something is rotten in the state of Denmark. We open on a dark, dreary, and propitious night. Two soldiers, Bernardo and Marcellus, are standing watch on the battlements outside Elsinore, the Danish castle. These sentries are a bit nervous. A ghost has visited the castle battlements three times and they believe he's coming back. Fearful, the guards ask Horatio, Hamlet's brainy friend and school chum from the University of Wittenberg, if he'll stand guard to await the ghost's return. They believe the specter is the spirit of the dead king, the young Prince Hamlet's father. Horatio surveys past conflicts between the elder Hamlet and Fortinbras, the king of Norway. We learn that Prince Fortinbras is getting ready to invade again. Horatio surmises the ghost is a sign, a bad omen of political problems that lie ahead. When the ghost does reappear, Horatio asks "if [he] is privy to [his] country's fate." But the ghost ignores him.

A Royal Death and Hasty Marriage

Inside the castle of Elsinore, we see that Claudius, the new king of Denmark, has just married Queen Gertrude, Hamlet's mother. Hamlet is gripped by melancholy, and his depression has gotten his mother and stepfather's attention. Claudius asks Hamlet, "How is it that the clouds still hang on you?" Then Gertrude reminds her son that "all that lives must die,/Passing through nature to eternity."

VERSE BY VERSE

Scholars puzzle over the printed editions of *Hamlet* from 1603, 1604, and the 1623 First Folio. The 1604 second quarto is the longest script we have, believed to be based on Shakespeare's original manuscript. Until recently, students read a conflated version of several *Hamlet* texts in school. But since editors at Oxford University Press suggested that Shakespeare revised the 1604 script to come up with the First Folio version, each script is studied as a separate text. (If you visit the British Library website, you can pull up the same page from different editions and compare them side by side on your computer screen!) In the Shakespeare Theatre Company's 2007 staging, director Michael Kahn carefully cut the full, four-hour script down to about 3 hours, 15 minutes. "I tend to excise topical sections, like the part where Hamlet talks about the children taking over the theatre business in London. The Elizabethans cared deeply about that, but it means less to us."

Chapter 20. Hamlet, Prince of Denmark

At Polonius' house, we're introduced to his family. As he prepares to sail to Paris, Laertes tells his sister Ophelia goodbye. In parting words, he advises her not to be too open and affectionate with Hamlet, reminding her that the prince may not be able to marry for love. After Polonius sends his son abroad, he begins quizzing his daughter about their conversation. He's suspicious of Hamlet's true intentions. Skeptical that Hamlet's intentions toward Ophelia are serious and honorable, Polonius orders her to stop seeing him. She consents.

The Prince of Denmark Vows Revenge

On a dreary night, Hamlet is poised on a platform, waiting for the ghost of his dead father to appear. All the while, the court carouses inside the castle. The ghost appears and urges Hamlet to follow him. King Hamlet's ghost reveals to his son in detail how his evil brother poisoned him. The suffering spirit doesn't spare Hamlet the poetic detail of Claudius' treachery: "Ay, that incestuous, that adulterate beast,/With witchcraft of his wit, with traitorous gifts,/. . . won to his shameful lust/The will of my most seeming-virtuous queen."

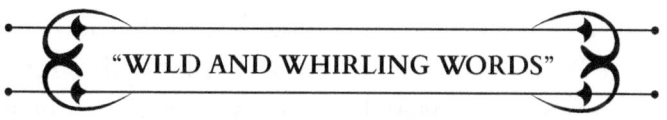
"WILD AND WHIRLING WORDS"

> When the ghost refers to Claudius as "that incestuous, that adulterate beast," you might ask why he characterizes the couple as committing incest. The Elizabethans might have believed that Gertrude and Claudius shouldn't marry, based on an Old Testament belief that a man who marries his brother's wife can't produce children. Or early audiences might have recalled Henry VIII's attitudinal change toward the validity of his marriage to Catherine of Aragon, who was his brother Arthur's widow when he married her in 1509.

Horrified, the prince is intent on avenging his father's murder. After the ghost disappears, Hamlet makes Marcellus and Horatio promise not to tell anyone what they've seen. If the prince should "put an antic disposition on," or act out of character or somewhat madly, they should remain quiet:

Hamlet:	Here, as before, never, so help you mercy,
	How strange or odd some'er I bear myself—
	As I perchance hereafter shall think meet
	To put an antic disposition on—
	That you, at such times seeing me, never shall,
	With arms encumb'red thus, or this headshake,
	. . .
	That you know aught of me—this do swear,
	(I.5.169-174; 179)

Hamlet Feigns Madness

Polonius plans to have his servant Reynaldo spy on Laertes while he's in Paris. (This scene, by the way, is frequently cut in stage versions.) When these two finish talking and Reynaldo leaves, a frightened Ophelia enters, disturbed by her recent encounter with Hamlet. She reports that his dress is bizarre and his expression is strange. She says, "as if he had been loosed out of hell/To speak of horrors, he comes before me." She also assures Polonius that she has not spoken to the prince, nor received his letters. Although she is not sure what is amiss, Polonius feels sure Hamlet's love for Ophelia is making him insane. (Mind you, during the Renaissance, lovesickness was seen as a genuine malady. But we know that Hamlet is pretending to be mad in front of Ophelia.)

Claudius Gathers His Spies and Hamlet Has a Brainstorm

Hamlet:	—the play's the thing
	Wherein I'll catch the conscience of the King.
	(II.1.604-05)

Back at the castle, amid the news that Fortinbras' army poses no imminent threat, Polonius gets the opportunity to tell Claudius and Gertrude that Hamlet has gone mad because Ophelia has refused to see him. Concerned, Claudius arranges for Hamlet's childhood chums, Rosencrantz and Guildenstern, to spy on him. Polonius and Claudius make plans to listen in on the next encounter between Hamlet and Ophelia. The action becomes complicated when a troupe of players arrives at the castle. Theatre is Hamlet's pastime, so he is temporarily distracted.

Chapter 20. Hamlet, Prince of Denmark

Hearing the players recite various dramatic speeches, Hamlet has an idea. He will stage *The Murder of Gonzago* and have the First Player insert a few extra lines. Saying, "O! what a rogue and peasant slave am I," Hamlet chastises himself for the inability to rouse himself into action, preferring instead to "unpack [his] heart with words." Still, Hamlet has a plan to get Claudius to expose his guilty conscience and erase his nagging doubts that the ghost is really the devil. He says, "I'll have these players/Play something like the murder of my father/Before mine uncle; I'll observe his looks;/. . . if he but blench/I know my course." (During Shakespeare's time, men of the theatre had faith that a play encouraged moral behavior. Hamlet hopes that when Claudius sees connections between the play and his actual murder, he'll openly show his guilt.)

"Get Thee to a Nunnery"

Act three begins with Hamlet's most famous soliloquy, as he muses about life, death, and suicide. After the speech, the prince runs into Ophelia. They exchange pleasantries, but when the young woman attempts to return Hamlet's letters, he denies that he ever gave her any. What's worse, he gets aggressive, asks her odd questions, denies having ever loved her, accuses her of being unfaithful, and orders her to enter a nunnery!

TIMELESS SOLILOQUIES

> When Ophelia returns Hamlet's letters, the prince becomes unhinged and appears to lose faith in life and those around him. In the following speech, he seems cynical and disgusted with women.
>
> Hamlet: I did love you once.
>
> Ophelia: Indeed, my lord, you made me believe so.
>
> Hamlet: You should not have believ'd me, for virtue cannot so [inoculate] our old stock but we shall relish of it. I lov'd you not . . .
>
> Ophelia: I was the more deceiv'd.

> Hamlet: Get thee to a nunn'ry, why would'st thou
> be a breeder of sinners?
> (III.1.114-118; 120-121)
>
> Language experts point out that Hamlet's use of *nunnery* is both cruel and ironic because it was a slang term for *brothel*. He seems sincere, though, in pushing her to join a convent.

During the lovers' poignant scene, Ophelia visibly suffers as Hamlet's message to her becomes more and more deranged. (You'll see this scene played in many ways onstage. Sometimes it begins tenderly until Hamlet begins to unravel; at other times, Hamlet appears distant toward Ophelia from the beginning of their conversation.) While this is happening, Polonius and Claudius are hiding, overhearing every word. Although Polonius is sure that love is causing Hamlet's madness, a shrewd Claudius suspects there may be another explanation for the prince's behavior.

Hamlet Lays His Trap

Hamlet stages a performance of *The Mousetrap* before the king and queen. (Read more about Hamlet's advice to the players later in this chapter.) Amazingly, the story resonates so powerfully with Claudius that he guiltily stomps out of the hall. After this outburst, Hamlet has evidence of the king's guilty conscience. Horatio has a similar perception. Now Hamlet is determined to follow the spirit's command to avenge his murder. Mentally, Hamlet feels more able now to spring into action.

After seeing the play, Claudius becomes suspicious of Hamlet's behavior and the motives behind it. He makes plans to send the prince to England, enjoining Rosencrantz and Guildenstern to go with him. Alone in the castle, Claudius is in an emotional state. He feels the urge to repent, but considering that he'll lose his kingdom and Gertrude, he comes to his senses. Hamlet comes upon the king in prayer. Vulnerable though he is, the prince refuses to take his revenge because, if Claudius is killed while praying, his soul will go to heaven. (Modern audiences often look upon this scene as another missed opportunity for Hamlet to get revenge!)

Chapter 20. Hamlet, Prince of Denmark

Hamlet Upbraids the Lusty Queen

> Hamlet: Frailty, thy name is woman!
> (I.2.146)

Hamlet has been summoned to his mother's apartment. In the famous "closet scene," the queen is perturbed with how her son has treated the king, so she confronts him openly. (Polonius, mind you, is listening to her from behind the *arras*, or wall hanging tapestry.) Hamlet impertinently accuses her of offending his father, the deceased king. They argue, but when Polonius cries out for fear that Hamlet will harm the queen, Hamlet sees the arras rustle. He impulsively stabs at the shape behind the tapestry, thinking it is the king. Hamlet has killed Polonius! The ensuing exchange between Hamlet and Gertrude is legendary. Next to Polonius' corpse, the prince cruelly upbraids his mother for marrying the man who killed her husband. She tells him that his "words [are] like daggers" to her ears. When the ghost suddenly appears before them, Hamlet speaks to him. Now Gertrude is certain that Hamlet is mad.

A Cycle of Revenge Destroys Two Families

Gertrude tells Claudius about Hamlet's bloody deed. After a search, Rosencrantz and Guildenstern find Hamlet and take him to Claudius. The king orders Hamlet to leave Denmark and travel to England with his two friends, who will carry a secret letter with Hamlet's death warrant for the English king. On a plain in Denmark, Hamlet crosses paths with Fortinbras' army, on its way to Poland. Here, he questions the merits and risks of war in light of his own inability to avenge his father's murder.

Ophelia's ensuing lapse into lunacy is poignant. Losing her father and knowing that her lover murdered him send her over the brink. Hearing the news of his father's death, Laertes returns to Claudius' castle to seek his own revenge. He is devastated when he sees Ophelia unhinged.

Meanwhile, Hamlet manages to get free of Rosencrantz and Guildenstern. He sends a letter to Horatio at Elsinore and returns home. Claudius, seeing that he can make Laertes into his ally, plots with him to kill Hamlet in the context of a prearranged duel. To carry out the murder, the two agree that Laertes will use a sword dipped in poison during the match. Before the last act, Gertrude announces that Ophelia has drowned as she attempted to hang her flower garlands on the branches of a willow tree.

As two gravediggers prepare the ground for Ophelia's burial in the churchyard, Hamlet and Horatio happen upon them. The two move away when the priest arrives to begin the funeral. When Hamlet sees his family at the grave and realizes they mourn for the dead Ophelia, he soon advances to the graveside. After he scuffles with Laertes in the grave, Hamlet confesses, "I lov'd Ophelia: forty thousand brothers/Could not, with all their quantity of love,/ Make up my sum."

A Fencing Match—"The Readiness Is All"

Hamlet learns from Osric that Claudius has bet Laertes that Laertes can't beat Hamlet in a fencing match by more than 12 to 9. When Horatio tries to forestall the duel with the excuse that Hamlet is not fit, the prince refuses to delay. In these famous lines, Hamlet concedes to a divine plan and his role in it.

> Not a whit, we defy augury. There is special
> providence in the fall of a sparrow. If it be [now],
> 'tis not to come; if it be not to come, it will be now; if
> it be not now, yet it [will] come—the readiness is all.
> (V.2.219-222)

Hamlet and Laertes fence in front of the court as the king and queen look on. Hamlet gets the first hit. After Laertes is hit a second time, Claudius drops a poisoned pearl into a cup of wine intended for Hamlet. Thirsty and excited that her son is winning, Gertrude takes this cup and drinks. Next, Laertes wounds Hamlet, but in the scuffle they exchange rapiers (thrusting swords) and Hamlet wounds Laertes. Looking on, Gertrude swoons and falls dead, warning her son that she has been poisoned. Next, Laertes falls, weakened from the poisoned sword. While dying, he confesses that Claudius is to blame for Gertrude's death and Hamlet holds the poisoned sword that fatally wounded him. So Hamlet takes the sword and drives it through Claudius' torso and pours a poisoned drink down his throat. The king dies. Soon Hamlet weakens and eventually dies himself. In the distance, Fortinbras marches on the castle. He enters the castle after Hamlet dies, to take back what his dead father lost to King Hamlet.

"A KINGDOM FOR A STAGE"

Jack Young is the artistic director of the Houston Shakespeare Festival and head of the Professional Actor Training Program at the University of Houston. Accredited by the Society of American Fight Directors, Young lends his expertise to actors who fight onstage. When considering Kenneth Branagh's 1996 film *Hamlet*, Young takes issue with the fencing match between Laertes and Hamlet in Act five. In Young's view, this version pushes aside the premise that Claudius has invited Hamlet to compete with Laertes in a bout of swordsmanship. "Claudius wagers that Hamlet will at least score nine hits on Laertes before Laertes can score 12. It's not like the fight between Mercutio and Tybalt in *Romeo and Juliet*; it's like a basketball one-on-one match. When Mel Gibson fights in Zeffirelli's film, you see a duel with protective armor and prescribed rules, that gets out of hand, as Shakespeare wrote it. In Branagh's film, Laertes and Hamlet are out to kill each other from the very start—why does it take so long for Claudius to try to stop them?"

Part 5. The Tragedies

From left, Laertes (Michael Maloney) fights with Hamlet (Kenneth Branagh) as Claudius (Derek Jacobi) and Gertrude (Julie Christie) look on from a distance. Some scenes from Kenneth Branagh's 1996 movie were shot at Blenheim Palace near Oxford.

(Photo courtesy of Photofest.)

Intriguing Patterns and Themes in *Hamlet*

To some, *Hamlet* can be more satisfying in the contemplation than the dramatic experience. Shakespeare creates myriad, meaningful patterns through character and action. The play's cycle of revenge has been put in motion from the very first scene. Framing the first appearance of the ghost, we're told that Fortinbras may be marching on Denmark to avenge the death of his father, the deceased king of Norway. Then the ghost of King Hamlet exhorts his son to avenge his own "foul murder." Next, Laertes learns of the fatal stabbing of his father Polonius, and soon he pledges to avenge the murder with Claudius' assistance. Three sons move to avenge the murders of their fathers—Fortinbras, in the background; Hamlet, between contemplation of being and seeming, suicide and action; and Laertes, after brief planning with an evil king.

CHAPTER 20. HAMLET, PRINCE OF DENMARK

Note the parallel between the lines of succession in the Danish and Norwegian courts. When the fathers of Hamlet and Fortinbras died, they were succeeded on the throne by their brothers, not their sons. Denmark and Norway elected their kings, so the crown did not automatically pass from the father to the son, as it usually did in England.

Shakespeare probably revised his early version of *Hamlet* in 1599 or 1600, only three or four years after his only son Hamnet died in 1596, at age 11. Following a connection first noted by James Joyce, critics speculate that the premature death of Hamnet inspired Shakespeare as he wrote his greatest play. The theory seems plausible, since in Elizabethan English, the name Hamnet was a variant of Hamlet.

Take note of the compelling ironies. Hamlet feigns madness to expose Claudius' and the court's culpability, while Ophelia is driven truly insane by Polonius' murder. In *The Riverside Shakespeare: The Complete Works*, Frank Kermode discusses other patterns: "We have Ophelia's madness as a foil to Hamlet's 'antic disposition,' and the factitious grief of the player who 'acts' without motive when Hamlet, with all the motive in the world—as he tells us—cannot act at all."

Reviewing how the Danish court atmosphere is tainted, Kermode notes: "the play is full of spying, of 'tricks'—a repeated word; and Hamlet does his share, setting Horatio to watch the King. Power is abused . . . Custom is maintained in bad instances, broken in good. The evil of the tyrant is a contagious blastment [*a blighting influence*] for Ophelia. One may infer that the heaven which rejects his prayers will also ensure . . . that the tyrant's life is a short one."

Hamlet's Theatricality

Hamlet is a highly theatrical play. This quality marks it as unique among Shakespeare's work and among Western plays written over the last millennium. Ultimately, Hamlet's masks and play-acting bring us closer to understanding his mind and what disturbs him. While swearing Horatio and Marcellus to secrecy in Act one, he hints that he might reveal his "antic disposition." Presumably this is the mask he will wear by pretending to be mad. By feigning madness around Ophelia, Polonius, and his parents, Hamlet is pretending in order to discover the truth.

In Act three, the players arrive, promising Hamlet and us a diversion from the court intrigue. Yet Hamlet has more than a passing interest in the troupe; he engages with them and instructs them in both speech and movement. He dispenses the following advice: "Speak the speech, I pray you, as I pronounc'd it to you,/Trippingly on the tongue; but if you mouth it, as many of our/Players do, I had as life the town-crier spoke my lines." Here, you can't help but feel that Shakespeare himself is using Hamlet as a mouthpiece for the advice he would give actors in the Lord Chamberlain's Men. (From this advice, scholars surmise that Elizabethan actors delivered Shakespeare's lines more quickly than modern actors do, and thus, the plays didn't run so long.) By telling the actors, "Suit the action to the word, the word to the action, with this special observance, that you o'erstep not the modesty of nature," Hamlet is warning the players not to overdo it!

Another theatrical touch in *Hamlet* is Shakespeare's use of the play-within-the-play and other stage entertainment. On the night Hamlet stages *The Mousetrap*, the king and court are treated to a pantomime prelude, called a "dumb show." Then, by staging *The Mousetrap*, Hamlet creates an illusion of Claudius' crime. Using *The Mousetrap*, Hamlet and Shakespeare raise questions about the differences between illusion and reality. Finally, Shakespeare culminates his highly theatrical story with a showy fencing match intended to entertain the king and queen, the court, and viewers of *Hamlet*.

Chapter 20. Hamlet, Prince of Denmark

Acclaimed Director Michael Kahn Talks About the Challenges of Directing *Hamlet* and Grappling with Shakespeare's Ambiguity

Michael Kahn has served as artistic director of the nationally recognized Shakespeare Theatre Company in Washington, D.C., since 1986. He frequently directed Shakespeare while serving as artistic director of the American Shakespeare Theatre in Stratford, Connecticut. An award-winning stage director whose groundbreaking world premieres are too numerous to mention, Kahn is internationally renowned for his work on Broadway and with top U.S. opera companies. His former classical acting students include William Hurt, Laura Linney, Harvey Keitel, Val Kilmer, Kevin Kline, Patti LuPone, Kelly McGillis, Christopher Reeve, and Robin Williams.

After directing the Shakespeare Theatre Company's 2007 production of *Hamlet*, Kahn spoke about some of the specific challenges that directing *Hamlet* presents to the director.

"There have been so many productions of *Hamlet* that it's difficult for directors and actors, as well as theatregoers, to clear their minds of all the versions they've seen in order to have a conversation with the author. The story of *Hamlet* and its exciting incidents are pretty clear. But the question of why things happen and what the character is actually like who is acting and reacting to what happens is not nearly as clear.

"When we watch the play, many of the questions we ask are left open: Is Hamlet mad or not? Does Gertrude ever know or believe that Claudius has killed her first husband? Does Claudius kill for love as much as power? What is the extent of Hamlet and Ophelia's relationship? What is Horatio's feeling for Hamlet? Is the Ghost benevolent or cold and harsh? Is Polonius a fool or not? Is Polonius a politician or just a fuzzy old man? These questions underscore much of the play's ambiguity, I think, which is the genius of the play. Shakespeare has left ambiguity surrounding all the characters and as a result, directors and actors have to make large and small choices all the time about why and how things happen while being faithful to the text. This is what makes *Hamlet* so exciting and challenging for the artists doing it.

PART 5. THE TRAGEDIES

"A KINGDOM FOR A STAGE"

When he produced the Shakespeare Theatre Company's 2007 production of *Hamlet* in modern dress, artistic director Michael Kahn was aiming for authenticity. Likewise, the Lord Chamberlain's Men, Shakespeare's acting company, wore Elizabethan-era doublet and hose—those old-fashioned vests and balloon-shaped bottoms—whether or not a play was set in ancient Rome or Renaissance Vienna and so were dressed like the audience, i.e. in "modern" dress. Kahn's production was cleverly modernized—Ophelia enjoys her iPod, one of the Players carries a cell phone, and Claudius gives small tape recorders to Rosencrantz and Guildenstern to help them spy on Hamlet effectively.

"Since I directed *Hamlet* 15 years ago, my sense of the play has changed, while my sense of the language is the same. For example, my interpretation of Hamlet's madness is different now compared to then, but both of my interpretations are faithful to Shakespeare. You can be faithful to the text and afford yourself wide latitude in addressing the ambiguity.

"Also, when I directed the play years ago, I didn't consider all of Claudius' lines about how deeply in love he is with Gertrude. He is guilt-ridden during his first real soliloquy in Act three when he's alone onstage, and he talks about how terrible his deed was. If you consider this scene closely in light of earlier lines that suggest his great love for Gertrude, it appears that Shakespeare made Claudius more complicated than a simple villain. All of these scenes suggest that his motives are as much about his love for Gertrude as about power.

"The 'closet scene' is a very hard one to play because Gertrude has almost nothing to say. I think this is when she begins to fall apart. In our 2007 production, I have her deliver her speech about Ophelia's drowning with her clothes all drenched, as if she's just come from trying to save her. Right after that, Laertes appears carrying the drowned Ophelia. That particular moment is usually not done onstage. This tragic scene marks the end of Claudius and Gertrude."

Chapter 20. Hamlet, Prince of Denmark

FACTS TO REMEMBER
- Unlike Shakespeare's later tragedies, *Hamlet* takes us into the mind of one man and his unwillingness to take action to avenge his father's death.
- While we listen, wait, and doubt along with Hamlet, we are privy to a great mind's contemplation of universal concerns about life, death, and despair.
- Two delays in Hamlet's revenge occur when he stages *The Mousetrap* to implicate Claudius and when he postpones the murder as Claudius prays.
- Director Jack Young notes that Shakespeare intended for the duel between Laertes and Hamlet to be a ritualized game with prescribed rules, not a blood sport.
- *Hamlet* is considered the world's greatest modern literary masterwork because the central character thinks, questions, and ponders his existence in a philosophical fashion.

Chapter 21:
Othello, the Moor of Venice

> **INTRODUCTION**
> - An introduction to *Othello*, a domestic drama for all time
> - Insights into *Othello*'s key characters and a synopsis of the action
> - Shakespeare's portrait of Othello as a dignified hero who lowers himself to murder and self-destruction
> - Tips about themes in *Othello*
> - A behind-the-scenes look at how one director created a production of *Othello* at the Texas Shakespeare Festival

Ever since the King's Men first performed *Othello* at St. James' court on November 1, 1604, it has enjoyed unceasing popularity onstage. A brilliant, tightly contained domestic drama, *Othello* is unique among Shakespeare's four greatest tragedies. The play does not concern itself with lofty matters of the court or state. Instead, it confines itself to the intimate emotional territory shared by a husband and wife who violate Venetian social mores and centers on a revenge plot against them.

In marvelous Shakespearean fashion, *Othello* radically departs from plays like *Henry IV*, *Hamlet*, and *King Lear* because it does not explicitly address the responsibilities of a king, prince, or duke. Nor does it look at how the state uses the law as a tool to govern, as in *The Merchant of Venice* and *Measure for Measure.* Instead it goes for the jugular, baring the soul of a respectable military leader, showing us the limits of his passion, pride, and trust, until he self-destructs.

There are several reasons *Othello* has remained popular onstage. First, its plot is tightly woven and fast-moving, free of a distracting subplot that complicates the scope of *Hamlet* and *King Lear*. Second, Othello has very few characters. Its action essentially revolves around the trio of Othello, Desdemona, and Iago. Third, in creating Iago, Shakespeare has given us his greatest, most irresistible villain—a monster who drives the action from start to finish. Finally, *Othello* elegantly shows the evolution of Shakespeare's masterful psychological realism, both in dialogue and soliloquy.

The Characters

Othello—A Venetian army general, Othello is a respectable Moor of noble birth and character considered an outsider in Venetian society because he is foreign and dark-skinned. Othello falls victim to the evil machinations of Iago, his ensign. No one agrees on what makes Othello vulnerable to Iago's manipulation, but the turning point seems to come in the third act when he loses faith in his wife's love and stops trusting her. The erosion of his faith makes Othello vulnerable to a despicable villain, whom he blindly trusts.

Desdemona—She is the wife of Othello who flouts the expectations of her powerful father and her society by marrying a black African. She is honest and loyal to her husband, from the moment he first doubts her fidelity until he goes raving mad with sexual jealousy.

Iago—Othello's ensign, a commissioned military officer, is the play's villain. He is probably Shakespeare's most famous villain, carrying the third-longest Shakespearean male role, according to the *Oxford Dictionary of Shakespeare*, edited by Stanley Wells. When Othello passes Iago over for promotion, promoting Cassio to lieutenant instead, Iago transforms his envy into a vile plan to get even. In fact, Iago is so cruel that Shakespeare is often criticized because the villain's apparent motive doesn't seem to justify his behavior. (By the way, Othello addresses Iago as his *ancient*, which is another word for *ensign*.)

Emilia—The wife of Iago is also Desdemona's loyal mistress. When she finds the coveted handkerchief that Desdemona carelessly mislays, she presents it to Iago. By doing so, she is the ironic instrument of the act that sets events in motion that will lead to her mistress's murder. Emilia is the harbinger of the truth during the play's final scene, memorably recounting the evil behind Desdemona's foul murder.

Cassio—Othello's lieutenant is an honorable man and loyal to Othello, but he has a few flaws himself. He drinks too much on occasion and talks indiscreetly about his sexual relationship with Bianca. Iago takes advantages of Cassio's weaknesses and finds ways to ensnare him in the plot to bring down Othello. After Cassio is stripped of his rank, he speaks profoundly about the importance of reputation, a subject we'll address later.

Roderigo—He is the gullible Venetian gentleman who is easily duped by Iago because he loves Desdemona. Iago tricks him into aiding his revenge plot by promising him that Desdemona's love is still within reach. Iago considers Roderigo expendable and easily sacrifices him when their plot to murder Cassio goes awry.

Brabantio—He is a Venetian senator and the father of Desdemona. Brabantio is angered when he learns his daughter has eloped with Othello. He unsuccessfully appeals to the Venetian senate to get her back. But his pleas prove fruitless when Desdemona is allowed to explain why she married the Moor. Feeling disgraced and furious, he disowns her and warns Othello that Desdemona is capable of deceiving her husband, just as she deceived her father.

Duke of Venice

Lodovico—Desdemona's kinsman; a Venetian nobleman

> Gratiano—Desdemona's uncle; a Venetian nobleman
>
> Bianca—A courtesan who is Cassio's mistress
>
> Senators of Venice
>
> Montano—The governor of Cyprus who is replaced by Othello
>
> Clown—A servant of Othello
>
> Gentlemen of Cyprus
>
> Messenger, Herald, Officers, Gentlemen, Musicians and Attendants
>
> *Setting: Venice and Cyprus*

A Secret Marriage in Venice

As the play opens, the mood seems strained because of a shift among the ranks of the Venetian Army. Othello, a noble Moor and army general, has just made the devoted Michael Cassio his personal lieutenant, passing over his ensign Iago, who holds the lowest rank granted to a commissioned officer. Needless to say, Iago is incensed. But he's not the only one. Roderigo, a suitor to Desdemona, has just found out that she has eloped with Othello, so he takes his anger out on Iago for withholding the news.

Both livid, Iago and Roderigo decide to alert Senator Brabantio, Desdemona's father, about the elopement. Shouting lewdly beneath Brabantio's window, the two speak in nasty, irreverent terms about Othello's sexual behavior with Desdemona. Brabantio is outraged over the news that his daughter has married a Moor.

"WILD AND WHIRLING WORDS"

> When you watch a performance of *Othello*, you'll be compelled by the jarring, profane images of animal sexuality uttered in an early scene. Iago tells Brabantio, "... an old black ram/Is tupping your white ewe!" referring to the sexual relationship between Othello and

Desdemona. Iago further shocks the senator when he says, "your daughter and the Moor are now making the beast with two backs."

Scholars often look at this imagery within a symbolic or allegorical reading of the play. They speculate that Venice is a decadent society that has fallen into chaos and disarray, after the fall of Adam and Eve. Othello and Desdemona are likened to the first couple of Genesis, while Iago is pegged as the serpent that destroys their life in paradise.

Meanwhile, the Duke of Venice is reacting to the news that Turkish ships are about to invade Cyprus. From the senate chambers, he has sent for Othello and is in the process of assigning him to a command in Cyprus, when who should interrupt but the angry Brabantio. The senator appeals to the Duke to arrest and imprison Othello on the spot. Later, he complains that the general has stolen his daughter from him and married her without her father's permission. Othello is prepared to defend himself, but also wants Desdemona summoned to tell her side of the story.

In the meantime, the general recounts how he courted Desdemona and how she became attached to him as he told stories about his military exploits. Further, he tells of how his and Desdemona's love developed. Desdemona had become captivated by the stories of his adventures and beguiled by his heroism. In this lofty speech, we also learn that Brabantio admired Othello and welcomed him into his home.

>Othello: She wish'd she had not heard it, yet she wish'd
>   That heaven had made her such a man. She thank'd me
>   And bade me, if I had a friend that lov'd her,
>   I should but teach him how to tell my story,
>   And that would woo her. Upon this hint I spake:
>   She lov'd me for the dangers I had pass'd,
>   And I lov'd her that she did pity them.
>   This only is the witchcraft I have us'd.
>   Here comes the lady; let her witness it.
>   (I.3.162-170)

As Othello defends his honor, we see there is nothing rash or unreasonable about his behavior, nor has he done anything immoral. When she arrives, Desdemona publicly explains how much she loves Othello and dotes on him. Othello is exonerated and urged by the Duke to make haste to Cyprus. He grants Desdemona's wish to accompany her husband. Othello decides that she should travel with Iago and puts her in the care of his wife, Emilia. Things start to get interesting when Iago secretly promises Roderigo that he shall soon have Desdemona back because it is likely that she'll begin to stray from her husband. In a soliloquy, Iago reveals details of a plot to get revenge on Othello, which involves making him believe that Desdemona is having an affair with Cassio.

In Cyprus, a Scheme to Entrap Cassio

Although a terrible storm destroys the Turkish fleet, all of Othello's ships arrive safely to his new command in Cyprus. Iago wastes no time in luring Roderigo, who doesn't know Cassio, in on his plot to damage Cassio's position in the army. Believing he may have a chance with Desdemona, Roderigo goes along with the plan. Then, in another soliloquy, the vicious Iago explains exactly how he plans to hurt Othello. Crediting his boss with a "constant, loving, noble nature," Iago confesses that he won't be content until he "puts the Moor/ At least into a jealousy so strong/That judgment cannot cure."

In Oliver Parker's 1995 film version, Kenneth Branagh (right) rendered Iago as sardonically comical and supremely confident.

(Photo courtesy of Columbia Pictures/Photofest.)

That evening, there is much for the soldiers to celebrate. Because of the storm, the Turkish threat has been eliminated. Othello orders Cassio to keep a close watch on the Venetian troops in Cyprus. Iago gets to work, though, and manipulates Cassio into drinking too much. Then Roderigo involves the lieutenant in a brawl that brings Othello into the mix. Guilty of impropriety, Cassio is in a delicate position. When Othello arrives on the scene and wants to know what's going on, Iago purposely holds back the details of the brawl and its escalation. This makes Othello suspect the worst of Cassio. Believing that Iago is withholding information that would implicate Cassio and failing to trust his own lieutenant, he demotes Cassio, stripping him of his coveted rank as lieutenant. Cassio, of course, is eager to mend his reputation. He tells Iago:

Cassio: Reputation, reputation, reputation! O, I have lost my reputation! I have lost the immortal part of myself, and what remains is bestial. My reputation, Iago, my reputation!
(II.3.262-265)

Afterwards, the weasel Iago secretly advises Cassio to get Desdemona to use her influence to restore his position. This is just the beginning of Iago's evil machinations. In yet another soliloquy, Iago keeps us abreast of his next plan to make Othello suspicious of Desdemona's efforts to help Cassio plead his case.

Planting Seeds of Sexual Jealousy

Emilia arranges a meeting between Cassio and Desdemona, her mistress. When the meeting takes place, Iago makes sure that Othello catches Cassio making his departure. Desdemona, of course, pleads with her husband on Cassio's behalf. (It may seem a little far-fetched, but physically, Iago is never very far away from this couple. This is one of Shakespeare's artificial conceits that prevent us from asking too many questions about the plot's believability.) Iago begins posing questions about the couple's relationship with Cassio during their courtship. Although Othello indicates that nothing unseemly or unlawful occurred between his wife and Cassio, Iago casts suspicion on Cassio's honesty. At the same time, he professes his love for Othello to reinforce the general's trust in him, so he can manipulate him with further revelations. When Othello asks for proof, Iago holds back but continues to plant

PART 5. THE TRAGEDIES

the notion that Desdemona and Cassio were sexually involved before Othello married her:

Iago:	Look to your wife, observe her well with Cassio, Wear your eyes thus, not jealous nor secure. . . .
Othello:	Dost thou say so?
Iago:	She did deceive her father, marrying you, And when she seem'd to shake and fear your looks, She lov'd them most.
Othello:	And so she did.

(III.3.197-99; 205-208)

Hmmmm. Not surprisingly, these revelations give Othello something to worry about. When Desdemona comes back into the room, Othello is seized by fresh doubts about her fidelity.

The Missing Handkerchief

Sometime later, Desdemona accidentally drops her handkerchief and leaves the room before she realizes it is gone. Emilia finds it and gives it to Iago, knowing he's asked her for it numerous times before.

TIMELESS SOLILOQUIES

Iago:	O, beware, my lord, of jealousy! It is the green-ey'd monster which doth mock The meat it feeds on. That cuckold lives in bliss Who, certain of his fate, loves not his wronger; But O, what damned minutes tells he o'er Who dotes, yet doubts; suspects, yet [strongly] loves!
Othello:	O misery! (III.3.165-171)

> Here is one of the play's most memorable speeches, partly because our image of jealousy as the "green-eyed monster" seems to have originated with Shakespeare. Iago's words are ironic because the villain is actually provoking Othello to feel the jealousy he warns him against. The passage also finds thematic echoes elsewhere. Later, when we discuss them, we'll explore how Othello's sexual jealousy may be the root of his undoing.

Now Iago has his chance to invent the proof he needs to convince Othello that there is something going on between Desdemona and Cassio. He plants Desdemona's handkerchief in Cassio's room. When Iago sees Othello again, the general is not doing well at all. His mind is in chaos, and he seriously doubts his wife at this point. Iago sadistically feeds this jealously with more lies. He tells Othello that he has overheard Cassio utter affectionate things to Desdemona during his sleep. Worse, he tells the general that he saw Cassio carrying the handkerchief. This latest fabrication pushes Othello nearer to the breaking point, and he is determined to get revenge against Cassio and Desdemona. When he learns that his wife cannot find the handkerchief, he believes he has genuine proof of her infidelity.

More Lies Until Othello Collapses into a Fit

The more Iago lies about Desdemona's fidelity, the worse it affects Othello's mental state. Desdemona is alarmed by Othello's mood changes. The general becomes enraged when Iago tells him a tale about how Cassio had acknowledged sleeping with Desdemona. Upon hearing this, Othello is physically overcome with rage and jealousy. Suddenly, he falls into an epileptic-like seizure, an episode that proves tricky for any actor playing Othello onstage.

Throughout the last two acts, Iago engineers two charades that show us the horrifying extent of his evil-doing. We witness how Othello's mistrust and jealousy have overcome him physically. In the first charade Iago sends Othello over the edge with more "proof" of Desdemona's infidelity. He has the Moor eavesdrop on a conversation between him and Cassio. Cassio indiscreetly talks about his affair with Bianca, and overhearing this, Othello wrongly assumes he is talking about being with Desdemona. Now livid, Othello speaks to Iago

PART 5. THE TRAGEDIES

about murder—a plan to murder his wife and her ostensible lover. Both men agree that Desdemona should be strangled, not poisoned.

"So Sweet Was Never So Fatal"

Order within Othello's household quickly dissolves into chaos. Lodovico arrives from Venice to issue an order for Othello to return to Venice and informs him that Cassio should take his command in Cyprus. In this scene Othello audaciously slaps and insults Desdemona in front of Lodovico and his men. In the next scene a fearful Emilia urgently defends her mistress. Though Desdemona forgives Othello for mistreating her, Emilia starts to smell a rat, and that rat, of course, is her own husband.

Iago's second charade occurs at the beginning of the fifth act. This time, he brings Roderigo into his and Othello's plot to kill Cassio, telling him to provoke a swordfight with the former lieutenant. The plan goes awry and Iago ends up fatally stabbing Roderigo to rid himself of an incriminating witness. The rest of the action moves at a breathless pace toward one of Shakespeare's most tragic conclusions. Inside the couple's bedchamber, when Desdemona finally stands up to her husband's accusations, he is provoked to murder her.

"A KINGDOM FOR A STAGE!"

Great directors differ in how they interpret the famous scene when Othello murders Desdemona. To experience the broad artistic license that Shakespeare's script gives the actor and director, check out three well-known screen adaptations. In one, directed by Orson Welles in 1952, Welles (as Othello) took a piece of Suzanne Cloutier's sheer nightgown and held it over her face until she suffocated. In one of Laurence Olivier's most frenetic Shakespearean roles, for the 1965 film featuring the National Theater of Great Britain, Olivier ranted at Maggie Smith's Desdemona as she sat up in bed, smothered her with a pillow, and finally choked her to death. In Oliver Parker's realistic 2001 film, Laurence Fishburne's Othello displayed tears and tender kisses before throwing Irene Jacob violently on her bed more than once before suffocating her with a pillow.

After Othello strangles his wife, Emilia enters the bedroom and finds her mistress gasping for life, still refusing to blame her husband! When Desdemona dies, the stage belongs to Emilia. She rages against Othello's murder, confronts her husband, and demands to know the truth; then she bravely insists on reporting it to Montano, Gratiano, and all the others on the scene. In a final flurry of madness, Iago fatally stabs Emilia; reeling from Iago's sadistic betrayal, Othello wounds the villain, who is taken away to be tortured and interrogated. When Lodovico relieves Othello of his power and his command, Othello offers his final speech:

> Othello: I have done the state some service, and they know't—
> No more of that. I pray you, in your letters,
> When you shall these unlucky deeds relate,
> Speak of me as I am; nothing extenuate,
> Nor set down aught in malice. Then you must speak
> Of one that lov'd not wisely but too well;
> Of one not easily jealous, but being wrought,
> Perplexed in the extreme; of one whose hand
> (Like the base [Indian]) threw a pearl away
> Richer than all his tribe; . . .
> (V.2.339-348)

Here, the fallen general acknowledges his errors and begs those listening to speak the whole truth about him, his past and recent deeds, and the circumstances that caused his fall from grace. Othello implies that despite his extreme love for Desdemona, he was provoked to extremes of jealous emotion that led him to sacrifice her. Afterward, he stabs himself to death and falls on the bed near her.

Looking at Othello as a Tragic Hero and Some Thoughts About Theme

Before you walk away from the play, it's important to remember that, despite the playwright's depiction of Venetian prejudice toward foreigners and blacks, Shakespeare has nonetheless depicted Othello in the play's first half as the image of nobility and military grandeur. In defending himself before Brabantio, Othello is nothing if not articulate. His anecdotal review of his experiences and how they impressed Desdemona leaves no doubt in our minds that he is a guiltless hero. Further, the fact that Shakespeare subjects him to the browbeating from Brabantio emphasizes his position and plight as an outsider in Venetian society. But it isn't until Othello and Desdemona leave Venice that their lives are torn apart. One key to the success of Iago's treachery may lie in Othello and Desdemona's insecure position in the unfamiliar territory of Cyprus.

"WILD AND WHIRLING WORDS"

By casting the hero of Othello as a Moor, we can safely assume that the general was born somewhere in North Africa, but Shakespeare doesn't tell us exactly where. Critics argue incessantly over whether Shakespeare intended for Othello to be a black-skinned African or a tawny-hued Arab. Stage productions have offered myriad interpretations, casting both white and black actors in the coveted role. But key images suggest that Shakespeare imagined Othello as a black man. He is described as being "thick-lipped" with a "sooty bosom." These and other images offer good internal evidence of how Shakespeare envisioned his hero.

Sadly, Othello is not without tragic flaws, and we can't help but see a little of ourselves in Shakespeare's once-dignified hero who ends up cruelly reduced to an untrusting, self-centered madman. Why does such an accomplished military figure recklessly abandon his deep love for and trust in a loyal wife and succumb to savage, bloodthirsty revenge? Why does Othello become so jealous? Perhaps it is because his sexual passion for Desdemona is so strong. His sexual jealousy seems to have caused him to spin out of control.

There are certainly no easy answers, but the root of Othello's undoing may lie in his excessive self-love or pride, a root cause of jealousy. Ironically, Othello loses faith in the person who loves him the most, the one whose love for him is the most honest and selfless. The fact that Desdemona has risked and incurred her father's ostracism proves the strength of this love. Sadly, Othello blindly ignores her constancy and wrongly places faith in one who merely pretends to be honest. When he places more trust in false Iago than he does in the true Desdemona, Othello is doomed.

Do you recall the value that Cassio placed on his military reputation and how devastated he was when Othello stripped him of his rank? In a commentary accompanying the Naxos AudioBooks 2000 version of *Othello*, director David Timson reminds us that reputation really mattered among seventeenth-century Venetians. To engage in commerce, merchants took risks and placed great faith in one another's reputations.

Creating a Production of *Othello* at the Texas Shakespeare Festival

Roseann Sheridan, artistic director of the Children's Theater of Madison and former associate artistic director of the American Players Theatre, directed *Othello* at the Texas Shakespeare Festival in 2007. While planning the production, she was involved in numerous decisions about set design and props. These decisions were important because they affected her creative team's vision and how she herself blocked the scenes with actors. In early meetings with her creative team, Sheridan opted against a set design and costumes that were too contemporary or too fixed in the Elizabethan period. "We wanted the play to feel timeless and, yet, suggestive of a time removed from our own. Influenced by time constraints, the creative team settled on the simplicity and lines of the Napoleonic era."

Aiming for Simplicity in Costumes, Scenery, and Props

The creative team adapted costumes to fit the simple, Napoleonic style. "We felt the play had a sensuality and sexuality, supported by a sense of black-and-white or polar opposites," Sheridan explained. "The male actors' pants are all tight-fitting polyester Wrangler jeans without the Wrangler label and belt loops. The enlisted men wore chef jackets, adapted to look more militaristic.

As the play's mood gets more chaotic, you see the costumes reflecting that breakdown. One of Desdemona's dresses has a long flowing slit up the side, and when Othello throws her down, it falls open."

To keep the environment simple, there was no flying scenery in the show, Sheridan said. "There are only two tables onstage, allowing us to convey a level of openness and comfort in Cyprus that doesn't exist in Venice. I wanted the scenes to feel intimate but not interior. Realizing that Shakespeare doesn't give us any stage directions, I had to add a prop to evoke Desdemona's domestic environment in Cyprus. Every now and then it's nice to have some kind of activity onstage. So I came up with the idea that she might give Cassio tea or prepare to give him tea. The tea set is our only other prop. With few props, the chaos is much more easily rendered."

Creating a Sense of Ritual Before Othello's Murder Scene

To stage Othello's climactic "It is the cause" scene, one of the greatest Shakespearean scenes for its blend of powerful poetry and heightened drama, Sheridan took pains to develop the motifs of sacrifice and ritual.

"We added ritualistic coloring to the 'It is the cause' scene. Desdemona sets up her own bed. Then Othello comes in to prepare for his own ritual, a ritual of murder. To show how his military world and North African origins were colliding, he was barefoot, clothed in a robe over military pants, wearing a medallion that appeared to be non-military, almost tribal. He had a saber, but he wasn't wearing it as a military weapon. He took what used to be a military sash and draped it around his neck to make him appear priest-like. He also had a basin so he could cleanse himself.

Woven throughout Othello's famous "It is the cause" speech are key Shakespearean clues to help the actor understand what the Moor is thinking. In *Shakespeare's Advice to the Players*, Peter Hall offers a close reading of this speech, particularly the ambiguity inherent in the word "cause."

Chapter 21: . Othello, the Moor of Venice

Othello: It is the cause, it is the cause, my soul;
   Let me not name it to you, you chaste stars,
   It is the cause. Yet I'll not shed her blood,
   Nor scar that whiter skin of hers than snow,
   And smooth as monumental alabaster.
   Yet she must die, else she'll betray more men.
   (V.2.1-6)

Hall explains: "Desdemona is the cause—the reason, the motive, the ground. She is the explanation, the occasion, the circumstance. She is also the business, the subject, possibly the court case, the legal process. Or her behavior violates the code of honor: a duel is justified. Finally she is Othello's matter of concern, his apprehension, his justification; and the disease, the illness, the sickness."

"To me Othello's repetition of the words 'It is the cause' felt ritualistic, like a chant or summoning. Once he goes over to Desdemona, he is struck by the reality of her; her infidelity is not just the problem in his mind. He puts his hand over the flame of the candle. All of these rituals color the scene. In our production, we took pains with Othello and Desdemona's preparation for bed, so that when Othello first enters the space where Desdemona lies and starts speaking, his words echo the couple's visual preoccupation with ritual, and the audience can really feel where Othello's words are coming from."

FACTS TO REMEMBER

- *Othello* stands apart from Shakespeare's other great tragedies because its action centers on the intrigue affecting a married couple who break social mores and later become estranged from one other.
- Although many critics believe he could have been an Arab from northern Africa, imagery in the play allows us to safely infer that Shakespeare envisioned Othello, the Moor, as a black African.
- Iago is one of Shakespeare's most brilliantly realized villains and the third-longest male role in all of Shakespearean drama.
- Othello's tragic flaw is exposed when he allows Iago to undermine his strong love for Desdemona, which causes him to stop trusting her.
- In a Texas Shakespeare Festival production of *Othello*, a director emphasizes the ritualistic mood of Othello's murder of Desdemona, which is implicit in the script.

Chapter 22
King Lear

> **INTRODUCTION**
> - Introducing *King Lear*, a great tragedy about two families destroyed by treachery, and what makes it timeless
> - Insights into the play's nine well-drawn characters
> - Key events in *King Lear*'s complex plot
> - The play's focus on filial ingratitude, estrangement, and its existential overtones
> - A fight director talks about choreographing stage violence in *King Lear* and Shakespeare in general
> - Two professionals talk about the challenges of performing and staging *King Lear*

Unlike most Western drama, *King Lear* feels personal and larger than life, concrete and mythical, immediate and timeless. But through the ages, *King Lear* has been criticized for being too dark and too difficult to stage. (One seventeenth-century rewrite of the play returns Lear to the throne and lets Cordelia live!) Few disagree, however, that the play is an artistic tour de force that surpasses all of Shakespeare's plays. Akira Kurosawa's classic film *Ran*, Ivan Turgenev's *A Lear of the Steppes*, and Jane Smiley's *A Thousand Acres* are among the great works inspired by Shakespeare's *Lear*.

Shakespeare's other tragedies inspire us because they explore treachery and the consequences of personal, communal, or political betrayal. But *King Lear* probes the truth of our human condition across every one of these realms. The play explores what happens when every imaginable human bond is broken: specifically, the bond between a king and each of his daughters, between a duke and each of his sons, between two selfish daughters, and between a good half-brother and an evil half-brother. In addition, a marriage bond is violated and a king exiles a loyal servant for being truthful. To modern playgoers born after the unspeakable horrors of two world wars, the Holocaust, and more recent genocide, *King Lear's* vision of human suffering and chaos is as germane as the bleak world of Sartre and Camus.

The Characters

King Lear—He is King of Britain, a proud, selfish monarch who foolishly decides to abdicate and divide his kingdom among his three daughters. After demanding that each prove her love through a formal declaration (and probably hoping to bestow the largest share on his favorite), Lear is offended by Cordelia's refusal. She says, "I cannot heave/My heart into my mouth." He misjudges her reluctance to express her love for impertinence. So, he disinherits her and banishes her from England. When the king hands over his lands and control to his two older daughters, he subjects himself to profoundly harsh consequences. By voluntarily and foolishly forfeiting his power, Lear finds his authority co-opted by Goneril, Regan, and Cornwall, whose regard for him diminishes greatly after he relinquishes his authority. Enraged by the injustice of his daughters' mistreatment of him, he ventures into the storm and goes mad.

Lear's Fool—He is as wise as the king is foolish. Lear's Fool is one of Shakespeare's witty, sardonic creations. Through his running repartee with Lear, the truth about the king's missteps and his lack of insight are revealed. During the storm, Lear empathizes with the Fool, signaling the king's movement toward selflessness.

Chapter 22. King Lear

Goneril—She is Lear's oldest daughter and the Duchess of Albany. She pretends to hold great affection for her father as he is dividing his kingdom. She mistreats him soon afterward, though, by refusing to board his large retinue of followers. She is the object of Lear's stinging curse. She lusts after Edmund, touching off disastrous consequences. After she poisons Regan, her vile deed is discovered and she kills herself.

Duke of Albany—He is Goneril's husband, as honest and upright as his wife is self-serving and evil. He disapproves of Goneril's treatment of Lear and vows to avenge Cornwall's horrific blinding of Gloucester. At the end of the play, we look to him and Edgar to put the country to rights.

Oswald—He is Goneril's loyal steward and her "yes" man, showing disrespect for Lear equal to that of his mistress.

Regan—She is Lear's middle daughter, the Duchess of Cornwall, who shows endearing sweetness to her father despite a cruelty that is often harsher than Goneril's. Before Lear ventures out into the storm, she refuses to sympathize with his anger toward Goneril; she insults him, condescends to him, and refuses to allow him to bring his horde of followers into her castle. Like Goneril, she has romantic designs on Edmund after Cornwall is killed. She is poisoned to death by Goneril.

Duke of Cornwall—He is Regan's husband and a despicably evil son-in-law. He, like Goneril and Regan, refuse to honor Lear's wishes immediately after he grants them equal halves of his kingdom. He betrays his king and father-in-law. To Lear's shock, he has the king's servant Kent put in the stocks. Heinously, he has Gloucester blinded to punish the elderly duke for helping the king. His servant mortally wounds him to stop him from gouging out Gloucester's second eye.

Cordelia—She is Lear's youngest daughter and, before the play begins, his favorite. By refusing to heap flattery upon him like her hypocritical sisters, she falls out of Lear's favor and is disowned. The King of France accepts her as his wife and marries her without a dowry. When her husband's army loses to the British, she and Lear are captured and she is hanged upon the villain Edmund's instructions.

Duke of Burgundy—A self-serving suitor of Cordelia who rejects her after she is disinherited. He only cares about her dowry.

King of France—A suitor of Cordelia who is unconcerned that her dowry has been stripped and marries her for love. Although he never appears again after the play's opening scene, we learn of his plan to invade England to restore Lear's power.

Earl of Kent—He is banished by Lear when he speaks truthfully and candidly to his king. He resurfaces, disguised as Caius, and becomes one of Lear's followers in order to watch out for him.

Gentleman loyal to Lear and Cordelia

Doctor

Earl of Gloucester—He is the father of Edgar and Edmund and the feudal vassal of the Duke of Cornwall. He is fooled by Edmund into believing that Edgar is plotting to murder him. Shakespeare creates him and his two sons as a foil to Lear and his three daughters. His physical blindness is symbolic of his failure to see the truth of his illegitimate son's treachery. He, like Lear, embarks on a journey of suffering that leads toward self-awareness and bitter assessments about the unjust suffering that humans experience.

Edgar—He is the legitimate, older son of Gloucester who is forced to flee from his father's castle after being framed by his evil half-brother. To escape persecution, he disguises himself as Tom O' Bedlam, a beggar. He stumbles upon Lear and his Fool, calling himself Poor Tom, and receives the king's profound sympathy. Later, he assumes the guise of a peasant after Gloucester tries to hurl himself off a cliff.

Edmund—He is Gloucester's smooth-talking younger son who is illegitimate. Also known as the Bastard and famous for being one of

Chapter 22. King Lear

> Shakespeare's greatest villains, he makes his father believe that Edgar is plotting against him. A ruthless opportunist who cares only for himself, he betrays his brother to inherit his father's dukedom and then exposes Gloucester as a traitor to Cornwall, subjecting him to unspeakable torture. He instructs his soldier to execute Lear and Cordelia in prison.
>
> An Old Man—A tenant of Gloucester
>
> Captain—One who is loyal to Edmund
>
> Curan—A courtier of Gloucester
>
> Two servants to Cornwall
>
> Other captains
>
> Knights of Lear's train, Officers, Messengers, Soldiers, and Attendants
>
> *Setting: Britain, during a period reminiscent of ancient times*

Lear's Foolhardy Test and Cordelia's Banishment

King Lear's opening scene feels like a parable. The aged King of Britain has gathered his three daughters, Goneril, Regan, and Cordelia, along with his two sons-in-law, the Dukes of Albany and Cornwall. Joining them are Cordelia's two suitors, the Duke of Burgundy and the King of France. The king tells his children that he plans to divide Britain into three parts. Posing the question, "Which of you shall we say doth love us most," the arrogant Lear promises to give the greater share to the daughter who demonstrates the greatest affection. Goneril and Regan declare their love flamboyantly, but Cordelia is averse to such display. She candidly tells him, "I love your Majesty/According to my bond, no more nor less," adding that she can't bestow all her love on her father when she is married. Incensed by her response, Lear disinherits her despite Kent's efforts to change his mind. Kent is cruelly banished, and the King of France agrees to marry Cordelia without a dowry. So Lear divides his kingdom in half, allotting one part to Goneril and Albany and another to Regan and Cornwall. (Accompanied by a hundred knights, he will take turns visiting

Goneril and Regan.) After Cordelia leaves, Goneril and Regan express concern that their father's senility may eventually backfire on them.

Edmund, the Bastard, Sabotages His Brother

Let's cut away to Shakespeare's subplot. The Earl of Gloucester is having a few problems of his own with Edgar and Edmund, his two sons. In a soliloquy, Edmund grouses about being illegitimate, with no hope of inheriting his father's dukedom. But this ambitious young man wants what he can't have. Using a forged letter and pretending to be loyal to his brother, Edmund convinces Gloucester that Edgar is plotting to murder him. Gloucester is fooled by Edmund's machinations.

Ungrateful Daughters

At the Duke of Albany's palace, the story of Lear gets interesting. As Goneril grows impatient with the king's imperious ways and the unruly behavior of his 100 knights, she tells Oswald, her steward, to give the king and his followers a chilly reception when they return from hunting. Behind his back, she disrespectfully calls Lear an "idle old man" and an "old fool." When Lear returns, Kent shows up, disguised as Caius, and joins the king's party so he can watch over him. In a lively scene, the Fool makes fun of Lear for getting himself into such a pickle, noting that he has "mad'st thy daughters thy mothers."

"WILD AND WHIRLING WORDS"

Over the years, students have read a conflated version of two different *Lear* scripts. The first, called *The History of King Lear,* appeared in an early quarto edition around 1605–1606. The second, known as *The Tragedy of King Lear,* was written in 1609–1610 and appeared in the 1623 First Folio. Many editions, including the *Oxford Shakespeare*, print both scripts, noting that the Folio version is Shakespeare's own revision. In the later Folio version, Shakespeare removed several short scenes, including Lear's trial of Goneril and Regan in Act three, scene 6.

Chapter 22. King Lear

Goneril tries to control her father by insisting that half of his followers leave her palace. Outraged by her insubordination, Lear puts a horrible curse on Goneril, underscoring the play's abiding concern with filial ingratitude:

> Lear: If she must teem,
> Create her child of spleen, that it may live
> And be a thwart disnatur'd torment to her.
> Let it stamp wrinkles in her brow of youth,
> With cadent tears fret channels in her cheeks,
> Turn all her mother's pains and benefits
> To laughter and contempt, that she may feel
> How sharper than a serpent's tooth it is
> To have a thankless child!
> (I.4.281-289)

The Duke of Albany is not happy with how his wife is treating the king, but Goneril persists. She sends Regan a letter to keep her updated on her plans to rid some of Lear's followers.

Cornwall Has Kent Put in the Stocks

Convinced that Edgar is a traitor, Gloucester decides to have him put to death and make Edmund his sole heir. Fearing for his life, Edgar flees from his father's castle. (At this point Shakespeare's two plots converge. Regan and her husband arrive at Gloucester's castle to escape from Lear and his followers. Of course, the manipulative Edmund cozies up to them!)

When Oswald and Kent (as Caius, the messenger) tussle outside Gloucester's castle, Cornwall has Kent put into the stocks. Gloucester isn't happy about it. When Lear arrives and sees his messenger in the stocks, he is enraged. It's hard for him to believe that Regan would do such a thing. When he questions her and Cornwall about who is responsible, he is interrupted by Goneril's arrival. Lear complains about how Goneril has been treating him, expecting Regan to take his side. Instead, she sides with Goneril, and this sends Lear over the edge. Then, both decide they're unwilling to shelter any of Lear's followers. Upset and enraged, the king flees the castle into the gathering storm.

Lear Rages Against His Daughters and the Elements

Kent learns that the King of France is sending an army to restore Lear to the throne. Joined by the Fool in the raging storm, a weeping Lear despairs of living in a universe where children are ungrateful and disloyal to their parents. He laments: "Regan, Goneril!/Your old kind father, whose frank heart gave all—/O, that way madness lies, let me shun that!" Sadly, the king begins to lose his wits. The storm rages and figuratively echoes the storm within Lear's mind. (Meanwhile, Edgar is on the lam, and to protect himself, he takes on the identity of a crazy beggar named Tom O' Bedlam.) Kent appears and helps the king search for shelter. They happen upon a hovel occupied by a miserable beggar who calls himself Poor Tom. In this poignant scene, a mad Lear takes pity on his Fool and Poor Tom, both of whom suffer from the extreme cold. (Actor Charles Krohn talks more about this moment later in this chapter.)

Gloucester Is Blinded

> Gloucester: As flies to wanton boys are we to th' gods,
> They kill us for their sport.
> (IV.1.36-37)

Meanwhile, Gloucester hears about Lear's suffering and secretly decides to help him. He also receives a letter informing him that the French king's army has landed at Dover to restore Lear to the throne. (He confides all of this to Edmund.) Then the worried Gloucester manages to find Lear and deliver him to warmth and shelter. As you might guess, Edmund betrays his father by telling Cornwall that his father has received news from the French army. Branding Gloucester a traitor, Cornwall has the old duke captured and tied to a chair and sets out to blind him. He gouges out one of Gloucester's eyes before Cornwall's servant tries to stop him. The servant fights his master, mortally wounding Cornwall before Regan murders him. Blinded by Cornwall in both eyes, Gloucester realizes that Edgar is innocent and Edmund is the villain. Next, an old tenant of Gloucester entrusts the old man to the care of Poor Tom (Edgar, remember?), who agrees to lead him to the cliffs of Dover.

Chapter 22. King Lear

Desperately Chasing Edmund after Cornwall's Death

After Lear goes mad and Gloucester is blinded, the palaces of Albany and Cornwall dissolve into chaos. Goneril learns from Oswald that her husband is happy at the news of Cordelia's invasion and unhappy that Edmund has exposed Gloucester as traitorous. When Goneril sends Edmund to tell Cornwall to ready an army, she gives him a loving goodbye and implies she is plotting to do away with Albany. As a seething Albany rails against his treacherous wife, this group learns that Gloucester is blinded and Cornwall is dead, leaving Regan a widow. (Now Goneril is worried that Regan will steal her Edmund!) Albany will not let Gloucester's torture go unpunished. At Dover, Kent learns that Cordelia worries about her father and has sent her attendants to fetch him. She gets word that the armies of Cornwall and Albany march toward Dover.

Now that Goneril is estranged from Albany and Regan's husband is dead, the two sisters fall out over Edmund's favor. Oswald arrives at Cornwall's palace and tells Regan that Albany will oppose the French invasion. Regan becomes jealous when she learns from him that Goneril is communicating with Edmund by letter. Revealing her own affections for Edmund, Regan asks the steward to give Edmund a token, along with Goneril's letter. Then she asks Oswald to offer Edmund a reward for killing Gloucester.

Back at Dover, Poor Tom has led Gloucester to believe he stands on the edge of a cliff. Before Gloucester throws himself over it, he says: "Oh you mighty gods!/This world I do renounce, and in your sights/Shake patiently my great affliction off." In a pathetic gesture, Gloucester flings himself over the precipice, hoping to commit suicide. When he doesn't die, Edgar (now disguised as a peasant, after the Old Tenant gave him a change of clothes in the previous scene!) convinces him he's been saved by a miracle.

Verse by Verse

Letters. Letters. Letters. The dramatic action of *King Lear* hinges on epistles of treachery and military overthrow. Like the forces in Lear's amoral universe, letters often serve a dark purpose. Edmund hands Gloucester a letter forged by his own hand, representing his half-brother Edgar as a traitor. Goneril has Oswald deliver Regan a letter about her plans to reduce Lear's knightly entourage. Gloucester receives a letter telling him the King of France is planning to invade England. After Edgar kills Oswald, he honors his request to deliver Goneril's duplicitous letter to Edmund, suggesting that he kill her husband after the battle and marry her.

Next, Lear arrives on the scene, raving mad and draped in weeds and flowers. At first, he doesn't recognize Gloucester. In this touching scene, a humbled Lear shifts between incoherence and lucidity, waxing insightfully about nature, adultery, his two daughters' betrayal, and a universe headed for ruin. (Read more about this scene's thematic overtones in the following.)

Lear flees when he sees Cordelia's attendants approach him. Suddenly Oswald shows up and prepares to kill Gloucester. The disguised Edgar comes to the rescue, killing Oswald before he does any harm. Later, Lear is brought to his beloved daughter's tent and we witness their tearful reunion. He confesses his sins and tells her he is ashamed of his actions. She tries to reassure him.

Two Wicked Sisters Are Undone

A disguised Edgar delivers Oswald's treacherous letter from Goneril to Albany. He asks mysteriously that, after the battle, Albany allow him to prove the truth of the letter by fighting Edmund. (Albany also determines to punish Goneril and Edmund after the battle with France.) In a soliloquy, Edmund hopes that Goneril will kill Albany after he wins the battle over Cordelia and Lear. He is determined to show no mercy toward the king and Cordelia when they're captured.

Sadly, the French army loses to the British and Cordelia and Lear are taken captive. At the British camp at Dover, Edmund sends instructions to have the prisoners killed. Albany, Goneril, and Regan show up. Albany demands that Edmund hand the captives over to him, but Edmund won't relinquish them. Meanwhile, Goneril has poisoned Regan and the poor woman is starting to feel sick! Supported by Albany, Edgar, his face hidden by armor, challenges his half-brother to a swordfight. The two men fight, and Edgar mortally wounds his half-brother. Finally, Edgar unveils his disguise.

Then a gentleman enters and announces that Goneril has committed suicide after confessing that she fatally poisoned Regan! A dying Edmund finally repents and confesses that he gave instructions to kill Lear and Cordelia. Albany sends someone to stop the execution, but it's too late! In the heartrending final scene, Lear carries his lifeless Cordelia, hanged upon Edmund's orders, across the stage. Grief stricken, Lear wails: "Why should a dog, a horse, a rat, have life,/And thou no breath at all?" Moments later, he dies, leaving Albany and Edgar to restore order.

What the Journeys of Edgar, Gloucester, and Lear Teach Us

Studies of *King Lear's* thematic vision fill hundreds of volumes. We can highlight a few. Early in Act five, when Edgar tells his father that Lear and Cordelia have been taken captive, Gloucester despairs, refusing to walk farther. Edgar replies:

> Edgar: Men must endure
> Their going hence even as their coming hither,
> Ripeness is all.
> (V.2.9-11)

Edgar's message would have struck Shakespeare's audiences differently from today. In *The New Cambridge Shakespeare: The Tragedy of King Lear*, Jay L. Halio notes, "In essence, Edgar tells Gloucester (as Hamlet tells Horatio) that Providence or the gods control our lives; hence, we must endure the time of our death even as, perforce, we endure the time of our birth. Providence, or the gods, not man, determines when the time is 'ripe', an idea which has little to do with modern theories of maturation or development."

The expression, "Ripeness is all," is informed by our modern sense of the words *ripe* and *ripen*, meaning mature and to grow. Nowadays, as many question the existence of God, the phrase resonates more darkly. "Ripeness is all" suggests that life is about being born, living, and dying, with no hope of an afterlife. Lear's questioning of God's decision to let animals live and Cordelia die reinforces the play's despair.

TIMELESS SOLILOQUIES

Clothing images pervade *King Lear*. Humble Lear's famous lament, "Through tattered clothes great vices do appear:/Robes and furred gowns hide all," has rich implications. Without opulent clothing, the vices of the poor are more conspicuous. Judges, kings, and men with legal and political authority can hide their vices underneath their outerwear, the protective shell of their dignity. Lear implies that without their robes and gowns, kings and other men of position would be like ordinary men. Lear's plainspoken plea after he rails about the injustice of Cordelia's death is poignant: "Pray you undo this button. Thank you, sir." Speaking this line, Lear shows a newfound deference, a respect for his fellow man. The King of Britain, stripped of his land, his sanity, and his beloved Cordelia, is both wise and broken in spirit before he dies.

Despite its tone of despair, we can be heartened by Lear and Gloucester's journeys toward enlightenment. Stripped of political respect and filial affection, Lear is cast out, reduced to a homeless creature like the insane beggar Poor Tom. Lowly and mad, he grows wise to his own folly, vice, and hypocrisy and that of others. When stripped of his throne, he comes to learn what a king owes the people of his kingdom. Gloucester, robbed of his sight, gains inner "sight," soulful enrichment, and self-awareness. The play explores human weakness and cruelty and nature's apparent indifference to human suffering. It offers truth about our human condition. In the following section, three prominent professionals, who balanced expertise in acting, directing, and university teaching, offer further insight into *King Lear*.

Actor Charles Krohn Muses about Performing Lear

Charles Krohn has been a member of the Alley Theatre's resident acting company for 30 years. He has performed in many Shakespeare productions at the Alley Theatre, while also directing and acting in Shakespeare plays for the Houston Shakespeare Festival. When he was approached about playing Lear in the Houston Shakespeare Festival's 1998 production of *King Lear*, he was eager to tackle it but felt apprehensive because of the role's challenges.

Before rehearsing the part, Krohn had taught the play several times and had seen great renderings of Lear on film by many actors, including Laurence Olivier and Michael Hordern. He talked about how his vision of Lear's character developed. "I try to let the character come to me during the rehearsal process. You should make bold choices at the outset but also be willing to give them up if the blocking process dictates. For me, the role develops as the play is blocked so you can link words with actions. As the lines become more familiar, the character has a chance to grow out of that.

"My most illuminating insight about Lear came late in rehearsal, as we worked on the lines between Lear and the Fool that occur around the storm scene in Act three. Up until that point Lear was beginning to accept responsibility for his past actions, but not completely. When we rehearsed scene 4, right after Lear addresses the Fool, he laments his neglect of the poor subjects of his kingdom: 'O, I have ta'en/ Too little care of this! Take physic, pomp,/Expose thyself to feel what wretches feel,' I realized that for the king to pay that act of deference through this remark indicated that he is rejoining the human race. The fact that this remark is an act of deference, that Lear is humbling himself to the Fool, was clarified for me during rehearsal and performance. It was something that transcended a simple reading of the lines. I understood then how Lear goes outside of himself, if not for the first time, for the first time in many years.

"Lear's journey is one that moves from pride to humility—from seeing himself as 'numero uno' to realizing that he is nothing. As soon as he sees himself as nothing, he becomes something. Compared to the other tragedies, I think that *King Lear* has a stronger grip on our personal human responses. Unlike *Hamlet*, a great play dominated by one character—Prince Hamlet—*King Lear* has nine fully developed characters who are all complex and interesting people."

Director Kate Pogue Talks about Staging *King Lear*

Kate Pogue brings a unique versatility to directing Shakespeare. A playwright, librettist, translator, drama instructor, and the author of *Shakespeare's Friends*, she directed 13 productions for the Shakespeare by the Book Festival in Richmond, southwest of Houston, and served as artistic director for 12 years. She has also directed for the Houston Shakespeare Festival and other university-sponsored productions. Pogue talked about the challenges of directing *King Lear* in 1998, particularly for audiences new to Shakespeare. "In directing for Shakespeare By the Book, it was my job to turn the play into a wonderful experience for the audience."

"*King Lear* is a very, very challenging script. The plot is dense and complicated, so the storytelling needs to be clarified. For example, the names of Gloucester's sons, Edmund and Edgar, both start with the letter *E*, which can be confusing. Edgar comes onstage relatively late and meets up with Edmund in a void. To clarify that for the audience, we came up with a non-speaking scene set to music in which Kent, Edgar, Edmund, and Gloucester make entrances at the court, so the audience could see Edgar connect with his family before he first converses with Edmund at the end of the play's second scene."

"A KINGDOM FOR A STAGE"

The 2002 Naxos AudioBook recording of *King Lear* is a veritable who's who of stage and film talent. Paul Scofield's involvement attracted leading film director/adaptor/actor Kenneth Branagh, who played the Fool; Alec McCowen, a leading film, Royal Shakespeare Company, and Broadway actor, as Gloucester; David Burke, famous as Watson opposite Jeremy Brett's Sherlock Holmes, played Kent; Harriet Walter, an award-winning stage and screen actress who appeared in *Sense and Sensibility*, *The Governess*, *Atonement*, and *The Crown*, played Goneril. Notable TV and film versions feature great actors performing Lear, including Laurence Olivier (1984) for TV's Mobil Theatre Showcase, Michael Hordern (1982) for BBC-TV, and Ian Holm (1998) also for BBC-TV.

"The fact that Kent and Edgar go in disguise can also be confusing to some. In our production, it was important for you to actually see Edgar and Kent's disguises and changes of character take place onstage, allowing you to keep each one's dual identity straight.

Chapter 22. King Lear

"In casting Lear, it is important to find an actor with a big voice and a ready access to deep emotion. It's important to remember that *King Lear* is the most humorous of all Shakespearean tragedies, but the play's humor is usually undervalued. If the director doesn't cast funny actors for the Fool, Kent, and Edmund, the play becomes a miserable experience for some. Most important, casting a real clown as Lear's Fool to bring out the script's humor is the secret of a successful *Lear* production.

"As a director you really learn *King Lear* in rehearsal and performance. I never used to like *King Lear* as a play, partly because of my dislike of Lear's character. That changed when I decided the play is a metaphor for the cost of human maturation and the difficulty of becoming truly generous and empathetic. Lear is caught in the two-year-old stage of ego-centrism. At the end he becomes a genuinely kind human being after a devastating journey. Witnessing that journey as a director gave me sympathy for Lear—he is acting out everyone's journey. Through him, we see the horrible costs of becoming a decent human being."

Artistic Director Jack Young Talks about Shakespearean Stage Combat

The challenge for a fight director is to make sure the physical staging of a violent scene helps move the story forward. *King Lear* has at least five scenes where people are beaten, blinded, or killed. Jack Young, artistic director of the Houston Shakespeare Festival and head of the University of Houston Professional Actor Training Program, helps Shakespeare directors stage violence in plays. He trained with the Society of American Fight Directors, an organization dedicated to promoting safe and effective stage combat. When Young works as a fight director, his job is to show actors how to use their weapons and to train them how to work together to give the audience an illusion of "real violence."

Putting together good stage combat takes time. "The great dance choreographer George Balanchine had a formula for his own modern dance pieces that I use to help directors understand how long it can take to put together a strong scene. For every minute a trained and talented actor fights onstage, it takes at least one hour to put it together, another hour to work through it, and a third hour to polish it, outside of regular rehearsals. The goal is to put together a set of moves between the 'combatants' that make the story clear to an audience who isn't used to seeing violence, while making sure all the actors stand together at curtain call completely unharmed. When metal goes against skin, metal wins. So stage fights have to work 11 times out of 10. Fight choreography is about illusion; it's a magic trick based on timing and distance. And the audience buys into it.

"There are other challenges. Fight directors usually don't have input on casting for every show. Some actors are good athletes; some aren't. Often actors who finally have the experience and 'name' to be cast in leading roles have also accumulated bad knees, sore backs, and aching shoulders. It takes special consideration to come up with choreography that makes them look good and doesn't wear them out over an eight-performance week. Once, when I directed fights for *Macbeth*, I worked with an actor who had made his reputation working in daytime TV. He was used to standing still to stay in the camera frame and he forgot how to move his feet. I worked the fight scene so the other actors came at him and he didn't have to move so much."

"A KINGDOM FOR A STAGE"

"One significant scene in Lear has the character of Cornwall pluck out both of Gloucester's eyes. A servant interrupts Cornwall, trying to defend Gloucester, but is killed by Cornwall's wife Regan. Once the servant is dead, Gloucester is revealed with whatever gore the company has devised to represent his blinded condition. Shakespeare shows his skill as a director by having the audience distracted by the fight between the servant and Cornwall so that they aren't watching the other people in the scene apply the makeup to make it appear that Gloucester's eyes have been gouged out."

—Jack Young, Houston Shakespeare Festival artistic director, fight choreographer, and associate professor at University of Houston School of Theatre

Chapter 22. King Lear

"The violence in *King Lear* spans a beating, a blinding, an attempted murder where the tables are turned on the murderer, a battle (sometimes staged, sometimes done as a shadow battle, sometimes presented as a sound-scape coming from offstage), and a formal trial by combat. The skills of the characters range from the older characters Kent, Cornwall, and Albany, who have fought in battles; to the young brothers Edgar and Edmund, who may have been trained as young gentlemen; to Oswald, a servant/courtier, who, depending on the director's idea for the play, may have no training as a fighter at all.

In the 2002 Turner Network TV drama, King of Texas *(a reimagining of* King Lear *for primetime audiences, which is filmed on a ranch), Uli Edel directs the iconic Patrick Stewart as the land baron John Lear. Screenwriter Stephen Harrigan appropriates Shakespeare's plot without his verse, and in this version, Lear divides his estate among three daughters who loathe him.*

(Photo courtesy of Turner Network Television/Photofest.)

FACTS TO REMEMBER

- Late seventeenth-century audiences couldn't abide *King Lear's* despair so they gave the play a happy ending. The experience of two world wars, however, has equipped contemporary audiences with an appreciation of the play's dark, nihilistic messages.
- *King Lear* looks at what happens when many kinds of familial bonds are broken.
- Shakespeare uses many letters of treachery in *King Lear* to advance and complicate his plot.
- For directors and fight choreographers, *King Lear* is one of Shakespeare's most challenging scripts, with its many well-rounded characters, overlooked humorous roles, and frequent and varied stage violence.
- Through its action and imagery, *King Lear* explores the consequences of filial ingratitude and follows the personal journey of two older men who grow wiser in spirit while questioning nature's indifference to suffering.

Chapter 23
Macbeth

INTRODUCTION

- An introduction to *Macbeth*, Shakespeare's exotic late tragedy and its appeal to James I, England's Scottish king
- A summary of *Macbeth*'s major characters and tips about how Jacobean audiences viewed witches
- A synopsis of *Macbeth*'s swift-moving plot
- Insights about character from actors Simon Russell Beale and Sian Thomas
- Highlights of three exceptional film versions of *Macbeth*

Macbeth, also known as *The Scottish Play*, is the last and shortest of Shakespeare's four greatest tragedies. Set in medieval Scotland amid bloody feuds at the time of Edward the Confessor, *Macbeth* predates the pivotal era that began when William the Conqueror left Normandy and invaded England in 1066. Steeped in poetry and the incantation of witchcraft, *Macbeth* possesses a distinct preternatural, Celtic exoticism that still intoxicates audiences. Like *King Lear*, Macbeth explores the psychological uproar within a divided kingdom. But *Lear* probes the workings of good and evil across a universal cosmos, whereas *Macbeth* focuses more narrowly on the psychology of evil and how ambition corrupts the souls of one man and his wife.

PART 5. THE TRAGEDIES

Shakespeare probably wrote *Macbeth* in 1606 when his company was known as the King's Men, about three years after James I, a Scot, took the throne of England. Adding to *Macbeth's* mystique is the likelihood that Shakespeare considered King James's fascination and belief in witchcraft when he wrote the play. The king issued a treatise called *Daemonologie* in 1597.

Simon Forman recorded seeing a performance of *Macbeth* in 1611, one of the earliest such records we have. The play was first published in 1623 in the First Folio of Shakespeare's plays. *Macbeth* remains popular today because Shakespeare's language brilliantly blends the proverbial and the everyday.

The Characters

THE REALM OF SCOTLAND

Duncan—He is the elderly King of Scotland, a kind and trusting monarch who has the Thane of Cawdor executed for treason in the play's first act. Unlike the much younger Duncan from Raphael Holinshed's *Chronicle's of England, Scotland, and Ireland*, Shakespeare's principal source, King Duncan is a sympathetic figure whose murder appears as foul as Claudius' murder of King Hamlet. When Shakespeare has Duncan proclaim Malcolm his heir to the throne, he deviates from historical fact because Scotland and Denmark elected their kings in the tribal fashion.

Malcolm—He is the older son of Duncan who, like his brother, fears for his life right after his father is murdered. He therefore escapes to England. The play concludes as he is elected King of Scotland.

Donaldbain—He is the younger son of Duncan who is afraid for his life after his father is killed. He flees Macbeth's castle for Ireland after the tragedy occurs.

Macbeth—He is a brave general in the king's army who is greatly admired for his military skill. As the play opens, he is a lord, the Thane of Glamis. Not long after he hears the witches' prophecy, he learns that he has been appointed Thane of Cawdor after King Duncan has the current Thane of Cawdor executed for treason. This news triggers a yearning within Macbeth that he calls "vaulting ambition" and tempts him to consider what it would take to become king, as the Weird Sisters predicted. Then his wife pushes him to carry out evil deeds to fulfill more of the prophecy. By the end of the play, his evil and villainy are boundless, his soul is hollow, and his life is meaningless. The only Shakespearean king who rivals him in villainy is Richard III.

Lady Macbeth—She is the determined wife of Macbeth who persuades her husband to strengthen his resolve and carry out the murder of Duncan. When she learns that the Weird Sisters predict her husband will be king, she imagines the weaknesses that might prevent her husband from fulfilling this part of the prophecy. Her will to "catch the nearest way" is so strong that actors often stereotype her as the evil queen who dominates her husband. Seeing her mentally break down after the murder, we realize that she failed to consider the implications of her plan. The stain on her conscience gives her no relief, and she commits suicide.

Banquo—He is a general of the king who serves with Macbeth. He seems to take the Weird Sisters' prophecy less seriously, leading us to believe that Macbeth is headed for a darker path right from the start. After Duncan is murdered, Banquo suspects Macbeth is involved but remains silent because he is part of his new court. It isn't long before Macbeth gets rid of his loyal friend, though. In the famous banquet scene, his blood-soaked ghost appears at Macbeth's table and pushes Macbeth into a distraught frenzy that upsets the guests.

Macduff—He is the upright Thane of Fife who first discovers King Duncan murdered in his bed. When he retreats to Fife to raise an army against Macbeth, Macbeth commits further atrocity by having Macduff's family slaughtered in cold blood. Unbeknownst to Macbeth, Macduff was "untimely ripped" from his mother's womb. As predicted in the Weird Sisters' final prophecy, he proves to be the evil king's undoing.

Part 5. The Tragedies

Rosse—He is a Scottish noble who serves as a messenger in several key scenes. He informs Macbeth that he will become Thane of Cawdor. He also tells Macduff that his entire family has been destroyed by Macbeth as retaliation for Macduff's defection.

Lady Macduff—She is the wife of Macduff who is cruelly slaughtered with her children when Macbeth learns that Macduff is recruiting English soldiers to support Malcolm's attack to regain the Scottish throne.

Lennox, Menteth, Angus, Cathness—Other noblemen of Scotland

Fleance—The son of Banquo who escapes while his father is murdered by Macbeth's hired men

A Gentlewoman

Seyton—An officer who works for Macbeth

Boy—A son of Macduff

A Scottish doctor

Sergeant

Porter

Old Man

Three Murderers

THE REALM OF ENGLAND

Siward—He is the Earl of Northumberland and the general of the English armed forces who support Malcom's rebellion.

Young Siward—His son

Doctor

Chapter 23. Macbeth

> **THE WEIRD SISTERS AND THEIR WORLD**
>
> The Weird Sisters—Referred to by some as witches, they are three women believed to manipulate supernatural forces for purposes of evil. These three issue two sets of prophecies during the play. Their name derives from *wyrd*, meaning *fate*.
>
> Three other witches
>
> Hecate—Queen of the witches
>
> Apparitions
>
> Lords, Gentlemen, Officers, Soldiers, Attendants, and Messengers
>
> *Setting: Scotland and England*

Three Hags on a Heath—An Uncanny Prophecy

> All: Fair is foul, and foul is fair,
> Hover through the fog and filthy air.
> (I.1.11-12)

Our tale begins amid thunder and lightning on a "blasted heath" in Scotland. The mood is unsettling, the atmosphere is dark, and we're reminded that all is not what it seems. Three witches chant in rhyme, foreshadowing their imminent meeting with Macbeth after a "hurly-burly," or battle, that's about to take place. From this very first scene, we surmise that the witches have powers greater than our own. When they utter "When the battle's lost and won," we are introduced to the first of the play's many equivocal expressions that muddle reality and confuse us. From this point on, note these kinds of language patterns in their prophecies and in the speech of Macbeth.

"Wild and Whirling Words"

To fully appreciate how the Weird Sisters function in *Macbeth*, you need a mini-lesson in etymology. Why does Shakespeare call them the *Weird Sisters* anyway? Today, the word *weird* is limited to *strange* or *bizarre*. For Shakespeare, the meaning was closer to the Old or Middle English *wyrd*, which meant fate or ones who determined fate. According to the First Folio version of *Macbeth*, the Weird Sisters occupy the "half world" or underworld of the play. Their presence, incantations, and spells affected Shakespeare's audiences profoundly because they believed that witches had supernatural powers akin to the devil. (When Shakespeare wrote *Macbeth*, many who were suspected of witchcraft were persecuted.) Throughout the play, Shakespeare often links the Weird Sisters to the powers of darkness.

In the next scene we learn that the Thane of Cawdor's rebellion against King Duncan has been squelched by Macbeth, the Thane of Glamis. Cawdor has surrendered and Duncan orders him to be executed. Duncan is stung by the betrayal and wastes no time conferring Cawdor's title, land, and power to Macbeth. He says, "No more that Thane of Cawdor shall deceive/Our bosom interest./. . . What he hath lost, noble Macbeth hath won." Cutting back to the heath amid the crackle of thunder, the witches are up to no good, "killing swine" and talking about it. As Macbeth and Banquo approach them, these hags address Macbeth as Thane of Cawdor and predict he will emerge as king of Scotland. Not surprisingly, these words shock the noble lords. When Banquo presses them for information about himself, they inform him that he will beget the future kings of Scotland.

Full of Ambition, Macbeth Is Tempted

As the witches leave Macbeth hankering for more information, Rosse and Angus arrive to inform Macbeth that he has been named the Thane of Cawdor after his impressive military victory. Macbeth and Banquo are stunned by this news and realize that the first part of the witches' prophecy has come true.

Chapter 23. Macbeth

Macbeth begins to ponder what it all means. In an aside to Macbeth, Banquo warns his friend that the "instruments of darkness" raise men's hopes and incite them to act in ways that ultimately cause great harm.

But even though Macbeth says, "If chance will have me king, why, chance may crown me/Without my stir," the allure of being king has gripped his spirit. He can't put it out of his mind. At the king's palace at Forres, Duncan praises Macbeth, saying, "More is thy due than more than all can pay." The king announces he plans to visit Macbeth's castle at Inverness. Addressing his kinsmen, he announces that his estate and the throne of Scotland will pass to his oldest son Malcolm, the new Prince of Cumberland. This news doesn't sit well with Macbeth and may well be the event that forces him to the dark side. In an aside, he says, "The Prince of Cumberland! That is a step/On which I must fall down, or else o'erleap,/For in my way it lies."

Spurred to Action by Lady Macbeth

> Lady Macbeth: Come, you spirits
> That tend on mortal thoughts, unsex me here,
> And fill me from the crown to the toe topful
> Of direst cruelty!
> (I.5.40-44)

Macbeth tells his wife the details of the witches' prophecy in a letter. She appears gleeful and determined that Macbeth shall become king. She fears, however, that her husband is "too full o' th' milk of human kindness" to do what has to be done to make it happen. When her husband arrives, she assures him that the king will spend his last night at Inverness. Macbeth isn't so sure about committing murder, but his wife assures him that he should leave the details to her. When Lady Macbeth tells her husband that his face "is a book, where men/May read strange matters," we are acutely aware of her self-conscious need to dissemble before the king. Eventually Macbeth resolves to follow her lead.

PART 5. THE TRAGEDIES

The stunning French actress Marion Cotillard is cast as the scheming Lady Macbeth in Justin Kurzel's cinematically inviting screen adaptation of Macbeth *(2015).*
Photo courtesy of The Weinstein Company/Photofest.

Duncan arrives at Inverness, Macbeth's castle, and is warmly greeted by Lady Macbeth. After the king greets Macbeth, the troubled thane grapples with his conscience. Murder would be the ultimate betrayal of Duncan because the king trusts Macbeth to keep him safe in his capacity as kinsman and host. He says:

> Macbeth: I have no spur
> To prick the sides of my intent, but only
> Vaulting ambition, which o'erleaps itself,
> And falls on th' other—
> (I.7.25-28)

When Macbeth expresses doubt about going forward, his wife berates him harshly, questions his change of heart, and calls him a coward. Resolute, she outlines the details of her plan to drug Duncan's guards and frame them with evidence of the crime, so they appear to be the guilty culprits. That night, the castle guests prepare for sleep. Banquo tells Macbeth that he dreamt of the

Weird Sisters the night before and notes that part of their prophecy has come true. Alone, Macbeth imagines he sees a bloody dagger and delivers a lengthy soliloquy, musing about its origins. He suggests that his vision stems from his "heat-oppressed brain" and projects the dark atmosphere of his mind onto the natural world outside.

After he stabs Duncan in the heart, Macbeth worries that God will punish him and imagines that he heard a voice cry, "Sleep no more!/Macbeth does murther sleep." When Lady Macbeth notices Macbeth forgot to leave the bloody daggers in the guards' hands as planned, she proceeds to do it herself. The next morning, Macduff and Lennox arrive at the castle. Macbeth greets them and acts as though he has just awoken. Macduff enters Duncan's chamber and discovers the king has been savagely murdered. He alerts everyone in the castle, and amid the confusion, Macbeth sneaks away, murders the two guards, and lays the blame on them. While the others are processing the horror and getting dressed, Malcolm and Donaldbain plot to flee Scotland, realizing that suspicion for the murder will fall on them.

Banquo's Fatal Suspicion

The disappearance of the king's sons looks fishy, suggesting they are guilty. But Banquo is the first to privately point the finger at Macbeth. Macbeth is soon crowned king, but it isn't long before the guilty king perceives that wise Banquo is a threat to his position as king because he knows too much: "To be thus is nothing,/But to be safely thus. Our fears in Banquo/ Stick deep." Macbeth is also worried about the prophecy that Banquo's children will rule Scotland. From this point on, Macbeth pursues his course of pure evil, provoking endless critical debate about his real motives.

Take a look at Act three, scene 5, and Act four, scene 1, in your edition of *Macbeth*. If you read them out loud, you might notice that the language of Hecate, for example, sounds different from the witches' language in Act one. Many scholars believe that Thomas

Middleton wrote these two scenes because they appear in the form of octosyllabic couplets, a style different from the rest of the play. These scenes also contain songs taken from Middleton's play *The Witch*, whose date is unknown. The edition of *Macbeth* inside *The Complete Oxford Shakespeare: Volume III Tragedies* credits Thomas Middleton with having adapted the play after it was written in 1606.

Macbeth arranges for Banquo and his son Fleance to be murdered. Macbeth's three murderers do away with Banquo, but Fleance manages to escape. Bloody murder continues to wreak havoc on Macbeth's psyche. No sooner has the first murderer reported that Banquo is dead than Macbeth sees his ghost seated at the banquet table with his guests. In this famous scene, Macbeth becomes unhinged at the sight of the ghost. Lady Macbeth tries to quiet and console him, telling the guests that he has long suffered from this malady. The spirit appears again, and Macbeth orders it to disappear: "Hence, horrible shadow!/ Unreal mock'ry, hence!" Macbeth's outbursts destroy the guests' merry mood and they leave abruptly.

Malcolm and Macduff Conspire

| Witches: | Double, double toil and trouble; Fire burn, and cauldron bubble (IV.1.10–11) |

We learn from Lennox that Malcolm is getting support from the King of England and Macduff himself, who has skipped the country, obviously convinced that Macbeth killed Duncan to get the crown. Feeling vulnerable, Macbeth decides to consult with the witches again to learn more about his fate. Joined by Hecate, their queen, they summon three apparitions that communicate what's in store for him. They tell him "beware the Thane of Fife." As he gazes at the image of the bloody child, they say, "for none of woman born/Shall harm Macbeth." And last they say, "Macbeth shall never vanquish'd be until/Great Birnan wood to high Dunsinane hill/Shall come against him." Afterward, Macbeth learns from Lennox that Macduff has deserted him and fled to England to gather an army. To punish him, Macbeth arranges for Macduff's family and supporters to be slaughtered. Back in England with

Chapter 23. Macbeth

Malcolm, Macduff learns his family has been cruelly sacrificed. Overcome with grief and anger, he promises to avenge the killings.

Two Portents Come to Pass

> Lady Macbeth: Out, damn'd spot! out, I say! One—two—why, then 'tis time to do't. Hell is murky.
> (V.1.35-36)

Fate finally catches up with the dastardly couple. Lady Macbeth has taken to walking in her sleep, plagued by hallucinations of blood-stained hands that won't come clean. Her gentlewoman and a doctor overhear her obsess about the deaths of Duncan, Lady Macduff, and Banquo. Meanwhile, we learn that Malcolm, Macduff, and Siward are leading an English army to a forest near Dunsinane castle, where Macbeth's men are encamped. Inured to his wife's mental suffering, Macbeth is confident that he will prevail against the rebels, in light of the recent prophecy.

When Macbeth learns from Seyton that Lady Macbeth has died, he delivers his darkest lament about life and its lack of meaning, one of Shakespeare's most moving and modern soliloquies.

TIMELESS SOLILOQUIES

> Macbeth: To-morrow, and to-morrow, and to-morrow,
> Creeps in this petty pace from day to day,
> To the last syllable of recorded time;
> And all our yesterdays have lighted fools
> The way to dusty death. Out, out, brief candle!
> Life's but a walking shadow, a poor player,
> That struts and frets his hour upon the stage,
> And then is heard no more. It is a tale
> Told by an idiot, full of sound and fury,
> Signifying nothing.
> (V.5.19-28)

William Faulkner found inspiration in this speech for the title of his Modernist masterwork *The Sound and the Fury* (1929). The book is written from the point of view of four narrators, and one of them is an idiot, a conceit that Faulkner derived from the speech.

....

Soon an incredulous messenger tells Macbeth that trees from Birnam Wood are creeping toward the castle. Macbeth recognizes the Weird Sisters' prophecy in this news and realizes he is doomed. As the rebels invade Dunsinane castle, Macbeth kills young Siward. Macduff pursues him, and when they begin to fight, Macbeth reiterates the prophecy that no man born of woman can kill him, only to hear Macduff say, "Macduff was from his mother's womb/ Untimely ripp'd." The two men fight. Macduff slays Macbeth and chops off the head of Scotland's usurping king.

Royal Shakespeare Company Actors Interpret the Macbeths

Simon Russell Beale, an acclaimed actor with the Royal Shakespeare Company and National Theatre, performed Macbeth in John Caird's production at London's Almeida theatre in 2005. In "Macbeth," an essay in *Performing Shakespeare's Tragedies Today*, edited by Michael Dobson, Beale reviews how Macbeth's language changes halfway through the play and echoes a profound change inside the man. In rehearsals for Caird's show, Beale discovered that from the moment Macbeth hears the Weird Sisters' prophecy, he grows more isolated and prone to self-analysis. In Act three, scene 2, Macbeth's speech to Lady Macbeth becomes "lyrical, loving, almost comforting," Beale notes, citing these lines:

> Macbeth: Light thickens, and the crow
> Makes wing to th'rooky wood;
> Good things of day begin to droop and drowse,
> Whiles night's black agents to their preys do rouse.
> Thou marvel'st at my words...
> (III.2.51-55)

Macbeth surprises his wife because he speaks in an unfamiliar voice, Beale says. "Macbeth is weaving a spell that is self-protective and excluding. He places himself in a landscape where the course of events is predictable and inevitable—a landscape in which his wife can no longer play a part." This new voice is unlike his public voice early in the play. "He is beginning to shut himself into a private world, a world that is, at this point, a refuge but that will become a prison."

"A KINGDOM FOR A STAGE"

Traditionally it's considered bad luck for actors to refer to the title of *Macbeth* while they are working inside the theatre. This has to do with the long history of accidents that have occurred in famous productions. Consequently, when they're inside the theatre, actors avoid Shakespeare's title and refer to the drama as *The Scottish Play*.

Sian Thomas played Lady Macbeth in a Royal Shakespeare Company production in 2004, directed by Dominic Cooke. In her essay "Lady Macbeth" in *Performing Shakespeare's Tragedies Today*, she offered numerous insights into her approach to performing the role and its challenges. Her decision to play Lady Macbeth as a "vulnerable, real woman" instead of an "evil queen" was influenced by the interpretation of British actress Sarah Siddons who performed in the late eighteenth and early nineteenth centuries. She says, "I think it is impossible to play Lady Macbeth as just an evil bitch, the 'fiend-like queen' referred to in the propaganda of the regime which supplants hers. From the start I knew I would be playing her as vulnerable, and once you grasp that as a starting point, you find she is also incredibly brave: considering she is not naturally as hard as nails, her willpower is extraordinary." She added that it was important to "keep her vulnerable, keep her volatile."

During rehearsal, Thomas also realized that her vision of Lady Macbeth conflicted with the image that her co-star expected. "I think he assumed I would just play her as an awful bad creature, so that he could get on with being a fascinating, vulnerable, flawed human being. So there was a slight contretemps when he discovered that I was not going to play her just as an evil queen . . ." Thomas also confirmed that actors playing the couple do come up with a back story to help them characterize the marriage. "We decided that we had been married at least ten years, and . . . that there had been a child, who had died."

Three Notable Screen Adaptations of Macbeth

Without a complicating subplot like *King Lear*, *Macbeth* carries us along as swiftly as a modern adventure tale. If you do a search on the Internet Movie Database (IMDB) at www.imdb.com, you'll find so many film and TV versions of *Macbeth* it will make your head spin. Macbeth appears to have been adapted for the big screen, television, and silent screen more than any other Shakespearean play. Three filmed versions, in particular, show contrasting approaches to characterization, visual imagery, and the use of Shakespeare's script.

"A KINGDOM FOR A STAGE"

One *Macbeth* adaptation on film, released in 2007, puts the imaginings of Australian writer/director Geoffrey Wright on display. The film featured Sam Worthington as Macbeth and Victoria Hill as Lady Macbeth. In *The New York Times*, film critic Matt Zoller Seitz characterized Wright's protagonist as "a longhaired, drug-addled gangster" and his kingdom as resembling an "MTV dreamscape of nymphet witches, smoky nightclubs and point-blank, slow-motion gun battles."

Trevor Nunn's 1976 production at Stratford-upon-Avon's The Other Place was conceived for television in 1979. Available on DVD, the show is a tour de force, featuring Ian McKellen, Judi Dench, and a cast on a bare, circular stage with tight framing and close shots.

In Charles Warren's TV version of *Macbeth* of 1988, Michael Jayston plays a convincing warrior/king who is widely admired and respected for his military prowess. As Lady Macbeth, Barbara Leigh-Hunt's long brunette locks starkly contrast with her pale skin, giving her a ghostly appearance. Her anti-heroine is strong-willed and domineering in the traditional sense.

Chapter 23. Macbeth

Roman Polanski shot his high-budget, panoramic *Macbeth* in North Wales, and the film was released in 1971. Polanski's is probably the most viable cinematic rendering of Shakespeare's script. Polanski offers a naturalistic tale of personal evil, highlighted by enough blood, gore, and authentic detail to capture the violence of feudal existence in medieval Scotland. The screenplay, co-written by Polanski and Kenneth Tynan, omitted more than 50 percent of Shakespeare's script. But as Kenneth Rothwell notes in *A History of Shakespeare on Screen*, what he lost in the cutting, Polanski made up for in his detailed visual rendering of animal life, feasting, bear-baiting entertainment, and general day-to-day movement inside and outside Macbeth's castle.

FACTS TO REMEMBER

- In writing a Scottish play featuring the prophecy of the Weird Sisters, Shakespeare no doubt appealed to King James's interest and belief in witchcraft.
- Sensing that Macbeth lacks the will to murder Duncan, Lady Macbeth goads him into doing the deed by insulting his sexuality and manhood.
- Pondering how part of the witches' prophecy has come true after Macbeth is named Thane of Cawdor, Banquo warns his friend that the Weird Sisters are "instruments of darkness" who often tempt men to act in harmful ways.
- Actors differ greatly in their interpretation of Lady Macbeth's true motives and vulnerability.
- In a 2005 production in London, actor Simon Russell Beale became inspired by how Macbeth's language reflected that of a lyrical poet who contemplates the prison of his isolation.

Chapter 24
Antony and Cleopatra

> **INTRODUCTION**
> - Introducing *Antony and Cleopatra*, Shakespeare's steamy, unsung tragedy about famous lovers of the ancient world
> - Descriptions of the play's major and minor characters
> - A synopsis of the action in *Antony and Cleopatra*
> - Interpretations of Cleopatra's fury on film
> - Director Joseph Graves talks about the challenges of staging and performing *Antony and Cleopatra*

If you've already dipped into *Hamlet* and *King Lear*, the pinnacle of Shakespearean tragedy, you may find Shakespeare's late Roman tragedy a little disappointing. Written around 1606-1607, *Antony and Cleopatra* doesn't address themes of political honor or heroism in the forthright manner of *Julius Caesar*, an earlier Roman tragedy (refer to Chapter 19).

But viewing *Antony and Cleopatra* through the lens of history is a mistake. Its central concern is the unpredictable love that rules the action of two lovers. As we see in *Othello*, a domestic tragedy, Shakespeare puts the lovers' intimate relationship in sharp focus. We get to see Antony and Cleopatra squabble, scream, and talk badly about one another, each behind the other's back, of course. Traversing the vast geographic expanse between Rome and Egypt,

PART 5. THE TRAGEDIES

Antony and Cleopatra explores how a man puts his public duty on hold to indulge in a love affair. By exploring how affairs of the heart can lead to the destruction of one's public position, the play resembles *Othello*, *King Lear*, and *Macbeth* more closely than *Julius Caesar*.

Shakespeare used Plutarch's *Lives of the Noble Grecians and Romans* as his main source. The protagonists are noble imperialists who meet an ignoble end after Octavius Caesar defeats them. Antony, in particular, allows his passion for Cleopatra to interfere with military strategy during the pivotal Battle of Actium. Antony still co-rules all-powerful Rome, but you sense that his glory days are gone. Antony often looks inward in this play, and for this, he resembles Hamlet, Othello, Macbeth, and King Lear, Shakespeare's most brilliant creations.

The Characters

THE ROMANS

Mark Antony (Marcus Antonius)—He is a great, highly respected general and one of Rome's three *triumvirs*, or rulers. He commands an extremely loyal following of advisors and soldiers who shudder to hear him downgrade himself in Act four. Despite his accomplishments and public esteem, he allows his desires for a much younger woman to cloud his military judgment during two key conflicts with Octavius Caesar. Octavius says of Antony, "You shall find there/A man who is th' [abstract] of all faults/That all men follow," suggesting that Antony's rise to glory and subsequent fall to temptation is typical of any man's personal journey. Fearing Antony will leave her, Cleopatra denigrates him at one point ("Or thou, the greatest soldier of the world,/Art turn'd the greatest liar.") and praises him later ("The demi-Atlas of this earth, the arm/And burgonet of men."), depending on his willingness to submit to her immediate desires.

Octavius Caesar—In the script, he is referred to as Caesar, but don't confuse him with his adoptive father and predecessor Julius Caesar.

Chapter 24. Antony and Cleopatra

At the actual Battle of Actium in 31 B.C.E., Octavius Caesar was only 20 years old. Though Cleopatra calls him "scarce-bearded Caesar" to cast aspersions on his youth, Octavius is a triumvir of Rome and a great rival to Antony. Whereas Antony appears warm and passionate, albeit in the twilight of his military career, Octavius appears cold and calculating. Octavius shrewdly prosecutes his military campaign against Antony, and, in triumph, he is respectful of the dead lovers.

Lepidus (M. Aemilius Lepidus)—He is the third triumvir of Rome and figures in the scene aboard Pompey's ship after the general has declared a truce. Octavius has him killed after he defeats Pompey.

Pompey (Sextus Pompeius)—He is a Roman general and the son of Pompey the Great. He foments Rome's internal strife. In his key scene, he honorably refuses a suggestion that he drown the three Roman rulers while they are carousing aboard his ship.

Domitius Enobarbus—Known as Enobarbus, he is Antony's loyal friend who offers us wise commentary on the action and the lovers until he dies. When Antony recklessly insists on fighting Octavius despite his severe losses in the naval battle, Enobarbus decides to desert him. Sickened by his own betrayal, he kills himself.

Octavia—She is the wife of Antony and sister of Octavius. Her marriage to Antony is arranged out of political expediency to solidify the tenuous bond between her brother and Antony.

Euphronius—One who taught Antony, who petitions Octavius for a possible surrender

ANTONY'S ALLIES

Ventidius—A loyal follower of Antony

Eros—The loyal bodyguard of Antony who kills himself, reluctant to obey Antony's command to assist in his suicide

Scarus—A loyal soldier

Canidius—Antony's lieutenant general who joins Octavius's side

Dercetas—A loyal follower of Antony

Demetrius—A follower of Antony

Philo—A follower of Antony who utters the play's opening lines

Silius—A soldier in Ventidius' army

OCTAVIUS CAESAR'S FOLLOWERS

Maecenas—A loyal follower of Octavius

Agrippa—A general of Octavius who proposes the marriage between Antony and Octavia, Octavius's sister

Dolabella—An emissary of Octavius who secretly tells Cleopatra of Octavius' plan to parade her ignominiously through Rome

Proculeius—An emissary sent by Octavius to make Cleopatra trust Octavius after Antony's death; he proves untrustworthy, contrary to what Antony tells Cleopatra before his death.

Taurus—A lieutenant general of Octavius

Thidias and Gallus—Friends of Octavius

POMPEY'S FOLLOWERS

Menas—A pirate in Pompey's service who advises the general to kill the three triumvirs while they are drinking aboard his ship

Menecrates—A follower of Pompey

Varrius—A follower of Pompey

THE EGYPTIANS

Cleopatra—Fourteen years younger than Antony, she is the inscrutable queen of Egypt, considered by some to be Shakespeare's greatest heroine. Mercurial and elusive, she is the consummate actress and someone we come to understand through the perspective of others. We learn she may be fickle when Charmian reminds her that she once loved Julius Caesar as much as she pretends to love Antony. When Antony says, "She is cunning past man's thought," we realize she indeed loves Antony, but only as far as that love serves her own and Egypt's interests. Enobarbus uses heightened metaphor when describing Cleopatra, making her seem larger than life. He tells us, "When she first met Mark Antony, she purs'd up his heart upon the river of Cydnus./. . . The barge she sat in, like a burnish'd throne,/Burnt on the water. The poop was beaten gold,/Purple the sails, and so perfumed that/The winds were love-sick with them."

Charmian—The maid of Cleopatra who stays close to the queen while she places the asps on her body. She ends her life in a similar fashion.

Iras—The maid of Cleopatra who dies by the asps' poison before her mistress does

Alexas—Attendant of Cleopatra

Diomedes—Attendant of Cleopatra

Mardian—A eunuch who is sent by the queen to lie to Antony by telling him she has committed suicide

Seleucus—Treasurer of Cleopatra who betrays his mistress by telling Octavius that Cleopatra is withholding information about her wealth

Soothsayer

A clown

Messengers, Officers, Soldiers, Guardsmen, Servants

Setting: Rome and Alexandria, Egypt

Rome Suffers While Antony Dallies with Cleopatra

When *Antony and Cleopatra* opens, approximately four years have passed since Julius Caesar was assassinated by Brutus and his conspirators. Three rulers, known as the triumvirate, co-rule the far-flung Roman Empire, and they include Octavius Caesar, Mark Antony, and Lepidus. General Pompey continues to wage civil war against Rome. In the opening scenes, we find Antony in Egypt, deeply smitten with Cleopatra. In the following lines, you'll hardly recognize the ally of Julius Caesar who brazenly provoked the Roman mob to civil war. All Antony seems to care about is dallying in bed with his lover Cleopatra, the fickle queen of Egypt. Rome's political well-being is the last thing on his mind.

> Antony: Let Rome in Tiber melt, and the wide arch
> Of the rang'd empire fall! Here is my space,
> Kingdoms are clay;
> (I.1.33-35)

But Antony soon learns that Rome suffers while he idly rolls in the hay. His wife Fulvia has instigated infighting against his ally Octavius, and Pompey and the Parthian leader have managed to conquer more of Rome's lands. He realizes that it's time to act: "I must from this enchanting queen break off;/Ten thousand harms, more than the ills I know,/My idleness doth hatch." When Antony learns that Fulvia has died, he experiences regret. This loss incites him to leave Egypt. Cleopatra isn't happy, of course, but he tells her he loves her, bids her goodbye, and sets off for Rome to help Octavius fight Pompey.

Pompey Challenges the "Triple Pillar of the World"

Throughout this play, Antony's affairs with Cleopatra are not very private. The couple almost never appear onstage alone with each other. Everyone from the couple's servants to Antony's military advisors seem to be talking about their affair. This includes Pompey, who is confident that his latest attack on Octavius and Lepidus will succeed because Antony will remain distracted by his royal Eastern lover:

Pompey:	He dreams; I know they are in Rome together,
	Looking for Antony. But all the charms of love,
	Salt Cleopatra, soften thy wan'd lip!
	Let witchcraft join with beauty, lust with both,
	Tie up the libertine in a field of feasts,
	(II.1.19-23)

When Antony arrives to meet with Octavius back in Rome, he denies being involved in his dead wife's rebellion and apologizes for not doing his part to prevent it. He acknowledges his irresponsibility and seems to want to make amends.

A Plan to Unite Octavius and Antony

Understandably, there are residual hard feelings between Octavius and Antony and a lack of trust. To bring them closer together, Agrippa proposes "To hold you in perpetual amity,/To make you brothers, and to knit your hearts/With an unslipping knot, take Antony/Octavia to his wife." At this point, we shudder at the thought of how Cleopatra will react to such a plan! But Antony goes for the idea, putting his political power and personal honor before everything else. Antony marries Octavia and promises to be faithful to her.

Cleopatra's Fury

Back in Egypt, Cleopatra is furious when she learns that Antony has married Octavia. She literally tries to kill the messenger who brings her the news!

"A KINGDOM FOR A STAGE"

Two screen adaptations of *Antony and Cleopatra* offer glimpses into the heart and passion of Cleopatra. In one emotionally fraught scene, the Egyptian queen beats the messenger who informs her that Antony has married Octavia. Believing that Antony belongs only to her after Fulvia's death, the venomous queen strikes the messenger repeatedly, saying: "Hence,/ Horrible villain, or I'll spurn thine eyes/Like balls before me, I'll unhair thy head."

In the 1983 Bard Productions stage play filmed by Hollywood Film Studios, when Lynn Redgrave's sensuous Cleopatra gets the news, she hauls off and kicks the messenger in the groin before thrashing him soundly. In the 1972 film version of Trevor Nunn's Royal Shakespeare Company version, Janet Suzman's sultry Egyptian queen grabs and whips the poor boy before drawing the dagger sheathed inside her wrist.

Back in Rome, Pompey declares a truce. He proceeds to entertain Octavius, Antony, and Lepidus on his ship. Left behind with Maecenas, Antony's lieutenant Enobarbus predicts that Antony will not ever leave Cleopatra:

> Enobarbus: Never, he will not:
> Age cannot wither her, nor custom stale
> Her infinite variety. Other women cloy
> The appetites they feed, but she makes hungry
> Where most she satisfies; for vilest things
> Become themselves in her, that the holy priests
> Bless her when she is riggish.
> (II.2.232-239)

Enobarbus believes that Octavia, the person brought in to unite Octavius and Antony, will eventually divide them.

Octavius and Antony's Rivalry Leads to War

Taking his new wife, Antony departs from Rome and heads for Athens to meet Ventidius and other triumphant soldiers. Meanwhile, back in Egypt, Cleopatra is relieved when the Messenger informs her that Octavia is not as beautiful as she is! Inevitably, Octavius and Antony's relationship begins to sour. Octavius has Lepidus murdered, and later, he rages when he learns that Antony is back with Cleopatra in Egypt. He takes the news of their newfound Eastern alliance as a hostile threat against his power. Consequently, he makes plans to retaliate.

Chapter 24. Antony and Cleopatra

Octavius: . . . He hath given his empire
Up to a whore, who now are levying
The kings o' th' earth for war.
(III.6.66-68)

"WILD AND WHIRLING WORDS"

Shakespeare invokes the names of Roman and Egyptian deities throughout *Antony and Cleopatra*. When Charmian invokes the name Isis, she refers to the great Egyptian goddess of nature. When Enobarbus suggests Cleopatra is more beautiful than Venus, he refers to the Roman goddess of love. When Antony alludes to the chariot of "holy Phoebus," he is talking about Apollo, the Greek and Roman god of the sun. Neptune is the Roman god of the sea, and Mercury is the Roman gods' messenger who invented the lyre.

Octavius marches against Antony toward Actium. Cleopatra is hanging around the military camp, and, of course, she can't help but distract Antony from serious war matters. When Octavius poses a sea battle, Antony's closest advisors warn against it, telling him that his strengths lie with his foot soldiers. Determined to combine sea forces with Cleopatra, Antony ignores these warnings. Sadly, this decision is the beginning of the end for Antony, who is visibly consumed by passion for Cleopatra. A frustrated Canidius says, "So our leader's [led],/And we are women's men."

Dishonored by Losses at Sea, Antony Dismisses His Followers

Antony's next defeat is abysmal. We learn that his ships might have had a chance against Octavius' forces, but as soon as Cleopatra's fleet retreats, Antony orders his to follow suit. Rather pitifully, a dishonored Antony tells his followers he's not worthy of their service. In spite of all that is lost, he hasn't given up on his love for Cleopatra. From the way he talks, Antony has allowed Cleopatra to steer the course for both of them:

Antony:	. . . Egypt, thou knew'st too well
	My heart was to thy rudder tied by th' strings,
	And thou shouldst [tow] me after. O'er my spirit
	[Thy] full supremacy thou knew'st, and that
	Thy beck might from the bidding of the gods
	Command me.
	(III.11.56-61)

Egypt's "False Soul"

Antony and Cleopatra are beholden to Octavius now, but Antony pleads with Octavius for a chance to rule in Egypt with the queen. Octavius turns him down. Then Octavius sends Thidias to promise Cleopatra anything she wants in exchange for turning Antony out of Egypt or murdering him. Knowing Octavius is the man to follow, the wily queen agrees to join Octavius' ranks. When an infuriated Antony catches Cleopatra with Thidias, he has the servant whipped and sends him back to Octavius. As you'd expect, Cleopatra manages to placate him, although she has just betrayed him. Enobarbus is so disappointed in Antony that he decides to desert him.

Act four consists of many short, touching personal scenes leading up to the next battle between Octavius and Antony. Enobarbus does desert Antony, but he commits suicide when he realizes he has made a grave mistake. Antony's forces perform well on land until Octavius mounts a naval offensive. The unthinkable happens when Cleopatra's ships defect to Octavius' side and Antony's fleet is forced to retreat. This time, an enraged Antony believes Cleopatra has betrayed him.

Finding Honor in Mutual Acts of Suicide

When Antony sees Cleopatra, he goes on a tirade and vows to kill her. Incensed, he says, "You have been a boggler ever," blaming her for his devastating military losses. Fearing for her life, she escapes, sending a servant to falsely report that she has killed herself. Hearing this news, Antony falls on his sword and mortally wounds himself. Antony spends his last, dying moments advising Cleopatra only to trust in Proculeius, of all Octavius's servants.

Chapter 24. Antony and Cleopatra

❦ TIMELESS SOLILOQUIES ❦

Harley Granville-Barker was a great director and critic who encouraged scholars to reimagine how Shakespeare's plays would have been performed in Elizabethan times. He calls *Antony and Cleopatra* a "tragedy of disillusion." In his *Prefaces to Shakespeare: Volume I*, he reminds us that Shakespeare's First Folio did not divide his plays into act or scene divisions. "There is . . . no juncture where the play's acting will be made more effective by a pause. On the contrary, each scene has an effective relation to the next, which a pause between them will weaken or destroy."

In the final poignant scenes, Cleopatra satisfies her "immortal longings," assisted in her preparations for suicide by a countryman who sneaks in a basket of poisonous asps. Her loyal Iras succumbs to the sting of the first snake and falls dead. Then Cleopatra puts an asp on her breast and her arm and dies while Charmian watches. After a touching eulogy, Charmian follows her mistress and ends her own life. Respectful of the love between Antony and Cleopatra, Octavius arranges for the lovers to be buried together in a common grave.

Director Eve Adamson directed Sarah Hartmann in the lead role of Cleopatra in the 1999 production of Antony and Cleopatra *at the Texas Shakespeare Festival. Actor/director Joseph Graves co-starred as Antony.*

(Photo Courtesy of the Texas Shakespeare Festival.)

Joseph Graves Talks About Staging and Performing *Antony and Cleopatra*

Joseph Graves has served as the artistic director of the Beijing Institute of World Theatre and Film, affiliated with Peking University, since 2004. On several Shakespearean productions in the United States, he collaborated with the late director Eve Adamson, who founded and ran the Obie Award-winning Jean Cocteau Repertory Theatre in New York City. In 2000, he performed the role of Antony in a Texas Shakespeare Festival production directed by Adamson. Graves discussed some of the challenges that *Antony and Cleopatra* presents to the director.

Chapter 24. Antony and Cleopatra

"Geographically, the play sprawls across the world," Graves said. "The scenes are also quite filmic, switching from one place to another very quickly, especially in Act four. The battle scenes on the ocean present monumental staging challenges. To simulate such battles in our production, we used huge pieces of Chinese silk attached to 40-foot poles, which were manipulated by actors and supernumeraries. When operated in conjunction with set pieces built from multipurpose oil barrels, we created highly stylized battle scenes evocative of a sea battle."

"A KINGDOM FOR A STAGE"

The Texas Shakespeare Festival took pains to evoke the steamy, sexual quality of Antony and Cleopatra's affair in its 2000 production of the play. Director Joseph Graves, who performed Antony, recalled, "When we opened, we were ostensibly coming from our bedroom into the court of people seen at the play's beginning. I, barefoot, wore Cleopatra's clothes and she wore mine, including my three-inch-heeled boots. Our faces were covered, so the audience thought for a moment that I was she and she was I. They soon realized our cross-dressing was a sexual game. Inescapably, the love between Antony and Cleopatra is a richly sexual one, and we wanted to express that in as theatrical a fashion as possible while avoiding the blatantly pornographic."

"Antony is a challenge for any actor," Graves said, "because he's a military man of power and pomp, caught in a mid-life crisis—and he's having a romantic fling with a more powerful, seductive woman. He's carrying on with Cleopatra at a time when his political and military prowess has seen better days. He gets easily caught up in her web of sexual politics, which makes it nearly impossible for him to take care of the political disintegration of his empire. Antony is only believable when you portray him as alternately enraptured with Cleopatra and furious with her. Although he is sophisticated, Anthony is truly no match for Cleopatra at playing games. Cleopatra is very complex because she's always putting on an act. Any actor should be savvy enough to know that in many profound ways, this is Cleopatra's play. Undeniably, she has deep affection for Antony, but an actress playing Cleopatra must give you the sense that she always wants to be at the top of her feminine, theatrical game."

> **FACTS TO REMEMBER**
> - In *Antony and Cleopatra* Shakespeare showcases the ever-changing passions between two powerful leaders of the ancient Roman Empire.
> - Cleopatra is a mercurial, inscrutable heroine and considered by many to be Shakespeare's greatest female role.
> - Antony allows his relationship with Cleopatra to cloud his judgment in prosecuting military campaigns against Octavius.
> - Cleopatra leads Antony to believe she is dead, which prompts him to commit suicide.
> - The play is challenging for directors because of its vast setting and the emotional range required of the two leads.

Part 6
The Romances

Part 6. The Romances

After he wrote his great tragedies, Shakespeare began a set of comedies after 1607 that were highly distinctive. The best of these include *The Winter's Tale* and *The Tempest*. Like his festive comedies, they focus on the vagaries of love and romance, but they lack the refreshing kind of realism found in festive comedies like *Much Ado About Nothing* and *As You Like It*.

Instead, these late comedies flesh out ancient tales from romance prose and poetry from the Latin and Greek tradition, which is why we now label them as romances. Shakespearean romances take place in exotic locales, and their plots are invigorated by elements of magic, the supernatural, or the bizarre. Providence can play a big role in the twists and turns of these plots. When you watch these plays, they contain the mood and machinery of a fairy tale.

In these otherworldly plays Shakespeare leans on typical motifs of romance poetry reminiscent of *The Iliad* or *The Odyssey*. The plots are driven by a shipwreck or a character's long journey, both of which can be followed by a tearful reunion. People are exiled from their kingdoms and families are broken apart. But after jarring separations, couples and families are usually united or reunited.

Chapter 25
The Winter's Tale

INTRODUCTION
- An introduction to *The Winter's Tale*, one of Shakespeare's most popular romances, and where his story originated
- A look at major characters in *The Winter's Tale*
- A summary of the main plot in *The Winter's Tale*
- Suspending our disbelief—Shakespeare uses the figure of Time to bridge a 16-year gulf of time
- Notable stage and TV productions of *The Winter's Tale*

The Winter's Tale belongs to a set of later Shakespearean plays known to modern theatre buffs as *romances*. These dramas are full of spectacle and set pieces and occasionally partake of supernatural beings to drive their plots. *The Winter's Tale* is both tragic and comic, but ultimately it transcends these genres by embracing fairytale themes of separation, reconciliation, and love.

Shakespeare composed *The Winter's Tale* around 1610-1611, only five or six years before he died. There is evidence that an early production was staged at the Globe on May 15, 1611. There were seven performances logged at court alone by 1640, which suggests the play was very popular during the early seventeenth century. Between the theatre closings in 1640 and the nineteenth century, its popularity waned. Today *The Winter's Tale* remains fairly well liked onstage, but it has rarely been adapted into film.

Structurally, *The Winter's Tale* is divided into two distinct halves, each of which contains symbolic echoes in contrasting seasons. Part one takes us through the "winter" of Hermione's death caused by Leontes' jealous passion. Part two deals with the "spring" of Perdita's birth, Hermione's resurrection, and the family's reconciliation. In writing *The Winter's Tale*, Shakespeare was inspired by a prose tale called *Pandosto, The Triumph of Time*, by Robert Greene, published in 1588.

The Characters

THE COURT OF SICILIA

Leontes—He is the King of Sicilia, an extremely jealous king who suspects his beloved wife Hermione of having an affair with Polixenes, his oldest friend. Theatregoers today often find his jealousy hard to fathom. In comparing Leontes to Othello, director Harley Granville-Barker calls Leontes' jealousy "a nervous weakness, a mere hysteria," adding, "He, poor wretch, moreover, even at his most positive, even while he sits in dignity and talks of justice, is conscious of this."

Hermione—She is the queen to Leontes and daughter of the King of Russia. For no apparent reason, she is suspected of being the lover of her husband's old friend. She is put on trial, convicted, and sentenced to prison. She shows tremendous patience and dignity throughout her ordeal.

Mamillius—He is Leontes' son and the young prince of Sicilia. He is dearly loved by both of his parents. He is overcome with a grief that kills him when Leontes refuses to believe that Hermione is innocent.

Perdita—She is the beautiful daughter of Leontes and Hermione who was born in prison, taken far away from home upon her father's orders and abandoned to die. Her figure and her fate are the true stuff of fairy tales. The name *Perdita* is Latin for "the lost one."

Paulina—She is the wife of Antigonus and a loyal friend and lady in waiting of Hermione. Hermione lives in her house for 16 years, as long as it takes for Leontes to show contrition. A bold figure, she makes Leontes think that he is responsible for his wife's death.

Camillo—A lord and counselor within Leontes' court who is embroiled in the king's false suspicions of his wife

Antigonus—A lord within Leontes' court, married to Paulina

Cleomines—A lord within Leontes' court

Dion—A lord within Leontes' court

Emilia—A lady attending on Hermione

Time (the Chorus)

A jailer

A sailor

Lords, Gentlemen, Officers, Ladies, Servants

THE WORLD OF BOHEMIA

Polixenes—He is the King of Bohemia who finds himself in a pickle when he visits Leontes' court in Sicilia. When the Bohemian king attempts to leave for home, Leontes' wife convinces him to stay (at Leontes' behest). Then Polixenes innocently agrees to stay after talking with Hermione and ends up incurring the bizarre wrath of Leontes, who suspects him of having an affair with the queen!

Florizel—The son of Polixenes and Prince of Bohemia, who goes by the name Doricles

Archidamus—A lord of Bohemia

Old Shepherd—The reputed father of Perdita

> Clown—The son of the Old Shepherd
>
> Mopsa and Dorcas—A shepherdesses
>
> Autolycus—A rogue
>
> Servant of the old shepherd
>
> *Setting: Sicilia and Bohemia**
> (*Because Shakespeare imagined his Bohemia on the sea, contrary to fact, some critics think he goofed. Others disagree, believing that the Bohemia of this play is completely imaginary.)

The Proverbial Storm—Leontes' Jealous Obsession

Leontes, the King of Sicilia, and Polixenes, the King of Bohemia, are longtime friends who have known each other since childhood. Polixenes has been visiting Leontes for nine months and decides it's time to head home. Leontes wants him to stay longer, but when he can't convince him to stay, he asks his wife Hermione to charm Polixenes into staying. When she is successful, Leontes becomes suspicious. But when he airs these suspicions to his counselor Camillo, he gets a chilly response. Camillo rightfully defends his mistress's honor. Still, Leontes is undetermined. In this excerpt his imagination seems to run wild:

> Leontes: Is whispering nothing?
> Is leaning cheek to cheek? is meeting noses?
> Kissing with inside lip? stopping the career
> Of laughter with a sigh? . . .
>   Is this nothing?
> Why then the world and all that's in't is nothing,
> The covering sky is nothing, Bohemia nothing,
> My wife is nothing, nor nothing have these nothings,
> If this be nothing.
> (I.2.284-287; 292-296)

Chapter 25. The Winter's Tale

"Wild and Whirling Words"

By titling his play *The Winter's Tale*, Shakespeare alluded to a "winter's tale," understood by Elizabethans as a story you'd snuggle up with on a long winter's night. The play has plenty of mythical, far-fetched qualities resembling an old-fashioned fairytale. Leontes' jealousy is wildly out of tune with reality. The king puts his wife on trial based on rash misjudgment, like a character from Aesop's fables. As in a fable, the harsh, jealous king is eventually forgiven for putting his wife and daughter through a harsh ordeal.

What is with this guy? Obviously deluded, he jumps to conclusions by suspecting his wife of acting immorally. Polixenes notices that his host is no longer cordial. Leontes becomes so consumed with jealousy that he orders Camillo to murder his guest with poison. Camillo refuses to carry out the king's bidding. Instead he tells Polixenes about the danger he is in, so he can escape Leontes' wrath. Accompanied by Camillo, Polixenes gets the heck out of Dodge.

Separation—Perdita Is Banished and Hermione Goes on Trial

| Hermione: | I am not prone to weeping, as our sex Commonly are, . . . but I have That honorable grief lodg'd here which burns Worse than tears drown. (II.1.108-109; 110-112) |

When the king learns that Camillo and Polixenes have escaped, he flies into a rage. Further convinced of Hermione's guilt, he formally accuses her of committing adultery and treason and has her arrested. When Hermione announces that she is going to have a baby, Leontes refuses to believe the child is his own. In spite of his wife's protests, Leontes throws his wife in prison. No amount of talk by Antigonus and the other lords will convince Leontes that he is wrong. Instead, the king sends a messenger to Apollo's shrine to receive an oracle about how he should act from this point on.

Part 6. The Romances

VERSE BY VERSE

When Leontes sends a messenger to the oracle of Apollo at Delphi, he is following a common practice familiar to readers of ancient Greek and Roman mythology. In this context, *oracle* is understood as a place where you consulted with a god. Or it was a medium through which one received a divine opinion or statement. An *oracle* was a prophecy or divine announcement.

Paulina, Hermione's lady in waiting, decides to visit her mistress in prison. She isn't allowed to see her, though, but she does learn from Emilia, her attendant, that Hermione has given birth there to a healthy baby girl. Paulina decides to take the baby to show Leontes, hoping that he'll see that the baby belongs to him. Her plan goes awry, however. When Leontes sees the child, his first notion is to have it burned. Antigonus begs Leontes to spare the child, so the king commands Antigonus to remove the child from the court, take it to a faraway location, and abandon it to the elements.

Leontes' couriers travel back to Sicilia from Delphi, the site of Apollo's shrine. Meanwhile, Hermione goes on trial for treason, accused of committing adultery and conspiring with Polixenes to do away with Leontes. In a long speech, Hermione attempts to defend herself, her behavior, and the solid reputation of her royal Russian family.

> Hermione: But thus, if pow'rs divine
> Behold our human actions (as they do),
> I doubt not then but innocence shall make
> False accusation blush,
> (III.2.28-31)

After she speaks, an officer enters with two lords and proceeds to read the oracle. It assures the innocence of Hermione and Polixenes and pronounces Leontes a "jealous tyrant!"

The Price of Obsession

Sadly, hearing the news from a divine oracle isn't enough for Leontes. In spite of the proclamation, he insists his wife is guilty. For his stubbornness, it appears that Leontes has gone too far and the gods may be punishing him! Leontes soon learns that his son Mamillius has died of grief over the news that his mother was found guilty. Leontes now believes that his son's death is a supernatural warning that the oracle was indeed true. Even worse, Pauline tells the king that Hermione is dead. (She's lying, of course, just to punish him, but now he thinks he's destroyed his entire family.) Leontes has no choice but to repent.

In director Matthew Ernest's modernized rendition of The Winter's Tale *for The Texas Shakespeare Festival in 2013, King Leontes' Sicilian castle appears as a stark, twenty-first-century-era glass house that complements the dark tone of the play's early scenes that are infused by the jealous monarch's brooding paranoia.*

(Photo Courtesy of John Dodd and The Texas Shakespeare Festival.)

A Foundling in Bohemia—Perdita's Awakening

Prompted by a vision from Hermione, Antigonus leaves the baby in Bohemia, the kingdom of Polixenes. He names her Perdita. On the way home, Antigonus is shipwrecked, marooned, chased by a bear, and eaten! (What a grim fairy tale this is . . .) Back in Bohemia, a shepherd discovers the baby and rescues her. His utterance to the Clown articulates an important theme in the play: "Thou met'st with things dying, I with things new-born."

At the beginning of Act four, Time delivers a Chorus, informing us that 16 years have passed since Perdita was abandoned.

In the play's second half, Shakespeare develops scenes of sheep-shearing and feasts characteristic of rural life in Bohemia. Perdita has blossomed into a young shepherdess who is being wooed by Florizel, Polixenes' son. In disguise, Polixenes visits the house of a shepherd where his son Florizel pays frequent visits. At the sheep-shearing feast the disguised king discovers that his son is in love with Perdita and he forbids him to see her. The king actually threatens to have Perdita killed if Florizel doesn't stop seeing her. Florizel refuses to obey, and the young couple soon flee from Bohemia on a ship, joined by the shepherd and his son.

 TIMELESS SOLILOQUIES

In the lines that open Act four, you can almost hear Shakespeare asking his gentle readers to forgive him for inserting a period of 16 years in the middle of a short drama:

> Impute it not a crime
> To me, or my swift passage, that I slide
> O'er sixteen years and leave the growth untried
> Of that wide gap, since it is in my pow'r
> To o'erthrow law, and in one self-born hour
> To plant and o'erwhelm custom.
> . . . Your patience this allowing,
> I turn my glass, and give my scene such growing
> As you had slept between.
> (IV.1.4-9; 15-17)

In his *Prefaces to Shakespeare*, Harley Granville Barker implies that Shakespeare took a risk with the above speech: "It is contrived that Time, in the middle of the play, shall definitely strike that note of tolerant understanding, the keynote of the whole play. A lesser artist, writing so, might stray toward indifference or cynicism; Shakespeare can sustain the tone of it beautifully. The very artifice of the device, moreover, attunes us to the artifice of the story; saves us, at this dangerous juncture, when Hermione is apparently dead, Antigonus quite certainly eaten by the bear, from the true tragic mood. Moreover, 'Time, as Chorus,' is the simple way to bridge dramatically the 16 years, and therefore the right one."

Reunion and Rebirth

Back in Sicilia, Paulina has urged Leontes not to remarry. The news gets around that Perdita, the king's long-lost daughter, has arrived in Sicilia. Leontes and his court receive her and Florizel warmly. When Polixenes arrives in Sicilia, Leontes decides to talk to him for Perdita and Florizel's sake. Later, both kings accompany Perdita, Florizel, and Paulina to look at a statue of the dead Hermione. Leontes continues to grieve for his dead wife. What happens next is one of Shakespeare's most uncanny stage tricks. Declaring that Apollo's oracle has been fulfilled, Paulina orders Hermione to descend from her pedestal. Suddenly, to the court's (and our own) disbelieving eyes, Hermione comes back to life! Leontes is overcome with happiness. As you'd expect, the queen is awed upon seeing that her daughter is alive. In the end, Paulina is urged to marry Camillo, Florizel marries Perdita, and Leontes is reunited with Hermione.

Reconciling the Play's Incongruities and Themes

For ages, readers and playgoers have struggled with thorny incongruities in *The Winter's Tale*. First, the way in which King Leontes treats his beloved wife Hermione is not simply cruel, it is highly far-fetched. At least in *Othello*, Othello's jealousy of Desdemona makes sense, because the villain Iago manipulates circumstances to perpetuate that jealousy. But Leontes' suspicions seem groundless. He appears to have no reason to suspect his wife of fooling around on him. Second, Shakespeare's apparent classic comic resolution to the play's highly tragic first half is as perplexing as Leontes' implausible actions.

Part 6. The Romances

"A Kingdom for a Stage"

Director Jane Howell's production of *The Winter's Tale* for BBC-TV has been recognized for its unusual visual appeal. Considered experimental and somewhat minimalist, Howell dressed Leontes in a bearskin hat and a cloak. The show starred Jeremy Kemp as Leontes and Anna Calder-Marshall as Hermione. Another notable stage production of the play featured Christopher Plummer as Leontes in Stratford, Ontario, in 1958. Judi Dench earned kudos for performing both Hermione and Perdita at a Stratford-upon-Avon production in 1969. Jeremy Irons performed Leontes in director Terry Hands' Royal Shakespeare Company production in 1986. In 1992, Adrian Noble directed a Royal Shakespeare Company production, in which Gemma Jones shined as Paulina.

To tackle these questions effectively, you need to look at *The Winter's Tale* differently from a tragedy like *Othello* or a realistic comedy such as *Much Ado About Nothing*. *The Winter's Tale* is deliberately infused with artifice—an implausible tyrant king; a 16-year time lapse between the play's first and second halves, and a heroine who "dies" and is reborn. The play's odd fairy-tale qualities and its culminating union of three couples offer unique moral perspectives.

Throughout the play various characters make reference to the divine, alluding to the existence of a higher power and a plan beyond what humans can apprehend. As an example, Shakespeare allows the oracle of Apollo to prove Leontes wrong in his judgment. Further, by allowing Leontes to lose a son and suffer the loss of his wife for 16 years, the play encourages us to question this king's rush to judgment and the strict ideal of justice embraced by monarchs of Shakespeare's day. We accept Paulina's power to create the illusion of Hermione's death and provoke the king to repent his actions. Only after Leontes repents can he regain the love of his virtuous Hermione. Not only is Hermione reborn, the love between her and Leontes is rejuvenated. Shakespeare complements this poignant sequence of events with the marriages of Paulina and Camillo and Perdita and Florizel. The latter union ensures the

Chapter 25. The Winter's Tale

longevity of Leontes' bloodline. While *The Winter's Tale* may sacrifice the trademark realism of tragedies like *Hamlet* and *King Lear*, its unique blend of the plausible, implausible, and the fantastic would have been appreciated by Shakespeare's audiences.

> **FACTS TO REMEMBER**
> - *The Winter's Tale* is Shakespeare's first successful romance and one of the last plays he wrote.
> - Although *The Winter's Tale* is performed less often than *The Tempest*, the play especially resonates with twentieth-century audiences.
> - When Paulina takes Hermione into her house for 16 years, she lies to Leontes and tells him the queen is dead.
> - By inserting a lapse of 16 years in the middle of the play, Shakespeare keeps the mood of the second half from seeming tragic, according to director Harley Granville Barker.
> - The two-part structure of *The Winter's Tale* underscores the thematic overtones of Shakespearean romance—the first half of the tale dwells on human strife and separation, while the second half emphasizes renewal, rebirth, and reconciliation.
> - Shakespeare's implausible plot and supernatural elements go hand in hand to reinforce his moral vision.

Chapter 26
The Tempest

> **INTRODUCTION**
> - An introduction to *The Tempest*, a magical romance that explores many faces of illusion and the artist
> - A look at the major characters in *The Tempest* and what they represent
> - A review of the principal events of *The Tempest*
> - Archetype, theme, and symbol in *The Tempest*
> - Traditional and experimental film versions of *The Tempest*
> - Actor Bree Welch muses about playing the role of Miranda for the Houston Shakespeare Festival

In writing *The Tempest*, Shakespeare has given us an inspiring and thought-provoking romance. In the play, he blends comedy and tragedy in a highly allegorical fashion, ending his tale with a positive message of forgiveness and hope for renewal and reconciliation. If you recall our universal journey to the Forest of Arden in *As You Like It* (refer to Chapter 12), each character in *The Tempest* likewise finds himself exiled or isolated from the civilized realm of the court. But instead of finding peace in the lively debate of an idyllic forest, in *The Tempest* we occupy an island inhabited by rough beings, humans with civilizing tendencies, and a realm of illusion where Prospero and his spirits work magic and determine the fate of the others.

Part 6. The Romances

Showing influences of Italian *commedia dell'arte*, *The Tempest* is full of music and glittering stage spectacle—masques, dancing, supernatural creatures who transform themselves, and an appearance by three goddesses. Prospero and Ariel use magic for a host of meaningful effects, and their actions become morally significant. Unlike in *The Winter's Tale*, Shakespeare's other popular romance, the playwright observes classical unities of drama in *The Tempest*. Limiting the time in which the play takes place to one day, Shakespeare also confines its place and action to a single island. The first recorded performance of *The Tempest* took place at court on November 1, 1611. The play first appeared in print in the 1623 First Folio.

The Characters

THE WORLD OF PROSPERO'S MAGIC ISLAND

Prospero—Prospero is the rightful Duke of Milan who has been exiled on an uninhabited island in the Mediterranean. With his tiny daughter, he arrived 12 years earlier, surviving the ordeal of being stripped of his dukedom by his brother Antonio. He calls himself "the prime Duke, being so reputed/In dignity, and most knowledgeable about the 'liberal arts.'" Prospero is a benign, benevolent ruler who learned magic from his books. Helped by Ariel, he manipulates the people and events on the island. He deliberately wrecks the ship of his usurpers in order to teach them lessons and force them to repent. He even intervenes to prevent Antonio and Sebastian from committing more treachery on the island! He causes his daughter and young Ferdinand to fall in love. Early on, we learn that he probably cared more about his books and the art of magic than he did about ruling his kingdom, when he says, "Me, poor man, my library/Was dukedom large enough." As the mastermind of all those around him, Prospero symbolizes the artist.

Miranda—She is the teenage daughter of Prospero, and one who has never had contact with a human other than her father. She is the picture of innocence, unsullied by any corrupting influences of civilized society. Unused to human contact, she falls head over heels in love with Ferdinand soon after she lays eyes on him.

Caliban—Caliban is portrayed as a savage, a "demi-devil," and a monster of the sea. Early on, we learn that Caliban tried to rape Miranda, which is why Prospero enslaved him. Feeling no remorse, Caliban tells Prospero he would have violated Miranda in order to procreate his own race, to have "peopled else/This isle with Calibans." To Prospero and Miranda, Caliban is baser than humans because he is incapable of moral improvement. Miranda teaches him the language of humans, but Caliban disparages his newfound knowledge of language and eschews the learning that Prospero has gained from books. In Prospero's view, Caliban is "a devil, a born devil, on whose nature/Nurture can never stick; on whom my pains/Humanely taken—all, all lost, quite lost!"

Ariel—He is an airy spirit indentured to Prospero, who the exiled duke rescued from imprisonment by the evil witch Sycorax. Prospero describes Ariel as "thou, which art but air," and calls him "chick," expressions that suggest he resembles a bird. Elizabethans recognized Ariel as a *sprite* similar to Puck, the spirit who waits on Oberon in *A Midsummer Night's Dream*. In the end, Prospero frees him after he has carried out his wishes.

Iris—A Roman goddess attending on Prospero; in Roman mythology, she was the goddess Juno's personal messenger

Ceres—Roman goddess of agriculture attending on Prospero

Juno—Queen of the Roman gods, attending on Prospero

Nymphs, Reapers, and other spirits attending on Prospero

THE SHIPWRECKED NOBLES WASHED ASHORE

Ferdinand—He is the prince of Naples and son of Alonso, the king. Despite being separated from his father and the others after the shipwreck, he safely wanders into the cell of Prospero and Miranda.

Part 6. The Romances

Although he falls in love with Miranda, he is closely monitored and supervised by Prospero.

Alonso—He is the King of Naples who becomes distraught when his son Ferdinand goes missing on the island after the shipwreck. He believes his son's disappearance is proof that God is punishing him for helping Antonio take Prospero's dukedom away from him.

Sebastian—He is the opportunistic brother of Alonso, the King of Naples. He has the audacity to plot his brother's murder and overthrow on Prospero's island!

Antonio—He is the usurping Duke of Milan who deposed his wise, bookish brother Prospero 12 years before the play begins. Always scheming and plotting, he is no sooner marooned on Prospero's island than he goes to work plotting more rebellion with Sebastian against Alonso.

Gonzalo—He is the councilor of King Alonso and, formerly, an honest and wise courtier of Prospero who is shipwrecked with Alonso's followers. Prospero appreciates him because he restored his books of magic and provided him and Miranda with food and clothing after they were exiled from Milan.

Trinculo—A jester, one of the clown roles

Stephano—A drunken butler, another clown role

Adrian and Francisco—Lords

Master of a Ship

Boatswain

Mariners

Setting: A ship at sea and an uninhabited island

Chapter 26. The Tempest

Prospero's Magic Isle

In the short opening scene, a ship is tossing on ferocious seas, in danger of going down. A group of nobles—including Alonso (the King of Naples), his son Ferdinand, his councilor Gonzalo, and Antonio (the usurping Duke of Milan)—is riding out the storm. Here we glimpse the ugly disposition of Antonio and Sebastian, the brother of Alonso. Soon, the ship sinks, however, and all are washed upon the shore of a seemingly uninhabited island.

A Banished Duke and His Young Daughter Go Native

A beautiful young girl named Miranda lives with her father, a magician named Prospero, on this same sparsely populated Mediterranean island. When she expresses concern over the fate of the seamen, Prospero reassures her about their safety. He explains how the two of them came to inhabit the island 12 years before. Once Duke of Milan, he had fallen in love with magic and neglected his duties as head of state. His brother Antonio plotted with the King of Naples to take away his dukedom. Father and daughter were banished to sea and luckily came upon the island once controlled by Sycorax, an evil witch who's dead. After freeing the good spirits that she controlled, Prospero could exercise his powers in peace.

VERSE BY VERSE

Prospero: So much of [Gonzalo's] gentleness,
Knowing I loved my books, he furnished me
From mine own library with volumes that
I prize above my dukedom.
(I.2.165-168)

Prospero's affinity for books and magic connect him to the world of the literary artist. In Prospero, Shakespeare may have even offered us a self-portrait. For centuries, Western poets, novelists, and critics have been drawn to *The Tempest*'s allegory and bookishness. Enduring literary works that show its influence include John Milton's *Comus*, T. S. Eliot's *The Waste Land*, W. H.

> Auden's *The Sea and the Mirror*, and Aldous Huxley's satirical *A Brave New World*. Samuel Taylor Coleridge delivered lectures on *The Tempest*, and Henry James weighed in on the play's brilliance in his *Complete Works of Shakespeare*.

Prospero tells Miranda that he has magically caused the shipwreck to force his enemies onto the island. Then he puts Miranda to sleep and bids Ariel, his favorite *sprite* and servant, to bring the nobles ashore and especially protect young Ferdinand, the king's son. So Ariel beckons young Ferdinand to leave the group and follow him into the safe care of Prospero. (Before he does so, he complains about having to take orders all the time, and Prospero reminds him that they have a bargain. If Ariel does the magician's bidding as he promised, as thanks for being rescued from Sycorax's imprisonment, Prospero will eventually free him.) Of course, Prospero orders him to stay invisible while carrying out his requests!

Miranda Spies a Prince

Prospero wakes up Miranda and who should appear but Caliban, the half-human monster who became Prospero's slave when he tried to rape Miranda. Surly and complaining, Caliban is not happy at all at his lot in life. The beast astutely points out that the island should rightly belong to him because he inherited it from Sycorax and occupied it before Prospero. When he complains of mistreatment, Prospero firmly reminds him that his own immoral behavior led to his enslavement. As Caliban grouses, we realize that the colonizers' peaceful existence on the island is not so idyllic for all of God's creatures.

But Miranda soon lights her gaze on the beautiful Ferdinand, a creature like no other.

> Miranda: There's nothing ill can dwell in such a temple.
> If the ill spirit have so fair a house,
> Good things will strive to dwell with 't.
> (I.2.458–460)

Chapter 26. The Tempest

She falls instantly in love with the young prince, and he returns the affection, of course. (We soon surmise that the two were destined to be lovers, as Prospero never stops working his magic!) Fearful that Ferdinand might take Miranda for granted, the magician proceeds to teach him a few lessons about valuing his daughter's honor and the merits of hard labor.

Subterfuge Against the King of Naples

We cut away to the beach on another portion of the isle. King Alonso mourns his missing son. Working behind the scenes, Ariel puts everyone asleep except Antonio and Sebastian. Not surprisingly, these two are already up to no good. They hurriedly plot to do away with the king in his sleep so Sebastian can overthrow the kingdom of Naples. Ariel stops them, though, before they do the evil deed.

Moving to a different piece of the island, we meet up with Caliban who makes the acquaintance of the king's jester (Trinculo) and the royal butler (Stephano). All are drunk, and Caliban bemoans his general servitude. In a scheme that parallels the treachery of Antonio and Sebastian, these three goofs hatch a plot to murder Prospero and take over the island! (Ariel, of course, is eavesdropping on their plan and divulges everything to his master.)

Two Lovers Pledge to Marry

We cut back to Ferdinand who has been ordered by Prospero to roll logs, much to Miranda's dismay. She interrupts the prince, against her father's wishes, and the two pledge to get married. Prospero trusts that Ferdinand has good intentions so he is content to leave them alone. Meanwhile, Ariel is up to more trickery, putting illusions of a grand banquet before the seamen and admonishing the nobles for committing treachery against Prospero, while disguised as a harpy. Ariel warns them they will be tortured unless they mend their evil ways. Alonso desperately searches for his presumed-dead son. The seamen are in a bad way!

Part 6. The Romances

"Wild and Whirling Words"

Familiar words in *The Tempest* can deceive you. Here are some key words and how Elizabethans understood them in context. When Miranda uses the expression "thy vile race" in addressing Caliban, the word *race* signifies a person's innate or inherited disposition or qualities, not our own physically determined classification. Ariel, called a *sprite*, is a fairy. In Greek mythology, a *harpy* is an ugly winged monster that has the body and head of a woman and the legs of a bird. In Act three Ariel disguises himself as a harpy.

Soon, Ferdinand is freed from his manual duties. Prospero goes along with Ferdinand and Miranda's engagement and has Ariel put together a masque to celebrate the couple's marriage. During the masque, different spirits dress up as goddesses Iris, Juno, and Ceres to bless the union, while nymphs and reapers provide entertainment. Ariel continues to punish Caliban and the drunken servants by tempting them to try on fine garments and giving them the imaginary impression that a pack of wild dogs is chasing them.

A Mystery Revealed and Prospero's Growth

Miranda: O wonder!
How many goodly creatures are there here!
How beauteous mankind is! O brave new world
That has such people in't!
(V.1.181-83)

Deciding that he has punished both groups of perpetrators sufficiently, Prospero decides it's time to show mercy to his enemies. He sends Ariel to bring Alonso, Antonio, and Sebastian back to him. He decides that after he has put his enemies on the right path he will give up magic once and for all. In a touching scene, Prospero dresses up in his duke's clothing and his enemies slowly recognize him. Alonso is the most contrite, repenting, confessing his treachery against Prospero, and giving back his dukedom. Alonso is uplifted even further when Prospero shows him a vision of his son Ferdinand playing chess with Miranda. Prospero declares that the young couple will rule Naples one day. Soon news comes that the wrecked ship has been found and is seaworthy enough to make it back home. As Ariel prepares good weather for the nobles' return home, Prospero prepares to entertain the visitors in his cave for one night and tell them the tale of his life on the island. In the end, Prospero sets Ariel free.

In her 2010 film version of The Tempest, *director Julie Taymor cast film and stage doyenne Helen Mirren (left) in the traditionally male role of Prospero, the rightful duke of Milan. In Taymor's experiment, "Prospera" works her magic on the uninhabited island where she lives in exile, alongside her daughter Miranda (Felicity Jones).*

(Photo Courtesy of Photofest.)

Exploring Illusion Versus Reality

Prospero: We are such stuff
As dreams are made on; and our little life
Is rounded with a sleep.
(IV.1.156-158)

Part 6. The Romances

The Tempest explores the nature of illusion and reality on many different levels. In creating false illusions of fine food and garments for the nobles and the drunken trio, Prospero and Ariel comically remind us that we can't always trust appearances. And even though Prospero and Ariel have created an illusory world using their magic, "the journey is no escape from reality, for the island shows men what they are and what they ought to be," notes David Bevington in his *Bantam Shakespeare: The Tempest*. In the famous passage noted previously, Prospero suggests that our lives are mere illusions, ephemeral and transitory until we sleep forever.

 TIMELESS SOLILOQUIES

In delivering the play's Epilogue, Prospero reminds us that his magical powers have disappeared. Now that the exiled duke has forgiven and freed his enemies and Ariel, it is time for him to return to reality, to his mortal life, and become a more responsible ruler of his dukedom.

> Now my charms are all o'erthrown,
> And what strength I have's mine own,
> Which is most faint. Now 'tis true,
> I must be here confin'd by you,
> Or sent to Naples. Let me not,
> Since I have my dukedom got,
> And pardon'd the deceiver, dwell
> In this bare island by your spell,
> But release me from my bands
> With the help of your good hands . . .

Using his charms, Prospero appeared God-like and in complete control of everyone. In renouncing magic, he chooses to return to the reality of mortals. Also implicit in this passage is the idea that Prospero resembles Shakespeare, the artist, mastermind of his plays and the illusions they create. As a stage artist, Shakespeare manipulates the playgoers by creating a dramatic vision to entertain us. Both Prospero and Shakespeare conjure illusions for us, their victims, and hold us in thrall. But only we have the power to break the spell through our applause.

"A Brave New World"—Theme of Freedom and Servitude

By making Prospero all-powerful, Shakespeare reminds us how the magician controls others. Although Ariel cheerfully does Prospero's bidding, he can't wait to be set free. He does have a certain amount of freedom, though, as he flies around and works his own magic! By contrast, Caliban is a slave, forced to do manual labor. At one level, Caliban reminds us that life wasn't so bad for him before Prospero and Miranda came along and tried to civilize him by teaching him their language. Miranda, too, experiences a kind of servitude to her father. While performing Miranda for the Houston Shakespeare Festival in 2006, Bree Welch was struck by how powerful and potentially dangerous Prospero was as a father. Through these three characters' individual prisms of existence, Shakespeare enlightens us about differing degrees of freedom and servitude.

Actor Bree Welch Interprets the Role of Miranda for the Houston Shakespeare Festival

When Bree Welch was asked to compare the role of Miranda to her past roles in Houston Shakespeare Festival (HSF) productions of *Love's Labor's Lost*, *As You Like It*, *The Taming of the Shrew*, and *Hamlet*, she realized her experience performing Miranda was unique. Before rehearsals, she was well aware that modern actors tend to interpret Miranda as somewhat ditzy and unintelligent, or even as overly juvenile. While performing in director Sidney Berger's HSF show in 2006, Welch settled on a view of Miranda that seemed more in line with Shakespeare's vision.

"A KINGDOM FOR A STAGE"

Princess Elizabeth, daughter of King James I, enjoyed one of the earliest showings of *The Tempest* at her wedding celebration in the winter of 1612-13. In the twentieth century *The Tempest* has inspired many TV and film versions. A good, traditional example was produced by BBC-TV in 1980 and directed by John Gorrie. It stars the talented Shakespearean actor Michael Hordern as Prospero and Pippa Guard as Miranda. After watching this, you can explore Derek Jarman's experimental 1980 film *The Tempest* or Peter Greenaway's 1991 self-reflexive movie, called *Prospero's Books*, starring John Gielgud. In it, Gielgud represents Prospero and Shakespeare self-consciously at work on their writing.

"I tried to characterize Miranda as a girl removed from social dictates," Welch says. "Miranda is very strong because she's been raised by Prospero, who's a powerful, intelligent man. He has been her only influence. Because she's very isolated, she's the epitome of innocence and naïveté. Walking in Miranda's shoes was intriguing for me because her experiences are so rare today. Our modern senses are overpowered by every imaginable influence—music and media especially. Because Miranda has been so isolated, she has strong, honest, emotional reactions to things. In the first act, when she discovers Ferdinand, the first human she's laid eyes on besides her father, she is completely speechless. At that moment, having only known her father, she shows her rare quality of innocence. One of the play's themes is the loss of innocence, and it's still relevant today. Parents want to keep their children innocent as long as possible.

"I think Miranda is the most unusual of Shakespeare's heroines. She's not a Juliet, nor is she an Ophelia or a Rosaline (from *Love's Labor's Lost*). Her own particular isolation and innocence make her stand apart. It's true that Juliet is innocent and feeling the overwhelming effects of her hormones at age 13, but she's strongly influenced by her mother and a host of societal constraints. Whereas Miranda, with no influence from the world, is able to completely find herself as an individual."

Chapter 26. The Tempest

FACTS TO REMEMBER

- *The Tempest*, Shakespeare's greatest romance and last solo work, is his second shortest play after *The Comedy of Errors*.
- By offering perspectives of how Prospero controls Ariel, Caliban, and Miranda, the play explores differing degrees of freedom and servitude.
- Prospero, a magician and master manipulator, embodies the artist and may be a self-portrait of Shakespeare.
- *The Tempest's* epilogue offers thought-provoking ideas about illusion versus reality, the role of the playwright, and life's transitory quality.

Appendices

Appendix A

Shakespeare's Lesser-Known Plays

(arranged alphabetically, not chronologically)

All's Well That Ends Well (1603–1606)

Type of play: A darker romantic comedy, also called a *problem comedy*. According to *The New Oxford Shakespeare* (2016), Shakespeare wrote the play between 1603-1606, Thomas Middleton adapted it for a revival after Shakespeare died, sometime between 1616-1621.

Sources: *The Decameron* by Giovanni Boccaccio (1353), translated by William Painter in *The Palace of Pleasure* (1566-67, 1575)

About the Play: Helena, an orphan and the opportunistic daughter of a physician, is crazy about Bertram, the snobby Count of Rossillion. Helena wants to marry Bertram. But in spite of the fact that his mother has raised her, the Countess is opposed to the match. Undaunted, Helena follows him when he leaves home to enter the care of the French king. Knowing a little about medicine (being a doctor's daughter), she deviously settles on a plan to cure the king of his sickness using her father's medicine. Her plan works! When the king rewards her by allowing her to choose her husband, she chooses Bertram. He rebuffs her, of course, and even though the king forces him to marry Helena, Bertram embarks on a series of plots to elude the marriage, beginning when he escapes to Florence. She suffers greatly throughout the ordeal, gets pregnant, but manages to wins him in the end.

The Comedy of Errors (1589–1594)

Type of play: An early comedy with a farcical, madcap feel and Shakespeare's shortest play

Sources: *Menaechmi* and *Amphitruo*, two ancient comedies by Plautus; *Midas*, by John Lyly (1589); *Supposes*, by George Gascoigne (1566); The Bible (St. Paul's *Acts of the Apostles* and *Epistle to the Ephesians*)

About the Play: Considering the play has two sets of identical twins, it won't be hard for you to imagine the mileage Shakespeare gets out of mistaken identity, his favorite comedic device. But here's a dark wrinkle—Egeon comes to Ephesus to look for his two missing sons. Solinus, the Duke, has him arrested and promises to behead him if he can't pay a ransom. After Egeon recounts his wild tale about how a shipwreck split up his entire family, the improbabilities never seem to stop.

Coriolanus (1607–1610)

Type of play: The latest Roman tragedy written by Shakespeare

Sources: Plutarch's *Lives of the Noble Grecians and Romans*, translated by Sir Thomas North (1579)

About the Play: The time is 490 B.C.E. The Roman aristocracy and starving lower classes are sharply divided. Caius Marcius, a successful soldier, despises both the plebeians and the powerful tribunes who represent them. The Roman tribunes hate him, too. When he defeats the Volscians at Corioli, he is dubbed Coriolanus in honor of the victory and offered the position of consul if he will humble himself publicly before the people. He refuses, flouting his distaste for the process. Wrong move—Sicinius and Brutus turn the people against him; he's then accused of treason and exiled. In Actium, his post as commander of the Volscian army backfires when Aufidius starts to feel threatened. His troops advance on Rome, but his family influences him to put a peace treaty with Rome in place. In the end, the Volscians declare him a traitor and he is murdered.

APPENDIX A. SHAKESPEARE'S LESSER-KNOWN PLAYS

Cymbeline (1610)

Type of play: Romance, a modern classification. *Cymbeline* was listed in the First Folio as a tragedy.

Sources: Raphael Holinshed's *Chronicles* (1587); *A Mirror for Magistrates*; *Frederyke of Jennen*, Anonymous (1560); *The Rare Triumphs of Love and Fortune* (1582); Apuleius, *The Golden Ass*

About the Play: *Cymbeline* is one of Shakespeare's four late romances. Its fantastical plot centers on Cymbeline's daughter Imogen, who has defied her father's wishes and married Posthumus Leonatus, a poor noble. Cymbeline has exiled Posthumus from Britain, and we are treated to a string of Imogen's fairytale adventures in the context of Britain's conflict with Rome. They include a plot to test Imogen's fidelity, a journey in which her life is threatened, her search for a Roman general (disguised as a boy), her sojourn in Wales under a different identity, the surprise appearance of two lost brothers, and her ruse to fake her death by taking sleeping medicine.

Henry IV, Part II (1597–1600)

Type of play: A history play and the second of a two-part sequence charting the education of Prince Hal and the iconoclastic knight Sir John Falstaff (refer to *Part I* in Chapter 16). Beginning with *Richard II*, *Henry IV, Part II* is also the third of Shakespeare's four-part saga covering the Hundred Years War, known as the *major tetralogy*.

Sources: Raphael Holinshed's *Chronicles of England, Scotland, and Ireland* and the anonymous *The Famous Victories of Henry V*.

About the Play: *Henry IV, Parts I and II* focus on England's civil war and how a young prince is tested on his journey toward the throne. *Part II* looks at the final days of Henry IV's reign. Both plays address related national and personal conflicts, laced with Shakespeare's rich portraits and verbal wit. You can enjoy *Part II* without knowing much about *Part I*'s rebellion and the Battle of Shrewsbury. *Part II* shines the spotlight on the irreverent Sir John Falstaff, who continues to thrive in our modern imaginations as strongly as the indecisive Hamlet.

APPENDICES

> **MEMORABLE LINES:**
>
> Hostess Quickly: He hath eaten me out of house and home, he hath put all my substance into that fat belly of his, . . .
> (II.1.74-75)

King John (1596; 1589-1598)

Type of play: Shakespeare's only stand-alone history play.

Sources: *The Troublesome Reign of King John*, an anonymous two-part drama published in 1591. Many scholars believe Shakespeare revised this source and created a very different play. Others say it is a bad memorial reconstruction of *King John*.

About the Play: Members of the court are not getting along with King John, who's not popular at all. Philip, the King of France, wants him to abdicate so John's nephew Arthur can take the throne. When John favors Philip, the Bastard (son of Richard, the Lionheart) in Philip's legal dispute with Robert Faulconbridge, John further provokes the bad blood between his court and France. The play centers on war between England and France; the marriage of John's niece and Lewis, the Dauphin; John's disagreement with the Pope and imprisonment of Arthur; and the French invasion of England (sanctioned by the Pope). The most famous event of King John's reign was the signing of the Magna Carta, remember? In *King John* Shakespeare omits any mention of this fact. (King John ruled England from 1199 to 1216.)

Love's Labor's Lost (1594–1597)

Type of play: A romantic comedy whose complement, *Love's Labor's Won*, seems to have been lost

Sources: No known source. For his plot and characters, Shakespeare may have borrowed from the Italian *commedia dell'arte* tradition.

About the Play: *Love's Labor's Lost* is very thin on plot, actually. King Ferdinand and three lords make a pact to get away from it all for three years, devoting themselves to quiet academic study. During this time, they vow not to admit any woman onto the court's premises. They soon weaken, of course, when the Princess of France shows up with three of her ladies to conduct official business. Misdirected letters, lyrical eloquence, masques, and masquerading dominate this light drama. The play parodies stuffy intellectuals of Shakespeare's day and overly idealized medieval love stories. It is unique among Shakespeare's plays, a dazzling displaying of the dramatist's poetical gifts.

MEMORABLE LINES:

Berowne: As, painfully to bore upon a book
            To seek the light of truth, while truth the while
            Doth falsely blind the eyesight of his look.
            Light, seeking light, doth light of light beguile;
            (I.1.74-77)

Love's Labor's Won (A Lost Play, 1594-1598)

Richard II (1595-1597)

Type of play: *Richard II* is the first drama of Shakespeare's four-part saga covering the Hundred Years War. The series, also called the *major tetralogy*, continues with *Henry IV, Parts I and II*, and *Henry V*. The play focuses on kingship and civil war during the late fourteenth and early fifteenth centuries.

Sources: Raphael Holinshed's *Chronicles of England, Scotland, and Ireland* and Edward Hall's *The Union of the Two Noble and Illustre Families of Lancaster and York*.

About the Play: *Richard II* is remembered more for its lyrical poetry than its ability to captivate us onstage. It's the story of a weak king's fall from power and grace, driven out by the usurping Henry Bolingbroke, his rival and spiritual opposite. Shakespeare presents King Richard as eloquent and self-aware but unable to act when necessary to overcome the seeds of rebellion. After Bolingbroke succeeds in deposing Richard, he takes steps that lead to his murder. Bolingbroke will live to regret and suffer for this act. Remorse troubles Bolingbroke in two subsequent dramas, *Henry IV, Parts I and II*.

Richard's deposition is significant historically and in Shakespeare because he is the first anointed king to be deposed; Henry's coronation signals a departure from the English rule of *primogeniture* (refer to Chapter 16 and Appendix A: *Henry IV, Part II*).

> **MEMORABLE LINES:**
>
> John of Gaunt: There is no virtue like necessity.
> (I.3.278)

Troilus and Cressida (1598–1603)

Type of play: A problem comedy or problem play; *Troilus* was labeled a tragedy in the First Folio.

Sources: *The Ancient History of the Destruction of Troy*, translation by William Caxton (1596); Homer's *Iliad*

About the Play: A bitter Trojan War drama that mixes dark comedy and bitter tragedy, the play's action occurs seven years after the Greek army lays siege to Troy to regain their lost Helen. Troilus, son of the Trojan king, loves Cressida, a Trojan woman whose father has joined up with the Greeks. Challenges are issued on both sides until the Greeks offer to exchange a Trojan captive for Cressida. The deal separates Troilus and Cressida, who seem ever loyal. In the Greek camp, Cressida's attention strays and Troilus discovers that Diomedes is courting his lover. He seeks revenge but is unsuccessful.

The Two Gentlemen of Verona (1587)

Type of play: An early comedy; *Two Gents*, as they say in the theatre business, is Shakespeare's least impressive drama.

Sources: *Diana*, by Jorge de Montemayor (1582); Arthur Brooke's prose romance, *Romeus and Juliet* (1562); *Midas*, by John Lyly (1589)

About the Play: Proteus, the first gent, supposedly loves Julia, but he leaves Verona to meet up with his close friend Valentine (the second gent) at the court

Appendix A. Shakespeare's Lesser-Known Plays

of Milan. There, Proteus forgets all about Julia (who dotes on him), falls in love with Valentine's girl, and proceeds to disparage Valentine by using his big mouth. This betrayal leads to Valentine's exile from the court. Julia is determined to get him back, though, so she disguises herself as a boy (of course) and sets out to find him. Julia's well-written role; the rich wit of Launce, the clown; and his dog Crab can't save the script's absurd, implausible twist when Valentine offers his beloved Silvia to Proteus, just after Proteus is about to rape her! What? Is this some lame attempt to put friendship on a higher plane than love? It's far-fetched and subverts the playwright's earlier design.

MEMORABLE LINES:

Valentine: What light is light, if Silvia be not seen?
What joy is joy, if Silvia be not by?
Unless it be to think that she is by,
And feed upon the shadow of perfection.
Except I be by Silvia in the night,
There is no music in the nightingale;
(III.1.174-179)

Appendix B
The Collaborative Plays
(arranged chronologically)

Titus Andronicus (1589; 1584–1594)

Authorship: Many scholars believe that Shakespeare collaborated with George Peele to write *Titus Andronicus* around 1593-94. They also suggest that *Titus* is Shakespeare's revision of an early Peele play (and they even speculate that he and Peele worked together on the revision). Bottom line—no one agrees on exactly when the play was written, but they do agree that it's not Shakespeare's (or Shakespeare and company's) best effort!

Type of play: *Titus* was written in the style of popular Elizabethan revenge tragedies similar to Thomas Kyd's *Spanish Tragedy* and Christopher Marlowe's *The Jew of Malta*. *Titus* is the first tragedy with Shakespeare's name on it.

Source: For the rape and mutilation of Lavinia, Shakespeare drew upon the mythical tale of Philomela from Ovid's *Metamorphoses*.

About the Play: If you're into the Elizabethan stage equivalent of slasher movies, *Titus* is your play. You have murder (lots of it), rape, horrific dismembering, decapitation, and even cannibalism. Not to mention that Titus' epic suffering won't elicit much sympathy because he repeatedly exercises poor judgment. Basically, you stop feeling sorry for the guy and pray that he'll manage to make one right decision.

The Roman general, Titus, has triumphed over the enemy Goths in a recent battle. His prisoners include the Goth Queen Tamora, her sons, and her lover Aaron, all of whom Titus carries back to Rome. Next, he orders the execution of Alarbus, Tamora's oldest son, to assuage the spirits of his dead sons who died in battle. Bad decision! This initial sacrifice is enough to ignite the passion and resolve of devious Tamora and her determined supporters. Then when the Romans encourage Titus to become emperor, he throws his support to Saturninus. Saturninus asks Titus if he can have Lavinia's hand in marriage, but this affair is thwarted when Saturninus' brother Bassanio (Lavinia's lover) steals her away. Steamed at Titus and his power, Saturninus then plans to marry Tamora. At this point, she sees her chance to consolidate her power and take her revenge on Titus' family.

Here's when the swirl of murder and mayhem spins out of control. With Aaron's help, Tamora's two sons kill Bassanio in the forest and brutally rape Lavinia, cutting off her hands and cutting out her tongue. Titus' surviving sons are tricked and arrested for murder, and Titus is duped into losing his hand! The rest of the play involves Titus' attempt to avenge the crimes against his family.

Henry VI, Part II (1587–1591)

Authorship: The editors of *The New Oxford Shakespeare* (2016) attribute the play to Shakespeare, Christopher Marlowe, and an anonymous playwright. Many experts agree that Shakespeare wrote Act three (scenes 9-12) and a speech by Young Clifford. Marlowe is credited with sections of Act four involving Jack Cade.

Type of play: A history play, the second of Shakespeare's four-part historical saga, or *minor tetralogy*, which culminates with the popular *Richard III* (refer to Chapter 15).

Sources: Raphael Holinshed's *Chronicles of England, Scotland, and Ireland* and Edward Hall's *The Union of the Two Noble and Illustre Families of Lancaster and York*

About the Play: Part II continues the bitter conflict known as the Wars of the Roses. By the end of the play, the Yorkists triumph at the Battle of St. Albans when the Duke of York's son Richard kills Gloucester.

Henry VI, Part III (1588–1591)

Authorship: The editors of *The New Oxford Shakespeare* (2016) attribute the play to Shakespeare, Christopher Marlowe, and an anonymous playwright. They assert that Shakespeare is believed to have written scenes 4-6, 8-12, 14, 23, and 25-29. Marlowe is credited as the principal author of scenes 1, 2, 7, 15-21, and 24.

Type of play: A history play, the third of Shakespeare's four-part historical saga, or *minor tetralogy*, which covers the Wars of the Roses and culminates with the popular *Richard III* (refer to Chapter 15).

Sources: Raphael Holinshed's *Chronicles of England, Scotland, and Ireland* and Edward Hall's *The Union of the Two Noble and Illustre Families of Lancaster and York*

About the Play: Early in Part III, Henry VI agrees to pass the crown to Richard, Duke of York, as long as Henry can continue to rule for the rest of his life. The bitter civil war between the Lancastrians and Yorkists continues, and events such as the Battle of Tewkesbury and the murder of King Henry by York's son Richard, Duke of Gloucester prefigure the younger Richard's ruthless climb to the throne in *Richard III*.

Edward III (1592; 1588–1595)

Authorship: An anonymous history play with mysterious authorship. It does not appear in the First Folio (1623). Many feel Shakespeare wrote several scenes involving the Countess of Salisbury; others believe he wrote the entire play. It was entered in the Stationer's Register in 1595, and bookseller Cuthbert Burby published it in 1596 with no author's name attached. Shakespeare's acting company did not claim it either. There are interesting arguments on both sides. Some say Shakespeare revised a play that was already well developed, which explains the lack of his signature comedy, flair for narrative structure, and character development.

Type of play: A history play that covers the beginning of the Hundred Years War (middle fourteenth century), which Shakespeare continued in his great four-part saga (*Richard III*; *Henry IV, Parts I and II*; and *Henry V*). It's often grouped with Shakespeare's Apocrypha because of its questionable authorship.

Sources: Jean Froissart's *Chronicles*.

About the Play: Set in England and France, *Edward III* dramatizes the political struggles of King Edward and his son, Edward, the Black Prince, who drew England into the Hundred Years War against France. It covers the pivotal Battle of Crécy in 1346.

Henry VI, Part I (1592; 1587–1592)

Authorship: The editors of *The New Oxford Shakespeare* (2016) attribute the play to Christopher Marlowe, Thomas Nashe (Act one), and an anonymous playwright. William Shakespeare is said to have adapted the play after it was written, and his hand is seen in Act two (scene 4), Act four (scene 2), and Act four (scenes 3-5). Marlowe is credited with writing Act five (scenes 4 and 5), among others featuring Joan.

Type of play: A history play, the first of a four-part sequence comprising Shakespeare's first chronicle, known as the *minor tetralogy*, which covers the Wars of the Roses and culminates with the popular *Richard III* (refer to Chapter 15).

Sources: Raphael Holinshed's *Chronicles of England, Scotland, and Ireland* and Edward Hall's *The Union of the Two Noble and Illustre Families of Lancaster and York*

About the Play: Part I centers on the start of the Wars of the Roses, referring to the political rivalry between the Earl of Somerset—head of the Lancastrians, represented by the red rose—and the Duke of York—leader of the Yorkists, whose emblem was the white rose. Part I also treats the final years of the English war against France, picking up where *Henry V* left off (refer to Chapter 17). This time the English are fighting Joan of Arc.

Appendix B. The Collaborative Plays

Timon of Athens (1606; 1603–1608)

Authorship: There's strong evidence that Shakespeare collaborated with Thomas Middleton on *Timon of Athens*. Some say Middleton wrote about one third of the play, specifically, scene 2 of Act one and the first six scenes of Act three.

Type of play: *Timon of Athens* is considered a tragedy of lesser quality than masterworks like *Hamlet*, *Othello*, *King Lear*, and *Macbeth*. But the play is actually a different beast. Its resolution resembles comedy that offers a lesson or moral. Some characters, or "stock types," represent vices and virtues found in medieval morality tales. Watching the play, you get the impression that Shakespeare, sensitive to his audience's craving for social satire, decided to experiment.

Sources and Influences: Plutarch's *Lives of the Noble Grecians and Romans* (*Life of Antony* and *Life of Alcibiades*), translated by Thomas North in 1579.

About the Play: Full of flaws and verse imperfections, the plot of *Timon of Athens* will remind you of Aesop's fables. Timon is a generous Athenian nobleman who is being taken advantage of by many friends and followers. Though he has given money to many people, these false friends refuse to reciprocate when his creditors come knocking. So he throws a party and exposes his false friends in an outrageous display. Afterward he retires to a cave outside of Athens to live as a misanthrope (hater of mankind). There he discovers a golden treasure, gives some of it to Alcibiades, and bestows the lion's share on his loyal steward Flavius. Before he dies, isolated from his fellow man, Timon rids himself of all parasites and sycophants.

Pericles, Prince of Tyre (1606–1608)

Authorship: Stylistic differences between the first two and last three acts of *Pericles* suggest that George Wilkins and Shakespeare both had a hand in it. A plausible hypothesis suggests that Shakespeare revised the second half of Wilkins's script and that they didn't collaborate. *The New Oxford Shakespeare* (2016) states that a majority of scholars agree that Wilkins is the main author of the play's first eleven scenes. The King's Men performed Shakespeare's revision at the Globe around 1607-08.

Type of play: A romance that adapts the ancient Greek tale of Apollonius of Tyre, a hero who interested Elizabethans.

Sources: *Confessio Amantis (The Lover's Confession)*, Book 8 (1385-93; 1554 edition), by John Gower, and *The Pattern of Painful Adventures–that Befell unto Prince Apollonius*, a prose romance by Laurence Twine (1576); the authors pay their debt to Gower by naming the Chorus after him.

About the Play: *Pericles* is a picaresque, allegorical tale that anticipates later symbolic romances like *The Tempest* and *The Winter's Tale*. Misfortune befalls the hero and spectacular elements abound–riddles, contests, exile, shipwreck, separation, pirate misdeeds, and reconciliation. It starts when the prince uncovers the answer to a riddle created by King Antiochus for men who court his daughter. Hinting that he knows the answer–that there is incest between the king and his daughter–Pericles leaves Antioch.

Pericles returns to Tyre, finds a lord to govern in his absence, and sets off for Tarsus to help hungry citizens stricken by famine. Antiochus' men are coming after him so he goes out to sea, but he's shipwrecked at Pentapolis. There he meets Thaisa, the king's daughter, and they marry. Back on the ship, Thaisa gives birth to baby Marina but is believed to be lost to Pericles in a tempest. Marina is raised by the governor of Tarsus and his wife, and all three are separated and endure more mishaps until the final reconciliation.

Cardenio (A Lost Play, 1612)

Authorship: John Fletcher and Shakespeare collaborated on a play called *The History of Cardenio*, which was lost. It may have been printed, but no copies exist. Editors of *The New Oxford Shakespeare* (2016) observe that Shakespeare wrote the initial half of the play, through Act three (scene 2), and Fletcher wrote all subsequent scenes. Evidence of the play comes from a Stationer's Register entry in 1653 that reads "The History of Cardenio by Mr. Fletcher and Shakespeare." Lewis Theobald, an early editor of Shakespeare, produced a play called *The Double Falsehood* in 1727. He reported that it was based on an English play by Shakespeare and centered upon two characters from Cervantes' *Don Quixote* (Cardenio and Lucinda).

APPENDIX B. THE COLLABORATIVE PLAYS

Henry VIII (1612–1613)

Authorship: There is strong evidence that John Fletcher and Shakespeare co-wrote *Henry VIII*. Most scholars agree that Shakespeare contributed Act one (scenes 1-2), Act two (scenes 3-4), Act three (first part of scene 2), and Act five (scene 1). Fletcher wrote the rest.

Type of play: *Henry VIII* was Shakespeare's last history play and the second-to-last play he collaborated on before he died.

Sources: Raphael Holinshed's *Chronicles of England, Scotland, and Ireland* and Edward Hall's *The Union of the Two Noble and Illustre Families of Lancaster and York*.

About the Play: Our contemporary view of the real Henry VIII comes from historians. It radically differs from Shakespeare's thinly drawn portrait of the famous Tudor king known for his many wives. Richer in pomp and ceremony than for its inspiring characters or engaging plot, the play explores the period when King Henry meets Anne Bullen, divorces Katherine, and makes Anne his queen. It also addresses Henry's power plays with the religious men who are opposed to his divorce.

The Two Noble Kinsmen (1613–1614)

Authorship: *The Two Noble Kinsmen* was listed in The Stationer's Register on April 8, 1634, as a drama co-written by John Fletcher and William Shakespeare. Experts tend to agree that Shakespeare wrote Act one, the first scenes of Acts two and three, and most of Act five.

Type of play: A romance in the style of *Pericles, Cymbeline,* and *The Winter's Tale*.

Sources: The play reenacts the *Knight's Tale*, from Chaucer's *Canterbury Tales* (1387).

About the Play: After marrying Hippolyta, Theseus fulfills the request of three queens mourning their husbands and attacks Creon, the king of Thebes. Capturing Creon's nephews, Palamon and Arcite, he puts them in prison. The two kinsmen fall in love with Emilia, Hippolyta's sister. Released and exiled from Athens, Arcite pretends to be Emilia's servant, while the jailer's daughter falls for Palamon and helps him escape. Eventually, Theseus orders them to settle their feud in single combat. The winner will get Emilia, while the loser will be executed. Arcite triumphs but is fatally injured after falling from his horse. Before dying he hands Emilia over to Palamon.

Appendix C
Glossary of Elizabethan English

Following is a list of Elizabethan words from Shakespearean quotations throughout this book, in addition to useful rhetorical and literary terms.

alliteration	The recurrence of an initial consonant sound in one or successive verse lines.
amity	Friendship; love.
anaphora	Repetition of the same word or phrase at the beginning of successive clauses or verses.
ancient	Ensign.
anon	Soon; shortly; immediately.
antic	Disguised; as in Hamlet's *antic disposition*.
antithesis	A contrast or opposition of thought in two phrases, clauses, sentences, or verse lines.
assonance	The recurrence of similar vowel sounds in one or more successive lines.
atomi	Plural of atom; a body so small as to be incapable of further division.

aught	Anything.
augury	The act of guessing or predicting the future.
blank verse	Unrhymed iambic pentameter lines, the medium of most English verse drama.
bond	A covenant or an agreement binding on him who makes it.
buck-basket	Basket for clothes washed in lye or soapsuds.
burgonet	A kind of helmet with a visor.
cadent	Falling.
casque	Helmet.
cipher	Nothing.
cloy	To fill up; to satiate.
corrival	One of several rivals.
courtier	An attendant at a sovereign court.
cuckold	The husband of an unfaithful wife.
descant	To comment on; to carp at or complain about.
disnatured	To be in a disordered condition; rendered unnatural.
dissembling	To cloak or conceal under a false appearance; to pretend or deceive; resemble falsely.
doff	To take off clothing or a hat; to put off; to lay aside.
ensign	A low-ranking military officer.
ere	Before; formerly.
evitate	Avoid; shun; shirk.
extenuate	Lessen; make less; or diminish.

Appendix C. Glossary of Elizabethan English

factitious	Not natural or genuine or spontaneous; forced or artificial.
feminine ending	A weak or unstressed extra syllable at the end of a line written in iambic pentameter.
forsooth	Truly.
gall'd	Vexed; annoyed; harassed; oppressed.
gormandizing	Devouring; practicing gluttony.
hoary	Grey or white with age; venerably old.
iambic pentameter	A verse line of five metric feet, each foot consisting of two syllables (stressed and unstressed).
impute	To assign blame; to charge with guilt or blame.
intemperate	Without measure or mean; immodest in behavior.
justice	The quality of being morally just or righteous; the administration of law, its forms, and processes.
lascivious	Inclined to lust; lewd; wanton.
maiden	A girl; a young unmarried woman; a virgin.
masque	A costume party or masquerade ball; a form of theatrical entertainment found in Shakespeare's romances.
mechanicals	Artisans; tradesmen who use machines or tools.
nunnery	Where nuns live under religious rule; a convent.
orb	A sphere of action or activity; the orbit or path or a planet; a circle.
ordnance	Engines for discharging missiles; artillery.
palmer	A pilgrim; an itinerant monk under a vow of poverty.
physic	Medicine, helping, or curing; the art of healing.

poop	The raised deck at the stern of a ship.
primogeniture	The right of succession or inheritance that belongs to the first-born child.
quarto	The earliest edition of Shakespeare's plays, so named because each sheet was folded twice, creating four leaves or eight pages to a sheet.
quit	To repay a person in exchange for something done; to depart or part from a place or person.
rheumatic	Full of watery mucus; pertaining to persons and their bodies.
riggish	Wanton; acting like a strumpet (*see* wanton).
rooky	Full of or abounding in rooks or crows.
shared line	A verse line shared by two or more characters.
sirrah	A form of address used with men or boys of an inferior position.
sprite	An airy spirit; fairy; elf; goblin.
surfeiting	Indulging excessively; drinking or eating too much.
teem	To bring forth or produce offspring.
triumvir	One of three co-rulers in ancient Rome.
tupping	Copulating (a ram or *tup* copulates with a ewe).
usury	The practice of lending money at interest; later, the practice of charging excessive interest rates for money on loan.
videlicet	Namely; that is to say; used to introduce a more precise explanation of a previous word or expression.
wanton	Undisciplined; ungoverned; unchaste; lewd.

Appendix C. Glossary of Elizabethan English

weird (adj.)   Having or claiming the power to control human destiny (the *weird* sisters); fate; suggesting the supernatural.

wight   A human being; a man or woman; a person.

will   Desire; wish; longing; an inclination to do something.

withal   Along with the rest; in addition; moreover; as well; at the same time; notwithstanding; nevertheless.

wracks   Wrecks.

Appendix D
Resources on Shakespeare's Plays

Following is a short list of suggested resources on Shakespeare's plays and how to appreciate them in a dramatic context. Some include lively discussions of what the plays mean or how to make sense of Shakespeare's verse. Others explore Shakespeare's life, his complete works, how he constructed his plays for performance, the commercial theatre business in his day, his fellow playwrights, and the political and social context in which he wrote.

Suggested Reading

Ackroyd, Peter. *Shakespeare: The Biography*. New York: Doubleday, 2005.

Bate, Jonathan. "The Mirror of Life: How Shakespeare Conquered the World," *Harper's Magazine*, April 2007.

Bate, Jonathan. *The Genius of Shakespeare*. New York: Oxford University Press, 1998.

Bate, Jonathan and Russell Jackson. *The Oxford Illustrated History of Shakespeare On Stage*. Oxford: Oxford University Press, 2001.

Bevington, David, ed. *The Complete Works of Shakespeare, Fifth edition*. New York: Longman, 2003.

Bloom, Harold. *Shakespeare: The Invention of the Human*. New York: Riverhead Books, 1998.

Brown, John Russell, ed. *Shakespeare in Performance: An Introduction Through Six Major Plays*. New York: Harcourt Brace Jovanovich, Inc., 1976.

Brown, John Russell. *William Shakespeare: Writing for Performance*. New York: St. Martin's Press, 1996.

Crystal, David and Ben Crystal. *Shakespeare's Words: A Glossary and Language Companion*. London: Penguin Books, 2002.

Delderfield, Eric R., ed. *Kings and Queens of England*. New York: Weathervane Books, 1978.

Edelstein, Barry. *Thinking Shakespeare*. New York: Spark Publishing, 2007.

Evans, G. Blakemore and J.J.M. Tobin, eds. *The Riverside Shakespeare: The Complete Works, Second edition*. Boston and New York: Houghton Mifflin Co., 1997.

Freeman, Neil, ed. *The Applause First Folio of Shakespeare in Modern Type*. New York: Applause, 2001.

Garber, Marjorie. *Shakespeare After All*. New York: Anchor Books, 2004.

Granville-Barker, Harley. *Prefaces to Shakespeare*. Princeton: Princeton University Press, 1946.

Greenblatt, Stephen, Walter Cohen, Jean E. Howard, and Katharine Eisaman Maus, eds. *The Norton Shakespeare: Based on the Oxford Edition, Second edition*. New York: W.W. Norton and Co., 2008.

Greenblatt, Stephen. *Will in the World*. New York and London: W. W. Norton and Co., 2004.

Greer, Germaine. *Shakespeare's Wife*. New York: HarperCollins, 2007.

Hall, Peter. *Shakespeare's Advice to the Players*. New York: Theatre Communications Group, 2003.

Kay, Dennis. *William Shakespeare: His Life and Times*. New York: Twayne Publishers, 1995.

APPENDIX D. RESOURCES ON SHAKESPEARE'S PLAYS

Kermode, Frank. *The Age of Shakespeare*. New York: The Modern Library Paperback Edition, 2005.

McDonald, Russ. *The Bedford Companion to Shakespeare: An Introduction with Documents, Second edition*. Boston and New York: Bedford/St. Martin's, 2001.

Meagher, John C. *Shakespeare's Shakespeare: How the Plays Were Made*. New York and London: Continuum, 1997.

Norwich, John Julius. *Shakespeare's Kings: The Great Plays and the History of England in The Middle Ages (1337-1485)*. New York: Simon & Schuster, 1999.

Papp, Joseph and Elizabeth Kirkland. *Shakespeare Alive!* New York: Bantam Books, 1988.

Rosenbaum, Ron. *The Shakespeare Wars*. New York: Random House, 2006.

Rothwell, Kenneth S. *A History of Shakespeare on Screen, Second edition*. Cambridge, U.K.: Cambridge University Press, 2004.

Schoenbaum, S. *William Shakespeare: A Compact Documentary Life*. Oxford: Oxford University Press, 1977.

Shapiro, James. *Contested Will: Who Wrote Shakespeare?* New York: Simon & Schuster, 2010.

Shapiro, James, ed. *Shakespeare in America: An Anthology From the Revolution To Now*. New York: The Library of America, 2013.

Shapiro, James. *A Year in the Life of William Shakespeare: 1599*. New York: HarperCollins Publishers, 2005.

Shapiro, James. *The Year of Lear: Shakespeare in 1606*. New York: Simon & Schuster, 2015.

Styan, J. L. *Shakespeare's Stagecraft*. Cambridge, U.K.: Cambridge University Press, 1967.

Taylor, Gary, John Jowett, Terri Bourus, and Gabriel Egan, eds. *The New Oxford Shakespeare: The Complete Works (Modern Critical Edition)*. Oxford: Oxford University Press, 2016.

Tillyard, E.M.W. *The Elizabethan World Picture*. New York: Vintage Books, 1959.

Wells, Stanley. *Shakespeare and Co.: Christopher Marlowe, Thomas Dekker, Ben Jonson, Thomas Middleton, John Fletcher and Other Players in His Story*. New York: Allen Lane, 2006.

Surfing on Shakespeare's Plays

Internet sites come and go, of course, so here are just a few authoritative websites for students and playgoers looking to brush up on Shakespeare's plays for class or before a performance, or in order to understand his life and times. You can find additional links on these sites.

- Shakespeare: His Works, Life, Theater, and other Resources for Students and Scholars (http://www.folger.edu/shakespeare)
- Folger Shakespeare Library: Online Resources for Students and Scholars (http://www.folger.edu/online-resources)
- Royal Shakespeare Company: About Shakespeare and Shakespeare's Plays (https://www.rsc.org.uk/shakespeare/)
- British Library: Treasures – Shakespeare in Quarto (http://www.bl.uk/treasures/shakespeare/homepage.html)
- Shakespeare Birthplace Trust: Explore Shakespeare (https://www.shakespeare.org.uk/education/)
- PlayShakespeare.com – The Ultimate Free Shakespeare (https://www.playshakespeare.com)
- Stratford Festival of Canada: Watch Plays on Demand (https://www.stratfordfestival.ca/WatchandExplore)
- Oregon Shakespeare Festival Play Study Guides (https://www.osfashland.org/experience-osf/education/study-guides.aspx)
- Shakespeare's Works (Folger Shakespeare Library) (http://www.folger.edu/shakespeares-works)

Index

A

Abhorson *(Measure for Measure)*, 186
Abraham, F. Murray as Nick Bottom, 89, 95, 101
Abraham Slender *(The Merry Wives of Windsor)*, character synopsis, 139-140
Abram *(Romeo and Juliet)*, 250
Acker, Amy, 125
acting companies, licenses, 14
acting troupes, noble sponsorship, 13
actors
    Benedick *(Much Ado About Nothing)*, challenges of playing, 133-134
    Elizabethan views on, 13-14, 33-34
    Henry IV, challenges of playing, 228-229
    Merchant of Venice, The, 115-116
    Midsummer Night's Dream, A, 101-102
    Richard III, challenges of playing, 213-214
    Rosalind, challenges of, 163
    Shakespearean actors, 14, 33-34
Actors on Shakespeare: *A Midsummer Night's Dream*, 95, 101
Adamson, Eve, 360
Adam *(As You Like It)*, 13, 154
Adrian *(The Tempest)*, 51, 380
Aeneid, 4
Affleck, Ben, 258
Age of Shakespeare, The, 90, 276, 417
Agrippa *(Antony and Cleopatra)*, character synopsis, 352
Alexander, Bill, 101, 215
Alexander Court *(Henry V)*, 234
Alexas *(Antony and Cleopatra)*, 353
Alice *(Henry V)*, 235, 243
Alleyn, Edward "Ned," 258
alliteration, 49, 50, 55, 252, 409
All's Well That Ends Well, 18, 19, 68, 183, 190, 393

Alonso *(The Tempest)*, character synopsis, 380
Amiens *(As You Like It)*, character synopsis, 153
anaphora, 53, 208, 409
ancient, 301, 409
Anderson, Mary, 163
Andrews, Anthony, 262
Angelo *(Measure for Measure)*, character synopsis, 184
Anne Page *(The Merry Wives of Windsor)*, character synopsis, 139
Annis, Francesca, 261
Antigonus *(The Winter's Tale)*, character synopsis, 367
antithesis, 49-50, 55, 409
Antonio *(The Merchant of Venice)*, character synopsis, 106
Antonio *(Much Ado About Nothing)*, character synopsis, 123
Antonio *(The Tempest)*, character synopsis, 380
Antonio *(Twelfth Night)*, character synopsis, 168
Antony and Cleopatra, 349-362
    characters, 350-353
    Egyptian deities in, 357
    genre, 349-350
    initial publication of, 61
    plot, 354-359
    proposed date written, 68, 349
    screen adaptations, 355-356
    setting, 353
    sources, 17
    staging, 360-362
Antoon, A. J., 35, 101, 134
Apollo, 357, 369, 370, 373, 374
Apothecary *(Romeo and Juliet)*, 250
Apparitions *(Macbeth)*, 337

Applause First Folio of Shakespeare in Modern Type, The, 65, 416
Arcadia, 58
Archibald (*Henry IV, Part I*), 220
Archidamus (*The Winter's Tale*), character synopsis, 367
Ariel (*The Tempest*), character synopsis, 379
Aristotle, 70
Armin, Robert, 160, 170, 178
Artemidorus of Cnidos (*Julius Caesar*), 267, 272
Ashcroft, Peggy, 163
assonance, 49, 55, 409
As You Like It, 151–165
   characters, 152–155
   initial publication of, 61
   pastoral poetry, 151
   plot, 155–159
   proposed date written, 68, 151
   satirical undercurrents, 156–157
   screen adaptations, 164
   setting, 155
   staging, 161–162
Atkins, Eileen, 163
Aubrey, Juliet, 195
audiences, Shakespearean plays, 31
Audrey (*As You Like It*), character synopsis, 155
Autolycus (*The Winter's Tale*), 368

B

Badel, Sarah, 88
Balanchine, George, 329
Balthasar (*Much Ado About Nothing*), character synopsis, 123
Balthasar (*Romeo and Juliet*), 250
Balthazar (*The Merchant of Venice*), character synopsis, 108
Banquo (*Macbeth*), character synopsis, 335
Baptista (*The Taming of the Shrew*), character synopsis, 76
Barabas (*The Jew of Malta*), 17, 106, 119
Bardolf (*Henry V*), 234
Bardolph (*The Merry Wives of Windsor*), character synopsis, 139
Barker, Harley Granville, 40, 359
Barnardine (*Measure for Measure*), 186

Barton, John, 215
Bassanio (*The Merchant of Venice*), character synopsis, 107
Bate, Jonathan, 19
Battle of Bosworth Field (Wars of the Roses), 8, 213
Beale, Simon Russell, *Macbeth*, on interpreting, 333, 344, 347
Bean, Jeffrey, xix, 133–134, 135, 178–179
Bean, Sean, 261
Beatrice (*Much Ado About Nothing*), character synopsis, 122
Beaumont, Francis, 19
Beckinsale, Kate, 135
Bedford Companion to Shakespeare: An Introduction with Documents, The, 7, 417
Beijing Institute of World Theatre and Film, 20, 360
Benedick (*Much Ado About Nothing*), 122, 133–134
Benvolio (*Romeo and Juliet*), character synopsis, 249
Berger, Sidney, xix, 85, 88, 118, 387,
Bergner, Elisabeth, 164
Bernardo (*Hamlet, Prince of Denmark*), 283
Bernstein, Leonard, 247
Bianca (*Othello*), 302
Bianca (*The Taming of the Shrew*), character synopsis, 76
Biondello (*The Taming of the Shrew*), character synopsis, 77
Blackfriars, purchase of, 18
blank verse, 33, 47, 48–49
Blenheim Palace, 292
Bloom, Harold, 53, 242, 261, 279
Boatswain (*The Tempest*), 380
Bogdanov, Michael, 244
Boito, Arrigo, 149
Book of Common Prayer, 9
Booth, Douglas, 254
Booth, Edwin, 227
Booth, John Wilkes, 277
Booth, Junius, 277
Borachio (*Much Ado About Nothing*), 123
Branagh, Kenneth, 42, 70, 101, 124, 131, 134, 162, 164, 244, 282, 291, 292, 304, 328

Index

Brett, Jeremy, 328
Brook, Peter, 101, 195
Brooke, Arthur, 260, 398
Brown, John Russell, 42, 126, 229, 252
Brutus, Marcus (*Julius Caesar*), 267, 271, 274-275
Buckingham (*Richard III*), character synopsis, 201
Burbage, Cuthbert, 27
Burbage, James, 25, 27-28
Burbage, Richard, 16, 26, 212
Burke, David, 328
Burton, Richard, 81, 86, 88

C

Cadfael, 134
Caesar, Julius, 265. *See also Julius Caesar*
Caird, John, 344
Caius Ligarius (*Julius Caesar*), 267
Calder-Marshall, Anna, 374
Caldwell, Raymond, xix, xx
Caliban (*The Tempest*), character synopsis, 379
Camillo (*The Winter's Tale*), character synopsis, 367
Campbell, Douglas, 100
Canidius (*Antony and Cleopatra*), 352
Canterbury Tales, The, 59, 84, 143
Cardenio, proposed date written, 69, 406
Carey, Henry, 16
Carlei, Carlo, 254
Carter, Helena Bonham, 180
Casca (*Julius Caesar*), 267
Celia (*As You Like It*), character synopsis, 153
Ceres (*The Tempest*), character synopsis, 379
Cesario, 168
Chamberlain (*Henry IV, Part I*), 221
Chapman, George, 19
character analysis, the actor's influence upon, 42-43
characters
   Antony and Cleopatra, 350-353
   As You Like It, 152-155
   Hamlet, 280-283
   Henry IV, Part I, 218-221
   Henry V, 232-235
   Julius Caesar, 266-268
   King Lear, 316-319
   Macbeth, 334-337
   Measure for Measure, 184-186
   Merchant of Venice, The, 106-108
   Merry Wives of Windsor, The, 138-140
   Midsummer Night's Dream, A, 90-92
   Much Ado About Nothing, 122-123
   Othello, 300-302
   Richard III, 200-202
   Romeo and Juliet, 248-250
   Taming of the Shrew, The, 76-77
   Tempest, The, 378-380
   Twelfth Night, 168-169
   Winter's Tale, The, 366-368
Charles (*As You Like It*), 153
Charmian (*Antony and Cleopatra*), character synopsis, 353
Chaucer, Geoffrey, 41, 62, 84, 143, 407
Chicago Shakespeare Festival, 44
Chimes at Midnight, 228
Chorus (*Henry V*), character synopsis, 232
Christie, Julie, 292
Christopher Sly (*The Taming of the Shrew*), 77
Chronicles of England, Scotland, and Ireland, 17, 231, 395, 297, 402, 403, 404, 407
Chronology of composition, Shakespeare's plays, 67-69
Cibber, Colley, 212, 216
Cicero (Roman orator), 4, 40
Cicero (*Julius Caesar*), 266
Cinna (*Julius Caesar*), 267
Claudio (*Julius Caesar*), 268
Claudio (*Measure for Measure*), character synopsis, 185
Claudio (*Much Ado About Nothing*), character synopsis, 122
Cleomines (*The Winter's Tale*), character synopsis, 367
Cleopatra (*Antony and Cleopatra*), character synopsis, 352-353
Clitus (*Julius Caesar*), 268
Clothier, Richard, 241
Cloutier, Suzanne, 308
Clown (*Othello*), 302
Clown (*Romeo and Juliet*), 250

Clown (*The Winter's Tale*), character synopsis, 368
Coast of Utopia, The, 41
Cobweb (*A Midsummer Night's Dream*), 92
Colley, Kenneth, 194
Comedies, The, 69
Comedy of Errors, The, 17, 67-68, 70, 176, 183, 389, 394
commedia dell'arte, 378, 396
Complete Oxford Shakespeare: Volume III Tragedies, The, 342
composition, order of Shakespeare's plays, 67-69
compositors, 60-61
Condell, Henry, 18, 59
Conrad (*Much Ado About Nothing*), character synopsis, 123
Constable of France (*Henry V*), 234
Cooke, Christian, 254
Cooke, Dominic, 345
Copernicus, 9
Cordelia (*King Lear*), character synopsis, 317-318
Corduner, Allan, 116
Corin (*As You Like It*), 4, 154
Coriolanus, 69, 394
Cornelius (*Hamlet, Prince of Denmark*), 283
Cotillard, Marion, 340
Court of Athens, The (*A Midsummer Night's Dream*), 90
Cravens, Rutherford, xix, 147, 177
Croft, Emma, 164
Cumberbatch, Benedict, 213
Curio (*Twelfth Night*), 169
Curtain theatre, 29, 258
Curtis (*The Taming of the Shrew*), 76
Cusak, Niamh, 261
Cymbeline, 69, 395, 407
Czinner, Paul, 164

D
Daniel, Phil, 88
Danner, Blythe, 134
Dardanius (*Julius Caesar*), 268
Day, Gillian, 213
de Witt, Johannes, 26
Decius Brutus (*Julius Caesar*), 267
Dekker, Thomas, 19, 418
Demetrius (*A Midsummer Night's Dream*), character synopsis, 91
Dench, Judi, 124, 195, 261, 346, 374
Denisof, Alexis, 125
Dennis (*As You Like It*), 154
Dickinson, Emily, 42
Diomedes (*Antony and Cleopatra*), 353
Dion (*The Winter's Tale*), character synopsis, 367
Dobson, Michael, 344
Doctor Caius (*The Merry Wives of Windsor*), character synopsis, 140
Doctor Faustus, 16
Dogberry (*Much Ado About Nothing*), character synopsis, 123
Dolabella (*Antony and Cleopatra*), character synopsis, 352
Domitius Enobarbus (*Antony and Cleopatra*), character synopsis, 351
Don John (*Much Ado About Nothing*), character synopsis, 123
Don Pedro (*Much Ado About Nothing*), character synopsis, 122
Donaldbain (*Macbeth*), character synopsis, 334
Dorcas (*The Winter's Tale*), 368
Drake, Fabia, 163
Droeshout, Martin, 18
Dromio (*The Comedy of Errors*), 176
ducats, 106, 107, 109, 110, 113, 115, 130
Duchess of York (*Richard III*), character synopsis, 202
Duke Frederick (*As You Like It*), character synopsis, 153
Duke of Albany (*King Lear*), character synopsis, 317
Duke of Beaumont (*Henry V*), 233
Duke of Berri (*Henry V*), 233
Duke of Bourbon (*Henry V*), 233
Duke of Britain (*Henry V*), 233
Duke of Burgundy (*Henry V*), 233
Duke of Burgundy (*King Lear*), character synopsis, 318
Duke of Cornwall (*King Lear*), character synopsis, 317
Duke of Exeter (*Henry V*), 233

Index

Duke of Orleance (*Henry V*), 233
Duke of Venice (*Othello*), 301
Duke of York (*Henry V*), 233
Duke Orsino (*Twelfth Night*), character synopsis, 169
Duke Senior (*As You Like It*), character synopsis, 152
Duncan (*Macbeth*), character synopsis, 334

E

Earl of Kent (*King Lear*), character synopsis, 318
Earl of March (*Henry IV, Part I*), 220
Earl of Richmond (*Richard III*), character synopsis, 201
Earl of Salisbury (*Henry V*), 235
Earl of Warwick (*Henry V*), 235
Earl of Westmerland (*Henry IV, Part I*), character synopsis, 219
Earl of Westmerland (*Henry V*), 233
Edel, Uli, 331
Edgar (*King Lear*), character synopsis, 318
Edmund (*King Lear*), character synopsis, 318
Edmund, Lord Mortimer (*Henry IV, Part I*), character synopsis, 220
Edward III, 68, 403-404
Edward IV (*Richard III*), character synopsis, 200-201
Edward Poins (*Henry IV, Part I*), 220
Edzard, Christine, 164
Egeus (*A Midsummer Night's Dream*), character synopsis, 90
Ehle, Jennifer, 215
Elbow (*Measure for Measure*), 186
Elizabeth (*Richard III*), character synopsis, 202
Elizabeth I, queen of England (1558-1603), 2, 3, 8-9, 10, 16, 41, 66, 201, 207, 261
Emilia (*The Winter's Tale*), character synopsis, 367
ensign, 300, 301, 302, 409, 410,
Ernest, Matthew, 371
Eros (*Antony and Cleopatra*), character synopsis, 351
Escalus (*Measure for Measure*), character synopsis, 184-185
Euphronius (*Antony and Cleopatra*), character synopsis, 351

Evans, Edith, 163
Evans, Frank, 215
Every Man in His Humor, 10, 13

F

Fabian (*Twelfth Night*), 170
fabliau, 141, 143, 149
Faerie Queen, The, 58
Fairbanks, Douglas, 87
Falstaff
  Henry IV, Part I, character synopsis, 220
  Henry IV, Part II, 395
  Henry V, 234, 237
  The Merry Wives of Windsor, character synopsis, 138
  opera by Verdi, 149
Faulkner, William, 344
Feast of the Epiphany, 174
Fellowes, Julian, 254
Ferdinand (*The Tempest*), character synopsis, 379-380
Feste (*Twelfth Night*), 170, 177, 178-179, 180
festivals, Shakespeare, 20, 44
Fields, W. C., 148
Fiennes, Joseph, 41
figures of speech, 49, 50-54
First Folio, 13, 15, 18, 43, 44, 59, 60-66, 69, 117, 199, 266, 284, 320, 334, 338, 359, 378
Fishburne, Laurence, 304, 308
Flavius (*Julius Caesar*), 267
Fleance (*Macbeth*), 336
Fleetwood, Susan, 163
Fletcher, John, 19, 66, 406, 407, 418
Florizel (*The Winter's Tale*), character synopsis, 367
Fluellen (*Henry V*), 234, 238
Folger, Henry Clay, 59
Fool (*King Lear*), character synopsis, 316
Fool (*King Lear*), inspiration for performance, 326-327
fools, Shakespearean, 176-179
formal rhetoric, *Richard III*, 209
Fourth Folio, publication, 66
Francis (*Henry IV, Part I*), 221
Francis Flute (*A Midsummer Night's Dream*), character synopsis, 92

Francis Ford (*The Merry Wives of Windsor*), character synopsis, 138-139
Francisca (*Measure for Measure*), 185
Francisco (*Hamlet, Prince of Denmark*), 283
Francisco (*The Tempest*), 380
Freedman, Gerald, 134
Friar Francis (*Much Ado About Nothing*), 123
Friar John (*Romeo and Juliet*), 250
Froth (*Measure for Measure*), 186
Fuller, Thomas, 15

G
Gadshill (*Henry IV, Part I*), 221
Garai, Romola, 162
George, Duke of Clarence (*Richard III*), character synopsis, 200
George Page (*The Merry Wives of Windsor*), character synopsis, 139
Gielgud, John, 100, 124, 195, 229, 262, 277, 388
Globe theatre, 3, 6, 10, 11, 17, 23-33, 35, 151, 167, 170, 232, 266, 276,
Goneril (*King Lear*), character synopsis, 317
Gonzalo (*The Tempest*), character synopsis, 380
Goring, Marius, 195
Gorrie, John, 388
Governess, The, 266, 328
Governor of Harfleur (*Henry V*), 234
Gower (*Henry V*), 234
Granville-Barker, Harley, 40, 359, 366
Gratiano (*The Merchant of Venice*), character synopsis, 107
Gratiano (*Othello*), 302
Graves, Joseph, xix, 20, 349, 360-362
Grayson, Kathryn, 87
Greenaway, Peter, 388
Greene, Robert, 15, 366
Greene's Groatsworth of Wit, 15
Greer, Germaine, 85, 416
Gregory (*Romeo and Juliet*), 250
Gremio (*The Taming of the Shrew*), character synopsis, 77
Grumio (*The Taming of the Shrew*), 76
Guinness, Alec, 214
Guthrie, Tyrone, 100, 195, 214

H
Halio, Jay L., 325
Hall, Edward (source), 17, 212, 397, 402, 403, 404, 407
Hall, Edward (director), 101, 277
Hall, Peter, 133, 188, 215, 312, 416
Hamlet, 13, 19, 20, 33, 44, 52, 89, 168, 279-297, 327, 375
 characters, 280-283
 genre, 69-70
 Hamlet as protagonist, 279-280
 Hamnet, as inspiration, 293
 plot and themes, 283-293
 proposed date written, 18, 68, 168
 screen adaptations, 70, 291, 292
 setting, 283
 staging and directing, 44, 291, 295-296
 theatricality, 294
 versions, quarto, bad quarto, and First Folio, 55, 64, 71, 284
Hammond, Antony, 214
Hands, Terry, 374
Harrigan, Stephen, 331
Hartmann, Sarah, 360
Hastings (*Richard III*), character synopsis, 201
Hayne, Victoria, 187
Hecate (*Macbeth*), 337
Helena (*A Midsummer Night's Dream*), character synopsis, 91
Heminges, John, 18, 59, 71, 117,
Henry, Deidre, 161
Henry, Lord Scroop of Masham (*Henry V*), 234
Henry, Prince of Wales (*Henry IV, Part I*), character synopsis, 218-219
Henry IV (actor's interpretation of), 217, 227-229
Henry IV, Part I, 198, 217-230
 characters, 218-221
 initial publication, 61
 plot, 221-226
 popularity of, 217
 proposed date written, 68, 217
 screen adaptations, 227, 228
 setting, 221
 staging, 228-229

Index

Henry IV, Part II, proposed date written, 68, 198, 227, 395-396, 398
Henry Percy, (*Henry IV, Part I*), character synopsis, 219
Henry Percy, Earl of Northumberland (*Henry IV, Part I*), character synopsis, 219
Henry V, 28-29, 134, 231-244
    characters, 232-235
    focus on war and patriotism, 231, 242, 244
    plot and themes, 235-242
    proposed date written, 68
    screen adaptations, 236, 241, 242-244
    setting, 235
    source, 231
    stagings, 191, 244
Henry VI, Part I, 15, 68, 404
Henry VI, Part II, 15, 68, 402-403
Henry VI, Part III, 15, 68, 403
Henry VII (Henry Tudor), king of England, (1485-1509), 8, 212
Henry VIII, 19, 27, 66, 69, 407
Henry VIII, king of England (1509-1547), 8
Henslowe, Philip, 26, 258
Henslowe's Diary, 27, 28, 67
Hepburn, Katharine, 124, 163
Hermia (*A Midsummer Night's Dream*), character synopsis, 90
Hermione (*The Winter's Tale*), character synopsis, 366
Hero (*Much Ado About Nothing*), character synopsis, 122
Heston, Charlton, 88
Heywood, Thomas, 19
Hicks, Greg, 277
Hiddleston, Tom, 241
Hill, Victoria, 346
Hippolyta (*A Midsummer Night's Dream*), character synopsis, 90
Histories, The, 69
History of King Lear, The, 320. See also *King Lear*
History of King Richard the Third, 212. See also *Richard III*
History of Shakespeare on Screen, A, 347
History of the Worthies of England, The, 15
Hoffman, Michael, 102
Holinshed, Raphael, 17, 212, 231, 334, 395, 397, 402, 403, 404, 407
Holm, Ian, 215, 328
Hordern, Michael, 262, 326-328, 388
Hortensio (*The Taming of the Shrew*), character synopsis, 77
Hostess Quickly (*Henry V*), 235
Hotspur (*Henry IV, Part I*), character synopsis, 219
Houston Shakespeare Festival, 54, 85, 119, 147, 177, 291, 326, 327, 329, 330, 377, 387
Howard, Bryce Dallas, 164
Howell, Jane, 374
Hughes, Bernard, 134
Humphrey, Duke of Gloucester (*Henry V*), 232
Hupp, Robert, xix, 179-180
Hurt, William, 295
Hussey, Olivia, 262
Hymen (*As You Like It*), 155
Hytner, Nicholas, 228

I

iambic pentameter, 49, 55, 255, 262, 410, 411. See also blank verse
Invention of Love, The, 41
Iras (*Antony and Cleopatra*), character synopsis, 353
Iris (*The Tempest*), character synopsis, 379
Irons, Jeremy, 374
Isabella (*Measure for Measure*), character synopsis, 185
Isis, 357
Isle of Dogs, The, 14

J

Jacob, Irene, 309
Jacobi, Derek, 124, 134, 292
Jaggard, Isaac, 60
Jaggard, William, 60
James I, king of England (1603-1624) and of Scotland, as James VI (1567-1624), 2, 3, 9, 10, 18, 27, 33, 333
Jamy (*Henry V*), 234
Jaques (*As You Like It*), character synopsis, 153

Jarman, Derek, 388
Jayston, Michael, 346
Jessica (*The Merchant of Venice*), character synopsis, 107
Jew of Malta, The, 106
John (*The Merry Wives of Windsor*), 139
John Bates (*Henry V*), 234
John, Duke of Bedford (*Henry V*), 233
John Falstaff. *See* Falstaff
John Rugby (*The Merry Wives of Windsor*), 140
Johnson, Celia, 262
Johnson, Samuel, 66
Jones, Felicity, 385
Jones, Gemma, 374
Jonson, Ben, 5, 10, 13, 14, 15, 19, 59, 62, 418
Juliet (*Measure for Measure*), character synopsis, 185
Juliet (*Romeo and Juliet*), 29-30, 51, 260, character synopsis, 249
Julius Caesar, 16, 17, 61, 71, 265-277, 349, 350
   characters, 266-268
   plot, 269-275
   proposed date written, 68, 266
   screen adaptations, 277
   setting, 268
   source, 275-276
   stagings, 265, 276-277
Juno (*The Tempest*), character synopsis, 379

K

Kahn, Michael, xix, 44, 279, 284, 295-296
Kate (*Henry IV, Part I*), character synopsis, 220
Katherina (*The Taming of the Shrew*), character synopsis, 76
Kay, Dennis, 5
Keel, Howard, 87
Keitel, Harvey, 295
Kemp, Jeremy, 374
Kempe, Will, 65, 160
Kenerly, Kevin, 161
Kermode, Frank, 276
Keystone Kops, the, 134
Kimbell, David, 149

King John, 51, 68, 396
King Lear, 18, 52, 89, 160, 170, 177, 299, 315-332, 333, 346
   audio book version, 328
   characters, 316-319
   genre, 69
   performing Lear, 326-327
   plot and theme, 319-326, 332
   proposed date written, 69
   screen adaptations, 328, 331
   script versions (conflated, quarto, and First Folio), 320
   setting, 319
   stage combat, 329-331
   staging, 327-328
King of Texas, 331
King's Men, 3, 9, 30
Kirk, Lisa, 88
Kirkland, Elizabeth, 31
Kiss Me Kate, (film), 87
Kline, Kevin, 102, 124, 134, 164, 295
Kökeritz, Helge, 149
Krohn, Charles, xix, *King Lear*, on performing, 322, 326-327
Kurzel, Justin, 340

L

Lady Anne (*Richard III*), character synopsis, 200-201
Lady Macbeth (*Macbeth*), character synopsis, 335
Lady Macduff (*Macbeth*), character synopsis, 336
Lady Mortimer (*Henry IV, Part I*), character synopsis, 220
Lady Percy (*Henry IV, Part I*), character synopsis, 220
Laughton, Charles, 195
Launce (*The Two Gentlemen of Verona*), 176
Launcelot Gobbo (*The Merchant of Venice*), character synopsis, 107
Laurenson, James, 241
Lazalde, Arthur, 193
Lear's Fool (*King Lear*), character synopsis, 316
Le Beau (*As You Like It*), 153
Leigh-Hunt, Barbara, 346

Index

Leighton, Margaret, 163
Leonard, Robert Sean, 135
Leonardo (*The Merchant of Venice*), character synopsis, 107
Leonato (*Much Ado About Nothing*), character synopsis, 122
Leontes (*The Winter's Tale*), character synopsis, 123
Lepidus (*Antony and Cleopatra*), character synopsis, 351
Lester, Adrian, 163
Lincoln, Abraham, 277
Linney, Laura, 295
Lives of the Noble Grecians and Romans, 17, 275
Lodovico (*Othello*), 301
Loncraine, Richard, 214
Looking for Richard, 214
Lord Chamberlain's Men, 3, 9, 11-12, 14, 16-18, 21, 27, 30, 33, 58, 160, 178, 232, 266
Lord Grandpré, 234
Lord Rambures (*Henry V*), 234
Lord Strange's Men, 16, 214
Lorenzo (*The Merchant of Venice*), character synopsis, 107
Love's Labor's Lost, 10, 68, 396-397
Love's Labor's Won, 396, 397
Lucentio (*The Taming of the Shrew*), character synopsis, 67, 77
Lucilius (*Julius Caesar*), 267
Lucio (*Measure for Measure*), 185
Lucius (*Julius Caesar*), 268
Luhrman, Baz, 262
LuPone, Patti, 295
Lysander (*A Midsummer Night's Dream*), character synopsis, 90

M

M. Aemilius Lepidus (*Julius Caesar*), character synopsis, 266
Maaske, Dee, 162
Macbeth, 18, 40, 71, 333-347
  characters, 334-336
  initial publication of, 61
  inspiration, 334
  plot, 337-344
  proposed date written, 69, 334
  screen adaptations, 340, 346-347
  setting, 337
  sources, 17, 334
  staging, 344-346
  Thomas Middleton (adaptation), 341-342
Macbeth (*Macbeth*), character synopsis, 334-335
Macduff (*Macbeth*), character synopsis, 335
Macmorris (*Henry V*), 234
Madden, John, 261
Maecenas (*Antony and Cleopatra*), 352
Mahood, M. M., 112
malapropisms, creating, 131
Malcolm (*Macbeth*), character synopsis, 270
Maloney, Michael, 292
Malvolio (*Twelfth Night*), character synopsis, 169-170
Mamillius (*The Winter's Tale*), character synopsis, 366
Mankiewicz, Joseph L., 277
Marcellus (*Hamlet, Prince of Denmark*), 283
Mardian (*Antony and Cleopatra*), character synopsis, 353
Margaret (*Much Ado About Nothing*), character synopsis, 123
Margaret (*Richard III*), character synopsis, 201
Maria (*Twelfth Night*), character synopsis, 170
Mariana (*Measure for Measure*), character synopsis, 185
Mark Antony (*Antony and Cleopatra*), character synopsis, 350
Marlowe, Christopher, 16, 19, 49, 58, 155
Mary I, queen of England (1553-1558), 8
Mason, James, 195
Master Fenton (*The Merry Wives of Windsor*), character synopsis, 139
Master of the Revels, 14
McCowen, Alec, 328
McDonald, Russ, 7
McEnery, John, 194
McEnery, Peter, 102
McGillis, Kelly, 295
McKellan, Ian, 214, 261, 346
McTeer, Janet, 101

Measure for Measure, 18, 19, 66, 70, 183-195, 299-300
   characters, 184-186
   genre, 70, 183
   plot and theme, 184-194
   proposed date written, 68
   screen adaptations, 194-195
   setting, 186
   stagings, 194-195
Mechanicals (*A Midsummer Night's Dream*), 91
Menas (*Antony and Cleopatra*), character synopsis, 352
Merchant from Mantua (*The Taming of the Shrew*), character synopsis, 77
Merchant of Venice, The, 7, 17, 105-120, 188, 299
   Antonio, challenges of performing, 115-118
   characters, 106-108
   controversy surrounding, 105, 117-119
   New Cambridge Shakespeare edition of The Merchant of Venice, 112-113
   plot, 109-114
   proposed date written, 68
   setting, 108
   Shylock, 16, 90, 96, 98-99
   staging, 118-119
Mercury, 246, 357
Mercutio (*Romeo and Juliet*), 29
Meres, Francis, 67
Merry Wives of Windsor, The, 5, 51, 137-149, 198
   characters, 138-139
   First Folio version, 140
   inspiration, 4, 137
   plot, 139-146
   proposed date written, 68
   setting, 140
   staging of, 147-148
Messala (*Julius Caesar*), 267
Metellus Cimber (*Julius Caesar*), 267
Metropulos, Penny, xix, *As You Like It*, staging, 161
Michael Williams (*Henry V*), 234
Michell, Keith, 277
Middleton, Thomas, 342

Midsummer Eve, 90
Midsummer Night's Dream, A, 5, 16, 24, 34, 53, 61, 89-103, 147, 379
   Bottom, performing, 101-102
   characters, 90-92
   initial publication of, 61
   play-within-the-play, 98-99
   plot and theme, 93-100
   proposed date written, 67, 68
   reputation, 89
   Samuel Pepys, diary entry of, 89
   screen adaptation, 102
   setting, 92
   staging, 100-101
Miller, Jonathan, 88, 164
Mineart, Mark, xix, Henry IV, playing, 228-229
Miranda (*The Tempest*), 377, 378-379, 387-388
Mirren, Helen, 102, 164, 385
Mirror for Magistrates, A, 17, 212
Mirror of Life, The, article in Harper's, 19
Mistress Alice Ford (*The Merry Wives of Windsor*), character synopsis, 138, 148, 149
Mistress Margaret Page (*The Merry Wives of Windsor*), character synopsis, 138, 148, 149
Mistress Overdone (*Measure for Measure*), 186
Mistress Quickly (*Henry IV, Part I*), character synopsis, 230
Mistress Quickly (*The Merry Wives of Windsor*), 4, 139
Mohinsky, Elijah, 102
Molina, Alfred, 162
Montano (*Othello*), 302
Montjoy (*Henry V*), 234
Mopsa (*The Winter's Tale*), 368
More, Thomas, 212
Most Lamentable Comedy and Most Cruel Death of Pyramus and Thisbe, The, 94
Moth (*A Midsummer Night's Dream*), 92
motion pictures. *See also* screen adaptations
Mowat, Barbara A., 187
Mr. William Shakespeares Comedies, Histories, & Tragedies, 60. *See also* First Folio

Index

Much Ado About Nothing, 61, 65, 121–135, 168, 176, 194, 364, 374
   Benedick, analysis, 133–134
   characters, 122–123
   initial publication of, 61, 122
   plot, 124–132
   popularity of, 121–122
   proposed date written, 68, 122
   screen adaptations, 125, 134–135
   setting, 124
   source, 132
   staging, 126, 134–135
Murellus (*Julius Caesar*), 267
Mussolini, Benito, 276
Mustardseed (*A Midsummer Night's Dream*), 92
misogynistic overtones, *Taming of the Shrew, The*, 75–76, 84, 85–86
My Own Private Idaho, 227

N

Nelligan, Kate, 194
Neptune, 357
Nerissa (*The Merchant of Venice*), character synopsis, 107
Neville, Anne, 201
Neville-Andrews, John, 148
New Penguin Shakespeare, The, 277
New Place estate, purchase, 4–5, 10
New York Shakespeare Festival, 31, 44, 95, 100, 101, 134, 214, 228
Ney, Chuck, 193
Nick Bottom (*A Midsummer Night's Dream*), character synopsis, 91, 102
Nickell, Paul, 88
Noble, Adrian, 374
Norman, Marc, 172
North, Thomas, 17, 394
Nunn, Trevor, 172, 180, 346, 356
Nym (*Henry V*), 234
Nym (*The Merry Wives of Windsor*), character synopsis, 139
Nymphs (*The Tempest*), 379

O

Oberon (*A Midsummer Night's Dream*), character synopsis, 92
Octavia (*Antony and Cleopatra*), character synopsis, 351
Octavius Caesar (*Antony and Cleopatra*), character synopsis, 350–351
Old Gobbo (*The Merchant of Venice*), character synopsis, 107
Old Man (*Romeo and Juliet*), 250
Old Shepherd (*The Winter's Tale*), character synopsis, 367
Oliver (*As You Like It*), character synopsis, 153
Olivier, Laurence, 42, 164, 213, 214, 229, 236, 242, 244, 308, 327, 328
Oregon Shakespeare Festival, 44, 161, 165, 418
Orlando (*As You Like It*), character synopsis, 152
Ostler (*Henry IV, Part I*), 221
Oswald (*King Lear*), character synopsis, 317
Othello, 18, 299–313, 349, 350, 373, 405
   characters, 300–302
   initial performance date, 299
   Othello as Moor, tragic hero, 309–311
   plot and themes, 302–311
   proposed date written, 68
   screen adaptations, 304, 308–309
   setting, 302
   staging and directing, 311–313
Owen Glendower (*Henry IV, Part I*), character synopsis, 220
Oxford Dictionary of Shakespeare, 15, 163, 184, 300

P

Pacino, Al, 116, 214, 215,
Page (*Romeo and Juliet*), 250
Palladis Tamia: Wits Treasury, 67
Paltrow, Gwyneth, 172
Pandosto, The Triumph of Time, 366
Papp, Joseph, 31, 100
Parker, Oliver, 304, 308
Pasco, Richard, 277
pastoral poetry, *As You Like It*, 151, 152
Paterson, Joseph, 241
Paulina (*The Winter's Tale*), character synopsis, 367

Peaseblossom (*A Midsummer Night's Dream*), 92
Peckhardt, Erika, 193
Pembroke's Men, 16
Penguin Opera Guide, 149
Pennington, Michael, 244
Pepys, Samuel, 89, 148
Perdita (*The Winter's Tale*), character synopsis, 366-367
Pericles, proposed date written, 69, 405-406, 407
Peter (*Measure for Measure*), 185
Peter (*Romeo and Juliet*), 250
Peter Quince (*A Midsummer Night's Dream*), character synopsis, 92
Peter Simple (*The Merry Wives of Windsor*), character synopsis, 140
Petruchio (*Romeo and Juliet*), 249
Petruchio (*The Taming of the Shrew*), character synopsis, 76
Pfeiffer, Michelle, 102
Philip, Earl of Montgomery, 62
Phillips, Robin, 100
Philostrate (*A Midsummer Night's Dream*), character synopsis, 91
Phoebe (*As You Like It*), character synopsis, 155
Phoenix, River, 227
Pickford, Mary, 87
Pigott-Smith, Tim, 194, 195
Pimlott, Steven, 215
Pindarus (*Julius Caesar*), 268
Pistol (*Henry V*), 234
Pistol (*The Merry Wives of Windsor*), character synopsis, 139
Platter, Thomas, 276
Plautus, 4, 17, 70, 394
plays by Shakespeare
  appreciation by Elizabethan audiences, 31-33, 35, 40-41, 45
  co-authorship and total output, 66-67
  chronology (proposed date written), 67-69
  genres, 69-70, 71
  characterization, inherent ambiguity of, 42-43
  interpretation by today's directors, 43-44
  modern editions, basis of, 66
  publication, contemporary attitudes toward, 58-59, 65
  publication, of First Folio, 60-63
  role of director, 34-35
  script versions, 63-64
  Second, Third, and Fourth Folios, 66
plots (and themes)
  Antony and Cleopatra, 354-359
  As You Like It, 155-159
  Hamlet, 283-293
  Henry IV, Part I, 221-226
  Henry V, 235-242
  Julius Caesar, 269-275
  King Lear, 319-326, 332
  Macbeth, 337-344
  Measure for Measure, 184-194
  Merchant of Venice, The, 109-114
  Merry Wives of Windsor, The, 139-146
  Midsummer Night's Dream, A, 93-100
  Much Ado About Nothing, 124-132
  Othello, 302-311
  Richard III, 204-212
  Romeo and Juliet, 250-260
  Taming of the Shrew, The, 78-83
  Tempest, The, 381-387
  Twelfth Night, 171-176
  Winter's Tale, The, 368-374
Plummer, Christopher, 214, 374
Plutarch, 17, 265, 275-276, 350, 394, 405,
Pogue, Kate, xix, *King Lear*, on staging, 327-328
Polanski, Roman, 347
Polixenes (*The Winter's Tale*), character synopsis, 367
Pompey (*Antony and Cleopatra*), character synopsis, 351
Pompey (*Measure for Measure*), 186
Pope, Alexander, 66
Popilius Lena (*Julius Caesar*), 266
Porter, Cole, 87
Portia (*The Merchant of Venice*), character synopsis, 108
Prather, Doug, 109
Prefaces to Shakespeare: Volume I, 359, 372
primogeniture, laws of, 221, 398, 412
Prince Edward, death, 204, 210

Index

Prince John of Lancaster (*Henry IV, Part I*), character synopsis, 219
Prince of Aragon (*The Merchant of Venice*), character synopsis, 108
Prince of Morocco (*The Merchant of Venice*), character synopsis, 108
Prince Richard, death of, 204, 210
Princess Elizabeth, daughter of King James I, *The Tempest*, viewing of, 387-388
Proculeius (*Antony and Cleopatra*), character synopsis, 352
Prospero (*The Tempest*), character synopsis, 378
Prospero's Books, 388
Ptolemy of Alexandria, 9
Publius (*Julius Caesar*), 266
Puck (*A Midsummer Night's Dream*), character synopsis, 92
Pyramus and Thisbe, 90, 91, 94, 99, 102

Q

quarto editions, 55, 57, 58-59, 60-61, 64, 199, 260, 284, 259, 320
Quayle, Anthony, 228
Queen Isabel (*Henry V*), 233
Queen's Men, the, 16, 75
Quintilian, 40

R

Radford, Michael, 116
Rakoff, Alvin, 262
Rape of Lucrece, The, 12, 21, 58
Reapers (*The Tempest*), 380
Redgrave, Corin, 195
Redgrave, Lynn, 356
Redgrave, Michael, 229
Redgrave, Vanessa, 163
Reeves, Keanu, 227
Regan (*King Lear*), character synopsis, 317
Rehan, Ada, 163
Richard, Earl of Cambridge (*Henry V*), 234
Richard II, 10, 14, 15, 51, 68, 241, 395, 397-398
Richard III, 10, 16, 32, 198, 199-215, 218, 402, 403, 404
  characters, 200-202
  Colley Cibber's version, 212
  formal rhetoric in character's speeches, 208, 209
  genre, 69
  plot and themes, 204-212
  political alliances (family tree), 203
  proposed date written, 68
  screen adaptations, 213, 214-215
  setting, 202
  sources and inspiration, 199-200, 212
  stagings, 214-215
Richard III, king of England (1483-1485), 8, 199-201, 203, 204, 212-214
Richard Scroop (*Henry IV, Part I*), 220
Rickman, Alan, 262
Rivals, The, 131
Robbins, Jerome, 262
Robert Shallow (*The Merry Wives of Windsor*), character synopsis, 140
Robin (*The Merry Wives of Windsor*), character synopsis, 139
Robin Goodfellow (*A Midsummer Night's Dream*), character synopsis, 92. See also Puck.
Robin Starveling (*A Midsummer Night's Dream*), character synopsis, 92
Robson, Flora, 195
Romances, 364
Romeo (*Romeo and Juliet*), 26, character synopsis, 248
Romeo and Juliet, 4-5, 16, 47, 48, 50, 52, 61, 64, 232, 247-263, 291
  actors, notable, 261
  characters, 248-250
  plot and themes, 250-260
  proposed date written, 67-68, 247, 260
  screen adaptations, 41, 172, 247, 258, 262
  script versions, 71, 260
  setting, 250
  source, 260
  staging and casting, 261-262
Rosalind (*As You Like It*), 130, character synopsis, 152
Rose theatre, 27
Rosencrantz and Guildenstern are Dead, 283
Rosse (*Macbeth*), character synopsis, 336
Rothwell, Kenneth, 347

Royal Shakespeare Company, 20, 101, 195, 261, 328, 344, 345, 356, 374, 418
Royal Shakespeare Theatre, 20, 215
Rush, Geoffrey, 258
Ryecart, Patrick, 262

S
Saire, Rebecca, 262
Salerio (*The Merchant of Venice*), 107
Sampson (*Romeo and Juliet*), 250
Sanchez, Guillermo, 66
Sanders, Norman, 277
Scofield, Paul, 328
Scott, George C., 214
Scott, Margaretta, 163
Scottish Play, The, 333, 345. *See also Macbeth*
screen adaptations
   Antony and Cleopatra, 355-356
   As You Like It, 164
   Hamlet, 70, 291, 292
   Henry IV, Part I, 228, 229
   Henry V, 236, 241, 242-244
   Julius Caesar, 277
   King Lear, 328, 331
   Macbeth, 340, 346-347
   Measure for Measure, 194-195
   Merchant of Venice, The, *116*
   Midsummer Night's Dream, A, 87-88
   Much Ado About Nothing, 125, 134
   Othello, 304, 308-309
   Richard III, 212-214
   Romeo and Juliet, 41, 172, 247, 258, 262
   Taming of the Shrew, The, 81, 86, 87-88
   Tempest, The, 385, 387-388
   Twelfth Night, 172, 180
   Winter's Tale, The, 371, 374
Sea Captain (*Twelfth Night*), character synopsis, 168
Sebastian (*The Tempest*), character synopsis, 380
Sebastian (*Twelfth Night*), character synopsis, 168
Second Folio, publication, 66
Seitz, Matt Zoller, 346
Sejanus, 10, 13
Seleucus (*Antony and Cleopatra*), character synopsis, 353
Senators of Venice (*Othello*), 302
Seneca, 70
Sense and Sensibility, 328
sexist overtones, *Taming of the Shrew, The*, 75-76, 84, 85-86
Sextus Pompeius (*Antony and Cleopatra*), character synopsis, 351. *See also* Pompey
Seyler, Athene, 163
Seyton (*Macbeth*), 336
Shakespeare, Anne Hathaway, 5
Shakespeare, Hamnet, 5, 12, 18, 293
Shakespeare, John, 4
Shakespeare, Judith, 5
Shakespeare, Mary Arden, 4, 154
Shakespeare, Susanna, 5
Shakespeare, William, 2, 3-21, 62
   alliteration, 48-49, 50-51, 252, 409
   anaphora, 53, 208, 409
   antithesis, 47, 50-51, 409
   as actor (player), 12-14
   as Globe shareholder, 16
   as poet, 12
   assonance, 49, 409
   asteismus, 53-54
   blank verse, 12, 15, 16, 33, 48-49, 55, 248, 410. *See also* iambic pentameter
   collaborations (as playwright), 19-20, 401-408
   early life, 4-6
   education, 4-5
   figures of speech, 49, 50-54
   legacy, 20
   London, move to, 5-6
   Lord Chamberlain's Men, as member, 16-19. *See also* Lord Chamberlain's Men
   Marlow, Christopher, influence, 16-17
   marriage of, 5
   peers (in playwrighting), 19-20
   plays, number credited, 66-67
   plays, publication of, 60-66
   punning, 44-45
   rhetorical devices, 47-54
   sources, 16, 393-399, 401-408. *See also* individual plays
   syntax, 42-43
   theatre career (as actor), 11-14

use of verse and prose, 51-52
verse line, artistry, 48-54
words, coining (impact on English vocabulary), 52
Shakespeare Alive!, 31
Shakespeare and Co., 14, 418
Shakespeare festivals, 44
Shakespeare in American Communities, 179
Shakespeare in Love, 7, 16, 41, 172, 258, 261
Shakespeare in Performance: An Introduction Through Six Major Plays, 229, 416
Shakespeare: The Invention of the Human, 261, 415
Shakespeare Theatre Company (Washington, D.C.), xix, 44, 284, 295, 296
Shakespeare's Advice to the Players, 188, 312, 416
Shakespeare's Friends, 327
Shaw, Fiona, 163
Shelley, Carole, 163
Sheridan, Richard Brinsley, 131
Sheridan, Roseann, xix, xx, 261, 311
Sherman, Alice, 148
Shylock (*The Merchant of Venice*), 17, 106-107, 111-114
Siddons, Sarah, 345
Sidney, Philip, 58
Silva, Vilma, 1162
Silvius (*As You Like It*), character synopsis, 155
Sir Andrew Aguecheek (*Twelfth Night*), character synopsis, 169
Sir Hugh Evans (*The Merry Wives of Windsor*), 5, 140
Sir John Falstaff (*Henry IV, Part I*), character synopsis, 230
Sir John Falstaff (*The Merry Wives of Windsor*), character synopsis, 138
Sir Michael (*Henry IV, Part I*), 220
Sir Oliver Martext (*As You Like It*), 155
Sir Richard Vernon (*Henry IV, Part I*), 202
Sir Thomas Erpingham (*Henry V*), 233
Sir Thomas Grey (*Henry V*), 234
Sir Thomas More, 63, 67
Sir Toby Belch (*Twelfth Night*), character synopsis, 169
Sir Walter Blunt (*Henry IV, Part I*), 219
Siward (*Macbeth*), character synopsis, 336
Smith, Maggie, 100, 163, 308
Snug (*A Midsummer Night's Dream*), character synopsis, 92
Solanio (*The Merchant of Venice*), character synopsis, 107
Sondheim, Stephen, 262
Soothsayer (*Julius Caesar*), 267
Spenser, Edmund, 58
St. John's Eve, 90
stagings
  Antony and Cleopatra, 360-362
  As You Like It, 161-162
  Hamlet, 44, 291, 295-296
  Henry IV, Part I, 228-229
  Henry V, 191, 244
  Julius Caesar, 265, 276-277
  King Lear, 327-328, 329-331
  Macbeth, 344-346
  Measure for Measure, 194-195
  Merchant of Venice, The, 118-119
  Merry Wives of Windsor, The, 147-148
  Midsummer Night's Dream, A, 100-101
  Much Ado About Nothing, 126, 134-135
  Othello, 311-313
  Richard III, 214-215
  Romeo and Juliet, 261-262
  Taming of the Shrew, The, 77, 85-86
  Tempest, The, 388-389
  Twelfth Night, 179-180
  Winter's Tale, The, 371, 374
Stephano (*The Merchant of Venice*), character synopsis, 108
Stephano (*The Tempest*), 380
Stephens, Toby, 180
Sterling, Vanessa, 148
Stevenson, Juliet, 163
Stewart, Patrick, 331
Stoppard, Tom, 41, 172, 283
Strato (*Julius Caesar*), 268
Stride, John, 261
Stubbs, Imogen, 180
Suzman, Janet, 163, 356
Swan theatre, 26

T

Tamburlaine, 16
Taming of the Shrew, The, 16, 32, 75-88, 135
   characters, 76-77
   Christopher Sly's dream, 78
   controversy surrounding, 75-76, 84, 85-86
   Elizabethan patriarchal context, 86-87
   genre, 67
   main plot, 78-82
   original cast, 77
   popularity of, 75
   proposed date written, 68, 75
   screen adaptations, 81, 86, 87-88
   setting, 77
   staging, 77, 85-86
   subplot, 82-83
Taylor, Elizabeth, 81, 88
Taylor, Sam, 87
Taymor, Julie, 385
Tempest, The, 19, 71, 364, 377-389, 406
   characters, 378-380
   genre, 69, 377
   initial publication, 61
   inspiration, 377
   plot and themes, 381-387
   proposed date written, 69
   screen adaptations, 385, 387-388
   setting, 380
   staging, 388-389
Texas Shakespeare Festival, 44, 148, 193, 195, 299, 311, 360, 361, 371
Thacker, David, 195
theatre, Elizabethan views on, 23-33
Theme of Persecution in Selected Plays of the Yiddish Art Theatre, The, 118
Theseus (*A Midsummer Night's Dream*), character synopsis, 90
Third Folio, publication, 66
Thomas, Duke of Clarence (*Henry V*), 233
Thomas (*Measure for Measure*), 185
Thomas, Sian, 333
Thomas Percy, Earl of Worcester (*Henry IV, Part I*), character synopsis, 220
Thompson, Emma, 101, 124, 135, 243
Thompson, Sophie, 163
Tiernan, Andrew, 164
Timon of Athens, 19, 69, 405
tiringhouses, 30
Titania (*A Midsummer Night's Dream*), character synopsis, 92
Titinius (*Julius Caesar*), 267
Titus Andronicus, 16, 60, 68, 401-402
Tom Snout (*A Midsummer Night's Dream*), 92
Touchstone (*As You Like It*), 153, 156
Toussaint, Lorraine, 95
Tragedies, The 69
Tragedy of King Lear, The, 325. See also King Lear
Tragicall Historye of Romeus and Juliet, The, 260. See also Romeo and Juliet
Tranio (*The Taming of the Shrew*), character synopsis, 77
Trebonius (*Julius Caesar*), 267
Trinculo (*The Tempest*), 380
Troilus and Cressida, 68, 69, 398
Troughton, David, 215
troupes (acting), noble sponsorship, 16
Tubal (*The Merchant of Venice*), character synopsis, 107
Tudor, Henry, 214
Tutin, Dorothy, 163
Twelfth Night, 18, 33, 51, 61, 70, 89, 160, 167
   characters, 168-170
   genre, 70
   initial publication, 61
   plot, 171-176
   proposed date written, 68
   screen adaptations, 172, 180
   setting, 170
   staging, 179-180
   symbolism of title, 174
Two Gentlemen of Verona, The, 16, 41, 67, 68, 398-399
Two Noble Kinsmen, The, 66-67, 407-408
Tynan, Kenneth, 347

U-V

Union of the Two Noble and Illustre Families of Lancaster and York, The, 13, 212, 397
Ursula (*Much Ado About Nothing*), character synopsis, 123
Utah Shakespeare Festival, 44
Valentine (*Twelfth Night*), 169

Index

Van Sant, Gus, 227, 228
Varrus (*Julius Caesar*), 268
Vaughan, Stuart, 214
Venus, 357
Venus and Adonis, 12, 21, 58
Verdi, Giuseppe, 149
Verges (*Much Ado About Nothing*), character synopsis, 123
verse lines, 20-55
Vincentio (*Measure for Measure*), character synopsis, 184
Vincentio (*The Taming of the Shrew*), character synopsis, 77
Vintner (*Henry IV, Part I*), 221
Viola (*Twelfth Night*), character synopsis, 168
Viramontes, Jos, 162
Virgil, 4
Visscher, Claes Jansz, 6
Voltemand (*Hamlet, Prince of Denmark*), 283
Volumnius (*Julius Caesar*), 268

W–X–Y–Z

Walter, Harriet, 328
Warren, Charles, 346
Wars of the Roses (1455-1487), 8, 198, 205, 213-215, 403
Washington, Denzel, 134-135, 215, 274
Waterston, Sam, 134
Watts, Cedric, 118
Weird Sisters (*Macbeth*), 271, 335, 338, 341, 344, 347, 413, character synopsis, 337
Welch, Bree, xix, 387-388
Welles, Orson, 228, 276, 308
Wells, Stanley, 14, 163
Wentworth, Scott, xix, 109, 115-116
Werstine, Paul, 187
Westwick, Ed, 254
West Side Story, 247
What You Will. See *Twelfth Night*
Whedon, Josh, 125
Wheeler, David, 215
Whiting, Leonard, 262
Wickwire, Nancy, 163
Widdoes, Kathleen, 134
Widow (*The Taming of the Shrew*), character synopsis, 77
Wilkinson, Tom, 195
William (*As You Like It*), character synopsis, 155
William, Earl of Pembroke, 62
William Page (*The Merry Wives of Windsor*), character synopsis, 139
William Shakespeare: His Life and Times,
William Shakespeare: Writing for Performance, 42
William the Conqueror, 333
Williams, Robin, 295
Winter's Tale, The, 19, 364, 365-375
  characters, 366-368
  genre, 69, 365
  incongruities, 373-374
  inspiration, 366
  plot and themes, 368-374
  proposed date written, 61, 69, 365
  screen adaptations, 371, 374
  setting, 368
  staging, 371, 374
  structure of, 366
  titling of, 369
Witch, The, 342
Wood, John, 214
Woolf, Virginia, 42
Works, 59
Worth, Irene, 163
Worthington, Sam, 346
Wright, Geoffrey, 346
Wriothesley, Henry, 12, 21, 58

Young, Jack, xix, 290, 329-331
Young Cato (*Julius Caesar*), 268
Young Siward (*Macbeth*), 336

Zeffirelli, Franco, 70, 81, 88, 262
Ziegler, Georgianna, xix, 59, 60

www.ingramcontent.com/pod-product-compliance
Lightning Source LLC
Chambersburg PA
CBHW060417010526
44118CB00017B/2252